INTRODUCTION
TO
EDUCATION

INTRODUCTION TO EDUCATION

Tom E.C. Smith
University of Arkansas

WEST PUBLISHING COMPANY
St. Paul • New York • Los Angeles • San Francisco

Cover Art: Mary Griep
Copyediting: Kathy Pruno
Interior Art: Alice Thiede/Carto-Graphics
Indexing: Sandy Schroeder

COPYRIGHT © 1987 By WEST PUBLISHING COMPANY
50 W. Kellogg Boulevard
P.O. Box 64526
St. Paul, MN 55164–1003

Library of Congress Cataloging-in-Publication Data

Smith, Tom E.C.
  Introduction to education.

  Includes index.
  1. Teachers—Training of—United States. 2. Education
—Study and teaching—United States. I. Title.
LB1715.S4847 1987   370'.7   86–26749

ISBN 0–314–28514–8

Photo Credits

1 Arleen Casto Lewis; **10** © Susan Lapides 1983/Design Conceptions; **13** © Laima E. Druskis/Jeroboam, Inc.; **19** Elizabeth Crews, Stock Boston; **25** © Olaf Kallstrom/Jeroboam, Inc.; **31** Arleen Casto Lewis; **44** Historical Picture Services, Chicago; **45** Historical Picture Services, Chicago; **47** Peter Vandermark, Stock Boston; **53** Arleen Casto Lewis; **60** Historical Picture Services, Chicago; **62** © Karen R. Preuss/Jeroboam, Inc.; **63** Jean-Claude Lejeune, Stock Boston; **69** David A. Krathwohl, Stock Boston; **74** © Peeter Vilms/Jeroboam, Inc.; **84** Norman Hurst, Stock Boston; **92** Arleen Casto Lewis; **97** Arleen Casto Lewis; **102** © Eileen Christelow/Jeroboam, Inc.; **113** © Susan Lapides 1985/Design Conceptions; **115** Bohdan Hrynewych, Stock Boston; **117** © Susan Lapides 1985/Design Conceptions; **124** Arleen Casto Lewis; **129** Elizabeth Crews, Stock Boston; **139** Bruce Wellman, Stock Boston; **142** Elizabeth Hamlin, Stock Boston; **159** Arleen Casto Lewis; **162** Cary Wolinsky, Stock Boston; **167** Peter Southwick, Stock Boston; **176** © Jonathon Fisher/Jeroboam, Inc.; **182** Arleen Casto Lewis; **186** Laimute E. Druskis, Stock Boston; **198** © Evan Johnson/Jeroboam, Inc.; **209** Elizabeth Hamlin, Stock Boston; **215** Arleen Casto Lewis; **225** © Frank Siteman/Jeroboam, Inc.; **230** © Tom Turner 1983/Design Conceptions; **234** Bohdan Hrynewych, Stock Boston; **241** Arleen Casto Lewis; **248** George Bellerose, Stock Boston; **254** George Bellerose, Stock Boston; **259** Arleen Casto Lewis; **262** Jeffry W. Myers, Stock Boston; **267** © Frank Siteman/Jeroboam, Inc.; **269** Jean-Claude Lejeune, Stock Boston; **279** Paul Fortin, Stock Boston; **285** Jeff Dunn, Stock Boston; **293** Jean-Claude Lejeune, Stock Boston; **294** © Suzanne E. Wu/Jeroboam, Inc.; **304** © Frank Siteman/Jeroboam, Inc.; **307** Peter Vandermark, Stock Boston; **312** Arleen Casto Lewis; **320** © Susan Lapides, 1986/Design Conceptions; **323** Fredrik D. Bodin, Stock Boston; **332** Arleen Casto Lewis; **339** Frank Siteman, Stock Boston; **340** Donald Dietz, Stock Boston; **345** George Bellerose, Stock Boston; **352** Richard Sobol, Stock Boston; **358** Arleen Casto Lewis; **362** Cary Wolinsky, Stock Boston; **365** Deborah Kahn, Stock Boston; **372** George Bellerose, Stock Boston.

To Bonnie and Jake

ABOUT THE AUTHOR

Dr. Tom E.C. Smith is currently a professor in the area of teacher education at the University of Arkansas, Fayetteville, where he has served on the faculty for eight years. Prior to coming to the University of Arkansas, Fayetteville, he taught two years at the University of Arkansas at Little Rock. Dr. Smith earned his Doctor of Education degree from Texas Tech University in 1977. He has taught at the elementary and secondary levels in public schools and community special education programs.

Dr. Smith has written three college textbooks and more than twenty articles published in reference journals. He has made numerous presentations at national, regional, and state conferences and is currently on the National Board of Directors, Division on Mental Retardation, Council for Exceptional Children. He has served on two national committees for Kappa Delta Pi as well as numerous committees within the Mid-South Educational Research Association. The College of Education Research Award and Service Award at the University of Arkansas have been awarded to Dr. Smith.

Currently, Dr. Smith is serving a Governor's appointment to the Board of Directors, Arkansas Developmental Disabilities Services. He has also been appointed to several task forces and committees in the state of Arkansas dealing with teacher education.

CONTENTS

Preface

Chapter 1
INTRODUCTION   1

    ADVANCE ORGANIZERS   3
    INTRODUCTION   3
    EDUCATION IN THE UNITED STATES TODAY   8
        Magnitude of Public Education   8
        Purposes of Public Education   9
        Current Trends and Problems in American Education   9
    FUTURE OUTLOOK OF EDUCATION   26
    ORGANIZATION OF THE TEXTBOOK   27
    SUMMARY   27
    IN THE FIELD   28
    REFERENCES   28

Chapter 2
HISTORY OF EDUCATION   31

    ADVANCE ORGANIZERS   33
    INTRODUCTION   33
    EUROPEAN FOUNDATIONS IN EDUCATION   33
        The Greek Period   34
        The Roman Period   34
        The Medieval Period   34
        Renaissance and Reformation   35
        The Enlightenment   35
    EDUCATION IN THE UNITED STATES   35
        The Colonial Period   35
        The National Period   37
        Education in the Nineteenth Century   39
        Education in the Twentieth Century   43
    SUMMARY   51

IN THE FIELD   51
REFERENCES   52

Chapter 3 ───
PHILOSOPHY OF EDUCATION   53

ADVANCE ORGANIZERS   55
INTRODUCTION   55
Definition of Philosophy   56
Purposes of Educational Philosophy   56
BRANCHES OF PHILOSOPHY   57
Metaphysics   57
Epistemology   57
Axiology   58
SCHOOLS OF PHILOSOPHY   58
Basic Philosophies   58
Educational Philosophies   63
PHILOSOPHY AND EDUCATIONAL PRACTICE   64
Teaching and Philosophy   65
SUMMARY   67
IN THE FIELD   67
REFERENCES   68

Chapter 4 ───
WHO CONTROLS EDUCATION IN THE UNITED STATES?   69

ADVANCE ORGANIZERS   71
INTRODUCTION   71
ROLE OF THE FEDERAL GOVERNMENT   71
Legislative Branch   71
Judiciary Branch   73
Executive Branch   79
NATIONAL ORGANIZATIONS   80
Teacher Unions   80
Other National Organizations   82
STATE LEVEL INFLUENCE   86
State Government   86
State Constitutions   87
State Legislatures   87
State Education Agencies (SEAs)   88
Voluntary Statewide Agencies and Groups   90
LOCAL INFLUENCE   91
School Boards   91
Local Advisory Groups   92
Local Associations   93
Teachers   93
School Administrators   94
CONCLUSIONS: WHO DOES CONTROL?   94

SUMMARY   94
IN THE FIELD   95
REFERENCES   95

Chapter 5
ELEMENTARY EDUCATION   97

ADVANCE ORGANIZERS   99
INTRODUCTION   99
ELEMENTARY SCHOOLS   99
    Purpose of Elementary Schools   99
    Administration of Elementary Schools   102
    Organizational Arrangements of Elementary Schools   104
    Philosophy and School Policies   107
    Curriculum in Elementary Schools   107
ELEMENTARY CLASSROOMS   110
    The Elementary Teacher   110
    Curricular Variations Within Classrooms   112
KINDERGARTEN EDUCATION   118
SPECIAL SERVICES   119
    Special Education Services   119
    Gifted Education Services   119
    Counseling Services   120
SUMMARY   120
IN THE FIELD   121
REFERENCES   122

Chapter 6
SECONDARY EDUCATION   124

ADVANCE ORGANIZERS   126
INTRODUCTION   126
STRUCTURE OF SECONDARY SCHOOLS   126
    Intermediate Schools   127
    High Schools   128
OBJECTIVES OF SECONDARY EDUCATION   129
ORGANIZATION OF SECONDARY SCHOOLS   131
CURRICULUM OF SECONDARY SCHOOLS   132
    Common Curriculum   132
    Specialized Curricular Areas   135
    Curriculum Development and Revision   138
    Extracurricular Activities   138
METHODS OF INSTRUCTION   141
    Lectures   141
    Classroom Discussion   141
    Independent Study   143
    Individual Instruction   143
    Other Instructional Methods   143

SCHOOL PHILOSOPHY AND POLICIES 145
  Discipline 145
  Appearance Codes 147
  Expulsion and Suspension 147
  Search and Seizure 148
  Other School Policies 148
PROBLEMS FACING SECONDARY SCHOOLS 148
  School Dropouts 149
  Declining Academic Performance 151
  Problems of Adolescence 152
SUMMARY 155
IN THE FIELD 156
REFERENCES 156

Chapter 7
VOCATIONAL AND CAREER EDUCATION

159

ADVANCE ORGANIZERS 161
INTRODUCTION 161
VOCATIONAL EDUCATION 161
  What Is Vocational Education? 162
  Purposes of Vocational Education 163
  History of Vocational Education 163
  Current Status of Vocational Education 164
  Effectiveness of Vocational Education 166
  Role of the Federal Government in Vocational Education 171
  Role of Business in Vocational Education 171
  The Reform Movements and Vocational Education 173
  Future of Vocational Education 173
CAREER EDUCATION 174
  Objectives of Career Education 175
  Components of Career Education Programs 175
  Career Education in Elementary Schools 177
  Career Education in Secondary Schools 178
RELATIONSHIP BETWEEN VOCATIONAL AND CAREER EDUCATION 179
SUMMARY 179
IN THE FIELD 180
REFERENCES 180

Chapter 8
SPECIAL EDUCATION

182

ADVANCE ORGANIZERS 184
INTRODUCTION 184
HISTORY OF TREATMENT OF THE HANDICAPPED 185
  Education and Treatment Prior to 1750 185
  Education and Treatment Since 1750 185

SPECIAL EDUCATION TODAY   188
    Students Served   188
    Legislation   189
    Litigation   195
MULTICULTURAL SPECIAL EDUCATION   196
    Multicultural Concerns   197
    Responding to the Multicultural Problem   197
HANDICAPPED CHILDREN   198
    Traditional Classification System   198
    Generic/Noncategorical Model   203
SPECIAL EDUCATION SERVICES   204
    Traditional Service Delivery Model   205
    Current Service Delivery Model   205
SUMMARY   210
IN THE FIELD   211
REFERENCES   212

Chapter 9
EDUCATIONAL ADMINISTRATION   215

ADVANCE ORGANIZERS   217
INTRODUCTION   217
ADMINISTRATIVE HIERARCHY   217
LOCAL BOARD OF EDUCATION   217
    Powers and Responsibilities of Boards   218
PROFESSIONAL ADMINISTRATIVE STAFF   220
    Districtwide Administrative Staff   220
    Building-Level Administrative Staff   223
CAREERS IN ADMINISTRATION   235
    How to Become an Administrator   235
    Benefits of School Administration   235
SUMMARY   238
IN THE FIELD   239
REFERENCES   239

Chapter 10
SCHOOL FINANCE   241

ADVANCE ORGANIZERS   243
INTRODUCTION   243
TAXES   244
    Classification of Taxes   244
    Tax Shifting   245
    Tax Sources   246
THE DEVELOPMENT OF SCHOOL FINANCE   246
    School Finance During Colonial America   246
    School Finance After the Colonial Period   247

LOCAL SUPPORT FOR SCHOOLS   248
   Property Tax   248
STATE AID FOR EDUCATION   252
   Minimum Foundation Programs   252
FEDERAL SUPPORT OF EDUCATION   254
   Formula Grants   255
   Discretionary Funds   255
   The Future of Federal Aid   256
SUMMARY   256
IN THE FIELD   257
REFERENCES   258

Chapter 11
EDUCATIONAL PSYCHOLOGY
259

ADVANCE ORGANIZERS   261
INTRODUCTION   261
HUMAN DEVELOPMENT   261
   The Development of Thinking   262
   The Development of Language   266
   The Development of Morality   268
PRINCIPLES OF LEARNING   270
   Behavioral Theorists   271
   Cognitive Theorists   275
   Eclectic Theorists   277
MOTIVATION   279
MEASUREMENT AND EVALUATION   281
SUMMARY   282
IN THE FIELD   283
REFERENCES   284

Chapter 12
CAREERS IN EDUCATION
285

ADVANCE ORGANIZERS   287
INTRODUCTION   287
TEACHING AS A PROFESSION   289
   Early Status of Teaching as a Profession   289
   Current Status of Teaching as a Profession   289
CHARACTERISTICS OF TEACHERS   291
   General Characteristics   291
   Characteristics of Good Teachers   292
STATUS OF TEACHING   295
   Supply and Demand   295
   Salaries   300
   Other Benefits   301

SHORTCOMINGS IN TEACHING   303
   Burnout   303
   Low Job Status   303
   Low Salaries   306
   Actions from Reform Movements   306
OTHER EDUCATION PROFESSIONS   307
   Educational Administration   307
   School Counseling   307
   Social Work   308
   School Health   308
   Other Professional Support Personnel   308
TEACHING: SUMMATION   308
SUMMARY   309
IN THE FIELD   310
REFERENCES   310

Chapter 13
TEACHER PREPARATION   312

ADVANCE ORGANIZERS   314
INTRODUCTION   314
TEACHER EDUCATION   314
   Status of Teacher Education   314
   Criticisms of Teacher Education   316
   Reforms in Teacher Education   320
TEACHER CERTIFICATION   325
   Traditional Certification Programs   325
   Alternative Certification Programs   327
TEACHER EDUCATION: CONCLUSIONS   329
SUMMARY   330
IN THE FIELD   330
REFERENCES   331

Chapter 14
EDUCATIONAL TECHNOLOGY   332

ADVANCE ORGANIZERS   334
INTRODUCTION   334
INSTRUCTIONAL TELEVISION   336
CLOSED–CIRCUIT TELEVISION   337
AUDIOVISUAL KITS   338
VIDEOCASSETTE TECHNOLOGY   339
COMPUTERS   340
   Computers in Education   341
   Uses of Computers in Education   343
   Teacher Training in Computers   351
OTHER EDUCATIONAL TECHNOLOGIES   353
EDUCATIONAL TECHNOLOGY: NEEDED DIRECTIONS   353

SUMMARY 355
IN THE FIELD 356
REFERENCES 356

Chapter 15
THE FUTURE

358

ADVANCE ORGANIZERS 360
INTRODUCTION 360
FUTURISM 360
GLOBAL CONCERNS AND THE FUTURE 361
Population Trends 361
Natural Resources 362
Food 363
Geopolitics 363
THE FUTURE OF PUBLIC EDUCATION IN THE UNITED STATES 364
Population Trends in the United States 366
Maintaining the School Reforms 367
Curriculum for the Future 367
Technology in the Future 369
PAST PREDICTIONS OF THE FUTURE OF EDUCATION 370
Predictions by Theodore Hipple (1974) 370
Predictions by Max Rafferty (1974) 370
Conclusions of Predictions of 1974 371
AUTHOR'S PREDICTIONS 371
SUMMARY 373
IN THE FIELD 373
REFERENCES 374

EPILOGUE

CONTROL OF AMERICAN EDUCATION 375
REFORM MOVEMENTS OF THE 1980s 376
ELEMENTARY AND SECONDARY EDUCATION 376
SPECIAL EDUCATION 377
VOCATIONAL AND CAREER EDUCATION 377
EDUCATION AS A PROFESSION 378
TECHNOLOGY IN THE SCHOOLS 379
ORGANIZATION AND FUNDING OF SCHOOLS 380
CONCLUSIONS 380

Appendix 1   AGENCIES AND PROFESSIONAL ORGANIZATIONS 382
Appendix 2   IN–THE–FIELD ACTIVITIES REPORT FORM 384
Appendix 3   FEDERAL LEGISLATION AFFECTING EDUCATION 385
Appendix 4   IMPORTANT COURT CASES AFFECTING EDUCATION 387
Appendix 5   IMPORTANT DATES IN AMERICAN EDUCATION 389
Glossary 392
Index 399

PREFACE

Education in the United States is at a crossroads. The American system of public education has received more attention during the past five years than at any other time in recent history. The critical reports issued in the late 1970s and early 1980s that questioned the quality of public education in the United States, and the reforms initiated as a result, brought education into the limelight. Politicians, educators, parents, and the general public have all joined in the movement to improve our educational system and respond to the suggestion that "our nation is at risk." There has never been a more exciting time for education in this country. The initiation of needed reforms along with the emerging profession of teaching make the field of education a challenging career.

The objective of this textbook is to provide students preparing to be teachers with a general overview of education. The text is designed for students who are beginning their coursework in education. The book clarifies many issues related to education and public schools and focuses on the positive aspects of our educational system and teaching as a profession.

This textbook is not intended to provide all available information concerning a particular topic. Rather, it presents information that enables the reader to acquire a general understanding of education, including the foundations of public education; the organization, administration, and financing of American schools; the specialized concerns of education; and the profession of teaching. Teaching is presented as an emerging true profession, made up of dedicated, skilled persons.

Two topics discussed throughout the text include multicultural education and special education. Information related to multicultural education is assimilated in several chapters, while content concerning special education is presented in a separate chapter. These two topics are covered because of their importance to education today, as well as the requirement by the National Council for the Accreditation of Teacher Education (NCATE) that content related to multicultural education and special education be included in teacher education curricula.

ORGANIZATION

The textbook is organized into fifteen chapters. Chapter one provides an introduction to education in the United States. The focus is on the magnitude of public education, as well as the status of the current reform movements started as a result of the critical reports issued in the late 1970s and early 1980s. Chapters two and three present information about the history and philosophy of education, providing the reader with a general understanding of the development of public education in this country. Chapter four deals with the complicated topic of who controls education in the United States.

Chapters five and six focus on elementary and secondary schools. Organization, purposes, curricula, and classroom methods are discussed. In chapters seven and eight, material is presented that deals with vocational education and special education. These two topics receive extensive coverage because of their relationship to general education and the large numbers of students enrolled in these two programs.

Chapters nine and ten focus on the administration and financing of public education. Roles of administrators and administrative staff, as well as methods of financing public education, are presented to give the reader an understanding of public school organization. Chapter eleven deals with educational psychology. This topic is included in the text because of the critical role of psychology in education. Learning theories, motivation, and human development are included in the discussion.

Chapters twelve and thirteen present information related to careers in education and teacher education. Teaching is presented as an emerging profession. Characteristics of good teachers and the status of teaching related to supply and demand, salaries, and fringe benefits are included. The chapter on teacher education focuses on how to become a teacher, including information on teacher education and current efforts to reform teacher education.

Educational technology is the topic of chapter fourteen. This chapter looks at the technological explosion that has occurred and its impact on education. Finally, chapter fifteen presents information concerning the future. Futurism as an area of study, as well as the future of education, is included. An epilogue is provided to tie together all content presented in the text.

INSTRUCTIONAL AIDS

Highlights, which focus on current newspaper and magazine articles related to education, are included in each chapter. These provide the reader with an up-to-date view of what is happening in education in the United States. Each chapter also includes an in-the-field section that provides students with questions to ponder and research during any field activity that might be associated with the course. A report form for the in-the-field activities is located in the appendix. At the beginning of each chapter are an outline, objectives, and advance organizers. These aids enable students to focus on the important content included in the chapter.

ACKNOWLEDGMENTS

I would like to gratefully acknowledge the contributions of the following individuals who contributed so much to the development of this textbook: Ms. Marilyn Smith, for her support and secretarial assistance; Drs. Max and Arleen Lewis, for their critiques and constant positive reinforcement; Ms. Libby Swindle, for her personal friendship during difficult times; Josie and Steve Sabo, for their unyielding support; and especially to my son, Jake, and wife, Bonnie, for their tolerance of my long hours and trying moments. I would also like to thank all those who provided formal reviews of the manuscript. Their many suggestions greatly improved the content of the text.

Jon Conescu, University of New Mexico-Valencia Campus

Larry Cozad, University of Wisconsin-LaCrosse

Everett Davis, University of Southern Maine

Dan DeLoache, Northeastern State University

Lucille Freeman, East Central Oklahoma State University

Thomas Gwaltney, Eastern Michigan University

Mary Legg, Valencia Community College

Jeremy Rakowsky, Lorain County Community College

Beryl Wellborn, Grinnell College

Finally, I want to thank the people at West Publishing Company for supporting this project. Special thanks goes to my editor, Mr. Clark Baxter, who always had uplifting comments, even during dismal times, and to Ms. Jean Cook, whose professionalism made the production of the text go very smoothly.

Tom E.C. Smith

Chapter 1
INTRODUCTION

OBJECTIVES

After reading this chapter, you will be able to

- describe the magnitude of public education in the United States;

- discuss the reform reports that emerged in the early 1980s;

- specify some of the reforms that have been initiated in states in response to the critical reports;

- define and discuss multicultural education;

- discuss the changing role of the federal government in education;

- describe the role of the conservative movement in public education;

- discuss some of the trends in public education in the United States.

OUTLINE

ADVANCE ORGANIZERS
INTRODUCTION
EDUCATION IN THE UNITED STATES
    TODAY
      Magnitude of Public Education
      Purposes of Public Schools
      Current Trends and Problems
        in American Education

FUTURE OUTLOOK OF EDUCATION
ORGANIZATION OF THE TEXTBOOK
SUMMARY
IN THE FIELD
REFERENCES

1. How many pupils are served in public education in the United States?
2. What were the major criticisms voiced in the reports on education that were published in the early 1980s?
3. What are the purposes of public education?
4. What role is the conservative movement playing in public education?
5. What has been, and is emerging as, the federal government's role in public education?
6. What is multicultural education?
7. Which teacher organizations have influence in education?

INTRODUCTION

Education in the United States has been taken for granted for many years. Since the common school movement of the mid-1800s, which paved the way for a publicly supported education for all children, parents have assumed that public education would be available for their children. Parents also assumed that these schools would provide a quality education that would prepare their children for the world of adulthood and a higher place in the social strata.

Beginning in the late 1970s, an increasing degree of criticism has been directed at schools about the quality of education provided. Attention has been drawn to adults who cannot read, write, or verbally communicate at a functional level after twelve years of public education. America's difficulty in maintaining technological leadership in the industrialized world has been pointed out; that students in some other countries achieve at a higher level than children in this country has caused concern; and students graduating from high school without adequate vocational or college preparatory skills have embarrassed educators. Schools have also been criticized for including too many extracurricular activities into the curriculum, diluting the quality of academic instruction.

In response to these highly publicized problems, reformers have come forward with myriad solutions. Suggestions include everything from lengthening school days and school years to competency tests and/or basic skills tests for teachers. Politicians, professional educators, parents, and other interested persons have offered advice. Not since the education panic of the late 1950s, caused by the Soviet Union's launching of the satellite Sputnik, has the American public engaged in such widespread evaluation and demanded such widespread reform of the educational system. An indication of public support for reforms can be found in the results of a survey conducted by Freeman, Cusick, and Houang (1985). The survey, from a nationwide sample of twelve hundred adults, found that more than 80 percent of the sample supported

1. a requirement that students pass high-school exams in reading and math;
2. a requirement that junior-high students pass exams in reading and math;
3. at least half of all classes being required courses;
4. a system to reduce unexcused absences from school;
5. a requirement that teachers pass state or national teacher exams;

6. a requirement that teachers spend one month each summer improving their teaching skills.

The Gallup Poll of the Public's Attitude Toward the Public Schools (1985) indicated that 43 percent of the respondents gave the schools either an A or B rating. This compared with only 31 percent of the public rating schools with an A or B in 1983.

The American system of public education needs to be supported by a higher degree of public confidence if the system of equal educational opportunities for all children is to become viable. To prevent further erosion of public confidence and to support more positive public attitudes toward education may take many years of serious efforts by educators, parents, and politicians. That attention has been called to problems in the educational system is a positive step to needed reform. Caution must be used, however, in implementing change. Much of the educational system today is excellent. There are excellent teachers, curricula, and buildings, and highly motivated students. The positive things about education must be developed to strengthen the system. Great American educators such as Dewey, Mann, Conant, and Goodlad, as well as many parents and professionals, have worked diligently over the years to build a sound system of public education. Much of this system should remain in place.

American education is, however, at a crossroads. Several critical reports issued in the early 1980s indicated that the educational system in this country has reached a point where major changes must be made if the United States is to maintain its role of leadership in the world. While isolated concerns about education have been voiced for many years, education's loss of credibility and prestige is now widely acknowledged by the public (Weiler 1982).

Although discounted by many professionals, the report that created the most concern was issued by the National Commission on Excellence in Education in 1983. The Commission, formed in 1981 by Secretary of Education Terrell Bell, published *A Nation at Risk* (1983) after a two-year study of the condition of education in the United States. The report began with the conclusive statement that "Our nation is at risk" and listed several indicators of this risk: (1) twenty-three million American adults are functionally illiterate; (2) 13 percent of all seventeen-year-olds in this country, and as many as 48 percent of minority seventeen-year-olds, are functionally illiterate; (3) scores on the Scholastic Aptitude Test (SAT) declined steadily from 1963 to 1980; (4) science achievement scores of seventeen-year-olds declined in testing in 1969, 1973, and 1977; and (5) remedial math courses in colleges increased 72 percent between 1975 and 1980. These are but a few of the findings included in the report that indicated that the effectiveness of American education has seriously declined.

The following statements further clarify why the Commission concluded that the nation was "at risk":

- The number of students taking a general curriculum in high schools increased from 12 percent in 1964 to 42 percent in 1979.

- Only 31 percent of high-school graduates completed intermediate algebra.

- Twenty-five percent of the credits earned by general track high-school students were in areas of health, physical education, remedial math, English, and work outside the school.

- Homework for high-school seniors had decreased while grades had increased and academic achievement decreased.

- Students in other industrialized countries spent up to three times as much time in math and science courses as students in the United States.

- Twenty percent of all four-year public universities had to accept all high-school graduates from state high schools.

- Fifty percent or more of the credits earned for graduation could be electives in thirteen states.

- The amount of time spent in school was less in the United States than many other industrialized countries.

- The average school provided only twenty-two hours of instruction per week to students.

- Too many teachers came from the bottom of their high-school and college graduating classes.

- The average salary for teachers with twelve years of experience was only $17 thousand.

The reforms called for in the Commission's report were far reaching. They ranged from lengthening the school day and school year to decreasing the amount of time allotted for nonacademic electives.

Many of the educational practices and perceived practices in our schools are being challenged (Campbell 1983). Several other reports were issued in 1982 and 1983 that focused on problems of public education in the United States (see table 1–1).

Although recent attention has focused on education's problems, there is good news: states have taken and are taking actions to respond to many of the concerns of critics. A report issued by the Education Commission of the States in July, 1984, noted that between June, 1983, and July, 1984, twenty-seven states initiated reforms, fourteen states were refining plans for reform, and five states had initiated reforms in the early 1980s (Action in the States 1984). These reforms were responses to recommendations made by the National Commission on Excellence in Education and other task force reports, and ranged from lengthening the school day to implementing merit pay plans for teachers.

While education in this country will not turn back the "rising tide of mediocrity," cited by the Commission's report, the improvement process has begun. The first step was simply to publicize concerns. The future will determine if the reforms called for in the various reports are implemented, and if implemented, whether the suggested reforms actually improve the quality of education.

Although no proof exists that the changes implemented thus far have had a significant effect, students' test scores have begun to improve. Stedman and Kaestle (1985) report that the decline in test scores that began in 1963 is over, with students' scores on the Iowa Test of Basic Skills improving dramatically between 1977 and 1984 and test scores on the American College Testing Program (ACT) and the Scholastic Aptitude Test (SAT) having bottomed out. Graham (1984) reports that verbal and math test scores on the SAT have increased slightly.

Not all professionals view the reports of the early 1980s as helpful to education. For example, Albrecht (1984) states that the report of the National Commission on Excellence in Education encouraged overgeneralization of the condition of public education. The Commission's report "... would have us believe that a school is a school is a school". Other criticisms of the Nation at Risk report include the following: (1) the report suggests that the welfare of the college-bound student should be the criterion for judging the success of schools; (2) action should be taken immediately, before thorough thought has been applied; (3) the report legitimizes a way to get rid of children who have difficulty with school; and (4) what is good for one student, such as more math and science, is good for all students (Albrecht 1984).

In addition to these criticisms of the Nation at Risk report, critics have also reacted to other national reports. Ornstein (1985) lists the following general criticisms of the reports:

1. Reports are too idealistic and too unrealistic.
2. Narrow nationalistic interests are served at the expense of the public interest.

TABLE 1-1 Selected Recommendations of Six Reports on Education (and Sponsoring Organization), 1982-1983

	Federal Role (or other support role)	School Practices	Curriculum Objectives
TIME FOR REFORM (Council for Basic Education, 1982)	School people, with parents and community members, should establish educational goals and academic standards. Role of federal government is minimal.	Increase time devoted to learning. Consider the role of the principal and community in reforming schools.	Strengthen academic standards; emphasis on liberal arts and science; raise college entrance requirements.
ACADEMIC PREPARATION FOR COLLEGE (The College Board, 1983)	Develop a national standard for academic achievement in secondary education.	Emphasize improvement of study and independent learning skills.	Improve preparation in English, math, science, computers, foreign languages, the arts. Improve student competencies in reading, writing, speaking, listening, reasoning, math, study skills. Raise college entrance requirements.
MAKING THE GRADE (Twentieth Century Fund, 1983)	Emphasis on the federal government providing special education programs for the poor, minority, immigrant and handicapped student. Similar emphasis on the federal government providing programs to develop scientific literacy among all citizens and advanced math and science training for secondary students.	No comparable provision.	Improve English language and advanced learning in math and science. Initiate alternative programs for students with learning problems, and a voucher program for disadvantaged students.

TABLE 1-1 (Continued)			
	Federal Role (or other support role)	*School Practices*	*Curriculum Objectives*
EDUCATING AMERICANS FOR THE 21ST CENTURY (National Science Foundation, 1983)	Federal government should maintain a national mechanism for measuring student performance; it should have input in establishing national goals for education.	Consider longer school day, week, and/or year.	Require one hour daily of math and thirty minutes of science in grades K–6. Devote more time to math and science in the secondary grades, and provide more advanced courses. Raise college entrance requirements.
ACTION FOR EXCELLENCE (Education Commission of the States, 1983)	Create policies which foster partnerships between the private sector and education. Federal government has an essential supporting role in financing education.	Consider longer school day. Emphasize order and discipline and more rigorous grading with periodic testing. Assign more homework. Revitalize the curriculum to encourage independent learning and reduce droputs.	Establish and improve minimum competencies in reading, writing, speaking, listening, reasoning, economics. Strengthen programs for gifted students. Raise college entrance requirements.
A NATION AT RISK (The National Commission on Excellence in Education, 1983)	Federal government, in cooperation with the states and localities, should help meet the needs of special populations such as the disadvantaged, minority and bilingual students, the handicapped, gifted, and talented. Advocates national standardized tests, and the identification of the national interest in education.	Consider 7-hour school day and 200-day school year. Tighten attendance and discipline. Provide periodic testing and more rigorous grading. Place and group students by performance rather than age. Assign more homework. Improve textbooks and other instructional materials.	Strengthen graduation requirements in the five New Basics; English, math, science, social studies, and computer science. Increase foreign languages for college-bound. Provide rigorous courses in vocational education and arts. Raise college entrance requirements.

Reprinted with permission. Ornstein, 1985.

3. Too much attention is focused on course requirements and standards.
4. Most of the recommendations reflect previous suggestions.
5. Most of the reports ignore knowledge about school change.
6. Elitist solutions are supported, such as advanced courses and programs for gifted and talented children.
7. Most of the recommendations are very expensive.

Although these criticisms have been expressed at various times by various people, the reports of the early 1980s caught the public's attention. State legislators, governors, and others got on the bandwagon to improve education, to restore it to its previous place with what some regard as "quick fix" solutions (Albrecht 1984). While few educators would suggest that all is right with education in this country, many would have suggested different modifications. Although some of the changes brought about by the reform movement in the 1980s will have positive effects on education, other changes may prove useless in improving the quality of education. One undeniably positive outcome of the reports is the focusing of national attention on public education in the United States. Before blindly implementing changes, however, professionals need to determine whether the reports are accurately presenting the situation, and if so, whether the recommendations cited in the reports are sound (Passow 1984).

The issues in education today are particularly difficult, because they are not clear-cut. They are matters of value. Since different people value different things, disagreement is inevitable. The need seems to be for compromise/consensus rather than winners and losers and forced agreement. The reform movements have hopefully pointed out these facts and will lead to a better educational system.

EDUCATION IN THE UNITED STATES TODAY

Magnitude of Public Education

Public education in the United States is big business. The number of individuals directly and indirectly affected by education is difficult to estimate. Directly, students and their families and professional educators are involved. Indirectly, many other groups must be considered when describing the magnitude of public education, including employers; citizens who support schools with their tax dollars; businesses that depend on schools for their existence, such as textbook companies, school supply businesses, and enterprises that provide transportation capabilities to schools. The list is endless.

Number of students in public education. To grasp the extent of public education, an understanding of the number of children involved is needed. In the 1985–86 school year, 39.4 million students were enrolled in public education programs in the United States. Of this number, 24 million, or 62 percent, were enrolled in elementary schools, while the remaining 38 percent were in secondary schools. Enrollment by states ranged from a high of 4.2 million in California to a low of 107,000 in Alaska (Estimates of school statistics: 1985–1986 1986). The public school population can further be described by racial composition, disabilities, and language skills (see table 1–2). Although enrollments in public schools have been declining since 1970, recent evidence suggests that the decline has ended. The 1985 enrollment in elementary schools reflected the first major enrollment increase in fourteen years (Elementary enrollment up 1985).

School districts. To provide public educational programs for the approximate forty million students enrolled in public school programs, states are divided into school districts. During the 1985–86 school year, there were 15,746 such districts. The number of districts per state ranged from one in Hawaii and the District of Columbia to 1,092 in Texas (Estimates of school statistics: 1985–1986 1986). In 1981–82, 54 percent of the districts had fewer than one thousand students enrolled, while approximately 42 percent had enrollments between one thousand and ten thousand. Only 4 percent had enrollments greater than ten thousand (National Center for Education Statistics 1983).

Private education. In addition to the approximately forty million students enrolled in public educational programs in 1983, nearly five million students, or 10 percent of all

TABLE 1–2   Public School Enrollment: Fall 1980 by Race/Ethnic, Disability, and Limited English Speaking

Category	Percentage
White Non-Hispanic	73.3
Black Non-Hispanic	16.1
Hispanic	8.0
American Indian Alaskan Native	0.8
Asian or Pacific Islander	1.9
Disabled	8.3
Limited-English Proficient	2.3

Source: The Condition of Education, 1983 Edition. National Center for Education Statistics.

students, were enrolled in private schools. In some states, 15 percent or more of students were in private schools, while other states had very few students enrolled in private programs (National Center for Education Statistics 1983).

Purposes of Public Schools

Unlike public schools of the 1800s, which were designed primarily for academic and religious training, today's schools are expected to accomplish many goals. Many believe that too much is expected of American schools.

Even the academic purposes have expanded. The original goal of developing students' skills in the basic academic areas of reading, writing, and arithmetic has expanded to include many areas of knowledge. Besides the academic purpose of schools, society expects schools to provide instruction and experiences in civic, vocational, and personal goals. The expectations of schools now range "from mechanics in the basic skills, understanding of social and natural phenomena, and the highest levels of cognition to getting along with others, relating to humankind, and developing personal interests and capacities" (Goodlad 1983, p. 468).

Not only are schools supposed to provide instruction and experiences in all these areas, but they are supposed to accommodate myriad children in the process. The purposes would be difficult enough if all students were equal in abilities, came from similar environments, and had the same needs. A condition much to the contrary exists in public schools. Students range from the low to the high end of the intellectual continuum; represent many different racial, cultural, linguistic, and socioeconomic groups; and have different attitudes concerning education. The task of being all things to all students has proved to be difficult and has led to much dissatisfaction.

Current Trends and Problems in American Education

Educators in this country always seem to be implementing one trend or another. Many critics have suggested that educators are more interested in fads and quick fixes than in thought-out, well-researched solutions based on empirical evidence. Concerning the recent reactions to the Nation at Risk report, Albrecht (1984) believes that reforms are being implemented too fast to answer some of the points made by the

Unlike the schools of the 1800s, today's public schools have many different purposes, including preparation for life after high school.

report. Effective change must consider the interaction among numerous variables, each of which may affect combinations of others. The remainder of this chapter will describe various conditions, goals, and problems that need to be addressed if change is to be effective.

Curricular reform. Back-to-the-basics started as a reform movement in the 1970s. Since then, the merits of emphasizing the three Rs at the expense of other curricular areas has been debated. The issue is whether to base the entire curriculum on these basic subjects or include them within other subject areas.

Critics often refer to current educational practices as moving away from teaching the skills necessary to develop competencies in these three basic areas. In reading, for example, Bussis (1982) believed that an emphasis on "essential" reading had greatly reduced the time spent on reading. To change this practice, it was recommended that teachers make a wide range of reading materials available to students, read to children daily, encourage writing, set aside a reading time, and work individually with children. Similar changes in reading, as well as in other basic curricular areas, are frequently recommended by others.

State initiatives in response to reports of the early 1980s. Many states have responded to the Nation at Risk report and other critical reports of the early 1980s. By the middle of 1984, more than 250 task forces had been established to examine the state of education and recommend changes. Many of the task forces responded to a report by the Education Commission of the States, which recommended actions in eight areas:

1. Develop and implement state plans to improve education in public schools.
2. Create broader partners for improving the schools.
3. Acquire the resources necessary for improving the schools.
4. Express a new and higher regard for teachers.
5. Make academic experiences more intense and productive.
6. Provide quality assurance in education.
7. Improve leadership and management in public schools.
8. Provide better services to those underserved and unserved. (Action for Excellence 1983)

The actions range from minimal to far reaching, all having the intent of responding to critics of public education in the early 1980s (see table 1–3).

Multicultural education. Multicultural education developed out of the racial turmoil of the 1960s (Banks 1983). Just what multicultural education is cannot be precisely agreed upon. What can be stated is that multicultural education "is a concept predicated upon a fundamental belief that all people must be accorded respect, regardless of age, race, sex, economic class, religion, physical or mental ability" (Grant 1982, p. 485). The term is sometimes used as a catchall for anything innovative dealing with the education of minorities (Ivie 1978).

Melting pot theory. The multicultural education movement began in the early 1960s when educators began to respond to the demands of ethnic and racial minority groups who wanted a more balanced presentation in textbooks about minority groups and more minority professionals involved in education (Banks 1983). The movement resulted from the realization that the melting pot theory of American culture had not occurred, and probably would not occur. This idea is called cultural pluralism. "Pluralists reject the traditional 'Americanizing' function of the public school because it has meant assimilation into the white, middle class pattern of American society" (Ivie 1978, p. 442). Educators need to acknowledge that assimilation has not taken place. Multicultural education is an attempt to realize this fact.

Our society appears to be growing more rather than less diverse. The recent immigration of Hispanics, Cubans, Haitians, Vietnamese, and others adds to our cultural diversity. Many parents and children still have strong ties to racial, linguistic, nationalistic, ethnic, or Waspish traditions (Ehlers and Crawford 1983). These strong ties probably will not change in the near future.

Purposes of multicultural education. The initial purpose of multicultural education was to promote racial equality and harmony. Correcting errors of omissions, stereotyping, and misinformation, as well as providing information about ethnic minorities, has been replaced by the promotion of ethnic pluralism. The purposes have moved from primarily political to pedagogical (Gay 1983). Multicultural education currently attempts to assimilate reliable information about cultural pluralism into the entire curriculum.

TABLE 1–3 Examples of Actions Taken by States in Response to Education Reports of the Early 1980s

State	Actions
Arkansas	• Approved most comprehensive education program in state's history in a special legislative session in 1983. • Passed sales tax increase to fund reforms • Adopted new standards that will — reduce student/teacher ratios — increase number of principals and counselors per district — increase course offerings in high schools — initiated competency testing in grades 3, 6, and 8
Tennessee	• Passed a comprehensive reform act in 1984 • Passed tax increases to fund reforms • Established a five-step career ladder for teachers with annual salary incentives ranging from $500 to $7,000
Florida	• Passed stiffer high-school graduation requirements • Established twenty-eight regional coordinating councils to review and recommend programs to assure timely and needed vocational education programs • Established new academic performance standards for graduation and participation in interscholastic extracurricular activities
Ohio	• Increased funding for public education 15.4 percent for FY 1984 and 7.3 percent for FY 1985 • Increased graduation requirements • Passed procedures for ensuring that students achieve minimum academic competencies • Lowered student/teacher ratios in grades 1–4
Massachusetts	• Established the Commonwealth Inservice Institute to fund inservice programs. Examples of funded programs: — Middle management training model focusing on time management, staff development, computer education, and curriculum planning for administrators — Program to assist elementary teachers in coordinating reading programs — Training to assist administrators in programs for gifted and talented students
California	• Developed the Mathematics, Engineering, Science Achievement (MESA) Program. Program objectives: — Increase minority students' participation in math, science, and engineering training programs — Promote career awareness in minority students

Source: *Action in the States, Task Force on Education for Economic Growth. Education Commission of the States, 1984.*

Components of multicultural education. Multicultural education is not accomplished in a simplistic, single course taught to high-school students. Rather, multicultural education includes

1. Professional staffing that reflects the pluralistic nature of our society;
2. Curricula that are unbiased and present appropriate information about individuals of different sex, race, ethnic background, socioeconomic class, and ability;
3. Acknowledgment of the knowledge and use of different languages as acceptable;
4. Instructional materials free of bias and representative of various groups. (Grant 1982)

Bilingual education is a component of multicultural education. It focuses not on teaching equal skills in English and another language, but rather attempts to teach

Multicultural education aims at affording all children respect, regardless of cultural background.

English skills to non-English speakers (Foster 1982). Students are taught in their native language until they become proficient enough in English to receive the majority of instruction in English (Ovando 1983). This model, used in the majority of cases, is referred to as the transitional model. An alternative model focuses on maintaining the child's native language by giving it equal attention to English. The goal in this model is to enable the child to continue to develop the native language as well as English (Foster 1982).

Beginning with a federal budget of $7.5 million in the early 1970s, bilingual education had reached federal expenditures of $160 million by 1982 (Foster 1982). The mere size of federal financial involvement in bilingual education indicates the importance of this program. The role of the federal government in bilingual education will affect its future.

The future of multicultural education. Positive results of multicultural education include more minority students graduating from high school, the acknowledgment in textbooks of contributions made by minority individuals, and a more accurate representation of minority groups in textbooks and other instructional materials. However, multicultural education is at a crossroads. Although teachers involved in multicultural education play a significant role in successfully implementing its concepts (Ehlers and Crawford 1983), the movement is confronted by two factors that could lead to its demise: economics and ideology. Economics could affect multicultural education, because in a time of budget cutbacks, government-supported multicultural education programs could be cut. Ideologically, the current movement toward conservatism and the promotion of the majority culture could limit multicultural programs (Gay 1983). If multicultural education is to continue to be a positive force in American education, it must have the support of government policy makers, as well as those in business and education (Banks 1983).

━━━━━━━━━━━━ HIGHLIGHT ━━━━━━━━━━━━

NEA Ignores Warning and Endorses Unbiased Tests for New Teachers

WASHINGTON (AP)—The National Education Association, ignoring a warning that it was inviting competency tests for all teachers, endorsed tests Wednesday for people entering the profession.

The 7,000 delegates, concluding the annual NEA convention, said unbiased tests should be part of "rigorous state standards" for all new teachers.

They spurned the advice of a Florida teacher leader who warned, "The proponents of testing will not stop with entry-level testing. It's you and I that they want."

The vote was a victory for NEA President Mary Hatwood Futrell, who had urged the delegates to put the NEA on record in favor of "the toughest possible" certification requirements for new teachers.

"It's very important," she said later. "It states more clearly and more positively what our positions are. . . . It says up front that we're for high standards."

The NEA reasserted its opposition to competency tests for veteran teachers. The testing resolution stopped short of saying there should be a single national certification exam, as Albert Shanker, president of the rival American Federation of Teachers, has proposed.

Now, the 1.7 million-member AEA policy is that "competency testing must not be used as a condition of employment, recertification or relicensing, evaluation, placement, ranking or promotion of certified teachers." It also opposed using student test scores to evaluate teachers.

Arkansas held the first-in-the-nation basic skills tests for already-certified teachers and administrators in March. Ninety per cent of those who took the test passed it.

The NEA delegates, in another move to bolster the NEA image, voted for the first time to support dismissal proceedings against incompetent teachers. The NEA said teachers should be given "sufficient time and opportunity for improvement" after a negative evaluation. Then, if "a teacher is formally re-evaluated and there is documentation of incompetence, dismissal proceedings with guaranteed due process should be initiated," the NEA said.

The delegates adopted the resolution on an amendment from the floor by Susan A. Stitham, a Fairbanks, Alaska, English teacher, who said the NEA must display its "utter intolerance of incompetence in America's classrooms."

A minority of the NEA's Resolutions Committee had proposed a similar resolution. The NEA has long favored formal, annual evaluations for teachers, but had never put in writing support for moves to dismiss incompetents.

Ruth D. Holmes, a Pensacola elementary school teacher and past president of the Florida Teaching Profession, tried to derail the test resolution. She proposed instead that teacher colleges be required to test students before they graduate.

But the delegates rejected her amendment. They inserted the word "state" in the call for "rigorous standards" and passed the rest of the plank intact.

Teacher candidates should have above-average grades, complete a period of student teaching and pass "appropriate pedagogical and subject matter tests," the NEA said. "Tests should be valid and unbiased."

Improved teachers. One of the reforms called for in the Nation at Risk, Action for Excellence, and other reports is improved teachers. The Nation at Risk document reported the following about teachers:

- Too many teachers come from the bottom quarter of graduating classes.

- Teacher preparation curricula are heavily weighted with educational methods courses.

- Average teacher salary after twelve years of teaching is only $17 thousand.

- Severe teacher shortages exist in some subject areas, most notably math and science.

- Half of the newly hired math, science, and English teachers are not qualified to teach these courses.

To improve the quality of teachers, many states have initiated reforms, which include increasing salaries, screening prospective teachers before they enter teacher education, providing merit pay for outstanding teachers, providing more flexibility in teacher certification, requiring teachers to pass competency tests to remain certified, and requiring teachers to pass tests before initial certification. In addition to these suggestions, a recent congressional task force called for school districts to develop sabbatical programs for teachers, for the federal government to fund leave time for study through a talented teacher fellowship program, and for school administrators to try different ways to improve the work environment for teachers (Congressional Report Waffles on Merit Pay 1983). Several initiatives have been implemented by states to improve the quality of teachers (see table 1–4).

Providing merit pay for superior teachers is being investigated by several states. The issue is controversial, but is generally supported by the public (Williams, King, Shirley, and Steptoe 1983). Most professionals agree that those teachers who do the best job should receive the most pay; questions concerning how such a system would be developed remain unanswered. Should teachers be rewarded based on their continuing education, the achievement levels of their students, ratings by supervisors, peer evaluations, or other measures?

Even though a merit pay plan that is without criticism may be difficult to develop, several states and local districts have implemented merit pay programs. Pipho

TABLE 1–4 Sample of Actions by States to Improve Teachers		
Action	*Number of States Initiated*	*Number of States Pending*
Salary increases of 8 percent or more	16	—
Programs to recognize outstanding teachers	17	—
Master-teacher, career-ladder, or merit pay plans	19	7
Financial incentives or training programs for retraining in teacher shortage areas	28	3

Source: Action in the States. Task Force on Education for Economic Growth, Education Commission of the States, 1984.

(1983) stated that as many as twenty states could propose legislation dealing with merit pay in 1984. Some of the states and their plans include the following:

California	Recommend rules, regulations, and guidelines for the California Mentor Teacher Program
Florida	Appoint the Florida Quality Instruction Incentives Council to develop and implement a plan for incentives for teachers
New Jersey	Develop a Master Teacher Program
Tennessee	Revamp the Master Teacher Plan
	Appoint an Interim Commission on Master Teacher-Administrator Certification
Virginia	Budget $500 thousand in 1984–86 to field test several performance-based teacher pay plans

Besides these statewide efforts, many local districts have taken the initiative to implement teacher incentive/merit pay plans. In Round Valley School District, California, teachers assist in the development of their own merit pay program. They can earn merit points for (1) teacher initiative, (2) teacher cooperation, and (3) principals' evaluations (Burke 1982). Various rewards are provided for teachers in the Catalina Foothills School District in Tucson, Arizona, for excellence in the classroom. The most popular reward for teachers in the program has been trips to professional meetings, although cash, instructional materials, and computers can also be earned (Frase, Hetzel, and Grant 1982).

A much publicized merit pay plan, the Second Mile Plan, was initiated in the Houston Independent School District in 1979. With this plan, teachers qualify for incentive pay through six different categories:

- teaching in secondary science or math

- service in a high priority school

- good teacher attendance

- outstanding educational progress by students in the school

- service at a unique campus

- professional growth

The plan cost the district approximately $11 million during the first year, in which two-thirds of the district's teachers received incentive pay. Average incentive pay was $936, with a range from $300 to $3,500. The school board has been supportive of the program and "sees the incentive pay plan as a viable method of rewarding those teachers who effectively meet the special needs of the district" (Say and Miller 1982, p. 271).

Although many states and districts are experimenting with merit pay plans, a great deal of controversy over the issue stills exists. Teacher unions, for the most part, do not support merit pay programs. Often, merit pay plans that are developed and implemented are not successful. One example of a failed merit pay plan is in Kalamazoo, Michigan. The plan was started in 1974 to reward administrators and teachers based on evaluations by administrators, peers, pupils, self, and pupil performance. The program ended with a great deal of controversy, having never achieved its goal (Doremus 1982).

The conservative movement. The political climate in the United States has been conservative since the mid-1970s. This conservative trend has had an impact on public education. Calls for returning to the basic purposes of public schools have been voiced by conservative educators, parents, and politicians. Some of the recommended changes include (1) a return to emphasizing the basic academic subjects; (2) a deemphasis on extracurricular activities; (3) an emphasis on moral education; (4) inclusion of school prayer; and (5) more control of the educational process by the family.

Most supporters of conservative reform of public schools are not extremists. They are well-intentioned, well-informed citizens who have the welfare of their children in mind. They are firmly convinced that the public schools of today have moved too far away from the appropriate purposes of public education. Some of the questions asked by these reformers include:

- Do parents have the primary rights and responsibilities in the education of their children?

- Do educators in public schools have the right to programmatically enter the "affective domain" of the child without the prior, informed consent of parents?

- What is the primary purpose of education—social and psychological development or academic and vocational achievement? (McGraw 1982, p. 94)

Parents who ask these questions want more of a say in the educational system than they currently feel they have.

Some professional educators also feel that public education has ventured too far from its original purposes. In Ebel's view (1982), much of what schools do today does not emphasize student achievement, and therefore, should be changed. His proposals for strengthening public education are similar to the ideas held by Horace Mann and other traditional educational theorists. To determine whether schools are promoting achievement, Ebel suggests asking: (1) Is there evidence of student learning? (2) Are teachers' instructional goals appropriate? (3) Are teachers' instructional methods effective? and (4) How can the school facilitate teachers' efforts?

The new right. In 1980, Park wrote that a new coalition was being formed among ultraconservative and right-wing groups in the United States. This coalition, called the New Right, includes traditional conservative groups and certain fundamentalist religious groups. The New Right is a potentially powerful force that deserves the attention of educators. The aim of the coalition is to change the ways children in this country are educated (Brodinsky 1982). People who hold New Right views differ from other conservative educational reformers in the extent to which they would go to alter public education. They agree with other conservative reformers, but would go further in implementing changes in schools.

The New Right has focused on public education as a target for change. Among the aims of the movement are

- developing and propagating "model" legislation for states;

- promoting prayer in public schools;

- promoting creationism;

- censoring textbooks and school library books;
- ending unionism and union tactics in education;
- promoting the interests of Christian schools;
- cutting taxes and school expenditures;
- nurturing conservative ideas;
- fighting "secular humanism" in public schools;
- channeling corporate gifts and funds into colleges and universities that promote "free enterprise." (Brodinsky 1982, p. 88)

Supporters of the New Right suggest that schools in this country "have been deliberately sabotaged by a core of elitist educators" who "through such exotic titles as values analysis, values clarification, situation ethics, death education, sex education, environmental education, and now the new global education ... are bent on totally stripping from children those traditional American values that parents and the majority of those who pay teachers' salaries still espouse" (Dixon 1982, p. 97). They believe that books expounding on traditional values have been banned from public schools (Gabler and Gabler 1982).

Censorship in school libraries is a major focus of the New Right; since the mid-1970s, individuals espousing New Right views have attempted to remove books from school libraries that are considered objectionable for a variety of reasons (Pincus 1984). The censorship activities have involved areas other than books. As a result of the attacks of right-wing groups, teachers are often questioned about classroom discussions, content of school plays and assemblies, and the circulation of materials (Kemerer 1984). Individuals identifying with the New Right want more control over what is presented to their children and press for the right to veto any information that they consider objectionable.

An area related to censorship is the desire by conservative groups to have creationism taught in lieu of or in combination with evolutionism. This area alone has caused a great deal of debate between individuals who believe in the scientific approach to creation and those who believe in the creationist view. Those who believe religion should be in the schools and those who strongly advocate strict adherence to separation of church and state are also at odds. Those who favor inclusion of creation science base their request on the fact that students have a right to know all sides to the creation question (Hahn 1982); those opposing creation science in public schools argue that creationism is not science but religion and should therefore be separate from education, which is an arm of the state (Strike 1982).

Home schooling. Another movement that parallels the conservative movement is home schooling. Parents in many parts of the country are beginning to formally educate their children at home, rather than sending them to public school programs. Although this might be viewed as encouraging truancy and breaking mandatory attendance laws, many states have given parents the legal right to provide home schooling.

Until just a few years ago, educating children at home was viewed as a subversive activity. Parents who educated their children at home would keep them in doors during school hours for fear that neighbors would report them to the local school

Most parents involved in home schooling are dissatisfied with the schools for not providing training in fundamental values.

authorities. Currently, however, home schoolers are speaking out; they are coming out of the "closet" and making the home schooling movement a public effort (Divoky 1983).

The majority of individuals involved in the home schooling movement are probably religious fundamentalists who believe that schools do a poor job of adequately educating their children, especially in fundamental values (Divoky 1983). A minority of home schoolers, however, provide educational programs in the home because they feel they can do a better job than the schools have done in educating their children. Regardless of the reasons for home schooling, more parents are trying it. With the movement picking up supporters, school officials should begin to cooperate with home schoolers and develop a close working partnership (Holt 1983).

HIGHLIGHT

Missouri Home Schoolers are Regulated

In the closing hours of this year's session, the Missouri legislature passed a controversial measure requiring parents who educate their children at home to provide at least 1,000 hours of instruction annually and to keep a written log on the education they provide.

The law, however, does not require "home schoolers" to register with local, county, or state authorities, according to William J. Wasson, the state's deputy commissioner of education.

The previous home-schooling provisions were deemed "unconstitutionally vague" last summer by a federal district judge, who asked the legislature to design more specific guidelines, Mr. Wasson said.

Under the measure, at least 600 of the required instructional hours must be spent on reading, language arts, mathematics, social studies, or science, and at least 400 hours must be spent at the home-school site.

Reprinted with permission from Education Week, Volume V, Number 36, 1986.

Technology. Our world is experiencing a technological explosion. New technologies are being developed that affect all aspects of our lives, including education. The most obvious technologies are in the area of machines and equipment (Hatch 1984). The advent of the microcomputer in the late 1970s and early 1980s has encouraged a great deal of interest related to its use in education. The use of microcomputers in education appears to have become a major force in education. The National Center for Education Statistics (1983) reported that the number of computers available in public schools tripled between 1980 and 1982. The number of schools with microcomputers increased from 13,986 in 1982 to 30,493 in 1983, an increase of over 200 percent in one year alone (National Center for Education Statistics 1984). In 1983, 27 percent of all elementary schools, 46 percent of all junior high schools, and 62 percent of high schools had microcomputers (National Center for Education Statistics 1984).

Closer investigation, however, indicates that the use of computers has not been as successful as the numbers might suggest. Problems that continue to block the widespread use of microcomputers in education include (1) availability of computers in schools, (2) lack of policy in schools related to computer usage, (3) adequate software, and (4) teacher training (Bonner 1984).

The potential of computers to revolutionize education may never be realized if computer purchases and program implementation precede adequate planning. To avoid this occurrence, Boyer (1984) suggests acceptance of three high-priority goals for computer usage by students. First, students need to learn about technology. This includes teaching students about the social impact of technology and computers, not hands-on instruction. The second priority is to teach students how to learn with computers or use computers to gather information. Finally, students should learn from computers. This requires interactive learning between students and computers, or "conversing" between students and computers to improve thinking skills.

While computers are capable of becoming a major force in education, some professionals argue that the over use of computers and other technologies can have a negative effect. For example, Hatch (1984) believes that the technology in education can "isolate us from the very processes by which we define our humanity." These human processes, defined as those things that differentiate humans from other living organisms, such as loving, knowing, and making decisions, can become devalued as a result of overdependency on technology.

Regardless of concerns, the use of technology in education today is definitely increasing. Microcomputers will likely continue to become a major instructional tool. While there are problems in the widespread use of this technology and concerns from some educators about dehumanizing the educational process, the future promises increased use of microcomputers in most aspects of education.

HIGHLIGHT

Education-Spending Rate Slows; Salary Gains Made, N.E.A. Finds

By J. R. Sirkin

WASHINGTON—Americans raised their spending for K–12 public education by an estimated $9.1 billion in 1985–86, pushing the average salary for classroom teachers to $25,257, according to a report to be issued this week by the nation's largest teachers' union.

Despite inflation and regional variations, the report, "Estimates of School Statistics, 1985–86," indicates slow but continued growth in public-school resources.

Due in part, however, to the first enrollment increase in more than a decade, the rate of growth in expenditures per pupil fell this year to its lowest level in 10 years—6.8 percent, for an increase of $235 per pupil, the report states.

Likewise, the rate of growth in school revenues, which had accelerated in the previous two years, declined from 8.4 percent a year ago to 7.1 percent in the current school year, according to the report.

"It is fair to question the future of many state-level education reforms in light of these revenue estimates, and to emphasize the need to examine local, state, and national revenue systems so that public-education improvements can be implemented fully and evaluated fairly," the report states.

The National Education Association, which prepares the annual report based on data provided by state education agencies, was scheduled to release it at a press conference here this week.

The report is generally considered the most reliable source of information on state education systems and their finances. Among this year's highlights:

- Enrollments increased nationwide by an estimated 109,000 students, to 39,468,269. Although secondary-school enrollments declined by an estimated 159,000, that decline was more than offset by an increase of 269,000 pupils in the elementary grades. Enrollments rose in 36 of 51 states, including the District of Columbia, although they fell in New England, the mid-Atlantic states, and the Great Lakes states. California and Texas each had increases of about 90,000 students.

- The number of classroom teachers increased by an estimated 13,670, raising the nation's public-school teaching force to 2,177,851. A decrease in the number of secondary-school teachers was more than offset by a bigger increase in teachers at the elementary level.

- Schools spent an average of $3,677 per pupil in 1985–86, although that figure varies widely within and among states. Alaska spent the most—$8,044 per pupil—while Utah spent the least—$2,297.

- Average salaries for classroom teachers rose by 7.3 percent, or $1,723. Average salaries for teachers in the highest-paying state—Alaska—topped $40,000, while teachers in South Dakota averaged the least—$18,095.

- Total expenditures for elementary and secondary day schools nationwide increased by 7.2 percent, from $125,524,891 to $134,604,869. Capital outlays exceeded an estimated $8 million, but the rate of growth fell from 15.6 percent to 7.1 percent. Interest on school debt rose by 8.9 percent, to $2.65 million.

- Revenues also increased by 7.2 percent, from $139,634,698 to $149,687,997, but the federal share fell for the seventh consecutive year, from 6.6 percent to an estimated 6.4 percent.

The state share rose for the fourth straight year, to an estimated 50.1 percent, while the local share fell from 43.7 percent to an estimated 43.5 percent.

The report's state-by-state data reveal significant spending hikes in three regions of the country—the mid-Atlantic, the Southeast, and the Far West, with more moderate gains in other regions.

It also indicates that the Southeastern states—which sparked the excellence movement—are closing the spending gap with the Southwest and Rocky Mountain states, but continue to lag behind New England and the mid-Atlantic states.

Even reform-minded states like Tennessee and Arkansas continue to trail all but four states in per-pupil spending, and two of those states—Alabama and Mississippi—are from the same region. Idaho and Utah were the two other states spending the least per pupil.

After Alaska, the highest-spending states were: New York, New Jersey, Wyoming, the District of Columbia, and Connecticut. The states that increased spending the most were: Wyoming, New Jersey, Montana, North Carolina, Delaware, Connecticut, New York, Rhode Island, and Georgia.

In percentage terms, salaries for classroom teachers increased most in the mid-Atlantic and Southwest states, sparked by big jumps in New Jersey and Oklahoma, respectively. Arkansas and Nevada also reported big percentage increases.

In absolute terms, the mid-Atlantic and Far West states led the way. New Jersey salaries increased the most—by some $3,400—while salaries in Nevada jumped by $3,100. In California and Mississippi, average salaries rose by about $2,500.

The highest-paying states were: Alaska, the District of Columbia, New York, Michigan, California, Rhode Island, New Jersey, and Wyoming. The lowest-paying states were: South Dakota, Mississippi, Arkansas, and Maine.

Mississippi, which has traditionally trailed all other states in this category, moved up only one notch, to 50th, despite raising teachers' salaries by a reported 15.8 percent—the largest percentage increase in the nation.

Education Week. April 23, 1986. Reprinted with permission.

Fiscal problems. In the fall, 1979, Chicago School Board members realized that they would not receive any bids on $124.6 million in general obligation notes that were required to keep the school system fiscally solvent. As a result, several things occurred: (1) more than forty thousand teachers and school staff did not know if they would receive paychecks, (2) the school board was unable to meet its payroll three times, (3) a one-week walkout by teachers occurred, (4) a full strike by teachers occurred, (5) 2,465 jobs in the district were lost, (6) the school superintendent resigned, and (7) a rescue plan was formulated by the state legislature, city of Chicago, and teacher unions (Banas 1980).

Other school districts have faced similar problems. The San Jose district in California, the eighth largest in the state, filed for bankruptcy when it faced a $14 million deficit after having closed fourteen schools and laying off five hundred teachers during the previous year (A California school district goes broke 1983). Money is the basis for public educational programs; without funds schools will discontinue to be a force in our society. Some reasons that schools today face increasing fiscal difficulties include:

- Constituency of the local community—fewer people with children; smaller families; population shifts from urban to rural, from industrialized to the sunbelt.

- Declining economy—the country has been experiencing economic decline, coupled with an astronomical federal deficit. Local communities have also experienced declining tax bases.

- Deemphasis of funding educational programs by the federal government.

- Inflation—increasing costs for transportation, utilities, building maintenance, and personnel.

In a time when state and local governments must assume a greater funding burden for public schools, their ability to do so is declining. A tax revolt, which began in the early 1970s, is having an impact on state and local governments. Between 1977 and 1980, sixteen states reduced sales taxes and twenty-two reduced income taxes. In the 1978 general election, tax reduction or limitation measures were voted on in thirteen states, with ten passing (Archambault and Duncombe 1979). States now provide the biggest share of the public school funding, approximately 47 percent, compared with less than 10 percent from the federal government. Unfortunately, during the past several years, state tax collections have not kept pace with inflation (National Center for Education Statistics 1983).

The tax revolt of the late 1970s is a reversal of the situation during the 1960s and early 1970s. From 1959 until 1976, 41 new taxes and 586 tax increases were passed in the states. This substantially increased the tax money available for public school programs (Adams 1982). Two of the biggest tax reversals occurred in California and Massachusetts. In 1978, California voters passed Proposition 13. This legislation limited property taxes to 1 percent of their 1975 assessed valuation (Hoban 1979). In Massachusetts, Proposition 2½ was passed in 1980. This act stipulated that no community could levy property taxes in excess of 2½ percent of its total assessed value. Furthermore, communities that already taxed at higher rates had to reduce taxes at a rate of 15 percent per year until the lower maximum was reached (Bumstead 1981).

These two tax measures had a major impact on education in both states. In California, Proposition 13 resulted in major reductions in personnel. Approximately eleven thousand educators, including teachers, support staff, administrators, and pupil support staff lost jobs. Another major result of the act was the low staff morale present after the cuts. Although difficult to define, morale is related to self-worth as professionals (Hoban 1979).

In Massachusetts, Proposition 2½ had similar results. One district, which had previously had a budget of over $14 million, was forced to reduce its budget by 15 percent, to just over $11 million. The results were that teachers had to be released, programs reduced or cut, and some schools actually closed (Bumstead 1981).

The reform movements of the 1980s have reversed the negative funding trends. Many states, responding to demands that education be improved and shocked by the reports indicating that schools were declining rapidly, passed substantial tax increases to fund new and improved programs. In July 1984 the Education Commission of the States reported that

- Fifteen states had passed or were considering increases in state sales or income taxes to support educational reform.

- Revenues increased from $69 billion in 1969 to $89 billion in 1984.

- Since 1982 increased state and local funding has offset part of the federal government's reduction in funding.

- Corporate, business, and foundation support for public education amounts to more than $50 million annually.

While the reform movements may have temporarily focused attention on school finance needs, local schools still need to develop strategies to convince local voters that schools need adequate funds to operate quality schools. Miller (1980) suggested several actions for schools to take to get tax increases. These included (1) providing massive amounts of information to the community, (2) justifying the needed fund increases, (3) forming voter coalitions that support increased funding, (4) soliciting citizens to canvass voters, and (5) informing the public of the consequences of no funding increases.

Declining enrollments. The enrollment in elementary and secondary public schools declined significantly during the 1970s and early 1980s. Between 1971 and 1981, overall enrollment in public schools dropped 13 percent, or 5.9 million students. Declines occurred in forty-two states and the District of Columbia. The decline in elementary schools was greater than in secondary schools, suggesting that the overall decline will continue (National Center for Education Statistics 1983). National population projections indicate that there will be 26 percent fewer 18-year-olds in 1991 than in 1978 (Wharton, Baudin, and Griffith 1981).

Although the enrollment decline should continue for several more years, the trend is reversing. In 1984 elementary schools recorded their first significant enrollment increase in fourteen years, resulting from an increase in the U.S. birth rate that started in 1977. The elementary enrollment increases are expected to continue through the early 1990s (Elementary enrollment up 1985).

Declining enrollments have major effects on the educational system, specifically: (1) reduced state aid, (2) hiring freezes or reductions, (3) smaller class sizes, (4) redistricting of school boundaries, and (5) remodeling or selling school buildings (King-Stoops and Slaby 1981). Negative attitudes on the part of school personnel is another result of declining enrollments. These negative attitudes result from uncertainty about job security, reduced resources to carry out the instructional program, and limited professional opportunities (Mazzoni and Mueller 1980).

Instructional programs are also affected by declining enrollments. Subject areas most affected include language arts, social studies, science, fine arts, and foreign

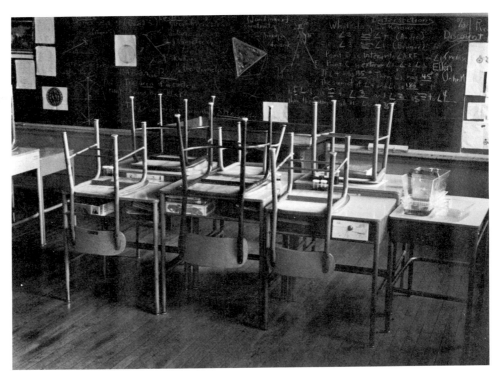

Declining school enrollments may lead to smaller class sizes and personnel reductions.

language, which results in reduced course offerings and fewer jobs in these subject areas (Gay, Dembowski, and McLennan 1981).

Accurate predictions of enrollments aids in planning and implementing quality educational programs. With declining enrollments, accurate predictions are even more critical. Unfortunately, being able to predict enrollments is not easy (King-Stoops and Slaby 1981). Variables such as the strength of the economy at the local, state, and national levels, also difficult predictions for economists, make predicting enrollments for schools even more difficult. Still, schools must attempt to accurately predict enrollment figures in order to adequately plan fiscal needs, personnel needs, and space needs.

Changing federal role. The role played by the federal government in education has been changing and should continue to change. Terrell Bell, the Secretary for the Department of Education during the first Reagan term, stated that "During the first two years of the Reagan administration, responsibility for administering the nation's educational system began to be returned to the states and localities" (Bell 1984, p. 531). A primary aim of the Reagan Administration was indeed to return to states and local agencies certain decision-making powers. Concomitant with this shift of responsibility came a shift of funding. The administration's request for federal funding for education in 1983 was $2.1 billion less than the previous year. Nearly 20 percent of the previous federal aid to education was cut (Clark, Astuto, and Rooney

1983). These budget cuts marked the beginning of a federal pullback from public education.

Besides sharply reducing the federal share of fiscal support to education, the Reagan administration also sought to decentralize federal education policy. A major avenue to effect this was through block grants. During the first Reagan term, twenty-nine categorical programs were consolidated into one block grant (Bell 1984). By consolidating programs, the administration succeeded in shifting more authority to states and local agencies to carry out educational programs. Although the future federal role in education cannot be accurately predicted at this point, the consensus is that the push to decentralize will continue (Clark, Astuto, and Rooney 1983).

Teacher unions. Teacher unions have grown in membership and influence. The two major unions are the National Education Association (NEA) and the American Federation of Teachers (AFT). The NEA has long held the distinction of being the larger and more powerful of the two organizations. Currently the memberships of both groups collectively are in excess of two million members.

Although considered to be a necessary force several years ago, the NEA and AFT are currently losing some power and credibility. Lieberman (1979), who advocated a collective bargaining role for teacher organizations in the early 1960s, now thinks that they have become too powerful and that their representational rights should be reduced. In clarifying this position, Lieberman points out the following:

- Teacher unions may have more than $500 million annually to support their causes.

- Pupil welfare is a secondary or tertiary consideration in teacher bargaining.

- The widespread use of collective bargaining techniques has made it virtually impossible for teaching to be considered a profession.

Many citizens now consider strong unions to be a barrier to educational reforms.

FUTURE OUTLOOK OF EDUCATION

Although attention has been focused on education in the past, the reform movements that began in the early 1980s have surpassed previous periods of interest. Not only are community members concerned about schools in their neighborhoods, but all segments of American society are concerned about the state of education and ways to improve education. Politicians, parents, professional educators, and other groups of people have all become involved in the reform of public education.

Several trends are already well entrenched and can be expected to continue during the next decade, including

- decreased role of the federal government

- decreased funding by the federal government

- increased emphasis on basic curricular areas

- increased emphasis on competency testing

- increased emphasis on teacher improvement

- increased need for local and state funds for education
- increased use of technology
- continued influence from conservatives
- continued opportunities for handicapped and other minority groups
- continued emphasis on accountability

We do not know whether the heightened public interest in education will continue. Interest generated by the many national reports may be replaced by more pressing issues. If so, the gains made by the recent attention to reform may have propelled American education into a position of providing children with an educational opportunity never attained. Whether the public educational system in this country has benefited from the reforms cannot be determined until the reforms have been evaluated.

ORGANIZATION OF THE TEXTBOOK

The remaining fourteen chapters include discussions on the history and philosophy of education; who controls American education; elementary and secondary education; vocational and career education; special education; educational administration; school finance; educational psychology; careers in education; teacher preparation; educational technology; futurism; and an epilogue that attempts to draw some conclusions concerning public education. Information on multicultural education is included in several chapters to provide an understanding of the concept and how it relates to public education.

Questions related to field observations are in each chapter for students to consider during field placements. Since many introductory education courses include a field component, these questions are included to encourage students to ask questions and make certain observations during their field experiences. The questions provide topics for classroom discussions following exposure to schools and students. They are also intended to raise issues relating to educational theory, policy, and practice.

SUMMARY

This chapter has provided general information about public education in the United States. The first part of the chapter focused on the current state of education, including discussions of the critical reports on public education issued in the 1970s and early 1980s.

The next section of the chapter included information on the magnitude of public education in this country. Approximately forty million students are enrolled in public schools each year. Various demographic information on these students was presented. The final section of the chapter focused on current trends in public education, including curriculum reform, improved teachers, multicultural education, the conservative educational movement, the New Right, technology, declining enrollments, and the reduced federal role in public education. Finally, a section on the future outlook for public education was included.

IN THE FIELD

1. Does the school district have a document stating the purposes of the schools? If so, where is it located and are teachers and students aware of its existence?

2. Have any district or school actions resulted from the critical reports issued in the early 1980s? Examples could include longer school days, longer school year, more required academic subjects.

3. Is there any evidence of multicultural education in the classroom through instruction or materials? What evidence did you observe?

4. Are teachers in the district on any kind of merit pay plan? If so, what are the provisions? If not, is there a plan to develop such a program?

5. Are teachers actively involved in professional organizations such as the NEA and AFT? Does one of these groups or another group represent the teachers in collective bargaining?

6. Are computers available for student use? If so, what kinds of computers and at what levels? Who makes the decision regarding adoption of particular kinds of computers and software?

7. Has the district been experiencing declining or increasing enrollments? What is the future projection concerning district enrollment? What are the reasons for the enrollment trends in the district?

8. What problems, concerns, and/or controversies exist in the school or district?

REFERENCES

A California school district goes broke. *Newsweek*, July 11, 1983, p. 26.

A nation at risk: The imperative for educational reform. The National Commission on Excellence in Education. U.S. Department of Education, 1983.

Action for excellence. Task Force on Education for Economic Growth. Education Commission of the States, 1983.

Action in the states. Task Force on Education for Economic Growth. Education Commission of the States, July, 1984.

Adams, E. K. 1982. The fiscal condition of the states. *Phi Delta Kappan 63*(9), 598–600.

Albrecht, J. E. 1984. A nation at risk: Another view. *Phi Delta Kappan 65*(10), 684–85.

Archambault, E. D., and H. S. Duncombe. 1979. Incompatible messages of the property tax revolt. *Phi Delta Kappan 61*(1), 26–27.

Banas, C. 1980. The Chicago school finance catastrophe. *Phi Delta Kappan 61*(8), 519–22.

Banks, J. A. 1983. Multiethnic education at the crossroads. *Phi Delta Kappan 64*(8), 559.

Bell, T. H. 1984. American education at a crossroads. *Phi Delta Kappan 65*(8), 531–34.

Bonner, P. 1984. Computers in education: Promise and reality. *Personal Computing 8*(9), 64–77.

Boyer, E. L. 1984. Education's new challenge. *Personal Computing 8*(9), 81–85.

Brodinsky, B. 1982. The new right: The movement and its impact. *Phi Delta Kappan 64*(2), 87–94.

Bumstead, R. A. 1981. One Massachusetts school system adapts to proposition 2½. *Phi Delta Kappan 62*(10), 721–25.

Burke, B. T. 1982. Merit pay for teachers: Round Valley may have the answers. *Phi Delta Kappan 64*(4), 265–66.

Bussis, A. M. 1982. Burn it at the casket: Research, reading instruction, and children's learning of the first R. *Phi Delta Kappan 64*(4), 237–41.

Campbell, R. F. 1983. Time for vigorous leadership in the public schools. In J. Frymier (Ed.), *Bad times, good times*. West Lafayette, IN: Kappa Delta Pi.

Clark, D. L., T. A. Astuto, and P. M. Rooney. 1983. The changing structure of federal education policy in the 1980s. *Phi Delta Kappan 65*(3), 188–93.

Congressional report waffles on merit pay. 1983. *The American School Board Journal 170*(12), 14.

Divoky, D. 1983. The new pioneers of the home schooling movement. *Phi Delta Kappan 64*(6), 395–98.

Dixon, G. 1982. The deliberate sabotage of public education by liberal elitists. *Phi Delta Kappan 64*(2), 97.

Doremus, R. R. 1982. What ever happened to Kalamazoo's merit pay plan? *Phi Delta Kappan 63*(6), 409–10.

Ebel, R. L. 1982. Three radical proposals for strengthening education. *Phi Delta Kappan 63*(6), 375–78.

Ehlers, H. and D. Crawford. 1983. Multicultural education and national unity. *The Educational Forum 47*(3), 263–77.

Elementary enrollment up, total enrollment still down. 1985. *Phi Delta Kappan 66*(10), 736.

Estimates of school statistics, 1985–86. National Education Association.

Foster, C. R. 1982. Defusing the issues in bilingualism and bilingual education. *Phi Delta Kappan 63*(5), 342–44.

Frase, L. E., R. W. Hetzel, and R. T. Grant. 1982. Merit pay: A research-based alternative in Tucson. *Phi Delta Kappan 64*(4), 266–69.

Freeman, D. J., P. A. Cusick, and R. T. Houang. 1985. Secondary school reform: What does the public say. *NASSP Bulletin 69*(483), 52–62.

Gabler, M., and N. Gabler. 1982. Mind control through textbooks. *Phi Delta Kappan 64*(2), 96.

Gallup, A. M. 1985. The 17th annual Gallup poll of the public's attitudes toward the public schools. *Phi Delta Kappan 67*(1), 35–47.

Gay, G. 1983. Multiethnic education: Historical developments and future prospects. *Phi Delta Kappan 64*(8), 560–63.

Gay, G., F. L. Dembowski, and R. L. McLennan. 1981. Preserving quality of education during enrollment declines. *Phi Delta Kappan 62*(9), 655–57.

Goodlad, J. I. 1983. A study of schooling: Some findings and hypotheses. *Phi Delta Kappan 64*(7), 465–70.

Graham, A. M. 1984. SAT results: Student achievement is up and the President's education policies are working. *American Education 20*(7).

Grant, C. A. 1982. *Bringing teaching to life*. Boston: Allyn and Bacon, Inc.

Hahn, G. E. 1982. Creation-science and education. *Phi Delta Kappan 63*(8) 553–55.

Hatch, J. A. 1984. Technology and the devaluation of human processes. *The Educational Forum 48*(2), 243–52.

Hoban, G. 1979. The untold golden state story: Aftermath of proposition 13. *Phi Delta Kappan 61*(1), 18–21.

Holt, J. 1983. Schools and home schoolers: A fruitful partnership. *Phi Delta Kappan 64*(6), 391–94.

Ivie, S. D. 1978. Multicultural education: The Mexican experience. *The Educational Forum 42*(4), 441–49.

Kemerer, F. R. 1984. Censorship, academic freedom, and the right to know. *Kappa Delta Pi Record 20*(3) 73–76.

King-Stoops, J., and R. M. Slaby. 1981. How many students next year? *Phi Delta Kappan 62*(9), 658–62.

Lieberman, M. 1979. Eggs that I have laid: Teacher bargaining reconsidered. *Phi Delta Kappan 60*(6), 415–19.

McGraw, O. 1982. Where is the public in public education? *Phi Delta Kappan 64*(2), 94–95.

Mazzoni, T. L., and V. D. Mueller. 1980. *Phi Delta Kappan 61*(6), 406–10.

Miller, I. 1980. Tax referendum strategies: A perspective for the eighties. *Phi Delta Kappan 62*(1), 22–23.

National Center for Education Statistics. 1983. *The condition of education, 1983 edition.* Washington, D.C.: U.S. Department of Education.

National Center for Education Statistics. 1984. *The condition of education, 1984 edition.* Washington, D.C.: U.S. Department of Education.

Ornstein, A. 1985. The national reports on education: Implications for directions and aims. *Kappa Delta Pi Record 21*(2), 58–64.

Ovando, C. J. 1983. Bilingual/bicultural education: Its legacy and its future. *Phi Delta Kappan 64*(8), 564–68.

Park, J. C. 1980. Preachers, politics, and public education: A review of right-wing pressures against public schooling in America. *Phi Delta Kappan 61*(9), 608–12.

Passow, A. H. 1984. Tackling the reform reports of the 1980s. *Phi Delta Kappan 65*(10), 674–83.

Pincus, F. L. 1984. Book bargaining and the new right: Censorship in the public schools. *The Educational Forum 49*(1), 7–21.

Pipho, C. 1983. Merit pay/master teacher plans attract attention in the states. *Phi Delta Kappan 65*(3), 165–66.

Say, E., and L. Miller. 1982. *Phi Delta Kappan 64*(4), 270–71.

Stedman, L. C., and C. F. Kaestle. 1985. The test score decline is over: Now what? *Phi Delta Kappan 67*(3), 204–10.

Strike, K. A. 1982. The status of creation-science: A comment on Siegel and Hahn. *Phi Delta Kappan 63*(8), 555–57.

Weiler, H. N. 1982. Education, public confidence, and the legitimacy of the modern state: Do we have a crisis? *Phi Delta Kappan 64*(1), 9–14.

Wharton, J. H., J. J. Baudin, and O. Griffith. 1981. The importance of accurate enrollment projections for planning. *Phi Delta Kappan 62*(9), 652–55.

Williams, D. A., P. King, D. Shirley, and S. Steptoe. The merits of merit pay. *Newsweek*, June 27, 1983, 61–62.

Chapter 2
HISTORY OF EDUCATION

OBJECTIVES

After reading this chapter, you will be able to

- trace the historical development of education in Europe;
- describe the educational systems developed in colonial America;
- describe the public school movement;
- trace the development of secondary education;
- discuss the role of litigation and legislation in the development of public education in the United States;
- describe the major criticisms of American education today;
- describe some of the recommendations made by critics for American schools;
- discuss the future of reforms currently being made in American schools.

OUTLINE

ADVANCE ORGANIZERS
INTRODUCTION
EUROPEAN FOUNDATIONS IN EDUCATION
    The Greek Period
    The Roman Period
    The Medieval Period
    The Enlightenment
EDUCATION IN THE UNITED STATES
    The Colonial Period

The National Period
Education in the Nineteenth Century
Education in the Twentieth Century
SUMMARY
IN THE FIELD
REFERENCES

ADVANCE ORGANIZERS

1. What was the system of education like in ancient Greece and Rome?
2. How were the Greek and Roman educational systems different and similar?
3. What were the differences in the educational systems established in the Colonies?
4. Why did the high school emerge as the model for secondary education?
5. What ideas existed that supported the Common School Movement?
6. What was the role of John Dewey in American education?
7. What legislation affected education in the twentieth century? How did this legislation impact public education and how did it relate to changes in society?
8. What were the Cardinal Principles issued by the National Education Association?
9. What major criticisms were leveled at American schools during the 1950s? Were they reactions to any events or publications?
10. What recommendations did James Conant make concerning the high school?
11. What is the status of reforms initiated during the 1970s and 1980s?
12. What do you predict will be the next reforms or changes in American education?

INTRODUCTION

Why study the history of education? Many prospective teachers ask this question, expecting the content to be uninteresting and to have little relevance to becoming a teacher. However, teachers need a general understanding of the historical foundations of education for many valid reasons.

John Dewey (1916, p. 251) wrote that "knowledge of the past is the key to understanding the present. History deals with the past, but this past is the history of the present." We understand what we are presently doing by understanding our past; current educational practices are partly explained by historical practices.

Many of the issues facing education today are not new. The relationship between education and government, providing adequate financing for public education, and efforts to ensure equal educational opportunity for all members of society are issues that have plagued education in the United States for over three hundred years (Fain, Shostak, and Dean 1979). By understanding the past, better solutions are likely to be made for the future. An understanding of the history of education can provide insight into education just as knowledge of the history of man can provide insight into society (Gutek 1970). This chapter presents an overview of the history of education in the United States, so the reader will have a basic understanding of the foundations of the current educational system.

EUROPEAN FOUNDATIONS IN EDUCATION

Education in the United States had its beginning in Europe. Therefore, a quick look at the way the European educational system emerged will provide a foundation for the present public educational system in the United States. The exact location and time of the beginning of education programs is impossible to determine. Formal schools existed in China and Sumer as early as 2000 B.C. (Johnson, Collins, Dupuis, and

Johansen 1982), however, educational systems that developed in Greece are considered the beginning of the framework for education in the United States.

The Greek Period

Education in Greece became somewhat formalized during the days of the Greek city states of Sparta and Athens. Since the Greek peninsula was politically organized around cities, the educational systems of the time reflected the basic philosophies of the city states. In Sparta, which was a militarized city, schools attempted to assist in making citizens totally obedient and subservient to the state. The content of the educational program was basically physical and moral, with little emphasis on academic subjects (Cordasco 1970). The goal of education was to educate children to serve the state.

The Greek city state of Athens was considerably different from Sparta, although it was in existence during the same period—approximately 800 B.C. Differences between the cities were reflected in the educational programs each devised. While the government of Sparta tried to destroy the family, the government of Athens preserved the family. Educational programs focused on reading, writing, and literary elements. Music, which was provided for students, included poetry, drama, history, oratory, and science as well as typical music education. (Cordasco 1970). The educational program in Athens was the beginning of a liberal arts curriculum. The emphasis was on educating for "wholeness": body, mind, and spirit.

The Roman Period

Roman education was heavily influenced by Greek education. Roman education can be divided into two distinct periods: that period without Greek influence and that period with Greek influence. From approximately 750 to 250 B.C., Roman education was not influenced by Greek education. Schools during this period offered rudimentary instruction in reading and writing. The home, however, remained the primary moral instruction center. Greek influence began about 350 B.C. and continued until 200 A.D. Schools were of several types, ranging from providing instruction in basic reading and writing to preparing students for public careers. The Latin Grammar School, which was developed during this period, remained the most persistent part of Roman civilization until the Roman Empire was destroyed. Subjects studied in the Latin Grammar School included literature (history, poetry, and scientific writings), math, music, and rudimentary dialectics. Gymnastics and dancing, which were found in Greek schools, were not included (Cordasco 1970).

The Medieval Period

The medieval period covers approximately 800 years, from A.D. 476 (the fall of the Roman Empire) to A.D. 1300. Education went into a severe decline during the first five hundred years of this period (the Dark Ages) and was somewhat revised during the last three hundred years.

During the Dark Ages, the Roman Catholic church became a powerful political force. By stressing gaining admission into heaven, the church deemphasized life on earth, including any knowledge acquired through education. Significant amounts of knowledge that had been generated were lost. During this period, Charlemagne came to power and attempted to infuse some life into education. However, despite his efforts, little progress was made and education continued to decline (Johnson et al. 1982).

The last part of the medieval period has been termed by some as the Age of the Revival of Learning. The reconciliation of religion and philosophy and the renewed interest in previous writings, mainly those of Aristotle, provided the impetus for many positive developments (Johnson et al. 1982).

Renaissance and Reformation

Education made significant gains during the Renaissance and Reformation, from 1300 to 1700. The Renaissance had a great impact on education through its emphasis on the need for educated individuals to know Latin (Ornstein and Levine 1981). This persisted in American education until well into the twentieth century. Teachers, often referred to as Renaissance humanists, were literary figures who taught through literature. They were critics of literature and used it as a base for most of the curriculum (Ornstein and Levine 1981).

Martin Luther's publication of ninety-five theses in 1517 generally marks the beginning of the religious reformation. During this period, marked by a revolt from the Roman Catholic church, various religious groups "developed their own educational theories, established their own denominational schools, structured their own curricula, and sought to convince their children of the rightness of the reformed gospels that were preached to them" (Ornstein and Levine p. 125). The main effect of the Reformation on education was the desire to expand literacy to the masses (Ornstein and Levine 1981). This created the need for schools in all cities and towns, and for their control to be other than the Roman Catholic church.

The Enlightenment

Following the Renaissance and Reformation came a period (eighteenth century) when reason emerged as a factor in schools. Also called the Age of Reason, this period focused on the use of the scientific method to formulate "natural laws" in science and the emergence of the idea that the common man should have an opportunity for improvement politically, economically, socially, and educationally (Johnson et al. 1982). This period was a revolt against the authoritarianism of the Reformation; education reflected the political, economic, and religious changes (Cordasco 1970).

EDUCATION IN THE UNITED STATES

Many historians divide American educational history into two major periods: the colonial period (1607–1788) and the national period (1787–present). The national period is further divided into the period from 1787 through the nineteenth century and the twentieth century (Cordasco 1970).

The Colonial Period

During the early days of the United States, the thirteen original colonies took on characteristics that were distinctly different. For the most part, the colonies were divided into three different groups: the New England colonies, the Middle colonies, and the Southern colonies. Much of the political practices in the colonies, and the educational systems as well, reflected the religious beliefs of the citizens of each section. New Englanders were predominantly Calvinists, following the dictates of John Calvin; the Middle colonies were composed of religious dissenters, including Quakers and Anabaptists; and the Southern colonies were mostly Anglican (Cordasco 1970).

The New England colonies. The New England colonies included Massachusetts, Connecticut, New Hampshire, Vermont, and Rhode Island. Massachusetts was settled by Puritans who followed the teachings of John Calvin (Gutek 1986). The educational system developed in the New England colonies was heavily influenced by Calvinism. Education was the primary method of indoctrinating children in the Calvinist dictates, the Bible, and the general laws of the colonies. A major motivating factor in the establishment of schools was to prevent Satan from corrupting an illiterate society (Gutek 1970). "The New England schools were designed to create educated Puritans who would perpetuate the religious, social, political, and economic beliefs of the adults" (Gutek 1986, p. 6). Education was to prepare an educated ministry and a literate and productive citizenry (Gutek 1986).

In order to combat the evils of illiteracy, Massachusetts passed the School Act of 1642, which marked the beginning of elementary education. This act was considered important in maintaining the commonwealth of Massachusetts (Commager 1983). It required that parents and guardians be responsible for ensuring that their children receive instruction in reading and understand religious principles and commonwealth law. The law did not order school attendance, but simply placed the educational responsibility on parents (Gutek 1970).

Massachusetts went a step further in 1647 when the General Court of Massachusetts passed the Old Deluder Satan Law. This act, which was designed to outwit Satan, required towns of fifty or more families to provide a teacher for reading and writing; towns of one hundred or more families also had to provide children with instruction in Latin (Gutek 1986). Similar laws were enacted in Connecticut in 1650 and New Hampshire in 1680. Rhode Island was the only New England colony that did not pass laws regarding education and allowing for taxes to be collected to support education (Cordasco 1970).

New England schools included town schools, or elementary schools, and secondary schools called Latin Grammar Schools. Town schools were governed by the community's selectmen. In addition to this basic academic school, other educational arrangements were available for young children, including apprenticeships, which had originated in medieval Europe, and dame schools. Dame schools were for very young children, were taught by women in their homes, and focused on simple skills such as learning the alphabet (Gutek 1986).

Puritan-influenced schools stressed reading (Gutek 1986). The major reading material used for education was the Hornbook, which was a paddle with a sheet containing the alphabet, vowels, syllables, the doctrine of the Trinity, and the Lord's Prayer. In 1690 another famous textbook, the New England Primer, became available. This book included twenty-four rhymes to assist in learning the alphabet, vowels, and syllables, as well as lessons for children such as "An Alphabet of Lessons for Youth," "The Dutiful Child's Promises," the Lord's Prayer, the Creed, the Ten Commandments, and "The Duty of Children Toward Their Parents." Memorization was the principal method of learning (Gutek 1970). The most important part of the New England Primer was an outline of Puritan theology (Gutek 1986).

Reading, writing, spelling, and arithmetic, or ciphering, were also subjects taught in New England elementary schools. Spelling required students to memorize long lists of difficult words, while arithmetic focused on basic computation, decimals, fractions, weights, and measures (Gutek 1986).

Unlike elementary education, secondary education in the New England colonies was not for the masses. Patterned after secondary schools in Europe, these schools were primarily designed to prepare students for college (Cordasco 1970). Students were mostly from economically well-to-do families.

The Middle colonies. The Middle colonies were composed of very divergent groups, having no common religion, language, or value structure. Contrary to the homogeneity of educational programs established in the New England colonies, programs developed in the Middle colonies varied considerably. In New York, which was controlled by the Dutch, the Dutch Reformed church operated schools that taught reading, writing, and religion. Some private schools, called academies, were established to prepare children for careers in specific trades or skills. The most famous of these schools was the Philadelphia Academy founded by Benjamin Franklin in 1751 (Ornstein and Levine 1981). Academies expanded very rapidly during the early 1800s and became the dominant secondary educational model during that era (Button and Provenzo 1983).

The Southern colonies. A major difference between the Southern colonies and those in the middle and New England regions was population distribution. While population centers were common in other parts of colonial America, the South was characterized by large, rural areas. The impact this had on education was that there were few areas where ample numbers of people lived to facilitate the development of school programs. The result was an emphasis on private and tutorial education. Landowners who could afford private tutors for their children did so, while poor white children and children of black slaves did without education.

The National Period

The success of the American Revolution and the adoption of the Constitution ended the colonial period and marked the beginning of the national period. Many major historical events occurred between 1787 and the beginning of the twentieth century, including the United States gaining independence from England, the Civil War, and the emergence of the United States as a great industrial and political power. During the nation's first fifty years, several important developments occurred that affected education.

Constitutional developments. In 1788 the United States Constitution was ratified. This document, which still provides the legal basis for our country, included many elements of Enlightenment political theory and British law. It provided for a system of checks and balances among the three branches of government, guaranteed basic individual rights, and established the principle of separation of church and state. The Constitution, however, did not specifically address education.

As a result of the Tenth Amendment reserving to states items not included in the Constitution, education was made a state responsibility (Gutek 1986). Several states made provisions for education in their constitutions. State constitutions of Pennsylvania (1776), North Carolina (1776), Georgia (1777), Massachusetts (1780), New Hampshire (1784), and Delaware (1792) included some provisions for the establishment of schools. In 1779 Thomas Jefferson, who thought education was critically important for a democratic society, introduced the Bill for the More General Diffusion of Knowledge in the Virginia Assembly. The bill would have made free public schools available for all children for three years, develop secondary schools, and establish a state university for higher education that would be free from religious influences. Although the bill was rejected in 1779 and later in 1817, it laid the foundation for public education in the United States (Cordasco 1970).

The federal government became involved in education even before the current Constitution was passed (Unks 1985). The new government under the Articles of Confederation passed the Land Ordinance of 1785, which required each township to reserve lot number 16 for the support of public schools. The Northwest Ordinance of 1787 reinforced the 1785 act by encouraging education as being important to good government and happiness. Article Three of the 1787 ordinance expressed a commitment for education by stating that "Religion, morality, and knowledge being necessary to good government and the happiness of mankind, schools and the means of education shall forever be encouraged" (Gutek 1986, p. 30).

Following the passage of the current Constitution, the federal government made outright financial grants to states to support education beginning with the Ohio Enabling Act of 1802, which returned 5 percent of the earnings from the sale of public lands to newly admitted states. This was followed by other acts that enabled states to use federal funds to support educational programs. "Federal grants to public education prior to the Civil War reflect the fusion of two basic Jeffersonian principles: the belief that government governs best when it governs least and the almost holy belief in the power of education to create a reasonable citizen for a democracy" (Unks 1985, p. 138).

The academy movement. Academies began in the mid-1700s and flourished until the Civil War, when high schools began to emerge. Between the years 1781 and 1825, academies were the most rapidly growing type of school in the United States. There were slightly more than one hundred academies in 1800 and more than one thousand in 1830 (Button and Provenzo 1983). Benjamin Franklin was instrumental in the development of the first academy in 1751 (Cordasco 1970). The focus of Franklin's academy was on a broad and practical curriculum. It was much more like an English Grammar School than the old Latin Grammar School (Gutek 1970).

Academies varied considerably in organization, control, and support. Some were operated for profit by private groups; some were under the control and support of churches; and still others received some support and were controlled by local government units. Programs offered by academies were diverse, including college-preparatory curriculum for students who would be attending college; English-language curriculum for students who would complete their formal education with the academy; and the normal curriculum, which prepared students to be teachers in common or elementary schools (Gutek 1986).

Courses provided at academies included

- Latin and Greek
- English
- Natural Sciences
- History
- Modern Languages
- Commercial Subjects
- Mathematics
- Music and Art (Gutek 1986)

Academies were the forerunner to the current comprehensive high school in the United States.

Elementary education. Because of states passing legislation for education and localities receiving funds from the federal government either through land grants or direct funding, elementary education began to grow in the United States during the first years following the American War of Independence. The infant school, which served children ages four to eight, was supported financially by the city of Boston in 1818. This practice was duplicated in many other communities and states, thus creating a network of elementary schools. After further development of elementary schools, infant schools became synonymous with the lower level of elementary schools (Cordasco 1970).

Another model developed during the first years of the Republic was called monitorial schools, where teachers would teach their brightest students who in turn would teach their peers. This model of education enabled one headmaster to teach many more students than the teacher alone could have taught. These schools, also known as Lancasterian schools after the founder of the idea, Joseph Lancaster, were started in many states after a Lancasterian school was opened in New York City in 1806 (Cordasco 1970).

Education in the Nineteenth Century

Public education in the United States made significant progress during the nineteenth century. Some of the reasons include (1) the common school movement, (2) state laws and state boards of education, and (3) permanent sources of funding.

The common school movement. Public education as it is known today had its beginnings with the common school movement in Massachusetts, led by Horace Mann. Proponents of mass education for all children defined the common school "as an institution that would provide its students with basic cultural and literary skills. . . . Common did not mean lowly or base-born, but expressed the idea of a cultural community in which ideas, experiences, beliefs, aspirations, and values would eventually become uniquely American" (Gutek 1970, p. 52).

Pre-nineteenth century forces contributed heavily to the common school movement. These included district schools in New England, the Massachusetts school laws of 1642 and 1647, and the ideals of the American Revolution. Along with state school laws, these forces helped lay the foundation for public education (Cordasco 1970).

Many arguments were heard both supporting and opposing universal education for all children. Arguments supporting the idea included

- education would benefit political enlightenment;

- individuals from diverse backgrounds could develop common values and loyalties;

- educated individuals would have job skills;

- education could lead to social improvement and economic advancement. (Gutek 1970)

Public education was thus viewed as a vehicle for preparing children from various ethnic and religious backgrounds for citizenship in the United States, as well as for participation in the economic system. The movement sought to mold citizens into a force with common values, ideals, loyalties, and purposes.

Many did not support the common school movement. Reasons for the opposition included the fact that class distinctions would be dismantled, cultural heritages would be lost, and religion would be removed from the schools (Gutek 1970). While some supported the common school movement for reasons of melting various heritages into one, others opposed the movement for the same reason.

The one individual who is given most of the credit for the success of the common school movement is Horace Mann. Mann was an attorney, legislator, and president of the Massachusetts senate. As president of the senate, Mann supported a law in 1837 that created the first Massachusetts State Board of Education. Prior to this bill, he had been supportive of a bill passed in 1834 that established the Common School Fund and a bill passed in 1836 that prohibited factories from employing children who had not spent at least three months of the previous twelve months in school (Field 1976). In 1837 Mann was appointed as the first secretary of education for the state of Massachusetts. Because of his efforts in establishing the common school, Mann is considered the father of American free public schools (Fain, Shostak, and Dean 1979).

When Mann was appointed as the secretary of education for Massachusetts, several problems were paramount in the public education system: incompetent teachers, poor physical facilities, inadequate curricula, and a lack of leadership by the local school committees. Mann viewed many of these problems as resulting from inadequate local control and saw two objectives as critical in the revitalization of public education: bringing back into public schools students in private education and limiting the control of schools by local citizens. That the State Board of Education had been created in Massachusetts indicated a direct challenge to local autonomy (Field 1976). Overall, Mann was very successful in his efforts to reform public education in Massachusetts. Other states were also making significant progress in their efforts in public education.

Several elements were necessary for the success of common schools. These included

1. The common school would be free and open to all.
2. The common school would be of such excellent quality that all parents and guardians would be willing to send their children.

3. The school would be common in the sense that all children would attend and that it would serve as a unifying force in welding communities together, assimilating the great numbers of immigrants pouring into the country. The premise was that if children from all classes of society would attend the same school, they would learn to understand and appreciate each other.
4. The common school would be publicly supported through taxation of the entire community.
5. The common school would be publicly controlled through elected or appointed public officials responsible to the whole community and not to any political, economic, or religious group.
6. The common school would be nonsectarian in character, with morality being taught without reference to the tenets of any particular sect.
7. The common school would provide the basic skills and knowledge essential for students of diverse backgrounds to assume the responsibility of citizenship. (Fain, Shostak, and Dean 1979, p. 34)

Horace Mann and others made the common school movement of the early 1800s successful. By 1860 approximately half of all elementary-aged children were being served in public school programs, and free school systems were established in most states (Armstrong, Henson, and Savage 1981). Although many children attended school sparingly, the system of public education at public expense had been established and was the framework for the current educational system.

State legislation. For the common school movement to be successful, states had to pass legislation that promoted public education and established permanent funding sources for public education (see table 2–1).

Development of secondary schools. The American high school evolved from the Latin Grammar School and academies. While the common elementary school was established by the late 1800s, high schools were just being developed. The Latin Grammar School, which focused on a curriculum emphasizing Greek and Latin writings, declined in popularity after the American Revolution because of a desire for a more utilitarian secondary school. Private academies appeared to meet the public demand for a more practical curriculum. While offering classical courses for college preparation, academies also included practical courses such as bookkeeping and

TABLE 2–1	State Legislation Supporting the Common School Movement
State	*Legislation*
New York	Passed legislation in 1784–1787 that established the University of the State of New York, a state school board
New York	Established a state school fund in 1805
New York	Established the office of the superintendent of common schools in 1812
Pennsylvania	Established the right to levy taxes for education in 1834
Massachusetts	Set up a state board and a state education superintendent in 1837

Source: Cordasco, F. A brief history of education, 1970.

surveying in their curricula. The broader based curricula of the academies was much more popular than the narrow opportunities of the Latin Grammar School (Gutek 1970).

In the late 1800s, private academies gave way to publicly supported high schools. This was a continuation of the trend started by the common school movement for elementary education. High schools in the United States formally date from 1821 with the founding of the English Classical School in Boston (renamed the English High School in 1824). Legislation supporting high schools was first enacted in Massachusetts with the Massachusetts Law of 1827, which required that towns with more than five hundred families have high schools (Cordasco 1970).

Although formally beginning in the early 1800s, high schools developed very slowly. In 1860 only 321 high schools existed in the United States (Cordasco 1970); New York State did not require the maintenance of high schools until 1864. As late as 1890 only 2,526 high schools were operational in the entire country (Commager 1983), and only 3.5 percent of all seventeen-year-olds graduated from high school (James and Tyack 1983).

In 1880 when enrollment in high schools surpassed the enrollment in academies, high schools grew significantly. Reasons for the rise of popularity of the high school included

- the change from an agrarian to an urban society where people were required to have certain skills;

- the industrialization that accompanied urbanization;

- the public's growing sensitivity of the needs of children and youth;

- the better financial capabilities to support public schools resulting from industrialization;

- the Kalamazoo court case of 1874 supporting the right of taxation for high schools. (Gutek 1970)

Although high schools made major gains during the latter part of the nineteenth century, they suffered from one major problem—a lack of standardization. High schools offered such a wide range of curricula that they almost repeated the demise of the academy. To rectify the situation, the National Education Association (NEA) established the Committee of Ten, a group of ten professionals, largely college presidents and professors, who were charged with the task of standardizing high schools (Cordasco 1970).

In 1893 the Committee of Ten made its report. Included in the recommendations were that

- children receive eight years of elementary school;

- children receive four years of high school;

- four separate curricula be offered: classical, Latin-scientific, modern language, and English;

- students be exposed to smaller number of subjects for intense study as opposed to many different subjects for shorter periods. (Gutek 1970)

Besides standardizing high-school curricula, the Committee of Ten was charged with improving the preparation of high-school students for college. In so doing, the committee members attempted to determine what scholarly content should be included in each of the four basic curricula offered in high schools (James and Tyack 1983).

The Committee of Ten was the first reform group for high schools. While many of its recommendations were never implemented, the process of having groups of professionals assess the needs of education was established as a precedent.

Education in the Twentieth Century

The growth of education in the United States during the twentieth century has been phenomenal. A comprehensive public education system has developed that supports all children from approximately five years of age to eighteen years. Unlike the educational programs in many countries, the American public education system attempts to provide twelve years of equal educational opportunity to all students, not only those with certain intellectual characteristics. "Schooling is available to a larger proportion of U.S. youth than is the case in other developed countries, yet the top 5 percent of U.S. young people attain the same high scores reached in nations where advanced schooling is reserved for an elite" (Tyler 1981, p. 307). Although the educational system in this country certainly has problems, as was amply pointed out in chapter one, it remains a model system for many countries to emulate.

Education from 1900 to World War II. During the early part of the twentieth century, public education began to take on its current form. By 1918 all states had mandatory attendance laws, and by 1930 the school year had increased to an average of 172 days (Cordasco 1970). The concept of elementary education for all children was widely accepted, and American high schools continued to grow rapidly.

The overriding influence over education in the United States during the first half of the twentieth century was John Dewey. Dewey was born in Vermont in 1859 and received his formal training in philosophy. He wrote several books that had a great impact on education, including *The School and Society* in 1898 and his classic text, *Democracy and Education*, written in 1916 (Gutek 1970), which was considered by a group of eighty-four curriculum specialists to be one of the two most important writings in education (Shane 1981).

In 1896, while at the University of Chicago, Dewey established an experimental laboratory school. In this setting he implemented some of his ideas in the classroom: (1) students should learn using the scientific process (Armstrong, Henson, and Savage 1981); (2) teachers should emphasize class discussions, sharing experiences, and testing ideas (Gutek 1970); (3) furniture should be movable to facilitate large and small group work; (4) activities should replace teacher-dominated drills; and (5) students should have available to them a large array of toys, materials, and books (Parker 1981).

Although Dewey's educational programs, which were based on his experimental philosophy, were not exactly like programs espoused by the progressive education movement, they were related. The major difference was that progressive education had a broader base among educators and was less specific than Dewey's ideas. Progressive education, supported by several of Dewey's followers, focused on the scientific method, the individual child, and society. However, some leaders of the progressive movement put more emphasis on the individual than society, which met with much criticism, especially during the depression years (Gutek 1970).

During the first half of the twentieth century, a major report was issued by the National Education Association that had a great impact on secondary education. The

John Dewey was the primary influence in American education during the first half of the 20th century.

report, issued by the NEA's Commission on the Reorganization of Secondary Education, identified seven goals for secondary education. These goals became known as the Cardinal Principles and included

1. Health
2. Command of fundamental processes
3. Worthy home membership
4. Vocational preparation

5. Citizenship
6. Worthy use of leisure time
7. Ethical character

These principles laid the foundation for current comprehensive secondary schools. They suggested that high schools have a greater purpose than simple academic instruction (Armstrong, Henson, and Savage 1981), and thus reflected Dewey's notion of "using secondary education as an instrument for transforming the everyday lives of citizens in an industrial democracy" (James and Tyack 1983, p. 402).

The Cardinal Principles emphasized a major thrust away from the purely academic high school. The report (1) stressed activities, democracy, and efficiency; (2) reflected the hope that schools could eliminate social problems; (3) brought focus on the drop-out rates of high schools; and (4) placed educators at the center of social reform. Overall, the Cardinal Principles won considerable public support and had a significant impact on secondary education (James and Tyack 1983).

Education in the United States during the depression era faced many problems. The depression hit all aspects of the country: (1) the gross national product dropped, (2) personal income declined, (3) unemployment soared, (4) stocks fell, and (5) corporate profits plummeted (Tyack and Hansot 1984). For school-age children, the

The depression affected all aspects of American society, including education.

depression meant unemployment, apathy, unrest, and despair (James and Tyack 1983). These problems abounding throughout the entire society should have produced a major blow to education. However, quite surprisingly, public education emerged from the depression in relatively good condition. Professionals were united, schools were viewed with a great deal of confidence by the public, and states had dramatically increased their contribution to public education (Tyack and Hansot 1984). Better guidance programs, more extensive social programs, and a more appealing curriculum were advocated by the teaching profession (James and Tyack 1983).

Although some of the tangibles appeared to have emerged from the depression on a positive note, the educational system still faced severe problems. For one thing, there was little equality of opportunity. School districts with strong economic bases continued to prosper, while those with unstable economic foundations were destroyed. The one positive thing to come out of this inequity was the recognition by many members of society that the American system maintained certain class differentials, that inequities existed (Tyack and Hansot 1984).

The belief that the public school system in the United States "owed all youths either an education through secondary school or guaranteed public service jobs" (James and Tyack 1983, p. 404) was a new philosophy that emerged as a result of the depression.

Education from 1940 to present. In the early 1940s, the progressive education movement was widely adopted. Individuals supporting this curricular approach referred to it as life-adjustment education. Emphasis on academic subject matter was limited, while other areas of the curriculum flourished (Armstrong, Henson, and Savage 1983).

Major criticisms of the schools began to emerge in the 1950s. Critics attacked low academic standards, which were considered a major reason for society's problems. Low academic standards were viewed as synonymous with life-adjustment education, child-centered learning, and other titles associated with the progressive movement. Targets for criticisms included watered-down curriculum, incompetent teachers, and a lack of programming for gifted children. The crest of public criticism came as a result of the launching of Sputnik, a Russian satellite in 1957 (James and Tyack 1983).

Reformers called for more science, more math, a stricter adherence to discipline, less individualization, fewer extracurricular activities, and fewer nonacademic subjects. One of the most ardent critics of the time was James Conant, former president of Harvard University. In 1959 Conant published *The American High School Today*, which presented twenty-one recommendations for American high schools. Among these recommendations were

- comprehensive counseling programs to assist students in selecting appropriate electives;
- more individualized instruction;
- ability grouping by subject;
- a core academic curriculum, consisting of English, social studies, and math and science;
- relevant vocational programs;

Following the launching of Sputnik, critics called for more science and math education.

- special programs for slow readers;

- programs for gifted students;

- more choices in science and foreign languages. (Conant 1959)

Responding to the critics, especially since the Sputnik launch concerned many Americans about national defense issues, the federal government passed the National Defense Education Act (NDEA) in 1958. This act was a major effort by the federal government to get involved in American education. It provided large amounts of money and stimulated curricular changes in science, math, and social studies. In addition, the NDEA supported teacher training, the development of better teaching materials, and an upgrade in the quality of textbooks (Armstrong, Henson, and Savage 1983).

The revolt against progressive education did not last long. In the mid-1960s social issues, such as racial segregation, poverty, equal opportunities for disabled children and women, and eventually the Vietnam War shifted attention from heavy

TABLE 2-2 Summary of Recent Research Evidence on the Effects of Desegregation

Study	Data	Independent Variable	Dependent Variable	Control Variables	Findings
Braddock (1980)	Survey in 1972 of black students attending four colleges in Florida (N = 253)	High school racial composition	Racial composition of college	Socioeconomic status, sex, high school grades, college costs and reputation, financial aid, and proximity to college	Black students from majority-white high school are more likely to enroll at majority-white four-year colleges.
Braddock and McPartland (1982)	Black subsample of the National Longitudinal Study (NLS) High School Class of 1972 (N = 3,119)	Elementary/secondary school racial composition	Racial composition of college	Socioeconomic status, sex, high school grades and test scores, region, and proximity to college	Black students from majority-white elementary/secondary schools are more likely to enroll in and persist at majority-white two- and four-year colleges.
Braddock, McPartland, and Trent (1984)	Black and white subsamples of the NLS Class of 1972 merged with survey data from their 1976 and 1979 employers (blacks = 1,518; whites = 1,957)	High school and college racial composition	Racial composition of employing firm	Sex, age, public vs. private employment, educational attainment, region, and community racial composition	Blacks and whites from desegregated elementary/secondary schools are more likely to work in desegregated firms; blacks from predominantly white colleges are also more likely to work in desegregated firms.
Crain and Weisman (1972)	Survey in 1966 of blacks living in North and West (N = 1,651)	Elementary/secondary school racial composition	Interracial contact, neighborhood racial composition, racial composition of occupation	Socioeconomic status, age, sex, region of birth	Blacks from desegregated elementary/secondary schools are more likely to have white social contacts, live in integrated neighborhoods.
Braddock and McPartland (1983)	Two-year follow-up of black subsample of NLS 1980–81 Youth Cohort (N = 1,074)	High school racial composition	Racial composition of co-worker groups and attitudes toward white supervisors and white co-workers	Sex, age, public vs. private employment, job status, and community racial composition	Northern blacks from majority-white high schools are more likely to have white co-workers. In the South, this relationship is also positive but confounded with community racial composition. Desegregated blacks evaluate white co-workers and supervisors more positively than do segregated blacks.

Study	Sample	Dependent variable	Independent variables	Controls	Findings
Green (1981; 1982)	Ten-year follow-up of 1971 black college freshmen surveyed by American Council on Education (N = 1,400)	High school and college racial composition	Racial composition of co-worker and friendship groups	Sex, high school grades, college major, etc.	Black adults who graduated from majority-white high schools or majority-white colleges and who grew up in majority-white neighborhoods are more likely to have white work associates and friends.
Crain (1984a)	Survey in 1982 of Project Concern participants (N = 660)	Elementary/secondary school racial composition	Interracial contact and neighborhood racial composition	Socioeconomic status, age, and test scores	Blacks who attend desegregated schools are more likely to move into integrated neighborhoods and to have a greater number of white friends.
Crain (1984b)	Survey of employers of NLS respondents (N = 4,080)	Inner-city school vs. suburban school	Employment decisions about applicants	Race, age, sex, education, and how applicant came to firm	Employers give preference to blacks from desegregated (i.e., suburban) schools.
Pearce (1980)	14 communities	Change in school segregation indices	Change in degree of desegregation in housing and in marketing policies in housing	Communities matched by size, region, racial composition	Communities with a communitywide school desegregation plan have more integration in housing and less "racial steering" by the real estate industry.
Pearce, Crain, and Farley (1984)	25 large cities	Change in school segregation indices	Change in housing segregation indices	City size, racial composition, previous level of segregation	Central cities where schools are desegregated have more desegregation in housing.

Reprinted with permission. Braddock, Crain, McPartland (1984) p. 260–261.

emphasis on academic educational programs and programs for selected students to programs aimed at wiping out poverty and inequalities. Diversity characterized the opinions held about public education: conservatives demanded more discipline and stricter academic standards, and libertarians and radicals declared that schools were unnatural and called for alternative schools, electives, and experience-based curricula (James and Tyack 1983).

An important set of events in public education during this period dealt with integration. Prior to the mid-1950s most minority racial children were educated in separate, segregated schools. This dual system of education was legally maintained, based on legal precedent in the case of *Plessey v. Ferguson* in 1896. The dual school systems provided minority racial children "putatively inferior training" (Braddock, Crain, and McPartland 1984, p. 260). This changed in 1954 when the United States Supreme Court issued its ruling in the *Brown v. Board of Education, Topeka, Kansas* case. The decision stated that separate is inherently unequal and required that schools desegregate with all deliberate speed. What followed was more than twenty-five years of turmoil, litigation, and disruption. By 1980, however, most of the nation's schools had been desegregated. Dual school systems, one for black children and one for white children, were mostly history. The actions from the *Brown v. Board of Education* case had a major impact on public education.

Studies investigating the effects of desegregation have abounded. For the most part, they prove that desegregation had positive outcomes for education and socialization. Braddock, Crain, and McPartland (1984) reviewed ten studies that show desegregation having a significant impact on socialization (see table 2–2).

During this period litigation became a major variable in public education. Court cases dealing with integration, programs for the disabled and disadvantaged, and student rights were heard in state and federal courts, from the district level all the way to the United States Supreme Court. In addition to the *Brown* case, a landmark court case dealing with handicapped children brought significant changes to schools. In the *PARC v. Pennsylvania* case, filed in 1971, a consent decree was reached in which Pennsylvania agreed to provide appropriate educational programs to mentally retarded children in the state. This case was followed by other similar right-to-education cases in which the majority were ruled in favor of handicapped children's rights to access public educational programs.

Concomitant with litigation, legislation was passed that greatly affected public education. Presidents Kennedy and Johnson, champions of civil rights and the rights of the disabled and disadvantaged, were leaders in enacting legislation that guaranteed these groups equal educational opportunities. A great deal of federal legislation was enacted during the 1960s and 1970s that supported programs for these minority populations. A prime example of this legislation was Public Law 94–142, the Education for All Handicapped Children's Act, which was passed in 1975. This act required all schools to provide a free, appropriate public education for all handicapped children, and when possible, this education was to be provided with nonhandicapped children.

As was discussed in the beginning of the text, national reform movements became pervasive in the late 1970s and early 1980s. Reformers of this current period reflect many of the same concerns and recommendations heard in the 1950s. Indeed, "The editorials and articles on public education in popular magazines of the 1950s might be reprinted today without any substantial change and be fashionable once again" (James and Tyack 1983, p. 406).

Whether the reforms initiated in the early 1980s have significant, long-term effects on public education remains to be seen. The public's lack of confidence in the public educational system in the United States has been extensively documented. Much of the public will likely be eager to grasp and encourage the implementation of recommended reforms. The fallacy in accepting reforms without adequate research will undoubtedly lead American education into still another swing of the pendulum. One of these days, educators, parents, government officials, and others must look at the history of education and learn from it. Constantly revolving on a never-ending cycle of change will not likely lead us to as sound an educational system as we could achieve with better planning and judgment.

SUMMARY

This chapter presented information concerning the history of education in the United States. The first section of the chapter discussed the importance of studying history and education. Information was then presented that traced education from the Greek city states of Athens and Sparta to the current educational activities in the schools. It was pointed out that education in colonial America was regionalized, with the New England, Middle, and Southern colonies differing significantly in their approach to public education.

Public education, as it is known today, had its beginnings in the common school movement of the mid-1800s. Its leader, Horace Mann, believed that public education should be available to all children during the elementary school years. From this beginning came mandatory public school attendance laws and the beginning of the public education system in the United States. Major events that affected education during the twentieth century were also presented.

IN THE FIELD

1. When were public schools first started in the school district? Who were some of the local founders of the school system and what were their motivations?

2. Were secondary schools started at the same time as elementary schools?

3. How many elementary, junior high, and high schools are in the district? Has the growth in the number of schools been steady, or was there a period when rapid growth was apparent?

4. How many professional teachers and administrators are employed in the district?

5. How many students graduate each year, and what percentage of these students go on to higher education programs?

REFERENCES

Armstrong, D. G., K. T. Henson, and T. V. Savage. 1983. *Education: An introduction.* New York: Macmillan.

Braddock, J. H., R. L. Crain, and J. M. McPartland. 1984. A long-term view of school desegregation: Some recent studies of graduates as adults. *Phi Delta Kappan 66*(4), 259–64.

Button, H. W. and E. F. Provenzo. 1983. *History of education and culture in America.* Englewood Cliffs, NJ: Prentice-Hall.

Commager, H. S. 1983. A historian looks at the American high school. *American Journal of Education 91*(4), 531–48.

Conant, J. B. 1959. *The American high school today.* New York: McGraw-Hill Book Company.

Cordasco, F. 1970. *A brief history of education.* Totowa, NJ: Littlefield, Adams & Co.

Dewey, J. 1916. *Democracy and education: An introduction to the philosophy of education.* New York: Macmillan.

Fain, S. M., R. Shostak, and J. F. Dean. 1979. *Teaching in America.* Glenview, IL: Scott, Foresman and Company.

Field, A. J. 1976. Educational expansion in mid-nineteenth-century Massachussetts: Human-capital formation or structural reinforcement? *Harvard Educational Review 46*(6), 521–52.

Gutek, G. L. 1970. *An historical introduction to American education.* New York: Thomas Y. Crowell Company, Inc.

Gutek G. L. 1986. *Education in the United States: An historical perspective.* Englewood Cliffs, NJ: Prentice-Hall.

James, T., and D. Tyack. 1983. Learning from past efforts to reform the high school. *Phi Delta Kappan 64*(6), 400–406.

Johnson, J. A., H. W. Collins, V. L. Dupuis, and J. H. Johansen. 1982. *Introduction to the foundations of American education.* Boston: Allyn and Bacon.

Ornstein, A. C., and D. U. Levine. 1981. *An introduction to the foundations of education.* Boston: Houghton Mifflin Company.

Parker, F. 1981. Ideas that shaped American schools. *Phi Delta Kappan 62*(5), 314–19.

Shane, H. G. 1981. Significant writings that have influenced the curriculum: 1906–1981. *Phi Delta Kappan 62*(5), 311–14.

Tyack, D., and E. Hansot. 1984. Hard times, then and now: Public schools in the 1930s and 1980s. *Harvard Educational Review 54*(1), 33–66.

Tyler, R. W. 1981. The U.S. vs the world: A comparison of educational performances. *Phi Delta Kappan 62*(5), 307–10.

Unks, G. 1985. The illusion of intrusion: A chronicle of federal aid to public education. *The Educational Forum 49*(2), 133–56.

Chapter 3

PHILOSOPHY OF EDUCATION

OBJECTIVES

After reading this chapter, you will be able to

- understand the branches of philosophy;

- understand the reasons for studying philosophy;

- define philosophy;

- list the purposes of educational philosophy;

- describe the components of the major schools of philosophy;

- relate the schools of general philosophy to the major schools of educational philosophy;

- describe the relationship between philosophy and teaching;

- discuss your philosophy of education as it relates to a formal philosophy.

OUTLINE

ADVANCE ORGANIZERS
INTRODUCTION
    Definition of Philosophy
    Purposes of Educational Philosophy
BRANCHES OF PHILOSOPHY
    Metaphysics
    Epistemology
    Axiology
SCHOOLS OF PHILOSOPHY
    Basic Philosophies

    Educational Philosophies
PHILOSOPHY AND
       EDUCATIONAL PRACTICE
    Teaching and Philosophy
SUMMARY
IN THE FIELD
REFERENCES

1. What is philosophy?
2. Why should educational philosophy be studied by prospective teachers?
3. What are the purposes of educational philosophy?
4. What are the three branches of philosophy?
5. What are the major schools of philosophy?
6. What are the major schools of educational philosophy?
7. Which schools of general philosophy gave rise to schools of educational philosophy?
8. What is the role of teachers?
9. How does educational philosophy influence teachers' actions?
10. How will you respond to interviewers and colleagues when they ask you "What is your philosophy of education?"

INTRODUCTION

Philosophy of education is a broad and complex subject. This chapter is not intended to provide students with an in-depth study of philosophy, but does provide an overview of philosophy and the philosophy of education. General philosophical concepts are presented to enable students to understand the role of philosophy in education.

Many students will ask why they must study philosophy and the philosophy of education. Just as the study of the history of education is relevant, so is the study of educational philosophy. First of all, "philosophy and education are not at all antithetical" (Phillips 1983, p. 3). Educational philosophy can help teachers clarify concepts, assess arguments, and expose assumptions (Phillips 1983). It can help teachers and other educators focus on questions that are speculative, prescriptive, and analytical; it can help enlarge thoughts so better personal choices can be made (Kneller 1971). Probably the most important reason for studying philosophy is that it helps in self-evaluation of beliefs and self-knowledge (Levison 1974).

Understanding educational philosophy requires some knowledge and understanding of general philosophy, because "many of the educational implications of philosophical views have not been made explicit. One needs to be familiar with philosophical problems to see their relevance to education" (Broudy, Parsons, Snook, and Szoke 1967, p. 7). When philosophy is related to problems in education, an understanding of general philosophy is required to see the relationship between these educational issues and philosophy (Broudy et al. 1967).

Although the basis for actions and beliefs, philosophy is often ignored or simply not considered essential in teacher education programs. Viewed in a general sense, philosophy is thought of as boring and meaningless. Opponents of teaching educational philosophy to prospective teachers rally around three basic arguments. Some think that teaching educational philosophy slows up the process of producing teachers. These individuals would encourage the emphasis of practical methods and materials courses or courses that give students something tangible to take with them into the classroom. Others feel that teaching philosophy confuses students. It might raise questions in students' minds whereas other courses give students ready-made answers to persistent educational questions. Others wonder why we should teach philosophy when philosophers themselves cannot agree. This argument fails to recognize that some philosophers do agree, in principle, and also that disagreement often leads to better understanding (Ozmon 1972).

A lack of a general understanding of philosophy precludes individuals from understanding how philosophy actually affects everyday actions (Marler 1975). Plato viewed philosophy as encompassing all knowledge into a "semireligious synthesis" (Park 1974, p. 3).

From a technical point of view, philosophy includes an interrelationship among activities, content, and attitudes. Synthesizing, speculating, prescribing, and analyzing are the activities in philosophy (Marler 1975). Synthesis enables educators to show the relationship of ideas to practice (Ward 1981). Speculative philosophy is a search for orderliness applied to all knowledge; it applies systematic thinking to everything that exists. The activity that attempts to establish standards for assessing values, judging conduct, and appraising art is prescriptive philosophy (Kneller 1971). It structures or restructures norms based on facts that have been synthesized (Marler 1975). Analyzing allows the use of language to analyze such words as *mind, freedom,* and *equality.* The analytic activity is currently the dominating activity of American and British philosophers (Kneller 1971).

Definition of Philosophy

Describing what philosophy is *not* might be more meaningful than describing what philosophy is. First, philosophy is not like science on three counts: It presents no proofs, there are no theorems, and there are no questions that can be answered with yes or no (Waismann 1969). Philosophy is an attempt to understand the world, discover how life should be lived, determine what things people should strive for, and improve social organization. Philosophy has been used to analyze almost every problem faced by man (Henderson 1947).

Purposes of Educational Philosophy

Viable philosophies of education are based on general philosophy. Any philosophy of education should answer three questions: (1) what is education? (2) what should education accomplish? and (3) how should it be accomplished? (Henderson 1947).

The study of philosophy will not dictate teachers' actions in classrooms, rather, it will give teachers

1. explications of philosophical assumptions commonly held in American culture that are of special import to the American school;
2. hypotheses concerning the possible contributions of philosophy to increasing the rationality of educational practices and opportunities to become involved in testing them;
3. speculative opportunities to analyze the philosophical reasons underlying observed professional practices and to synthesize these reasons with nonphilosophical factors that also contributed to the practices;
4. opportunities to explicate personal assumptions as to the basic problems of man and his world, thus taking one more step in relating beliefs, knowledge of facts, and habitual practices;

5. opportunities to become involved in a most systematic, comprehensive, penetrating, and open-minded inquiry into the present state and future possibilities of American education, which, it is suggested, is one important function of any truly professional educator. (Marler 1975, p. 21–22)

Educational philosophy, therefore, has many purposes. Power (1982) indicates that these include (1) planning for the best education; (2) providing directions for the best education in various political, social, and economic contexts; (3) correcting mistakes about educational policy and practices; (4) focusing on educational activities that require resolutions; and (5) inquiring about the entire process of education. Teachers need to be involved in educational philosophy and go beyond simply teaching skills to students based on textbook organizations. An understanding of various educational philosophies will help clarify the role of teachers in classrooms.

BRANCHES OF PHILOSOPHY

Metaphysics, epistemology, and axiology are the three basic branches of philosophy. These branches focus on different subjects in philosophy.

Metaphysics

Metaphysics is the branch of philosophy that deals with ultimate reality. It is primarily within the speculative activity. With the avalanche of scientific knowledge, metaphysics was considered unnecessary by many who felt that scientifically verifiable truths deleted the need for metaphysical assumptions about reality. Today, however, metaphysics has once again emerged as an important area. Scientists, Albert Einstein being the most noted, have even made metaphysical assumptions based on scientific fact. Currently metaphysics and science are considered as two separate activities, both with relevance for the other (Kneller 1971).

Metaphysics focuses on four concepts and assumptions: (1) basic reality, (2) human nature, (3) free will and determinism, and (4) God and faith. The concept of human nature can be described as inherently evil, inherently good, inherently superior or inferior, or as resulting from experiences or internal choices (Marler 1975). A teacher's view of human nature will undoubtedly affect trust, disciplinary methods, and daily interactions with students. If a teacher holds the view that people are inherently evil, classroom rules will reflect this mistrust. On the other hand, teachers who believe that the human nature is inherently good will rely less on structured classroom rules and more on individual responsibility.

Epistemology

Epistemology deals with knowledge. As an epistemologist, the philosopher would ask questions such as:

- What is there that is common to all the different activities that are involved in knowing?
- What is the difference between knowing and, say, believing?
- What can we know beyond the information provided by the senses?

- What is the relation of the act of knowing to the thing that is known?

- How can we show that knowledge is "true"? (Kneller 1971, p. 18)

Concepts of epistemology include the mind, ideas, experience, objectivity, frame of reference, and knowledge and truth (Marler 1975). Educators' views of knowledge have an immediate effect on the way information is transmitted. If the teacher believes that experience is the key to all knowledge, the teacher attempts to have children participate and actively experience everything. On the other hand, teachers who believe that knowledge can be acquired without direct experiences will be more inclined to instruct children using a lecture approach or simply by having children read materials.

Axiology

The third branch of philosophy, axiology, is the study of values. The basic questions in axiology include: are values personal or impersonal, changing or constant, and are they hierarchical in nature? Ethics deals with moral values, while aesthetics focuses on the value of beauty (Kneller 1971). Concepts and assumptions of axiology include (1) value: its nature and locus, (2) value judgments: validation, (3) values: classifying and ordering, (4) morality, (5) obligation and conscience, and (6) ends, means, and process (Marler 1975). In education the area of values has received a great deal of attention. Should schools teach values, and if so, which values? Is moral education something schools should provide or should this domain be left to parents? Teachers' views on these topics will affect their classroom behaviors regardless of a school's policies. If teachers feel that they should have a part in moral education, they may provide instruction on a variety of topics that they would not include in their curriculum if they did not support the idea of moral education. Values clarification is a good example of the relationship between education and axiology.

SCHOOLS OF PHILOSOPHY

Several schools of thought, or orientations to philosophy, have endured for centuries; others are relatively new. Some of these are related to general philosophy, while others have emerged as specific philosophies of education. Ozmon (1972) dichotomizes the schools of philosophy into basic and educational (see table 3–1). The five basic schools include idealism, realism, pragmatism, existentialism, and behaviorism. Educational philosophies that have evolved from these basic philosophies include perennialism, essentialism, progressivism, reconstructionism, existentialism, and behavioral engineering. A brief description of each of the basic and educational philosophies will provide a basis for understanding each viewpoint.

Basic Philosophies

Idealism. Idealism had its roots in ancient Indo–European culture; Plato is considered the "Father of Idealism." Idealism was assimilated into the Christian movement and was dominant throughout the Middle Ages. The philosophical base of colonial education in the New England colonies was idealism; it spread with the advent of the common school movement. Idealism suffered a severe blow with Darwin's scientific

TABLE 3-1   Schools of Philosophy

Basic Philosophy	Educational Philosophy
Idealism	Perennialism
Realism	Essentialism
Pragmatism	Progressivism Reconstructionism
Existentialism	Existentialism
Behaviorism	Behavioral Engineering

Source: Ozmon, 1972.

approach to knowledge and did not recover until the 1930 attack on progressivism, when it was more commonly known as essentialism (Marler 1975).

The basis of idealism is that there are certain universal, absolute concepts, such as Truth and Honor. These concepts are considered "higher truths" and are not to be questioned by scientific inquiry. Deductive logic, going from a universal truth to a specific conclusion, is used to develop knowledge (Marshall 1973). Idealism can be related to metaphysics, epistemology, and axiology of the traditional schools of philosophy (see table 3–2).

Realism. Realism also has ancient roots, and Aristotle is considered the "Father of Realism." Because idealism had such a monopoly on thought, through religion, realism remained a rather uninfluential philosophy until the expansion of science

TABLE 3-2   Metaphysics, Epistemology, and Axiology of the Traditional Schools of Philosophy

Idealism	
Metaphysics	• Ultimate reality is spiritual, not physical
Epistemology	• True knowledge comes from reason
Axiology	• Values and ethics are absolute
	• Good and beautiful do not change but are constant from society to society
Realism	
Metaphysics	• Matter is the ultimate reality
	• Matter exists even when it has not been discovered
Epistemology	• The world is as it is, not as it has been created by man
	• True knowledge is that which corresponds to the way the world is
Axiology	• Fundamental values are permanent
Pragmatism	
Metaphysics	• Reality is what we experience
	• Reality results from experience
Epistemology	• Knowledge results from the interaction of man and the environment
Axiology	• Values are relative
	• Worth of values should be tested, not simply accepted

Source: G. Kneller. 1973. Introduction to the philosophy of education. New York: John Wiley & Sons, Inc.

Aristotle is considered the "Father of Realism."

during the Enlightenment period in Europe. Realism gained a foothold in the United States during the eighteenth and nineteenth centuries. It was the dominant philosophy underlying education in the Middle colonies; several academies were founded by adherents of realism. In the twentieth century, realism expanded rapidly with the scientific movement. It was influential in the development of educational testing and educational psychology. In the 1930s realists and idealists both attacked progressive education; following Sputnik in the late 1950s, realism became popular and was a force in the push for more science education (Marler 1975).

Realism holds the position that reality exists without knowledge of its existence. The world is a physical world, governed by various laws, which exist even if they have not been discovered. Individuals discover these laws through scientific study. Realism also can be related to the three branches of philosophy (see table 3–2).

St. Thomas Aquinas combined the philosophy of Aristotle realism and church doctrine to develop religious realism, or scholasticism. Some philosophers label this Neo-Thomism. Scholasticism is the official philosophy of the Roman Catholic church. It is based on the belief that matter and spirit were created by God (Kneller 1971). Reason was considered the basis of the organization of the universe, but any conflict between conclusions arrived at by reason and faith were the result of inaccurate reasoning (Johnson et al. 1982).

Pragmatism. Pragmatism is primarily an American philosophy. Its beginnings can be traced to an essay published in 1878 by Charles S. Peirce (Leight 1984). The development of pragmatism into a philosophy occurred during the late nineteenth century and early twentieth century. In comparison to idealism and realism, this is a modern philosophy. Although it had some roots in ancient Europe, Darwin, Newton, the progressive movement, and social philosophy in the United States were the bases for its development (Marler 1975).

Pragmatism is a philosophy based on scientific analysis. It "ideally aims at intellectually honest solutions based upon an objective and dispassionate scientific analysis of all the evidence before any solution is even considered" (Marshall 1973, p. 47). Pragmatists consider the human mind as a tool to be used to discover knowledge. John Dewey is considered the foremost pragmatist. Although pragmatism and the progressive education movement occurred during the same period, they should not be considered the same. Dewey, for example, had some major reservations about the progressive education movement. He did not agree with some of the leaders in the progressive movement who encouraged child-centered and overly permissive schools. Dewey always felt that schools and society were to be closely coordinated within education (Leight 1984). Pragmatism can be related to the branches of philosophy also (see table 3–2).

Existentialism. Although existentialism had origins in ancient Europe, modern existentialism developed in Europe following the morass of two world wars. Basic themes of existentialism include the following:

1. The human situation is one of meaninglessness, alienation, anguish, and death.
2. Man has both absolute freedom and absolute responsibility to authenticate himself, make meaning in the world, and avoid meaningless, unauthentic life.
3. In so doing, he must have the courage to be, make decisions in the face of despair, and realize that truths and values are created by his subjective choice.
4. The Other represents a great danger to self-actualization, but a meaningful relationship with him is probably necessary to the achievement of one's own self. (Marler 1975, p. 382)

True existentialists would have students direct much of what occurs in schools, from setting the curriculum to the methods and rate it is presented (Marler 1975). While science would be a part of the curriculum, science would be taught as a tool, not as a decision maker. Man must retain control over science rather than science over man. Like pragmatism, existentialism would have students use psychology and

Existentialism allows students to direct their own learning activities.

sociology as a base. Students would be encouraged to learn about the diversity of cultures rather than be praised for stereotypical behavior patterns (Marshall 1973). While the effect of existentialism on education will likely remain minimal, it will continue to affect small pockets, such as the Summerhill school, which is based on existentialism philosophy (Marler 1975). Also, existentialism will undoubtedly continue to influence individuals' philosophies to a great extent.

Behaviorism. Individuals adhering to the philosophy of behaviorism favor manipulating people through the use of rewards and punishments. Operant conditioning and classical conditioning are the two primary methods used in behaviorism. Well-known individuals who advocate this philosophy include Pavlov, Watson, and Skinner.

Some proponents of behaviorism do not use punishments, but use a combination of positive and negative reinforcers. Positive reinforcers are pleasant things that occur following a behavior that will act as a reward. After being rewarded, or positively reinforced, the individual is more likely to repeat the appropriate behavior than if no reward were given. Negative reinforcers, on the contrary, are negative consequences that are removed when an individual performs in an appropriate manner. This differs from punishment in that punishment is something unpleasant that is provided following an inappropriate behavior, whereas a negative reinforcer is removed when the behavior is appropriate. For example, if a child cries because of a loud noise and the loud noise goes way, the child stops crying. This is a form of negative reinforcement. Punishment would be if the child cries and is spanked for crying.

Behaviorists are not concerned about eternal truths or causes of certain behavior. They believe that behavior is learned and can be extinguished with proper stimulus/ response interventions.

Educational Philosophies

Perennialism. Perennialism is a developed form of realism that had its beginnings with St. Thomas Aquinas. It is based on Aristotle's realism and the belief that there are certain everlasting values. As a result of this orientation, perennialists based the entire college curriculum on the "Great Books" of the world (Marshall 1973).

The basic principles of perennialism include the following:

- Human nature is the same everywhere, therefore, education should be the same.
- Man must use rationality to control his instincts.
- Education must teach knowledge of eternal truth.
- Education prepares man for life.
- Students should be taught about the world's permanence.
- Great works of literature, philosophy, and other subjects should be a major component of the curriculum. (Kneller 1971)

Progressivism emphasizes problem-solving by students.

Essentialism. Essentialism had its beginnings in the early 1930s. Like perennialism, essentialism holds that subject matter should be the center of education. Essentialism differs from perennialism, however, in denying the existence of everlasting values. Essentialism focuses on (1) learning as hard work, (2) teacher-directed learning, (3) assimilation of knowledge, and (4) mental discipline (Kneller 1971). Back-to-the-basics, the three Rs as a curricular focus, should be considered the core of the school curriculum in essentialism philosophy (Marshall 1973).

Progressivism. Advocates of progressivism are in favor of individuals learning effective problem-solving techniques. Progressivists do not believe there is a need to search for eternal truths, either through philosophy or science. In application, it is a practical approach to learning and education (Ozmon 1972).

Reconstructionism. The philosophy of reconstructionism was developed in the mid-twentieth century. It called for schools to get involved and support social reform. Although they did not believe that schools should take the lead in developing a new social order, reconstructionists thought that schools should cooperate with social reform movements. Adherents to this philosophy believe that schools should help establish a new social order that brings to realization basic cultural values. The new society should be truly democratic and directed by the people; the role of teachers should be to encourage students to identify with and support such a social revolution (Kneller 1971).

Behavioral engineering. Behaviorial engineering is a philosophy of education that focuses on controlling the learner's environment. Through manipulating the environment with rewards and punishment, behavior can be changed in the desired direction. "Behavior engineers feel that much of human behavior reflects attitudes and actions already conditioned by the environment, and that these attitudes and actions should be engineered along paths that are more useful and productive" (Ozmon 1972, p. xiv). The leading promoter of behavior engineering has been Skinner.

Practitioners of behavior engineering arrange reinforcers to encourage repeated appropriate behavior. Operant conditioning, sometimes referred to as behavior modification, is the primary methodology that implements this philosophy. Although this strategy is used extensively with disabled learners in special education programs, it has also been shown to be very effective with all students.

PHILOSOPHY AND EDUCATIONAL PRACTICE

The influence of philosophy on educational policies and practices cannot be overemphasized. Philosophical beliefs do affect education (see tables 3–3 and 3–4). A teacher's philosophical beliefs greatly affect what occurs in classrooms. Administrators' philosophies affect policies and the implementation of policies. Building principals' philosophies affect the manner in which students are disciplined and teachers are entrusted with professional responsibilities. For example, if teachers hold the view that all men are inherently evil, they will likely distrust students routinely. Similarly, if they support the ideas of perennialism, they are likely to include in their daily teaching activities information from the "Great Books" of history.

Table 3-3   Examples of the Influences of Philosophy on Educational Practice

Practice	Base Philosophy
Students are mistrusted and expected to cheat when they get the chance	Idealism
Curriculum is based on the "Great Books"	Perennialism
Students should choose what they want to learn and how they want to learn it	Existentialism
Teachers should arrange learning through experiences	Pragmatism
The three Rs should be the primary focus of education	Essentialism
Students and teachers should support social changes that will lead to a new social order	Reconstructionism
Well-defined values should be taught to children by teachers	Realism
Students should be taught enduring values and how to live with them	Idealism
Ideas are judged as true only after they have been tested	Pragmatism

Source: G. F. Kneller, 1973.

Teaching and Philosophy

In understanding the relationship between educational philosophy and teaching, the role of teachers must be clarified. Often the responsibilities of teachers are too narrowly considered. Some think of teachers only as employees of schools who cope with administrative bureaucracies, students who act out, difficult parents, and aging school plants. Others consider the only important role of teachers as focusing on teaching math, English, reading, and a host of other academic subjects. Another view is that teachers only deal with the social problems of students, including drug abuse, vandalism, truancy, and learning and behavior problems (Simpson and Jackson 1984).

TABLE 3-4   Philosophy and Teaching Methods

Philosophy	Basic Method(s)
Idealism	Lecture Discussion
Realism	Demonstration Recitation
Neo-Thomism	Formal drill Memorization
Experimentalism	Problem solving Project method
Existentialism	Individual study Individual questioning

Source: Morris and Pai, 1976.

Just about anyone can read a teacher's guide and present information in a sensible order. Understanding why it is presented in a particular way, if it should be presented in a particular way, or if it should be presented at all require a different kind of knowledge. Educational philosophy can provide a background for questioning practices, which should lead to better educational programs for students.

Without the desire and ability to question, teachers are often at a loss concerning how to deal with various issues that confront students and schools. Ethnic, religious, and ideological controversies require that teachers make decisions. They must be able to evaluate these kinds of issues and deal with them effectively in the educational process (Ozmon 1972).

As educational philosophers, teachers need to be involved in analytic, normative, and synoptic philosophy. Analytic philosophy involves clarifying educational matters by raising questions about what is meant by certain statements about education. For example, the statement "educating the whole child" may mean different things to different people; the teacher as an analytic philosopher would want to know the real meaning of this statement (Simpson and Jackson 1984).

Normative philosophy involves teachers finding reasons to support the things they do while understanding why they do not do certain things. Examples of questions include:

- Why should mathematics be required of everyone rather than swimming? Why should either be required? Indeed, why should schooling be required?

- In another vein, why should a student be suspended from school for vandalism? Are the reasons relevant? Are they cogent? If not, what ought to be done?

- What is the best way to teach my subject to these students? Does this show respect for the rights of my pupils? Will I educate them or indoctrinate them?

- Which applicant should be hired for the position in elementary education? What particular reasons can be given for employing one person over another? Should I recommend this applicant over the other ones?

- Is it true that ability grouping is undemocratic? If so, is it undemocratic to classify students as handicapped or gifted? Are undemocratic practices in the classroom necessarily wrong? How does one know? Is equity in education a vital concern? Why? If we wish to be humane teachers, does this of necessity mean we are obligated to have so-called child-centered classrooms? (Simpson and Jackson 1984, p. 18–19)

Teachers may also be involved in synoptic philosophizing. In this role, teachers attempt to understand the gestalt of education, the whole. Understanding how various pieces of the educational process fit together is a major part of synoptic philosophy. "The emphasis of synoptic philosophy is on seeing relationships, removing inconsistencies, suggesting new perspectives, and discerning a gestalt" (Simpson and Jackson 1984, p. 19).

The philosophies held by students themselves affect education. Students believing that they should have a major part in the development of the school curriculum and what occurs in individual classrooms are likely to find difficulties in most classrooms in public schools. On the other hand, if students feel that they should have limited input into the educational process, they will more than likely fit into the expectations of the school and will have little difficulty in dealing with teachers and administrators.

SUMMARY

This chapter has presented information concerning the philosophy of education in the United States. Philosophy, it was discussed, is an all-encompassing field. The three branches of philosophy are metaphysics, the study of the nature of reality; epistemology, the study of knowledge; and axiology, philosophy dealing with values.

The many different schools of philosophy include general philosophies—idealism, realism, pragmatism, existentialism, and behaviorism—and educational philosophies that have evolved from these basic philosophies—perennialism, progressivism, existentialism, essentialism, reconstructionism, and behavioral engineering. The chapter discussed the relationship among the different branches of philosophy and the schools of philosophy, pointing out the different orientations for each school. Finally, the role of philosophy to educational practice was presented. Philosophy affects policies and practices at all levels of education: administration, teaching, and learning. With such direct and important relationships, professional educators should determine what their individual philosophies are and determine if there are unwanted effects in the classroom from this philosophical base.

IN THE FIELD

1. Does a written statement of philosophy for the school system exist? If so, where is it located and do teachers and students have access to it?

2. Did you observe an instance of

   behavior modification?

   inquiry/problem solving?

   values clarification?

   drill and rote memorization activities?

   lecturing?

3. How can you perceive a person's philosophy by classroom actions?

4. Would you say the school and classroom reflect a general liberal or conservative philosophy or something in between? How did you determine this?

REFERENCES

Broudy, H. S., M. J. Parsons, I. A. Snook, and R. D. Szoke. 1967. *Philosophy of education.* Urbana, IL: University of Illinois Press.

Henderson, S. V. P. 1947. *Introduction to philosophy of education.* Chicago: The University of Chicago Press.

Johnson, J. A., H. W. Collings, V. L. Dupuis, and J. H. Johansen. 1982. *Introduction to the foundations of American education.* Boston: Allyn and Bacon.

Kneller, G. F. 1971. *Introduction to the philosophy of education.* New York: John Wiley & Sons, Inc.

Leight, R. L. 1984. Three pragmatic philosophers. *The Educational Forum 48*(2), 191–206.

Levison, A. B. 1974. The uses of philosophy and the problems of educators. In J. Park, Ed., *Selected readings in the philosophy of education.* New York: Macmillan Publishing Co.

Marler, C. D. 1975. *Philosophy and schooling.* Boston: Allyn and Bacon.

Marshall, J. P. 1973. *The teacher and his philosophy.* Lincoln, NE: Professional Publications, Inc.

Morris, V. C., and Y. Pai. 1976. *Philosophy and the American School.* New York: Houghton-Mifflin.

Ozmon, H. 1972. *Dialogue in the philosophy of education.* Columbus, OH: Charles E. Merrill Publishing Company.

Park, J. 1974. *Selected readings in the philosophy of education.* New York: Macmillan Publishing Company.

Phillips, D. C. 1983. Philosophy of education: In extremis? *Educational Studies 14*(1), 1–30.

Power, E. J. 1982. *Philosophy of education: Studies in philosophies, schooling, and educational policies.* Englewood Cliffs, NJ: Prentice-Hall.

Simpson, D. J., and M. J. B. Jackson. 1984. *The teacher as philosopher.* Toronto: Methuen.

Waismann, F. 1969. How I see philosophy. In R. S. Guttchen and B. Bandman, Eds., *Philosophical essays on curriculum.* Philadelphia: J. B. Lippincott Company.

Ward, S. A. 1981. The philosopher as synthesizer. *Educational Theory 31*(1), 51–72.

Chapter 4

WHO CONTROLS EDUCATION
IN THE UNITED STATES?

OBJECTIVES

After reading this chapter, you will be able to

- describe the way the federal government controls public education;
- discuss teacher organizations and other national controlling influences;
- list the methods used by the state government to control education;
- discuss local influences in public and private education;
- discuss state influence in public and private education.

OUTLINE

ADVANCE ORGANIZERS
INTRODUCTION
ROLE OF THE FEDERAL GOVERNMENT
    Legislative Branch
    Judiciary Branch
    Executive Branch
NATIONAL ORGANIZATIONS
    Teacher Unions
    Other National Organizations
STATE LEVEL INFLUENCE
    State Government
    State Constitutions
    State Legislatures

    State Education Agencies (SEAs)
    Voluntary Statewide Agencies and Groups
LOCAL INFLUENCE
    School Boards
    Local Advisory Groups
    Local Associations
    Teachers
    School Administrators
CONCLUSIONS: WHO DOES CONTROL?
SUMMARY
IN THE FIELD
REFERENCES

1. What does the United States Constitution say about education? Why is there no mention of education, learning, teaching, or related concepts in the Constitution?
2. How different would our educational system be if there were explicit statements about education in the Constitution?
3. What federal legislative acts have affected education?
4. Which federal court decisions have affected education and how have they affected education?
5. What role do teachers' organizations play in control of education?
6. What groups in state government influence education?
7. How do accreditation agencies and textbook publishers influence education?
8. What is the role of local boards of education?
9. Who does control public education in the United States?

INTRODUCTION

The control of education in the United States has been debated for decades. Although initial consideration of the question suggests a simple answer that local school boards control the schools, more extensive investigation into the issue indicates that the control of education in this country is a complex arrangement. Various groups and agencies that exert some control include the federal government, state governments, local school boards, and local communities. Other less obvious include accreditation agencies, textbook publishers and authors, teachers' unions, curriculum reform groups, and the press.

Who actually controls education in the United States is very difficult to determine. With so many different groups exerting influence, perhaps no one group controls education, but a number of groups and factors collectively provide the control. This chapter will investigate the various groups that have some influence over what occurs in our schools and will attempt to conclude which forces exert the most significant control over education in the United States.

ROLE OF THE FEDERAL GOVERNMENT

The role of the federal government in public education in this country has been controversial. Many individuals believe that the federal government should have nothing to do with public education, because the Tenth Amendment to the United States Constitution reserves for states matters not specifically given to the federal government. Since education is not a topic in the Constitution, the conclusion is drawn that education is the responsibility of the states, not the federal government. This should have ended the debate (Harder 1983).

Legislative Branch

Although this argument has been expressed for years, the federal government has been increasing its involvement in education for many years. This increased involvement started early in the history of the country with several pieces of legislation. The first legislation related to education passed by the national government was enacted by the Continental Congress. This act, the Land Ordinance Act of 1785, required that every township set aside one section for the establishment of public schools. While not far reaching, this legislation enabled Congress to establish "an early precedent for making its voice heard in education whenever it is desired" (Koerner 1968, p. 4).

The Northwest Ordinance of 1787 further indicated a commitment from the federal government by stating that "education shall forever be encouraged," because religion, morality, and knowledge are necessary for good government and mankind's happiness. The next federal legislative action affecting education was the Morrill Land Grant Act of 1862. The passage of this act gave federal land to states to establish land grant colleges. The federal government ended up giving seventeen million acres of land to states for this purpose. Sixty-eight land grant colleges exist today (Koerner 1968). A second Morrill Act was passed in 1890, which provided funding to land grant institutions for instruction in various subject areas.

The Smith-Hughes Act of 1917 was unprecedented, with the primary purpose of providing categorical aid to vocational education programs in public schools. The act was passed as a result of three factors: (1) international rivalry, (2) decline of the teenage work force, and (3) desire from educators for a differentiated curricula (Kaestle and Smith 1982). The legislation met the needs of both state and federal governments in that it recognized and supported vocational education (Harder 1983). The legislation differed from previous federal legislation in that it did much more than provide land; it provided money for programs.

Other federal legislative actions related to education were enacted during the depression and World War II years. They were considered temporary and affected education only indirectly. Some of these included (1) the use of funds from the Public Works Administration to construct schools, (2) payment for some teachers from the Federal Emergency Relief Funds, and (3) the Lanham Act of 1941 that reimbursed local schools for serving military dependents (Kaestle and Smith 1982).

By 1950 federal involvement in education continued to be limited to such things as vocational education, school lunches, aid to military dependents, and aid to native Americans. Although various lobby groups, such as the National Education Association, advocated general federal aid to education, Congress resisted (Kaestle and Smith 1982). In 1958 the National Defense Education Act (NDEA) was passed. This was in response to the launch by the Soviet Union of two satellites, Sputnik I and Sputnik II. Fearing that the United States was falling behind the Soviet Union in scientific endeavors, Congress passed the NDEA, which gave money to state universities to strengthen science education and education in the foreign languages (Koerner 1968).

The 1960s marked the beginning of significant federal involvement. During this period, Congress became involved in education through the passage of numerous acts. These included the Manpower Development Training Act of 1962, the Vocational Education Act of 1963, the Economic Opportunity Act of 1965, the Higher Education Act of 1965, the Elementary and Secondary Education Act (ESEA) of 1965, the Bilingual Education Act of 1968, and the Education for All Handicapped Children Act of 1975, as well as amendments to the ESEA.

The most comprehensive act affecting public education was the Elementary and Secondary Education Act of 1965 and its subsequent amendments. This act provided funds for economically disadvantaged children, demonstration programs, innovative programs, libraries, and assistance to improve secondary education programs. Subsequent amendments have provided funds for supporting educational programs for non-English-speaking students, handicapped students, and gifted and talented students (McCarthy and Cambron 1981).

The Elementary and Secondary Education Act of 1965 started out small compared with its current provisions. Initially, there were only five titles and twelve programs. Currently there are thirteen titles and over one hundred different programs. With each program having its own director, staff, and procedures, the bureaucracy grew with the proliferation of programs (Kaestle and Smith 1982).

Civil rights legislation. In addition to legislation passed by Congress that attempted to improve programs, another group of legislative acts were passed that were designed to ensure equal opportunities in education. These included Titles VI and VII of the Civil Rights Act of 1964, Title IX of the Education Amendments of 1972, and the Rehabilitation Act of 1973. Other legislation previously described that relates to civil rights includes the Bilingual Education Act of 1968 and the Education for All Handicapped Children Act of 1975 (see table 4–1).

Judiciary Branch

The judiciary branch of the federal government has been involved in litigation dealing with education during the past twenty-five years. Prior to the landmark *Brown v. Board of Education* civil rights case in 1954, educational issues and legal issues were kept separate. Even the Supreme Court, through its various decisions, indicated that it had no desire to become a "super school board" (Fischer 1979, p. 109). During the past fifteen years, however, courts have become involved in most aspects of educa-

TABLE 4–1	Description of the Bilingual Education Act of 1968 and the Education for All Handicapped Children Act of 1975
Act	*Description*
Bilingual Education Act of 1964	• Amended Title VII of the Elementary and Secondary Education Act • Provided funds for school district to develop and operate special programs for students with limited English-speaking skills who were low-income students • The Bilingual Education Act of 1974 removed the stipulation that students be from low-income families
Education for All Handicapped Children Act Public Law 94–142	• Mandated that public schools provide a free appropriate public education for all school-aged, handicapped children • Required that handicapped students be served with nonhandicapped students as much as possible • Required that individual education programs be developed for handicapped students • Provided parents, students, and schools with due process safeguards

The Judicial Branch has become very involved in education during the past 25 years.

tion, "including students' rights to free expression, compulsory attendance, and mandatory curriculum offerings, school finance reform, employment practices, student discipline, educational malpractice, sex discrimination, collective bargaining, employees' rights to privacy, desegregation, and the rights of handicapped and non-English-speaking students" (McCarthy and Cambron 1981, p. 13).

Through the process of litigation, the courts seek to exercise judicial review, establish legal principles, and settle disputes using principles of law. Courts do not deal with issues until there is a conflict or controversy. Further, the decisions of courts only apply to the geographic area where courts have jurisdiction. Therefore, two different courts might issue conflicting opinions, and those opinions are binding in their jurisdictional areas until and unless the United States Supreme Court makes a ruling on the issue. The rulings of the Supreme Court are the only ones that have national application (McCarthy and Cambron 1981).

Court structure. The United States has two court systems: federal and state. The federal court system comprises three levels. The lowest federal court level is the trial court, called district courts. There are approximately ninety-two district courts in the country. This is the entry level for litigation in the federal court system. There are eleven circuit courts of appeal (see figure 4–1). Federal circuit courts of appeal have between three and fifteen judges, depending on the caseload for that particular district. Decisions rendered in circuit courts are binding only on the geographic area

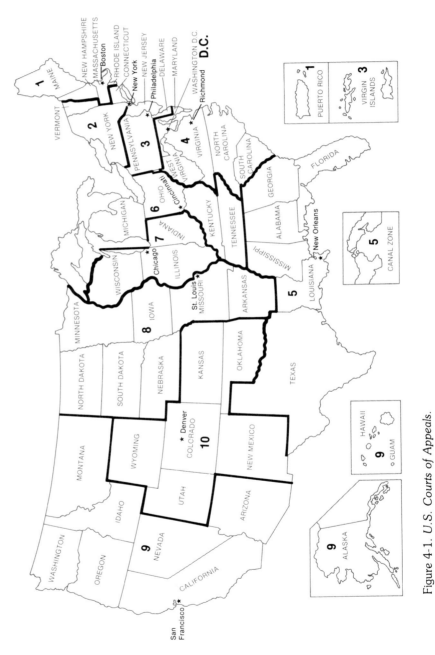

Figure 4-1. *U.S. Courts of Appeals.*

in that district. These decisions are extremely important, however, because they may be used as precedents in similar cases in other districts (McCarthy and Cambron 1981).

The highest federal court, and the ruling court of the United States, is the United States Supreme Court. No appeal can be made beyond the Supreme Court. Decisions rendered by the Supreme Court are binding on the entire country and may overturn previous decisions, as well as bring consensus to issues resolved differently by various courts of appeal (Valente 1980).

The United States Supreme Court deals with approximately five thousand cases per year. A written opinion is issued in fewer than 5 percent of these cases, with the remaining cases being considered by the Court to be inappropriate or of too little significance to require review (McCarthy and Cambron 1981).

Litigation in federal court. Most educational issues are resolved in state courts (Valente 1980). However, the federal court system has become increasingly involved in education cases as a result of federal legislation protecting students' rights and guaranteeing certain groups of children educational opportunities. An analysis of student litigation dealing with civil rights cases filed between 1977 and 1981 cataloged 1,632 cases (see table 4–2). Cases involving handicapped children were the most numerous, with discipline, regulation of sports, and equal protection also having large numbers. Approximately 45 percent of the cases were filed in federal court (Marvell, Galfo, and Rockwell n.d.).

That federal courts have become a factor in public education in the United States should be obvious. Some critics would say that the courts have become too involved. In cases such as *Brown v. Board of Education* (1954), which struck down segregated schools, and *PARC v. Pennsylvania* (1973), which required schools to provide appropriate educational opportunities to handicapped children, the federal courts have made a major impact on public education (see table 4–3).

Prior to the federal court's intervention in education, public schools were primarily responsive to the needs and desires of the white and financially middle and upper-

TABLE 4–2 Student Litigation Dealing With Civil Rights Cases, 1977–1981	
Case Categories	*Number Cases*
Handicapped/Special Education	769
Discipline	290
Regulation of Sports	186
Equal Protection	165
Religion Cases	73
Freedom and Privacy	65
Benefits and Services From Schools	121
Academic Matters	30
Other Categories	1

Source: Marvell, Galfo, and Rockwell, n.d.

TABLE 4–3   Significant Federal Court Decisions

Case	*Description*
Issue: School Finance/Organization	
Attorney General of Michigan v. Lowrey (1905)	Upheld the right of state legislatures to make and change boundaries of school districts
San Antonio Independent School District v. Rodriquez (1973)	Upheld a state funding model where local property taxes are used to provide a minimum educational program for all students
Issue: Church-State Relationships	
Illinois *ex rel.* v. Board of Education (1948)	Court ruled as unconstitutional a school program that permitted students to attend religious instruction in school during school hours
Abington School District v. Schempp, Murray v. Curlett (1963)	Ruled as unconstitutional a law that required the reading of ten Bible verses and recitation of the Lord's prayer during school hours, on school grounds, conducted by school personnel
Epperson v. Arkansas (1968)	A law forbidding the teaching of evolution was ruled unconstitutional
Sloan v. Lemon (1973)	The Supreme Court ruled as unconstitutional, a law allowing for partial reimbursement by the state for tuition paid by parents sending their children to private schools
Issue: Student Rights	
Tinker v. DesMoines Independent Community School District (1969)	The ruling was that it was unconstitutional to suspend students from wearing arm bands or other symbolic expressions unless such interferes with school
Issue: Race, Language, and Sex Discrimination	
Sweatt v. Painter (1950)	U.S. Supreme Court ruled that a black student could not be denied admission to the University of Texas Law School for the sole reason of race
Brown v. Board of Education, Topeka, Kansas (1954)	The Court ruled that children could not be denied admission to public schools on the basis of race; ruling declared segregated public schools to be unconstitutional
Green v. County School Board (1968)	Ruling declared that a "freedom of choice" plan in a previously segregated school district offers little likelihood for desegregation; required that an effective plan for desegregation be implemented
Swann v. Charlotte-Mecklenburg Board of Education (1971)	Upheld busing as a legitimate means for desegregating schools; gave district courts wide discretion in remedying long standing segregated school systems
Pennsylvania Association for Retarded Citizens (PARC) v. Pennsylvania (1971)	Required local schools to provide a free appropriate public education for all school-aged handicapped children

Source: Zirkel, 1978.

middle class. "Court decisions altered the balance of authority" (Kirp and Jensen 1983, p. 207). The decisions gave rights to individuals and groups that had previously been ignored and caused schools to make attempts to provide appropriate services for a broader population of students.

Since the landmark decisions that guaranteed certain rights and access to public education, the legislative and executive branches have assumed a greater role in shaping educational policy. Still, the federal court system is involved in public education. The system still creates rights and "may offer a forum for challenges to proposed federal cutbacks." Federal courts may continue to create rights, respond to challenges of federal cutbacks, and expand their domain (Kirp and Jensen 1983, p. 207).

HIGHLIGHT

Court Gives State Control of Cleveland Desegregation

By Janet Kolodzy
Special to Education Week

CLEVELAND—A federal district judge has ordered Ohio's chief state school officer to assume control over the Cleveland schools' desegregation program.

The May 13 order gives Franklin B. Walter, the state superintendent, authority to order or veto any action by the Cleveland school board or the district's superintendent, Ronald A. Boyd, regarding implementation of the federal court's remedial orders in the district's 12-year-old desegregation case.

The desegregation orders affect the district's entire educational program, including curriculum, student discipline, guidance and counseling, testing, and vocational education.

The Ohio Board of Education, the state superintendent, and the Cleveland board were all found liable for the segregation of the city's schools in 1976.

The state has been providing Cleveland with about $20 million in desegregation aid annually, but its involvement in district operations has been minimal.

The new order represented the latest attempt by the federal court to accelerate compliance with its previous orders in the case.

Six years ago, U.S. District Judge Frank J. Battisti appointed a desegregation administrator after he found the school board in contempt for failing to comply with his orders.

That post was eliminated in 1982 after the board promised swift compliance with the orders.

But testimony before Judge Battisti in early April and reports from the federal court's desegregation monitor indicated that the board was failing to live up to its promises.

"At the rate of compliance progress since 1983, the board will complete the remaining unfinished compliance work in 1992, nine years after the remedy-implementation deadlines set by the court," according to a report last February by the court's monitoring office.

That report also recommended that the state assume control over the desegregation program. *(See Education Week, Feb. 19, 1986.)*

Mr. Walter, Mr. Boyd, and the Cleveland school board's president, Joseph G. Tegreene, concurred in testimony before the court that efforts to comply with the desegregation orders had not been moving as quickly as they would have liked.

But the Cleveland school board and superintendent argued that the state should not be given control of desegregation. Instead, they suggested that the state should be required to promote further compliance with the orders by providing the district with additional funds and technical assistance.

But Judge Battisti adopted the monitoring commission's recommendation and ordered direct state control over the program.

Shortly after the decision was announced, Mr. Boyd and Mr. Tegreene both said they would be very willing to cooperate with state officials.

The state's presence in Cleveland will be in the form of an advisory team of education specialists, which will work with Cleveland school officials in areas including transportation, management and finance, vocational education, guidance and counseling, and community involvement.

Mr. Walter will not personally oversee the daily operations of the team. Instead, he has named one of his former state assistant superintendents,

Roger J. Lulow, to head the advisory team, which is composed of six state school officials and two former school superintendents.

Mr. Lulow, superintendent of the Willoughby-Eastlake School District in suburban Cleveland, served as the city schools' deputy superintendent in 1982–83. As a state assistant superintendent, he guided Cleveland in its administrative reorganization in 1982.

Mr. Walter said one of the major tasks facing the team will be the development of a 1986–87 budget for the district that must be completed by July 1.

He added that the panel will be responsible for the implementation of a facilities-use plan that calls for the creation of middle schools spanning grades 7 and 8 and changes in the district's curriculum.

Reprinted with permission Education Week, Volume V, Number 36, 1986.

Executive Branch

The executive branch of the federal government has also been involved in public education and has expanded its involvement since the late 1960s. No federal agency dealt with education until 1867, when Congress created the Federal Department of Education. The department was created to

- collect statistics and facts on the condition of education;

- disseminate information concerning organization and management of schools and teaching methods;

- promote the cause of education.

After an unproductive first year of operation, the department was downgraded to an "office" (Koerner 1968).

During the first one hundred years of operation, the United States Office of Education (USOE) had minimal impact on public education. In fact, it never efficiently accomplished its purpose of collecting and disseminating information. Following the launch of Sputnik by the Soviet Union in 1958, the USOE took on greater significance and grew greatly in size and power. Although Congress continued to identify the general purposes of programs administered by the USOE, detailed guidelines and qualifications were established by the Office (Koerner 1968).

The USOE was hampered by many different variables. Silberman (1980) indicated that a major problem in the USOE was the constant competition among three groups: elite reformers, power brokers, and professional educators. Elite reformers included the higher level bureaucrats in the Office of the President, department deputies and their assistants, consultants, and individuals from federal budget offices. Members of Congress and their powerful constituents made up the power broker group, while the professional educator group included civil service managers and their grantees. Constant bickering among these three groups created major problems for the USOE (Silberman 1980).

In 1979, supported by the Carter administration, Congress passed legislation authorizing the Department of Education as the eighth department in the federal government. The passage of the legislation authorizing this department was difficult, with many opponents to the concept. Those in opposition basically focused their arguments on the department's creation as adding to the federal budget and federal bureaucracy. As late as June 1979 the likelihood that the legislation would be passed by the House of Representatives was no better than fifty-fifty (Neill 1979a). The bill authorizing the establishment of the Department of Education did pass, however, and was signed into law in 1979. Provisions in the legislation stated that the department was to be operational within 180 days after the law's passage, and on May 7, 1980, the department was officially opened.

Creating the Department of Education was a major step forward in consolidating federal programs dealing with education. More than 150 agencies and programs that had operated in six different departments—Department of Health, Education, and Welfare; Department of Justice; Department of Defense; Department of Housing and Urban Development; Department of Labor; and Department of Agriculture—were placed in an agency that was without precedent (Neill 1979b). Indeed, this was a major shift in education policy at the federal level.

The five purposes listed for the Department of Education were the following:

1. To ensure equal educational opportunities for all citizens.
2. To strengthen the federal commitment to support state and local efforts to meet educational needs.
3. To encourage increased involvement of the public, parents, and students in federal education programs.
4. To promote improvements in the quality of education through research, evaluation, and information sharing.
5. To improve coordination, management, and accountability of federal education programs. (Neill 1980, p. 670)

To accomplish such a broad range of purposes, the department is organized into several different units (see figure 4–2).

Following the opening of the Department of Education, many critics continued to challenge its purposes. Indeed, one of President Ronald Reagan's campaign goals was to dismantle the entire department and create an educational foundation. The new Foundation for Educational Assistance was to administer (1) block grants and consolidated aid, (2) student financial aid, (3) compensatory programs for the disadvantaged, handicapped, and others, (4) informational, statistical, and research services, and (5) investigations of complaints and compliance (Rosenau 1982). Contrary to President Reagan's wishes, Congress did not accept the removal of departmental status for education.

NATIONAL ORGANIZATIONS

Teacher Unions

Teachers want some control over education, and they are as capable of developing sound education policy as are lay school boards (Retsinas 1982). As individuals, however, teachers have limited power. Therefore, they have banded together into teacher organizations to become a major force in controlling public education in the United States. Currently, the two major teacher organizations in this country are the National Education Association (NEA) and the American Federation of Teachers (AFT).

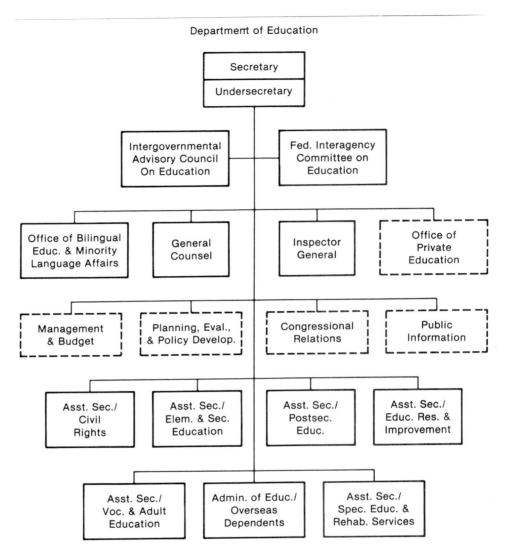

Department of Education

Key: Solid lines indicate offices stipulated in legislation.
    Dotted lines indicated offices not stipulated in legislation.
Source: Office of Management and Budget.

Figure 4-2. *Organization, United States Department of Education. Reprinted with permission, G. Neill, Observers see danger, challenge in building Education Department.* Phi Delta Kappan *1979, 61 (4), 236.*

Teachers' organizations began in 1794 when the Society of Associated Teachers of New York City was founded. In the early 1800s several similar groups were developed, primarily in urban areas. With the growth of these urban organizations came the ability to organize on a state level. By 1860 approximately thirty such state organizations were in existence. In 1857 the National Teachers Association was formed in Philadelphia. This group combined with the National Association of School Superintendents and the American Normal School Association in the 1870s to become the National Educational Association. In 1906 the organization changed its name to the National Education Association (Armstrong, Henson, and Savage 1983).

The American Federation of Teachers (AFT) was formed in 1916 when teachers' organizations in Chicago and the upper Midwest joined together. Unlike NEA, which was originally dominated by administrators and university professors, the AFT has always been primarily for teachers. While the NEA focused mainly on a broad array of educational issues, the AFT has always aimed its activities at teachers' benefits. Although never as large as the NEA, the AFT has had a major impact on education (Armstrong, Henson, and Savage 1981).

Both the NEA and AFT have grown dramatically since 1960. In 1957 the NEA had only seven hundred thousand members (Elam 1981); in 1978 the membership had grown to over 1.6 million (Lieberman 1981). AFT membership increased from forty thousand in 1940 (Armstrong, Henson, and Savage 1983) to five hundred thousand by 1978 (Lieberman 1981). The number of members in these organizations has enabled the groups to influence legislation at the state and national levels and policy at local levels. The NEA, with an average of six thousand members per congressional district, spent nearly $350,000 on the 1980 national elections (Elam 1981). At the 1983 NEA convention alone, a record $125,000 was raised for political contributions (Ficklen and McCormick 1983). Although their influence has been less than expected in some situations, both teachers' groups will continue to influence educational policies and legislation at the local and national levels.

Other National Organizations

Besides teachers' organizations, several other groups at the national level exert some control over public education. These include testing agencies, accreditation agencies, curriculum reform groups, textbook authors and publishers, foundations, citizens' advisory groups, and professional organizations.

Testing agencies. As a result of the development of national, standardized tests, various testing agencies influence education. School boards, administrators, and teachers want students in their districts to perform well on such tests as the Scholastic Achievement Test (SAT), American College Test (ACT), and other group achievement measures. The emphasis for students to perform well on these tests leads some schools to modify curricula and teaching objectives to better prepare students to perform well.

Many countries, use a national testing program that requires students to pass certain exams before completion of formalized schooling. These tests greatly affect the content of courses. While such a national testing program does not exist in the United States, the fact that only a few companies market most of the college entrance tests has a similar controlling effect on curricula. The ramifications are such that high schools have no choice but to offer their best students the majority of courses related to the subjects on college board exams (Koerner 1968).

The organization that is most important in college entrance testing is the Educational Testing Service (ETS) of Princeton (Koerner 1968). Most universities require that students complete the SAT, which is designed by ETS. Schools not requiring the SAT normally require the ACT, which is developed by the American College Testing Program (Jencks and Crouse 1982).

In 1900 several colleges attempted to relieve the burden of screening applicants for their schools by establishing the College Entrance Examination Board to administer one standardized test. As a result, the first SAT was administered in 1926. Since this beginning, colleges and universities have looked to ETS and others to a lesser degree to help determine which students to admit (Jencks and Crouse 1982). Indeed, the SAT "is being presented to the public—and apparently is increasingly accepted—as both the gatekeeper of college admissions and the single most important indicator of academic health at the college entry level" (Bracey 1980, p. 197).

Although recent studies have raised important issues about the ability of the SAT to predict college success, many high schools still attempt to formulate their curricula to prepare students for these entrance tests. If students do not do well on college entrance tests, students and their parents may be outraged. Schools, therefore, feel as though they have little to do other than try to prepare students to score well on the SAT and other admissions tests. Therefore, in effect, ETS and other test developers, are controlling education to some degree.

Accreditation agencies. Like testing agencies, accreditation agencies exert influence over public education in an unofficial manner. Accreditation of public schools has been done by universities, voluntary regional associations, and state education agencies. Universities began accrediting high schools in 1871 when the University of Michigan issued a notice to high schools that after a visit to the school by university faculty, the school could be designated as meeting the quality standards that would allow its graduates to be admitted to the University of Michigan without further examination (Saylor 1982).

The accreditation of high schools by universities continued until after World War II. The University of Nebraska maintained the only authority to accredit high schools in that state until 1950 when the state legislature passed legislation granting the State Department of Education this responsibility (Saylor 1982).

With the discontinuation of accreditation of high schools by universities came the requirement of standardized tests for university admission and the growth of voluntary regional accreditation agencies. Accreditation by regional agencies serves to

- provide standards for the public to compare its schools;

- assure that schools will undergo periodic self-study;

- assure that faculty and teaching conditions meet certain minimum standards;

- indicate a commitment to quality education by schools. (Partners in Quality Education 1982)

The first voluntary regional accreditation agency was the New England Association of Secondary Schools, which started in 1885. As with later voluntary agencies, the New England Association was "extra-legal and not under public control" (Saylor 1982, p. 48). Following the establishment of the New England Association, several other regional agencies were developed (see table 4–4). Of the regional associations, the North Central and Southern Associations have become dominant (Saylor 1982).

Accreditation of schools follows an on-site review by team members.

The accreditation of teacher training programs by voluntary agencies also influences public education. The National Council for Accreditation of Teacher Education (NCATE) is the primary accreditation agency that accredits teacher training institutions. Founded in 1954, "NCATE was created in an attempt to establish a national, voluntary accreditation process for teacher education" (Watts 1983, p. 646).

Although voluntary, NCATE accreditation is sought by many institutions for reasons such as (1) prestige, (2) reciprocal transfer of credit among member institutions, (3) student recruitment, (4) job placement of graduates, and (5) certification (Watts 1983). Accreditation of teacher training programs supposedly adds credibility to the assumption that its graduates are competent (Huffman 1982). Some consider NCATE accreditation as essential in maintaining quality teacher education programs, while others consider it unnecessary, expensive, and contributing little to quality teacher education.

TABLE 4-4   Regional Accreditation Agencies

Agency	Year Established
New England Association of Colleges and Secondary Schools	1885
Association of Colleges and Preparatory Schools in the Middle States and Maryland	1888
Association of Colleges and Preparatory Schools of the Southern States	1895
North Central Association of Colleges and Secondary Schools	1895
Northwest Association of Secondary and Higher Schools	1918
Western College Association	1948

Source: Saylor, 1982.

Curriculum and reform groups. Other groups that affect public education in this country also do not have official sanctions, but provide information and impetus for change. Among these are curriculum reform groups, often assembled by professional organizations, and other actions by professional organizations.

Curriculum reform groups have been impacting education in this country for only a brief time. The beginning of involvement by scholars in public education started in 1952 when a group of university professors and public school teachers founded a group to reorganize the teaching of math in public schools. While this action was small, it led to larger groups, such as the Physical Science Study Committee (PSSC), which was formed at the Massachusetts Institute of Technology to reform the high school physics curriculum. PSSC was the major curriculum reform group of the time and was the inspiration for many others that followed. As a result, high school physics classes changed dramatically and up to 25 percent of students studying physics in high schools used the PSSC program (Koerner 1968).

Individuals involved in PSSC created Educational Services Incorporated (ESI), which was the umbrella organization for PSSC and other reform efforts. In 1962 the focus of ESI was expanded from the sciences to include social sciences. ESI is the largest group in the country focusing on curriculum reform and research (Koerner 1968).

In addition to private groups such as PSSC and ESI attempting to revise curricula, various professional groups have also made efforts to influence the curriculum (see table 4-5).

Textbook authors and publishers. Another national force in education comes from the private sector relating to textbooks. Textbooks contain the majority of the content presented to students and often include suggestions for teaching style and methods. Although numerous textbook publishers prepare books for educational purposes, a few companies appear to control the market. The influence of these publishers and authors should not be discounted.

The influence of textbooks varies depending on the subject matter taught and the age groups of students. Limited influence results from textbooks at the kindergarten level while at the secondary level the content contained in books can be very influen-

---

TABLE 4-5 Professional Groups Influencing Curriculum

Group	Actions
Modern Language Association	• Established a Committee of Twelve in 1896 that submitted a report in 1898 that continues to influence curriculum in secondary schools and colleges. • Established the Modern Foreign Language Study in 1924 that published seventeen volumes related to teaching foreign language.
American Historical Association	• Established the Commission on the Social Studies in 1929 that prepared and published twelve volumes over a five-year period. Volumes on *The Social Studies as School Subjects* and *Methods of Instruction in the Sciences* provided guidelines for planning at the local and state levels.
National Council of Teachers of English	• Published, in 1935, a broad, flexible plan for teaching English. The book, *An Experience Curriculum in English*, was one of the best guides ever prepared by a national committee for curriculum planning in a subject field.
Progressive Education Association (PEA)	• Carried out curriculum experimentation with about thirty selected high schools in which schools chose their activities and received consultative services from PEA. This was called the Eight-Year Study. • The PEA Commission on Secondary School Curriculum established five committees to develop curricula for art, language and literature, science, math, and social studies. The reports from these committees did not have a great impact.

Source: Saylor, 1982.

tial. Subjects such as music, physical education, and vocational education are less influenced by textbooks than are biology, economics, history, and other more content-oriented subjects where the textbook may be the only external curriculum plan available (Saylor 1982).

An example of the influence of textbooks would be in the teaching of economics. Some books might overemphasize capitalism as the only moral, appropriate economic system while others would fairly present other economic systems, including those that deviate greatly from capitalism. In the teaching of reading, textbooks that emphasize the phonics approach would influence the reading program in an elementary school. Textbook publishers and authors, therefore, have a great influence on education. While this influence may be hidden, it definitely pervades the educational system (Koerner 1968).

STATE LEVEL INFLUENCE

Many different groups at the state level exert a great deal of influence over education, including state legislatures, teacher associations, administrator associations, and groups representing specific populations of students (Rosenthal and Fuhrman 1982). The power of these groups varies from state to state.

State Government

State government influences education in the following different ways:

1. Provisions in state constitutions
2. Enactment of statutory law

3. Court decisions
4. Powers granted state department/state boards of education
   a. Legal and regulatory powers
   b. Accreditation/standardization of schools
   c. Selection of textbooks and instructional materials
   d. Issuance of curriculum syllabi and guides
   e. Competency examinations (Saylor 1982, p. 78)

State Constitutions

All state constitutions include some provisions related to public education. Early constitutions contained limited details concerning education, with the primary focus being on the establishment of a public school system. However, many states are rewriting their original constitutions to contain more detailed guidelines on education. Even the rewritten constitutions most often give vast authority over education to state legislatures and do not include many specifics about educational systems. The granting of this power to legislatures, and the provisions made for taxes, enable state constitutions to influence education (Saylor 1982).

State Legislatures

Although many state-level groups affect education, in many states the legislatures have emerged as the powerful force. In some states, they are even referred to as "the big school board" (Rosenthal and Fuhrman p. 4). For the most part, legislators who have been in office for the past ten to fifteen years and have been supportive of education are being replaced by new representatives and senators. While most legislators in the past were stable in their offices, today's legislators are likely to stay in office only four to eight years. As a result, they do not develop an advocacy role for many areas, education being one of them (Rosenthal and Fuhrman 1982).

Legislators influence education via two legislative functions: budget and oversight. As state funds have diminished during the past decade, the budget appropriation role has become extremely critical. All state programs want more money. Prisons, social programs, higher education, transportation, and law enforcement have developed strong lobbies and demanded their fair share of state revenues. This leaves less for education, an area that often has had a fragmented lobbying effort (Rosenthal and Fuhrman 1982).

The oversight function of state legislatures enables legislators to evaluate previously approved programs to determine if they are effective and if schools are implementing them as intended. Such oversight functions now occur in thirty-five states. Because of the recent uproar over the quality of public education, legislators are more likely to get involved in oversight functions than in the past, making their impact on public education greater than ever.

> The professional dominance of education policy ended some years ago, and it is unlikely to recur. No longer will legislatures rubber-stamp policy decisions made by educators, by their associations, or by state departments of education. Currently, legislatures shape education policy—for better or for worse—and educators must reconcile themselves to that fact. (Rosenthal and Fuhrman 1982, p. 49)

State legislatures are heavily involved in the educational reform movements that began in the early 1980s. Several states have passed legislation implementing educational reforms ranging from teacher testing to school-year extensions. Legislatures probably will not give up their role in education; since they come from and represent a concerned constituency, they could not if they desired to.

State Education Agencies (SEAs)

State departments of education are found in all fifty states. These agencies, which are entrusted by state legislatures to "carry out the educational policies of the legislature and the board of education . . . are supposed to supply educational leadership for the state as well as to keep the legislature educationally informed, act as inspectors of schools, dispensers of aid, licensers of teachers, and a source of expert guidance in general to local school systems" (Koerner 1968, p. 91). SEAs derive their power from state constitutions and legislatures (Saylor 1982).

SEAs vary greatly from state to state. Some are extremely large with massive budgets, while others are relatively small with only a minimal amount of funding. SEAs may also vary over the following:

- SEAs organize themselves to become more or less actively involved in the policies and practices of all local education agencies (LEAs) within their boundaries.

- SEAs organize themselves to provide something between a very high and a very low amount, as well as quality of, technical assistance to LEAs.

- SEAs vary greatly in the emphasis they give to the determination and the attempt at regulation of LEA policies and standards of practice.

- SEAs vary widely along a continuum that ranges from low to high organizational efficacy. (Dentler 1984, p. 151–52)

Although SEAs vary greatly, most lack the necessary resources to be effective. They are hampered by limited budgets and rigid civil service requirements for employees. While many SEAs continue to maintain tight control over such areas as teacher and administrator certification, they are limited in their ability to perform more important roles such as inspecting schools, research and data gathering, long-range planning, and providing educational leadership (Koerner 1968). A recent study by Dentler (1984) confirms these facts. After visiting the SEAs, the conclusion was that only fifteen to twenty of the fifty SEAs are capable of influencing positive changes in the quality of schools.

Even though many SEAs appear to lack the necessary components to effect major changes, they have the necessary power to do so in most states. Primary methods of influencing local education programs are in the areas of (1) accreditation/standardization schemes, (2) textbook selection, (3) issuance of curriculum syllabi and guides, and (4) competency exams (Saylor 1982). The effectiveness with which SEAs influence education through these avenues varies from state to state.

SEAs, therefore, have the power if not the means to greatly influence education. The educational reform movements begun in the early 1980s will likely provide more means to SEAs to accomplish reforms. "A great deal of effort in curriculum formulation will be mandated and directed by the state departments of education as they seek to dictate the educational outcomes to be attained by students in at least a portion of the instructional program of the school" (Saylor 1982, p. 115).

─────────────────── HIGHLIGHT ───────────────────

States Have Much Control
Over Content Of Textbooks

LITTLE ROCK, Ark. (AP)—State governments are rich consumers with power over textbook publishers, who thrive by printing what states want, an industry official says.

Donald Eklund, vice president of the school division of the Association of American Publishers, trade association for the industry, also says there are so many publishing companies competing in the market, one state usually can find what it's looking for in textbooks and avoid another state's influence on their content.

For instance, if a state wants heavy emphasis on evolution in biology textbooks, at least one publisher will be eager to accommodate the buyer of the books, Eklund said.

"A publisher has to make decisions all the time as to what goes in and what doesn't go into a book because his first consideration is to make sure he meets the requirements set up by that state," Eklund said in a recent telephone interview from New York. "If he doesn't, he's not going to be considered. He'll just be thrown out of the game before it starts."

Eklund said a prominent Wall Street analyst of the publishing industry says no publisher is more responsive to the market than a textbook publisher. "You have to be. It is so competitive that you really have to respond to that market demand or they're not going to buy your books. There's so much to choose from," he said. States use various methods of choosing textbooks that school districts may buy using state funds. In Arkansas, a committee of practicing teachers examines books in one area every five years. This year, social studies books are being examined and chosen. Sue Owens, who supervises the committee, said in a recent interview that the committee doesn't try to find one book to meet the schools' curricula; instead, it tries

to eliminate unsuitable ones. That way, schools can choose a book that best fits its needs.

Eklund said some other states do the same thing. Georgia, for instance, put 15 biology books on its approved list, "and those range all the way from very heavy on evolution to those that are very light. It depends on what the local school district wants," he said.

Mel Gabler of Longview, Texas, and his wife, Donna, who run Educational Research Analysts, have long been active in testifying at textbook hearings. Gabler said recently by telephone that he is accused of being a censor and of representing a narrow special interest.

"We represent mainstream America. Surveys show that the mainstream holds traditional values, that lying, cheating, stealing and so on are wrong. That's censored out of textbooks," he said. Textbooks teach situational ethics, Gabler said, and teachers are told in some manuals not to insist on correct answers. Gabler said he receives more requests for information from outside of Texas than from within the state.

The Gablers also have received attention for their influence on evolution in textbooks. "We want evoluton taught as a theory," he said. "It's not treated like other sciences. There's no evidence shown against it."

Ed Bullington, a Little Rock social studies teacher and president-elect of the Arkansas Education Association, a teacher lobbying group, said a colleague in 1981 told him a psychology book that, in the draft version, referred to the evolution of the brain. The colleague said the version delivered to the school talked about development of the brain. Bullington said he called the publisher in Texas, who admitted that the Gablers had influenced the treatment of evolution.

Bullington said he believes parents have the right to control what their children read, but he opposes parents who try to control what all children read. "It doesn't give children the chance to examine several issues," he said. "It's denying them a pluralistic view of the world."

Eklund said such influence on textbooks is one reason that selection of books must be made carefully. But Bullington said those problems can go undetected. "If you're a beginning teacher, you may not know what should and should not be in there," he said.

Influence of people like the Gablers is limited, Eklund said. "A publisher has to look at the entire United States," he said. "He's not going to be influenced by one little pocket of protesters."

Eklund said that not only do textbook adoption committees choose what books may be bought with state funds, but they also choose who serves on the committee, "so the states have a great deal of control over what goes in the books."

Although publishers try to meet local needs, small states like Arkansas have less influence than larger states simply because it won't spend as much money on textbooks. "If you're going to write a book and make a buck off of it, in Arkansas 400,000 people might use it. You're also not going to sell an Arkansas history book in New York. That limits you to start with," Sherman Peterson, associate director for instructional services in the Arkansas Department of Education, said in a recent telephone interview.

Ms. Owens said large states like California and Texas have been leaders in the push for higher quality textbooks, so smaller states like Arkansas would benefit.

Defining quality poses problems, Eklund said. "I published a book one time that all the academics told me was the greatest thing since sliced bread. But it was a bomb because the teachers couldn't read it."

Eklund said there should be enough textbooks available for several levels of ability. "If you took a so-called rigorous textbook and put it in the hands of a child who's reading two grade levels below his grade, and being taught by a teacher who can't pass the minimum competency test, is that a really quality textbook? Disaster!"

Less than a penny out of every dollar spent on education goes for textbooks, he said. "If you're in a poorer school system and you have five classes of algebra, maybe you can afford only one set of textbooks. Where do you buy it? You buy it right down the middle. The kids above that and below that are getting cheated."

When studies criticize education, everyone involved in education tries to blame someone else, he said, but recently there has been a greater spirit of cooperation.

"It's something that's not going to be solved overnight. It's not a simple problem, but it's one where everybody has to work together," he said. *Northwest Arkansas Times.* May 26, 1985. Used by permission of the Associated Press.

Voluntary Statewide Agencies and Groups

Several agencies and groups at the state level wield influence over public education. One group in most states that influences educational practices is the state organization of teachers, usually the state chapters of the National Education Association or the American Federation of Teachers. The state affiliates of the NEA are the most powerful of these state groups; state affiliates of the AFT have as yet not developed into a powerful group in most states. The state NEA groups exert tremendous power with the legislature in many states. Often their executive offices are in the capitol cities, and they are heavily involved in legislation affecting education (Koerner 1968).

One reason state affiliates are so powerful is that membership is greater at the state level than it is at the national level. Many states, including Kansas, Iowa, and Illinois, have a tradition of large, active state NEA associations. In these states, legislatures often have a great deal of difficulty getting legislation passed without the approval of the state NEA affiliate (Koerner 1968).

Other state groups that affect education include state professional associations such as the state federation of the Council for Exceptional Children, which focuses on special education. Professional associations attempt to influence legislation and educational practices that are related to their own specific concerns. The effectiveness of the groups varies from state to state depending on the particular power of each organization in each state.

LOCAL INFLUENCE

Many local groups influence education in this country. Indeed, many people believe that local groups control public education. Among these local groups are school boards, local teachers' organizations, local advisory boards, and the general public.

School Boards

Each of the approximately sixteen thousand school districts in the United States is under the control of a local school board. Although many forces exert control over public education, local boards still have some powers in setting policies and priorities and providing the necessary incentives to ensure the quality of local educational programs (Nelson and Crum 1983). The three primary functions of local school boards are (1) long-range planning, (2) setting priorities, and (3) evaluating the superintendent (Moberly and Stiles 1978).

Many school boards control districts with fewer than five hundred students while a few govern districts with several thousand students. While individual board members have no power or authority, as a collective group, boards exert significant influence over local educational practices. Although school boards vary significantly, some generalizations can be made:

- Rights and responsibilities of boards are rarely clearly defined.
- Five to seven members serve on boards.
- Board members are elected on a nonpartisan basis.
- Majority of members are men.
- Professional and business groups are generally represented.
- Many board members have three to four years of experience.
- Board members are solid citizens.
- Boards meet regularly, weekly, biweekly, or monthly (depending on state laws and regulations) and in special meetings as needed. (Koerner 1968)

School boards set policies that affect the local district. In a study of 130 school districts representing nearly six thousand schools and 3.5 million students, it was determined that school boards often set policies that are more stringent than state requirements in such areas as graduation requirements and teacher qualifications (Nelson and Crum 1983). Boards do have power, therefore, to set their own more rigorous standards even though state departments of education and legislatures also set standards. A great deal of ambiguity exists concerning the relationships between

Local school boards have traditionally been thought of as the major controlling agency of schools.

SEAs and LEAs (Dentler 1984). As a result, some local boards exercise a great deal of power and control while others tend to relinquish these powers to the SEA.

Local Advisory Groups

In addition to exerting influence over local educational practices through local boards of education, community members also exert power with advisory groups. These groups are often developed with the leadership of the school administration. Establishing advisory groups (1) creates strong ties between the community and the school, (2) helps in information dissemination, (3) promotes public confidence, and (4) encourages evaluations by community members (Else 1983).

School districts can benefit directly from advisory groups. A vocational education advisory council in the Petersburg, Virginia, school district helped to determine the vocational needs of the community, identify goals and objectives, and more importantly, assisted in developing and maintaining appropriate vocational programs (Murphy 1983). Therefore, although not a legally formulated group with actual powers, local advisory groups can exert influence over educational practices.

Through the use of advisory groups, schools can gain useful information and support from local community members by involving them in the planning process for the school. A good way to elicit support is to first ask community members what they think are the most important goals and objectives for the school. By surveying community members in Lewisville, Texas, the superintendent's advisory committee determined that skills considered to be the most important for students, decision-making skills and future planning, were ranked only seventh and eighth in the school's performance (Killian 1983). By collecting such information from community members, schools are better able to stay in touch with their constituency and meet the needs deemed highest by the community.

Local Associations

The Parent Teacher Association (PTA) has been a major force in local educational policy from time to time and from community to community. In some communities, PTAs are very active and involved while in others the organization is barely visible. In districts where the PTA is active, administrators and school boards must pay attention to the group's wishes as it can exert a great deal of influence over local educational practices and policies.

Teachers

Certainly, at least in many districts, teachers influence local educational practices. This can be accomplished on an individual basis in the classroom or collectively when teachers are organized and express their views to the administration and school board. Local teacher organizations, often the local chapter of the NEA or AFT, have begun to wield more power over local educational practices than before these organizations became as sophisticated as they are now.

In many states, teachers have earned the legal right to collective bargaining. Even in states where this right has not been legally guaranteed, teachers often exercise the right through "sick outs" and other collective bargaining methods (Koerner 1968). As a result of teachers' bargaining powers, their ability to influence education at the local level has increased dramatically. Not only are teachers bargaining for salaries and fringe benefits, but they are also negotiating issues such as class size, extracurricular duties, and their rights to participate in local policy development.

Individually, teachers exert a great deal of control over what occurs in their classrooms. In this respect teachers are the ultimate curriculum planner. "All else is ancillary to the teacher's role in determining the nature, quality, meaningfulness, and appropriateness of the educational experiences being experienced by students under his or her direction" (Saylor 1982, p. 159).

Even with this amount of control over their classrooms, teachers still must adhere to certain district and state policies, utilize adopted curriculum guides, and follow certain rules that govern all instructional personnel (Saylor 1982).

School Administrators

School administrators, namely superintendents, assistant superintendents, and building principals, are obviously key individuals in local educational practices. Indeed, administrators are ultimately responsible for all that occurs in the schools. Therefore, the success of local schools depends a great deal on the quality of administration.

The role of administrators has changed in American education. Whereas these individuals were initially considered primarily as expert teachers and curriculum experts, their roles now include a vast array of functions, including fiscal planning and management, business management, personnel management, and school law (Podemski, Price, Smith, and Marsh 1984). This change of roles now mandates that school administrators assume a major leadership role in all aspects of education.

Although administrators work for school boards, they are still in a unique position to influence educational practices and policies in the local district. Most school board members are not educational specialists, but professional members of the community. As a result, they will often weigh very heavily the recommendations made by administrators when discussing school policies and practices. This, in effect, makes administrators the primary force in educational policy and implementation (Koerner 1968).

CONCLUSIONS: WHO DOES CONTROL?

The control over education in the United States is obviously a complex question. Although the belief has long been held that local boards of education exert ultimate control, investigating the influences at the state and national levels shows that local boards of education are very limited in their control. The control of our schools is shared by many different groups, both formal and informal. Certainly the federal government's influence has grown dramatically during the twentieth century. Although the early 1980s saw an effort to shift the trend away from federal influence and back to states and local units, federal involvement in public education is so broad that any such efforts will undoubtedly result in only minor changes.

No one group controls American education. All three levels of government, local, state, and federal, are heavily involved; publishing companies, teachers' organizations, and testing companies exert indirect influence; the judiciary has set precedence of ruling on education issues; and local teacher and parent groups are gaining influence. The only conclusions that can be drawn are that (1) control of education in the United States is and will continue to be shared by a multitude of individuals and groups, and (2) although the levels of influence may shift among groups, most of the variables influencing education currently will continue to have some impact in the future.

SUMMARY

This chapter has focused on the issue of control over American education. Many different forces exert influence. At the federal level, the executive branch, legislative branch, and judiciary branch are all involved. State legislatures have been gaining in involvement during the past two decades. At the local level, school boards still influence specific practices in local schools. In addition to government, many informal groups exert influence. These include testing agencies, accreditation agencies, and book publishers. Groups such as the right-wing coalition have become powerful influences. Teachers' organizations, through collective bargaining and strike actions, have added to their influence over what occurs in classrooms.

Control over education was shown to be a complex issue. No one group or level of government dominates public education in the United States. Rather, schools are influenced and controlled by a combination of government, lay, professional, and corporate groups.

IN THE FIELD

1. Do teachers feel they have a major role in decision making in the district? If so, how do they access the decision-making process?

2. Should teachers have a role in decision making? Why?

3. Do teachers primarily follow a teacher's guide or curriculum guide in their instructional activities? If not, what do they follow?

4. Do teachers use any state or district document relating to classroom objectives?

5. Does the district have a citizen's advisory group that is active? If so, what is its role?

6. Are school board policies available for review by teachers and students?

7. Is there a local teachers' organization? If so, does it have a role in district decision making?

8. Is the school and district accredited by a regional accreditation agency? If so, what agency and when was the last accreditation visit?

9. How does the school district ensure compliance with state and federal regulations in areas such as special education?

REFERENCES

Armstrong, D. G., K. T. Henson, and T. V. Savage. 1983. *Education: An introduction.* New York: Macmillan.

Bracey, G. W. 1980. The SAT, college admissions, and the concept of talent: Unexamined myths, unexplained perceptions, needed explorations. *Phi Delta Kappan 62*(3), 197–99.

Dentler, R. A. 1984. Ambiguities in state-local relations. *Education and Urban Society 16*(2), 145–64.

Elam, S. M. 1981. The national education association: Political powerhouse or paper tiger? *Phi Delta Kappan 63*(3), 169–74.

Else, D. 1983. Productive advisory committees keep parents happy and curriculums current. *The American School Board Journal 170*(6), *34+.*

Ficklen, E. and K. McCormick. 1983. Repeated attacks on education put unions on the defensive. *The American School Board Journal 170*(10), 31–34.

Fischer, L. 1979. Law and educational policy. *Educational Forum 44*(1), 109–14.

Harder, J. C. 1983. The federal-state relationship: A traditionalist's view. *Education and Urban Society 16*(1), 81–93.

Huffman, J. 1982. The role of accreditation in preserving educational integrity. *Educational Record 63*(2), 41–44.

Jencks, C., and J. Crouse. 1982. Should we relabel the SAT . . . or replace it? *Phi Delta Kappan 63*(10), 659–63.

Kaestle, C. F., and M. S. Smith. 1982. The federal role in elementary and secondary education, 1940–1980. *Harvard Educational Review 52*(4).

Killian, M. G. 1983. Community poll defines key skills and assesses schools' performance. *Phi Delta Kappan 65*(3), 218–19.

Kirp, D. L., and D. N. Jensen. 1983. The new federalism goes to court. *Phi Delta Kappan 65*(3), 206–10.

Koerner, J. D. 1968. *Who controls American education? A guide for laymen.* Boston: Beacon Press.

Lieberman, M. 1981. Teacher bargaining: An autopsy. *Phi Delta Kappan 63*(4), 231–34.

McCarthy, M. M., and N. H. Cambron. 1981. *Public school law: Teachers' and students' rights.* Boston: Allyn and Bacon, Inc.

Marvell, T., A. Galfo, and J. Rockwell. (n.d.) *Student litigation: A compilation and analysis of civil cases involving students 1977–1981.* Williamsburg, VA: National Center for State Courts.

Moberly, D. L., and L. J. Stiles. 1978. Getting a school board to address its primary tasks. *Phi Delta Kappan 60*(3), 236–37.

Murphy, M. C. 1983. How advisory councils can help. *Vocational Education 58*(4), 34–35.

Neill, G. 1979a. Department of education nears showdown in house. *Phi Delta Kappan 60*(10), 701–702.

Neill, G. 1979b. Observers see danger, challenge in building education department. *Phi Delta Kappan 61*(4), 236–37.

Neill, G. 1980. Education department explains its structure and purposes. *Phi Delta Kappan 61*(10), 670.

Nelson, J. L., and L. R. Crum. 1983. The power and challenges of local school boards. *American Education 19*(10), 10–16.

Partners in quality education. 1982. The community, its schools, and the north central association. *The North Central Association Quarterly, 57*(2), 27–29.

Podemski, R. S., B. J. Price, T. E. C. Smith, and G. E. Marsh. 1984. *Comprehensive administration of special education.* Rockville, MD: Aspen Systems.

Retsinas, J. 1982. Teachers: Bargaining for control. *American Educational Research Journal 19*(3), 353–72.

Rosenau, F. S. 1982. Administrative proposal for dismantling ED awaits congressional action. *Phi Delta Kappan 63*(8), 509.

Rosenthal, A., and S. Fuhrman. 1982. State legislatures and education policy: An overview. *Educational Horizons 61*(1), 4–9+.

Saylor, J. G. 1982. *Who planned the curriculum? A curriculum plans reservoir model with historical examples.* West Lafayette, IN: Kappa Delta Pi.

Silberman, H. F. 1980. Working in Washington. *Phi Delta Kappan 61*(7), 449–51.

Valente, W. D. 1980. *Law in the schools.* Columbus, OH: Charles E. Merrill Publishing Company.

Watts, D. 1983. Four views of NCATEs role and function. *Phi Delta Kappan 64*(9), 646–49.

Zirkel, P. A. 1978. *A digest of supreme court decisions affecting education.* Bloomington, IN: Phi Delta Kappa.

Chapter 5
ELEMENTARY EDUCATION

OBJECTIVES

After reading this chapter, you will be able to

- describe the purposes of elementary schools;
- discuss how elementary schools are administered;
- describe how elementary schools are organized;
- relate how curricula are developed;
- list the roles of elementary school teachers;
- discuss curricular variations within elementary classrooms.

OUTLINE

ADVANCE ORGANIZERS
INTRODUCTION
ELEMENTARY SCHOOLS
    Purpose of Elementary Schools
    Administration of Elementary Schools
    Organizational Arrangements
        of Elementary Schools
    Philosophy and School Policies
    Curriculum in Elementary Schools
ELEMENTARY CLASSROOMS
    The Elementary Teacher

    Curricular Variations Within Classrooms
KINDERGARTEN EDUCATION
SPECIAL SERVICES
    Special Education Services
    Gifted Education Services
    Counseling Services
SUMMARY
IN THE FIELD
REFERENCES

1. What are the purposes of elementary schools?
2. How do principals provide instructional leadership?
3. What are the advantages and disadvantages of graded and nongraded schools?
4. What is the role of philosophy and policy in elementary education?
5. What influences elementary school curricula?
6. What do elementary teachers do?
7. How can teachers utilize classroom space?
8. What are the primary modes of instruction in elementary classrooms?
9. What special services are available in elementary schools?

INTRODUCTION

Elementary schools in the United States are the beginning point for public education. The elementary school was the basis for the common school movement of Horace Mann in the mid-1800s and has become the foundation of free, public education. While many children do not attend vocational schools, do not graduate from high school, and may attend junior high school only with a well-documented record of failure, the vast majority of American children attend elementary schools, and without experiencing academic failure.

ELEMENTARY SCHOOLS

Elementary schools are the first and most important educational opportunity for many children. Although many children of middle- and upper-middle-class families attend day-care programs before reaching school age, for many others the public elementary school is their first organized educational experience. Even for the many children who attend several day-care programs, public elementary schools provide the first academic training they receive. Several factors help shape elementary schools in the United States. Among them are (1) the administration, (2) organizational arrangements, (3) philosophy and school policies, (4) curriculum, and (5) teaching styles and methodologies.

Purpose of Elementary Schools

Elementary schools in the United States have many different purposes. Those most frequently stressed include

1. literacy
2. citizenship education
3. personal development (Jarolimek and Foster 1981)

Literacy. Public schools in the United States have always had the responsibility to develop literacy in children. This began initially as reading instruction, but expanded to include writing and arithmetic. Currently schools focus not only on instruction in the three basic academic areas, but on knowledge of the world, science, and cultural awareness. "There is no way that an elementary school can receive a high rating without doing a respectable job of teaching children the fundamental skills of literacy" (Jarolimek and Foster 1981, p. 4).

HIGHLIGHT

Elementary Gains Seen in Testing Review

By Lynn Olson

Achievement in the elementary grades is by some measures at its highest level in three decades, according to a report on testing trends released this week by the Congressional Budget Office.

The report, *Trends in Educational Achievement*, states that the decline in test scores among students in the upper elementary grades actually ended as early as the mid-1970s, despite a "widespread misconception" that test scores stopped declining only a few years ago.

This trend in student performance in the early grades gained "relatively little attention," the report notes, "[p]erhaps because of the greater notice accorded to tests at the senior-high-school level."

The report is not particularly sanguine, however, about the overall level of student achievement. The report includes data showing that American students still fare poorly on international comparisons, and that many American students are not performing well even on fairly easy questions.

And although the test scores of high-school students have also improved, the C.B.O. analysis points out, scores on such examinations as the Scholastic Aptitude Test remain relatively close to their low points of the late 1970s.

On some tests, gains also appear to have been greater on lower-level as opposed to higher-level skills, such as problem-solving. But the study notes that there have been improvements in both areas. For example, the percentage of S.A.T. mathematics scores above 700 rose steeply between 1980 and 1984, although it was still small in absolute numbers.

The report also concludes that the gap in test scores between black and nonminority students has been "slowly but appreciably narrowing in recent years."

Although the difference in the average test scores of black and nonminority students remains large, improvements have been consistent from year to year, it states, "and could prove substantial over the long run."

The test scores of Hispanic students have also improved, although there is less data available on this group, according to the C.B.O.

There have also been substantial gains in the performance of students from inner-city schools, the report says, noting that by 1981, a fourth to a third of the gap in test scores between disadvantaged urban communities and the rest of the nation had been overcome.

The budget office prepared the study at the request of the Subcommittee on Education, Arts, and Humanities of the Senate Committee on Labor and Human Resources.

The first volume of the study assesses trends in the achievement-test scores of American elementary- and secondary-school students over the past 30 years, based on a variety of measures—including the National Assessment of Educational Progress, the "High School and Beyond" study, the S.A.T., the American College Testing Program, the International Association for the Evaluation of Educational Achievement, and the annual Iowa assessment of student achievement.

A companion volume, *Educational Achievement: Explanations and Implications*, will be published this summer or fall. It will examine the most common explanations for the changes in students' test scores, and the implications of those changes for educational policy.

Daniel Koretz of C.B.O.'s human-resources and community-development division, prepared the analyses for both volumes.

According to the report, scores on achievement tests first began a "sizable drop" in the mid-1960s.

"The decline was widespread," the report says, "occurring among many different types of students, on many different tests, in all subject areas, in private as well as public schools, and in all parts of the nation."

The largest drops tended to occur for students in the higher grades. At the end of the decline, for example, the typical student in grades 6 and above performed at a level comparable to the 38th percentile of students before the decline began.

The report cautions, however, that the size of the decline differed so greatly from test to test that a different mix of tests—or a larger and more representative sample of tests—might have yielded a very different figure.

In general, test scores for students in grades 3 and below dropped little, if at all, during the same period.

The study found that test scores first began to improve with those children who entered elementary school in the late 1960s, with each subsequent group of children typically outscoring those who began school the year before them. Test-score improvements have also been moving into the higher grades as these cohorts of children have aged.

Trend data from the annual Iowa assessment indicate, for example, that scores for students in grades 3 through 6 are at their highest point in 30 years; those for students in grades 7 through 10 have rebounded strongly, but are not yet at the previous highs for those grades; and scores for students in grade 12 have begun rising, but remain near the low point.

Recent data from NAEP suggest, however, that the upswing in test scores is, for the moment, over in the youngest age groups and may end fairly soon in the higher grades, the C.B.O. reports.

Scores on NAEP tests administered to 8th graders are expected to level off between 1983 and 1987, while scores of seniors would level off between 1987 and 1991.

Because no other national data are available, the report cautions that it is "not clear" whether this leveling off is a general phenomenon.

It also suggests that although declining test scores during the 1960s and 1970s have often been cited to justify recent educational initiatives—some of which have even been based on theories about what caused those declines—many of the reform efforts "are not fully consistent with either the trends or the limited information on their causes."

For example, the report notes, a number of recent proposals are aimed at improving curricula in the basic skills, even though test scores show some of students' greatest problems to be in higher-order thinking skills.

The report adds that "the results of standardized tests must be interpreted cautiously." In particular, it says, trends that appear only on one test, or only among a set of very similar tests, "should be considered questionable."

Copies of the report can be obtained free of charge by calling the Congressional Budget Office's publications division at 202–226–2809 or writing to C.B.O. Publications, C.B.O., U.S. Congress, Washington, D.C. 20515.

Education Week. April 23, 1986. Reprinted with permission.

Citizenship education. The second goal of elementary schools is to provide citizenship education. Like literacy training, this goal has been present in elementary schools since the development of publicly supported educational programs. Citizenship education is provided through formal classes such as history and civics; children also experience citizenship training through informal activities with children from a cross section of society (Jarolimek and Foster 1981).

Personal development. The final goal of the elementary school is personal development. Although not a primary focus of elementary education until this century, personal development is now thought of as a major responsibility of schools. Emotional, social, and physical growth are aspects of personal development that elementary schools attempt to facilitate (Jarolimek and Foster 1981). Another area of personal

Citizenship education is a major purpose of elementary schools.

development includes multicultural education. Elementary-aged children need an awareness of the various cultures and ethnic groups that are represented in this country. Children from these racial and cultural minority groups need to be able to identify with their groups; multicultural education can greatly facilitate this process.

Administration of Elementary Schools

As in all educational programs, the administration of elementary schools is vital to all elements of the school. Superintendents, building principals, and educational supervisors all participate to some degree in the administration of elementary schools. While the board of education and school superintendent are major administrative forces in elementary schools, principals have the most direct administrative and supervisory role in the total school program.

Principals perform many different roles and functions in elementary schools, including instructional leadership and management, personnel management, financial management, plant management, community relations, and student management. Actual roles and priorities are viewed differently by principals, who use different operational definitions to describe what they do each day (Hall, Rutherford, Hord, and Huling 1984). With all these roles and functions, the principal's workday is very busy and unpredictable; it is often spent going from one task to the next, having to shift gears constantly (Morris, Crowson, Hurwitz, and Porter-Gehrie 1982).

Principals are bound by the administrative hierarchy of the school, by the chain of command. In school districts, principals usually report to the superintendent, unless the district is large enough to employ assistant superintendents. The larger the school bureaucracy, the more principals must concern themselves with groups of individuals in the chain of command rather than single individuals (Brieschke 1985). Regardless of the size of the administrative structure, principals are still directly in control of the actions that occur in their schools. As a result, the many functions performed by principals in elementary schools are critical to the functioning of the school.

Principals as instructional leaders. One of the most important functions of the principal is in the area of instructional leadership. Broadly defined, instructional leadership includes all actions taken by principals, or delegated to others, that promote learning in students. These actions generally include

- setting schoolwide goals;

- providing resources necessary for learning;

- supervising and evaluating teachers;

- organizing staff development;

- facilitating staff interactions. (De Bevoise 1984)

The many variables involved in instructional leadership include community factors, the principal's beliefs and management style, and institutional influences such as district, state, and federal policies. The relationships among these variables eventually affect student outcomes (see figure 5–1).

Although the principal is still considered the instructional leader of the school, actions by teacher organizations have made this role more difficult. By isolating the principal from the instructional staff, teacher organizations have, to some degree, encouraged the principal to fill a managerial and adversarial role (King-Stoops 1977).

Hierarchy of administration. The state's right and responsibility for providing public education is inferred from the United States Constitution, which did not reserve this right for the federal government. States, in turn, have granted the power to operate local schools to local boards of education. Boards of education hire superintendents to carry out board policy, and superintendents employ other administrative personnel, such as assistant superintendents and principals, to assist in carrying out board policy.

At the top of the administrative hierarchy of public schools is the district superintendent. From this point, school districts vary considerably in their organizational structure. For example, in large districts, several administrative levels may exist between the superintendent and the principal. In small districts, on the other hand, principals report directly to the superintendent, because the district does not employ assistant superintendents or curriculum coordinators.

In addition to the formal power structure, or the administrative hierarchy, there is an informal power structure. The formal power structure can be described as the traditional hierarchical design where power flows from top to bottom, whereas the informal power structure comprises interpersonal relationships among school staff and community members (Wood, Nicholson, and Findley 1979). The two structures

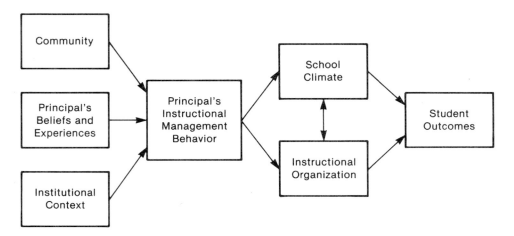

Figure 5-1. *The Principal's Role in Instructional Management. Reprinted with permission. D.C. Dwyer. 1984. The search for instructional leadership: Routines and subtleties in the principal's role.* Educational Leadership, *February, 32–37.*

also differ in that the formal structure describes the responsibilities for decision making, and the informal structure does not; communication channels in the formal structure are well-defined, but the informal structure depends on communication methods such as the infamous "grapevine" (Lipham and Hoeh 1974). Individuals in the formal power structure, such as superintendents and principals, must pay attention to the informal structure and consider its influence in decision making.

Organizational Arrangements of Elementary Schools

The movement of students in elementary schools is both vertical and horizontal, which requires schools that are organized both vertically and horizontally.

Vertical organization. "Vertical organization is the plan of the school for identifying when and who is ready to enter, as well as the procedures for regulating pupil progress through the elementary school to a completion point" (Ragan and Shepherd 1977, p. 109). Without vertical organization, there would be no set beginning time for students, no plan as to when to move students to higher curricular areas, and no set time for the completion of the program. Most organizational strategies can be dichotomized into *graded* and *nongraded*.

The general concept of the graded elementary school is to move students through the school in groups in a series of steps called grades. Each step, or grade, is usually one academic year in duration, with the number of grades varying among schools. During colonial America, graded schools did not exist; students with wide age ranges were simply assigned to a teacher, usually in a one-room schoolhouse with only one teacher. The notion of grouping students into grades based on chronological age was developed in Germany. American educators liked the idea, and after the Civil War, there was a rapid growth of graded schools. The general concept was to assign students to groups based on chronological age and keep these students together from year to year (Jarolimek and Foster 1981). Characteristics of the graded school are the following:

1. The graded school recognizes chronological age as the primary, if not the only, determiner of entry. Chronological age and years in school are the major ingredients of the decisions that locate the child within the vertical sequence.
2. The graded school has identified a body of skills, knowledge, and appreciations and has placed them in a sequence of six or seven positions called "grades." Each position equals one school term, or approximately nine months.
3. As a result of these positions and their sequence, graded textbooks were developed. Textbooks are typically assigned to a position within the sequence, and pupils at that position study the assigned text.
4. The decisions governing the vertical movement of pupils through the sequence are made at the end of the school term. Some variations have been introduced to provide for quarterly or semester promotions.
5. Promotion from one position to the next higher position within the sequence is dependent upon the pupil's having completed, with average or above success, all the work of the preceding position.
6. Graded schools may utilize the horizontal organizations of the self-contained classroom, departmentalization, platoon, or team.
7. The symbols expressing a graded organization are 1–6, or K–3 and 4–6, as applied to a building. For a school district the symbols, elementary through secondary, might be: K–5, 6–8, 9–10, and 11–12, or K–8 and 9–12. These symbols represent the vertical organization and the commitments of the district to kindergarten, middle school, mid-high, and high school.
8. At its lowest level, gradedness is essentially a lockstep system. (Ragan and Shepherd 1977, p. 111–12)

The graded organization has some definite strong points: (1) it reduces some variability among students; (2) it exposes all children to the same curriculum; (3) educational materials can be developed for chronological age interests; (4) similar chronological age among students facilitates social interactions; (5) it is efficient; (6) teachers are able to specialize their teaching focusing on a particular age group; and (7) minimum standards can be established for each grade level. Limitations of the graded approach include locking students into certain groups, regardless of ability levels and encouraging teachers to teach to the group with a rigid curriculum (Jarolimek and Foster 1981).

The aim of the nongraded school is continuous progress. Rather than locking students into a step system, nongraded schools allow students to progress through a curriculum at their own pace. The advantages of a nongraded approach are obvious, the greatest advantage being that students are not locked into a level irrespective of their skills and abilities. Capable students are able to progress through two or more traditional grade levels in one year. Likewise, students whose progress is slower than average avoid the stigma of having to repeat a grade or be passed onto the next grade without having mastered the competencies required for that level. While nongraded programs vary in name and type, the following features are common to most:

1. Students progress at their own rates throughout the school year.
2. Identification of skills, knowledges, and appreciations in content areas, not length of time, are the key to moving on to higher curricular levels.

3. Competencies, not number of years in school, are used to determine pupils' locations along the curricular sequence.
4. Extensive reporting and record keeping is required to chart student progress.
5. Students are provided with successful experiences regardless of their location in the curriculum. (Ragan and Shepherd 1977)

At first glance, the nongraded approach would appear to have many advantages over the graded system. Although as many as 25 percent of elementary schools have tried the nongraded organization, fewer than 10 percent maintained the system (Ragan and Shepherd 1977). Probable causes for the lack of popularity of the nongraded system include (1) too much record keeping, (2) deviates a great deal from the traditional graded approach, (3) teachers are more likely trained for the graded system, and (4) many parents do not understand the nongraded format.

Horizontal organization. Besides organizing the way students move through elementary schools, students and teachers need to be organized into instructional groups. This is called horizontal organization. The two basic approaches to horizontal organization are self-contained classrooms and departmentalization.

Students placed in self-contained classrooms receive the majority of their instruction in the same classroom from one teacher. This is the traditional approach and the most popular. A 1968 survey of more than two thousand elementary principals determined that more than 95 percent of the schools used self-contained classrooms in primary grades, 88 percent in the fourth grade, 80 percent in the fifth grade, and 71 percent in the sixth grade (National Education Association 1968).

Many arguments support the self-contained classroom. First, by having the same group of students all day for all subjects, teachers have a great deal of time to learn about, observe, and evaluate their students. Self-contained classrooms also facilitate an interrelated curriculum. Teachers are better able to tie material together across subject areas. In self-contained classrooms, students also have a better opportunity to participate in group activities, and there is a great deal more flexibility with time than in departmentalized schemes where students must go to another classroom at a certain time (Ragan and Shepherd 1977). The most viable argument for maintaining self-contained classrooms is tradition. Just as tradition makes nongraded vertical organization difficult to implement, it also helps to maintain the self-contained classroom that was used in the one-room schoolhouse.

The self-contained approach does have limitations:

- Pupils and teachers are isolated from other students and teachers.

- Students are primarily forced to interact with students in the same classroom.

- Cliques are easily established.

- Many teachers are not capable of teaching all subject areas.

- Leaders remain leaders and followers remain followers.

In departmentalized elementary schools, teachers specialize in a particular curricular area or areas. In contrast to the teacher in a self-contained classroom who must be somewhat of a generalist, teachers in a departmentalized scheme have time to concentrate on one or two teaching areas. Rather than teaching all subjects to twenty to thirty children daily, they may teach one or two subjects to one hundred children daily. The advantage of the departmentalized approach is that teachers have the opportunity to become experts in a limited number of subject areas.

Most of the disadvantages of the departmentalized approach relate the advantages of the self-contained approach. Namely, teachers in a departmentalized school have less time to get to know students well, subject matter may not be coordinated among the different teachers, and teachers and students are locked into specific time restraints.

Philosophy and School Policies

The philosophy and policies of schools give each school a unique personality. What occurs in schools and classrooms has a direct relationship to the underlying philosophy of the school and classroom. "Decisions about goals and curriculum rest solidly upon the school's ideas and beliefs about the nature of the child and how the child learns; about ethics, economics, and other great issues" (King-Stoops 1977, p. 5). For example, some schools may have the reputation of being tough on discipline and academic requirements, while others may be more lax and include some extracurricular opportunities in the curriculum. While the philosophy and policies of individual schools reflect the philosophy and policies of the local school board and superintendent, principals and teachers can influence these two elements to some degree, thereby giving the school a different personality than other schools.

The philosophy and policies of schools affect disciplinary methods, academic expectations and requirements, dress codes, curriculum, and school climate. People who influence the philosophy and policies of schools include administrators, teachers, school staff, parents and other community members, and students.

Although many would say that school boards and superintendents dictate school philosophy and policies, many variations exist among schools in the same district. Administrative leadership style is a key factor in how individuals are brought into decision making and school district philosophies and policies are implemented. Administrators can affect district philosophy and policies by choosing to implement directives, at the expense of the school, or refusing to implement directives for the sake of the school (Brieschke 1985).

Refusing to implement district directives, or policy, is called creative insubordination. It can be accomplished either by attempting to directly go against policies or by two or more principals agreeing to not implement certain directives. A third method is to openly refuse to meet deadlines. Regardless of the modes of insubordination chosen, administrators must believe that their actions are better for the school than the results of following district guidelines (Brieschke 1985).

In addition to building administrators influencing district philosophy and policies, the actions of many groups have an impact (see table 5–1).

Curriculum in Elementary Schools

The curriculum adopted and implemented by a school is more than a listing of subjects to be taught. The curriculum includes not only the intellectual content of subjects, but the methods used to teach, interactions that occur between teachers and students, and school-sponsored activities. A curriculum includes all student experiences for which the school accepts responsibility: formal courses, school-sponsored clubs, athletics, and band. A basic assumption underlying the curriculum is that

---

TABLE 5–1   Groups Influencing District Philosophy and Policies

Group	Influence
Parents	Actions by parent groups
	Actions by individual parents
Teachers	Actions by teacher organizations
	Actions by individual teachers
	Actions by teacher committees
State Department of Education	Development of curriculum guides
	Development of policies
Professional Groups	Curriculum suggestions in publications
	Development of standards
Accreditation Groups	Development and monitoring standards

---

informal learning experiences are as important to the growth and development of students as are formal ones (Ryan and Cooper 1980). In looking at what the future holds for school curricula, Wassermann (1984) indicates a preference for including areas that cannot be taught using computers and technology: (1) nurturing of children's feelings, (2) promotion of interpersonal skills, (3) promotion of higher-order cognitive skills, (4) nurturing of creativity and imagination, and (5) development of moral integrity.

The school's curriculum is derived from several different sources. Tyler (1949) suggested that a curriculum results from society, subject-matter specialists, and students (see figure 5–2). The role of society in curricular development is essential; what a particular society values must be incorporated into public school programs. After all, members of society are the taxpayers who support public education. Subject-matter specialists are needed in curricular development to help determine how much of a particular subject should be included in each grade level. Students participate, not by deciding what they should and should not learn, but by others determining the needs of students as viewed by society and subject-matter specialists (Fain, Shostak, and Dean 1979).

The elementary school curriculum is in a constant state of change; it never remains static but changes relative to the outside world. Throughout history, various influences have had an impact on school curricula (see table 5–2). A school's curriculum reflects the attitudes, values, and concerns of society. As a result of this relationship between curriculum and external forces, the current curriculum used in schools can be expected to undergo changes during the coming decades.

Although every school district may have a slightly different curriculum, most elementary schools provide basic academic instruction in similar areas. These include reading, mathematics, and writing, commonly referred to as the three Rs. "Most teachers believe that the three Rs are cornerstones of education; so do the majority of parents and other nonprofessionals" (Rogers 1982, p. 236). Therefore, most elementary school curricula focus on these basic academic subjects. Other subjects included

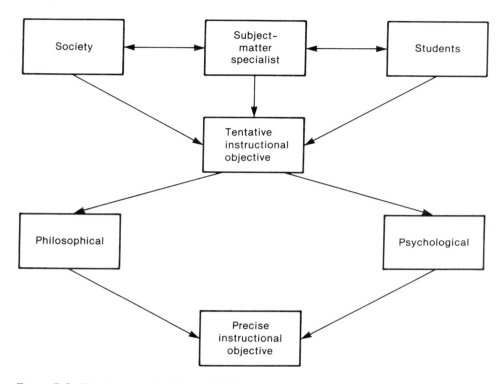

Figure 5-2. *Tyler's rationale. (Tyler, 1949).*

in most elementary schools are science, social studies, spelling, physical education, foreign language, music, and art.

Elementary school curricula in the future must take into consideration the needs of society; it must be responsive to the rapidly changing world. In view of the rapid growth of knowledge and increased specialization, a task force studying future trends in curriculum planning recommended that common themes be treated in an interdisciplinary fashion, that facts as well as processes be stressed, and that materials in addition to textbooks be used in education (Troutman and Palombo 1983). Another important component of the curriculum of the future should be an emphasis on teaching students to relate language to culture. This need will become more pronounced as daily interactions among culturally diverse individuals increase (Miel 1984). The curriculum should reflect multicultural education components to enable children to understand, accept, and identify with cultural and ethnic groups other than their own.

Variables that affect what a district includes in its elementary curriculum include the size and location of the district, socioeconomic factors in the community, priorities of the district, pupil-teacher ratios, and desired student outcomes. For example, small districts located in rural, agricultural communities likely stress different subjects than large, urban, industrialized districts.

TABLE 5-2	Major Influences on Curriculum
Time	*Influence*
1635–1770	Religion; schools expected to promulgate the religious beliefs in the country.
1770–1860	Political; schools should educate the public to ensure the preservation of democracy.
1860–1920	Economic; schools should educate people to fill new jobs in a rapidly expanding economy.
1920–present	Mass Education; schools should provide equal educational opportunity to all citizens.
1957–present	Excellence in Education; schools should do a better job in educating American youth. This movement resulted from the discovery in World War II that many graduates were very weak in mathematics and science. Sputnik also was a major influence.

ELEMENTARY CLASSROOMS

Individual classrooms comprise the structure of the schools. If the vertical organization of the school is graded, these classroom units will represent various grades. In schools that use a nongraded organization, classroom units represent a level of subject matter. Regardless of the organizational structure, the elementary classroom unit is a crucial element in elementary education.

The Elementary Teacher

The elementary teacher is the professionally trained individual who is in charge of the education of students. Although aides may be present in the classroom, individual teachers are still responsible for the educational accomplishments of students.

Roles of elementary teachers. Elementary teachers perform many roles in facilitating the education of their students: (1) a social model, (2) an evaluator, (3) a walking encyclopedia, (4) a moderator, (5) an investigator, (6) an ombudsman, (7) a morale builder, (8) a leader of the group, (9) a substitute parent, (10) a target for frustrations, and (11) a friend (Jarolimek and Foster 1981) (see table 5–3). King-Stoops (1977) listed the roles of elementary teachers as the following:

- planning the program

- organizing and managing the classroom

- individualizing the action

- working with other adults for a success-oriented classroom

Wassermann (1984) described the roles of the elementary teacher as diagnosing learning problems, facilitating independent learning, and developing curricula. While these lists differ somewhat, they illustrate the numerous roles that elementary teachers play in the education of children. Being an elementary teacher is no easy task; elementary teachers are busy people.

While teachers must perform many varied roles, their primary role is that of instructor. As an instructor, the elementary teacher imparts knowledge, guides students' learning experiences, and determines students' progress. Many of the other roles of elementary teachers are required to facilitate the overall role of instructor.

Characteristics of good teachers. Being an effective elementary teacher requires various professional competencies and personal characteristics, such as:

1. ability to organize
2. likes children
3. understands teaching modes and strategies
4. ability to adjust teaching strategies to specific children
5. maintains a healthy self-concept (Jarolimek and Foster 1981)

Instructional behaviors that enhance achievement include the ability to present information clearly, the use of variety in planning learning experiences, enthusiasm, task

---

TABLE 5–3   Roles of Elementary Teachers

Role	Description
Social Model	Models appropriate moral values and social values, life styles and career goals expected by the community
Evaluator	Includes formal and informal evaluation of all aspects of students' performance, including academic, behavior, and social
Walking Encyclopedia	Has a vast amount of knowledge to impart to children, but more importantly provides a model for children to find information on their own
Moderator	includes moderating personal differences among children; teacher actions must be viewed as fair
Investigator	Determining who is at fault, if thefts occur, etc.; should be performed in a very constructive manner
Ombudsman	Enables students to confide in the teacher concerning various anxieties and problems
Morale Builder	Provide successful learning experiences for children; helps build self-confidence in students
Group Leader	Includes classroom management and instructional planning for a group of children as opposed to one-on-one activities
Substitute Parent	Especially important with young children; teacher becomes the child's daily "parent" during school hours
Target for Frustrations	Attempt to understand children's frustrations and adverse behavior directed at teacher
Friend	Serve as the child's friend without becoming so friendly that the teacher-student role cannot be maintained

Source: Jarolimek and Foster (1981).

orientation, and the presentation of repeated opportunities for learning (Jarolimek and Foster 1981).

Teacher education. Being able to perform the many varied tasks of an elementary teacher requires considerable training. Most states require that a qualified elementary teacher complete a program of study at a college or university with an approved teacher education program. Upon successful completion of the college or university training program, individuals are eligible for certification as an elementary teacher. Teacher training programs vary somewhat, as do state certification requirements for elementary certification. While there are variations, teacher training programs and certification programs have much in common. Most states require that students complete coursework in the following general areas before being eligible for certification as an elementary teacher:

- language arts
- teaching reading
- teaching social studies
- teaching math
- teaching science
- measurement
- learning theory
- psychology
- elementary curriculum
- student teaching/practicum

Some training programs have individual courses for the above topics, while others combine several areas into one course. For example, a training program may have only one methods course for elementary teachers rather than specific methods courses for each subject.

As trends come and go, variations in competencies are recognized and reflected in required coursework. A good example is the changes in elementary teacher training programs as a result of Public Law 94–142, which required that many mildly handicapped students be mainstreamed into regular classrooms for a portion of each school day. Since regular classroom teachers now have responsibility for educating mainstreamed handicapped children, most university training programs and state certification departments mandate some training in special education for elementary teachers.

Curricular Variations Within Classrooms

Although school boards, superintendents, and building administrators adopt the curricula they want implemented in individual classrooms, elementary teachers can have a dramatic impact on the ways the curriculum is carried out. Methods of modifying the curriculum include (1) use of textbooks, (2) use of materials, (3) use of space, (4) teaching strategies or methods, and (5) grouping for instruction. The teacher is also largely responsible for the classroom milieu.

Use of textbooks. Textbooks for elementary schools are usually selected by a textbook committee appointed to act for the local school district. In many states, schools must select books that are on a state approved list of acceptable textbooks. Although teachers may be asked to provide input into the selection process, and many elementary teachers may actually serve on the local district selection committee, some

Teachers have a great deal of control over the types of materials used in classrooms.

elementary teachers have limited impact on the books adopted by the district. Even in these situations, teachers can modify the curriculum to some degree.

Teachers may use a great deal of supportive materials to reinforce the content of textbooks, to supply additional information, or to present information in a different manner than is found in the adopted text. Teachers do not have to follow the content of the state and district adopted text without using supplemental materials. As long as students are achieving at appropriate levels, teachers will probably not be asked to explain why they are teaching material differently than is prescribed by an adopted textbook.

Use of classroom materials. Unlike textbooks, which may have been selected with limited teacher input, other teaching materials are largely left up to the teacher. School budgets are usually very limited for teaching materials, and teachers often make their own materials or modify materials given to them by local businesses and other groups to fit the needs of children in classrooms. By making or modifying materials, teachers control the kinds of materials available for student use.

Materials can be easily modified for all students in an elementary classroom. Methods of modifying materials include (1) presenting different amounts of material to different students; (2) varying the difficulty level of the materials; (3) altering the sequence of the presentation of materials; (4) using different modes of presentation of the materials, and (5) allowing students to respond with alternative methods (Goodman 1978).

Elementary teachers often will be asked to suggest materials for purchase by the school. In these situations, teachers should ask several questions before determining that materials are appropriate for classroom use. Boland (1976) suggested the following checklist for help in determining whether materials are appropriate for handicapped students. They would also apply to materials for any elementary classroom.

1. Is the material suitable for the ages and interests of students in the school/ classroom?
2. Are materials appealing to look at?
3. Are directions easily understood?
4. Do materials require multisensory involvement?
5. Are materials simple, easy to use, durable, consumable, easily stored?

In addition, some states have developed guidelines to assist teachers in determining which materials have appropriate multicultural and nonsexist content.

Use of space. As with materials, teachers have a great deal of flexibility in their use of classroom space. The way space is used may be directly related to the success of students. Modifications in space may be required to take advantage of various activities and meet the particular needs of individual students. Many elementary classroom teachers organize their classrooms in the traditional row-by-row design. While this organization may facilitate structure, a more flexible approach may better suit various types of children found in the classroom. Berkowitz and Sheridan (1979) suggest that the utilization of space in a classroom be determined using a trial-and-error method. By becoming sensitive to the relationships between children's stimulation levels and the physical environment, teachers found that (1) rugs could be added or taken away to adjust noise levels, (2) furniture could be moved to create open or closed spaces for

Learning centers enable students to work on different activities throughout the classroom.

various type of activities, (3) certain toys should be removed if they are too distracting, and (4) some activities could best be conducted outside the classroom.

Another method of adjusting classroom space is through the use of learning centers, spaces for individuals or small groups that include materials about specific topics. A learning center "enlarges the learning environment, contributes to the development of self-actualizing learning, and provides for a greater range of learning rates, styles, and developmental levels" (Ragan and Shepherd 1977, p. 210). Learning centers permit teachers to occupy children with various learning activities while working with other children more intensely.

Individual learning should be encouraged with learning centers. Students are able to go to a learning center, perform the required activities, evaluate the work, and move on to another center or back to the base desk. Teachers can develop learning centers by pushing extra desks together in a corner of the room, acquiring small tables, or even using the teacher's desk (King-Stoops 1977). Materials at learning centers can be commercial, teacher-made, or student-made. Typical learning centers include science, math, language arts, and sensory training. Learning centers do not need to be elaborate, expensive, or difficult to make. Used properly, learning centers can take advantage of limited space in classrooms and create opportunities for individual initiative.

Methods of instruction. Instructional methodology includes the procedures, techniques, and manipulations of content and environment performed by teachers (Ragan and Shepherd 1977). Teaching requires a complex repertoire of instructional behaviors, because different students require different instructional approaches. There are several basic methodological approaches used in elementary schools; some teachers feel more comfortable with certain methods than others. One method is not necessarily superior to others in all circumstances. Jarolimek and Foster (1981) describe several teaching methods or modes frequently used by elementary teachers, including the expository mode, inquiry mode, demonstration mode, and activity mode (see figure 5–3).

Grouping for instruction. Students can be grouped either heterogeneously or homogeneously. Heterogeneous grouping does not attempt to categorize students on any specific criteria such as ability or interest. Students are randomly placed in instructional groups (although grouping by age is characteristic of a graded system) without any preselection for other characteristics. The advantages of heterogeneous grouping include:

- Students can interact with a broad range of students.

- Teachers must take into consideration several levels of academic abilities.

- Students have a wider variety of peer role models.

- A heterogeneous classroom closely resembles the characteristics of society.

Inquiry Mode

asking questions	interpreting	testing hypotheses
coming to conclusions	classifying	observing
stating hypotheses	self-directed study	synthesizing

Expository Mode

lecture	explanation	audio recording
telling	panels	motion pictures
sound filmstrip	recitation	discussion

Demonstration Mode

experiments	simulation and games	field trips
exhibits	modeling	

Activity Mode

role playing	preparing exhibits	processing
construction	dramatizing	group work

Figure 5-3. *Teaching Modes and Techniques. Source: Jarolimek and Foster. 1981. Teaching and learning in the elementary school. New York: Macmillan Publishing Co.*

The disadvantages of heterogeneous grouping include: (1) teachers may teach to the middle, leaving brighter students and students who require extra help to make it on their own; (2) the same students are in leadership roles; and (3) teachers have many different academic levels to teach.

Homogeneous grouping places children with similar characteristics together. The one characteristic normally considered when grouping is academic ability. However, other characteristics that could be used include cultural background, psychomotor development, age, personal and social adjustment, and interest (Jarolimek and Foster 1981). Using age as the criterion for grouping is most common when entry into the first grade is mandatory for children in certain age groups and admission before the target age is reached is prohibited.

The major advantage of homogeneous grouping is that teachers have similar students to teach. When grouping is based on academic abilities, teachers can gear instruction to the students' level of intellectual development without needing to consider students at extreme ends of the continuum. The disadvantages are that students in homogeneous classes do not get a chance to interact with a variety of children and often teachers of low academic students expect less from those students than they should, which often leads to less output than is possible.

Classroom milieu. The milieu, or environment, in elementary classrooms is largely determined by the teacher. Does the teacher have an open, trusting environment, or is the teacher continuously suspicious of all students, thinking that they are ever plotting to circumvent class rules? Does the teacher lavishly give out praise and "warm

Homogeneous grouping allows teachers to work with students with similar characteristics.

fuzzies," or does the teacher expect students to work on-task and recognize students only when their behavior is inappropriate? These variables, along with many other subtle and overt influences by the teacher, compose the classroom milieu.

Environmental factors that are the most critical include the definition of a good student, classroom rules, student-teacher interactions, and student-student interactions. The following statements briefly describe each component:

1. Definition of a good student. Teachers like some students better than others. This is probably determined by values held by the teacher related to what constitutes a "good" student.
2. Classroom rules. Classroom rules and teacher behaviors definitely affect student behavior. Students need to be aware of the classroom rules and the probable consequences of breaking the rules. Classroom rules must be applied to all children equally.
3. Student-teacher interactions. Teachers vary a great deal in their interactions with students. Some are very warm and interactive; others are more formal, rarely hugging, touching, or smiling. This aspect of milieu can affect feelings of stress and anxiety by students.
4. Student-student interactions. Peer interaction is a basic part of milieu. Some students are ostracized by peers, and others are very popular. Teachers should recognize these relationships and encourage positive interactions among all students.

KINDERGARTEN EDUCATION

Many public school districts operate kindergarten programs designed for five-year-old children as a preparation year for the first grade. The kindergarten year is an extremely important one. Children still have a high motivation to learn and the various environmental conditions that later impede learning have not yet taken hold. The kindergarten year is a rare time when enthusiasm and ability have not been daunted by the system (Barbe, Milone, Lucas, and Humphrey 1980).

Kindergarten programs are relatively new, having their roots in Western Europe in the early 1800s. In 1837 Friedrich Froebel established the first kindergarten in Germany (Johnson, Collins, Dupuis, and Johansen 1982). Froebel's kindergartens were developed "as a symbolic, growth-producing (flower-unfolding) concept (as well as a religious-oneness-with-God kind of orientation)" (Margolin 1976, p. 8). Child-care centers were later developed in Europe and the United States, not to help the child to "unfold," but primarily to assist mothers of low-income families (Margolin 1976).

Today there are two schools of thought regarding kindergarten education. One focuses on a traditional viewpoint that an unstructured environment rich with linguistic stimulation will provide children with preparation for more academic training. The other orientation relies more on structured, formal academic activities. Skills normally taught during the kindergarten year may use both approaches. For example, cognitive and psychomotor skills might rely more on formal instructional programs, while affective and linguistic activities may occur in more informal, unstructured settings (Barbe et al. 1980).

SPECIAL SERVICES

Elementary schools serve some children who require services beyond those provided for the majority of children. These include special education services, services for gifted and talented children, and counseling services. Without the provision of these services, equal educational opportunities would not be possible.

Special Education Services

Approximately 10 percent of the school population is handicapped to such a degree that special services are warranted. As a result of federal and state legislation and litigation, schools are now required to provide appropriate educational services to all school-age children, regardless of their disabilities. The major federal legislation that mandated these services was Public Law 94–142, which was passed in 1975. This legislation required that schools

- locate handicapped children;
- individually assess handicapped children;
- develop individual educational programs for handicapped children;
- provide appropriate services to handicapped children in the least restrictive setting (with nonhandicapped children);
- annually review the progress of handicapped children to determine the effectiveness of the services provided.

Elementary schools serve many handicapped children, mostly those with mild disabilities such as educable mental retardation and learning disabilities. The resource room model, where students attend regular classrooms part of each school day and receive extra help in the resource part of the day, is the primary model used to serve handicapped children (Friend and McNutt 1984). Since this is primarily the model used in schools, regular elementary teachers and school administrators must share in the responsibility of educating handicapped children. Chapter seven focuses entirely on special education and provides a great deal of information concerning services to handicapped children in public schools.

Gifted Education Services

Gifted children have been in and out of favor more than any other group of children. In the late 1950s gifted education received much emphasis and money following the launch of Sputnik by the Soviet Union. This was short-lived, however, because the federal emphasis shifted to disadvantaged and handicapped children. Recently programs for gifted and talented children have been revived.

Whereas gifted children were previously defined only in terms of academic abilities, current definitions include high performance in creativity, leadership, and visual and performing arts (Gallagher 1985). As a result of this broader concept, elementary school programs must be expanded to provide meaningful experiences in a variety of areas.

The following depicts various program adaptations that can be made in elementary schools for gifted students:

1. Enrichment in regular classes—Special materials and lessons are provided to enhance learning.
2. Consultant teacher—Specially trained teachers act as consultants to regular classroom teachers to suggest activities for gifted children.
3. Resource room—Gifted children go to a resource room for a portion of the school day to work with a gifted-education specialist.
4. Mentor—Community members with specialized skills work with gifted students either individually or in small groups.
5. Independent study—Gifted students are allowed to carry out independent studies under the supervision of a teacher.
6. Special-interest class—Classes in specialized content fields are offered to gifted students.
7. Special class—Gifted students are homogeneously grouped in self-contained classes or subject areas.
8. Special schools—Gifted children attend schools specifically designed for gifted students. (Gallagher 1985)

Although gifted education in elementary schools grew substantially during the early 1980s, the gains made in providing appropriate educational programs for these children may not be permanent. If history repeats itself, an emphasis on programming for gifted children may diminish as other, more pressing needs of the schools surface.

Counseling Services

Although counseling programs were originally developed for secondary schools, they have recently become common in elementary schools. Professionals realized that young children also have counseling needs. Children with emotional problems, and those with characteristics that suggest the eventual development of problems, have been targeted for intervention. Although many schools still do not have elementary counseling programs, the trend is that such programs will be available in most schools within the next few years.

Unfortunately the need and benefits of elementary counseling programs have not been greatly documented. Gerler (1985) reviewed studies published in *Elementary School Guidance and Counseling* from 1974 to 1984. Conclusions from this review revealed that elementary counseling programs can have positive effects on the affective, behavioral, and interpersonal skills of children, and therefore impact positively on academic performance. Elementary school counselors need to use these data to increase support for their programs.

SUMMARY

This chapter has focused on the elementary school. Elementary schools were the first to develop in this country, and they remain as the beginning point of education for most children. Although training in the basic academic skills was the original purpose of elementary schools, other areas have been added, including citizenship education and personal development. Currently elementary schools are asked to do much more than simply academic instruction.

As in all school organizations, the administration of elementary schools is a critical element. Without administrative support for programs, the likelihood that elementary-aged children will receive appropriate educational experiences is significantly reduced. Elementary school principals do not function in a vacuum, but must administer schools within the administrative hierarchy of the district. Still, the success of schools greatly depends on the skills and attitudes of building principals.

Elementary schools are organized both vertically and horizontally. Vertical organizational arrangements include graded and nongraded schools, and horizontal organizations are either self-contained or departmentalized; each organizational structure has several advantages and disadvantages. Elementary school curriculum focuses on academic training, as well as other experiences directed at child growth and development. Although every school district may have a different curriculum, most include academic instruction in the basic subject areas of reading, writing, and arithmetic. The curriculum of a given elementary school is affected by many different variables, including the community, financial resources, and philosophy.

The second section of the chapter focused on the elementary classroom. Within the classroom, the teacher is the key professional, being responsible for implementing school policies and philosophies. Although instruction is a primary role for elementary teachers, they must also address the personal growth of students, evaluate students' progress, and do a host of other duties. Teachers have a great deal of flexibility in their classrooms concerning how they implement the curriculum and how they teach children.

The final section of the chapter discussed some special services available to students in elementary schools. These included special education, gifted education, and counseling services. Students enrolled in elementary schools in the United States make up a very diverse group. They come from all kinds of backgrounds and require different services to enable them to benefit from school programs. Special services provided in elementary schools attempt to provide for the unique needs of many children.

IN THE FIELD

1. Are there stated purposes for the elementary school and district elementary education program?

2. Describe activities performed by the principal related to the role of instructional leadership.

3. What is the practice in the school related to the principal visiting classrooms?

4. Is the school graded or nongraded? How long has the organization been in place?

5. Describe one instructional behavior by the teacher you observed that seemed to be particularly effective.

6. Does the school have a school counselor? If so, what activities are performed by this individual?

7. Are there any administrators other than the principal at the school? If so, what are their job responsibilities?

8. Does the school use the self-contained or departmentalized model? How long has the model been in place?

9. Does the school's curriculum primarily result from state guidelines?

10. What kinds of educational materials are available in classrooms?

11. What kinds of materials are available in the school library?

12. Does the school have audio materials? If so, what kinds of equipment and materials?

13. Are students grouped for instructional purposes? If so, what criteria are used for grouping?

14. Does the school have a program for gifted and talented students? If so, what is the nature of the program?

REFERENCES

Barbe, W. B., M. N. Milone, V. H. Lucas, and J. W. Humphrey. 1980. *Basic skills in kindergarten: Foundations for formal learning.* Columbus, OH: Zaner-Boser, Inc.

Berkowitz, J., and M. Sheridan. 1979. Group composition and use of space in a preschool setting. *Teaching Exceptional Children 11*, 154–57.

Boland, S. K. 1976. Instructional materialism—or how to select the things you need. *Teaching Exceptional Children 8*, 156–58.

Brieschke, P. A. 1985. Principals in schools: Insubordination in discretionary decision making. *The Educational Forum 49*(2), 157–69.

De Bevoise, W. 1984. Synthesis of research on the principal as instructional leader. *Educational Leadership 41*(5), 14–20.

Dwyer, D. C. 1984. The search for instructional leadership: Routines and subtleties in the principal's role. *Educational Leadership 41*(5), 32–37.

Fain, S. M., R. Shostak, and J. F. Dean. 1979. *Teaching in America.* Glenview, IL: Scott, Foresman & Company.

Friend, M. and G. McNutt. 1984. Resource room programs: Where are we now? *Exceptional Children 51*(2), 150–55.

Gallagher, J. J. 1985. *Teaching the gifted child.* 3rd Ed. Boston: Allyn and Bacon, Inc.

Gerler, E. R. 1985. Elementary school counseling research and the classroom learning environment. *Elementary School Guidance and Counseling 21*(1), 39–48.

Goodman, L. 1978. Meeting children's needs through materials modification. *Teaching Exceptional Children 10*, 92–94.

Hall, G., W. L. Rutherford, S. M. Hord, and L. L. Huling. 1984. Effects of three principal styles on school improvement. *Educational Leadership 41*(5), 22–29.

Jarolimek, J., and C. D. Foster. 1981. *Teaching and learning in the elementary school.* 2d ed. New York: Macmillan Publishing Co., Inc.

Johnson, J. A., H. W. Collins, V. L. Dupuis, and J. H. Johansen. 1982. *Introduction to the foundations of American education.* Boston: Allyn and Bacon.

King-Stoops, J. 1977. *The child wants to learn: Elementary teaching methods.* Boston: Little, Brown and Company.

Lipham, J. M., and J. A. Hoeh, Jr. 1974. *The principalship: Foundations and functions.* New York: Harper & Row Publishers.

Margolin, E. 1976. *Young children: Their curriculum and learning process.* New York: Macmillan Publishing Co.

Miel, A. 1984. Making room for the future in the curriculum. *Kappa Delta Pi Record 21*(1), 14–16.

Morris, V. C., R. L. Crowson, E. Hurwitz, Jr., and C. Porter-Gehrie. 1982. The urban principal: Middle manager in the educational bureaucracy. *Phi Delta Kappan 63*(10), 689–92.

National Education Association. 1968. *The elementary school principalship in 1968: A research study.* Washington, DC: Department of Elementary School Principals.

Ragan, W. B., and G. D. Shepherd. *Modern elementary curriculum.* New York: Holt, Rinehart & Winston.

Rogers, V. R. 1982. What research tells us about the three Rs. *Phi Delta Kappan 64*(4), 236.

Ryan, K., and J. M. Cooper. 1980. *Those who can teach.* Boston: Houghton-Mifflin Company.

Troutman, B. I., and R. D. Palombo. 1983. Identifying future trends in curriculum planning. *Educational Leadership 41*(1), 49.

Tyler, R. W. 1949. *Basic principles of curriculum and instruction.* Chicago: The University of Chicago Press.

Wassermann, S. 1984. What can schools become? *Phi Delta Kappan 65*(10), 690–93.

Wood, C. L., E. W. Nicholson, and D. G. Findley. 1979. *The secondary school principal: Manager and supervisor.* Boston: Allyn and Bacon.

Chapter 6
SECONDARY EDUCATION

OBJECTIVES

After reading this chapter, you will be able to

- describe the growth of secondary education in the United States;
- discuss the structure of secondary schools;
- list the goals and objectives of secondary education;
- describe the different ways secondary schools are organized;
- list the courses generally found in the common curriculum;
- describe some specialized curricular areas;
- list advantages and disadvantages of specific teaching methods;
- relate the need for school policies to actual policies that currently exist in secondary schools;
- discuss current problems facing secondary education.

OUTLINE

ADVANCE ORGANIZERS
INTRODUCTION
STRUCTURE OF SECONDARY SCHOOLS
    Intermediate Schools
    High Schools
OBJECTIVES OF SECONDARY EDUCATION
ORGANIZATION OF SECONDARY SCHOOLS
CURRICULUM OF SECONDARY SCHOOLS
    Common Curriculum
    Specialized Curricular Areas
    Curriculum Development and Revision
    Extracurricular Activities
METHODS OF INSTRUCTION
    Lectures
    Classroom Discussion
    Independent Study

    Individual Instruction
    Other Instructional Methods
SCHOOL PHILOSOPHY AND POLICIES
    Discipline
    Appearance Codes
    Expulsion and Suspension
    Search and Seizure
    Other School Policies
PROBLEMS FACING SECONDARY SCHOOLS
    School Dropouts
    Declining Academic Performance
    Problems of Adolescence
SUMMARY
IN THE FIELD
REFERENCES

1. What is the structure of secondary education in the United States?
2. What are the purposes of middle schools compared with junior high schools?
3. What three curricular tracks are found in most secondary schools?
4. How are secondary schools organized vertically?
5. What subjects are generally included in the common curriculum?
6. What is the current status of science and math education?
7. What are some objectives of death education?
8. How can teachers improve their lecturing method?
9. How can teachers establish a positive learning environment?
10. What problems exist in secondary schools?

INTRODUCTION

Public secondary education in the United States is a relatively recent occurrence. The early education provided in colonial times through the common school movement of the nineteenth century focused on young children in elementary schools. Although high schools date from Boston in 1821 and the Massachusetts Law of 1827, large numbers of secondary schools became operational much later. New York State required high schools in 1864, and by 1890 only 2,526 high schools were operational (Commager 1983).

Since the late nineteenth century, growth has been phenomenal. The number of students enrolled in high schools doubled each decade from 1880 to 1930 (Clark 1985). More than twelve million students are currently enrolled in grades 9–12 and postgraduate public school programs (National Center for Education Statistics 1983).

While public secondary education in this country is relatively recent, it still set the trend internationally. Great Britain's secondary schools had an enrollment of only 109,000 in 1900 and did not provide secondary education for children who could not afford fees until 1907. After World War II Great Britain began public educational programs for fourteen- to eighteen-year-olds. Other European countries, with the possible exceptions of Holland, Switzerland, and the Scandanavian countries, followed similar patterns of development (Commager 1983).

Secondary education in the United States today is big business. Virtually all students enter the ninth grade, and approximately 75 percent graduate from high school (Clark 1985). At the end of the 1979–80 school year, more than three million students graduated from American high schools (National Center for Education Statistics 1983) (see figure 6–1). The number of students in high schools has increased by over 2000 percent since 1900 (Digest of Education Statistics 1980).

STRUCTURE OF SECONDARY SCHOOLS

Secondary education in the United States comprises two different levels: intermediate schools and high schools. The high school was the first to develop, starting in the late nineteenth century. This was followed by the development of intermediate schools in the early twentieth century.

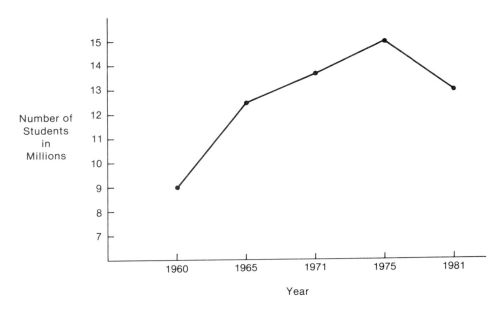

Figure 6-1. *Enrollment in high schools in the United States. Source: National Center for Education Statistics. 1983. Tyack and Hansot, 1984.*

Intermediate Schools

Intermediate schools were initially designed to bridge the gap between the relatively easy curriculum of elementary schools and the demanding academic curriculum of high schools. Many psychologists also began to recognize the need to provide students in their preadolescent and early adolescent years with experiences that were more appropriate for their maturational levels. Children develop in a sequential manner, and many pre- and early adolescent children have unique needs that differ significantly from those of older children (Armstrong and Savage 1983). Two different types of intermediate schools have developed.

Junior high schools. The first form of intermediate school to be developed was the junior high school. In the beginning the appropriate name for these schools was an issue. Names such as "subhigh school," "upper grammar school," "higher primary school," "departmental school," and "intermediate school" were used. Junior high school, however, became the predominant label for these early intermediate schools (Armstrong and Savage 1983).

By the early 1920s junior high schools were clearly established as an intermediate step between elementary schools and high schools. Although some emphasis was still placed on the special needs of young adolescent children, junior high schools soon came to focus almost entirely on academic preparation for high schools. This shift of purpose created a situation where unique psychological and social needs of these children were not being met. Critics began to question the overemphasis on academics and the limited focus on personal development. These critics, armed with research from developmental psychologists and physiologists proposed a reorganization of the intermediate school to enhance the focus of child growth and development during the pre- and early adolescent years. The name chosen for the reorganized school was borrowed from European education—middle schools (Armstrong and Savage 1983).

Middle schools. The specific rationale for middle schools includes:

- Children are reaching pubescence earlier.

- Many ninth grade students are more like their high-school peers than like seventh and eighth graders.

- Sixth grade children, and possibly fifth grade children, are more like seventh and eighth graders than early elementary children.

- Basic academic skills are learned in the first four grades, with older children being ready for more content-oriented classes. (Clark and Starr 1981)

A strong movement began for intermediate schools to be renamed middle schools and include grades 6, 7, and 8, or possibly 5, 6, 7, and 8. Middle schools were supposed to be an actual halfway station between elementary schools and high schools (Clark and Starr 1981).

High Schools

Secondary education actually started with public high schools. These schools, which evolved from private academies, were developed to provide educational opportunities for children beyond the elementary school years. High schools have developed into a stable educational institution to prepare adolescents for higher education or the world of work.

American high schools today no longer solely focus on academic preparation, but include activities that deal with socialization, vocational preparation, homemaker preparation, and a host of extracurricular activities such as clubs and athletics. The basic pattern found in most high schools today has been in existence for many years, which includes

- courses targeted to students whose futures after graduation vary;

- electives;

- subject-based instruction;

- schedules that permit students to take enough courses to earn a diploma acceptable in the business community or in college admissions offices;

- between twenty-five and thirty students in a class;

- a teaching load of five to six classes daily, with two to three different lessons to prepare for those classes. (Cuban 1982, p. 113)

High schools attempt to provide the right educational experiences for all adolescents in the system. While this is an ideal goal, it presents many problems. With such diversity in American society, high schools that attempt to provide programs for all students face a nearly overwhelming task.

Although high schools differ in some respects, most are similar. In general adolescents attend high school and are grouped horizontally by age and vertically by program track; programs comprise various subjects taught by teachers certified in those areas; students are exposed to subjects in various classes each day; and the social activities of students are many and varied (Sizer 1983).

OBJECTIVES OF SECONDARY EDUCATION

A constant problem in secondary education has been to define its goals and objectives. In the 1800s it was assumed that elementary schools should focus on teaching basic skills, such as reading, writing, and arithmetic, while the limited number of secondary schools should prepare students for higher education or entry into vocations. In 1918 the Commission for Reorganization of Secondary Education issued its report, The Cardinal Principles of Secondary Education, which indicated that secondary schools should prepare students for (1) health, (2) command of the fundamental processes, (3) worthy home membership, (4) vocational efficiency, (5) civic competence, (6) worthy use of leisure time, and (7) ethical character (Clark and Starr 1981).

These objectives laid the foundation for the comprehensive high school focusing on much more than academic training. Gross (1978) modified these seven principles into what he called "Seven New Cardinal Principles." These included personal competence and development, family cohesiveness, skilled decision making, moral re-

Secondary schools attempt to meet the varied needs of all students.

sponsibility and ethical action, civic interest and participation, respect for the environment, and global human concern.

The debate continues: should public secondary schools attempt to educate all children in all aspects of life, or should they restrict their efforts to more academic tasks? Boyer (1984) studied state legislation in all fifty states to determine the legal mandates of secondary schools. The results indicated a variety of mandated missions (see table 6–1).

Secondary schools must have a well-defined mission and set of purposes to be effective. These should include

1. Training students in thinking and writing skills;
2. Educating students using a core curriculum that should include literature, the arts, foreign language, history, civics, science, mathematics, technology, and health;
3. Preparing students for work;
4. Preparing students for community service. (Boyer 1984)

Secondary schools attempt to meet the needs of a variety of students: academically talented, academically deficient, college-bound, vocationally oriented, disadvantaged, and the majority of students who fit in the middle group of intellectual abilities and career aspirations. Some schools attempt to meet the needs of these students through a multifaceted program; others offer specialty areas such as the arts and vocational training. Many people have been critical of the comprehensive high school, including Admiral Hyman G. Rickover and Werner von Braun, who believed that academically talented students were being neglected as a result of comprehensive programs attempting to be all things to all students. Because of these kinds of criticisms, many people have advocated splitting the comprehensive high school into specialized programs, such as vocational schools, alternative schools, and even private schools supported by tax dollars (Tanner 1979). The future of comprehensive

TABLE 6–1   State Mandated Mission of High Schools

State	Mandate
Idaho	The school program shall be organized to meet the needs of all pupils, the community, and to fulfill the state objectives of the school.
Mississippi	The purpose of education is to provide appropriate learning experiences to promote the optimum growth and development of youth and adults throughout life.
Oregon	Each individual will have the opportunity to develop to the best of his or her ability the knowledge, skills, and attitudes necessary to function as an individual ... a learner ... a producer ... and a family member.
Maine	The public school must teach virtue and morality for not less than one-half hour per week. This includes principles of morality and justice and a sacred regard for truth, love of country, humanity, a universal benevolence, sobriety, industry and frugality, chastity, moderation and temperance, and other virtues that ornament human society.
California	Each teacher shall endeavor to impress upon the minds of the public the principles of morality, truth, justice, patriotism, and a true comprehension of the rights, duties, and dignity of American citizenship, including kindness toward domestic pets and the humane treatment of living creatures, to teach them to avoid idleness, profanity, and falsehood, and to instruct them in manners and morals and the principles of a free government.

Source: E. L. Boyer. Clarifying the mission of the American high school. Educational Leadership, 1984, 41(6), p. 20.

high schools is in question. However, the success of this secondary model has been such that any significant changes will likely come slowly, if at all.

There is no consensus concerning the goals and objectives of secondary schools in the United States. While the debate will continue, secondary education in this country will probably remain comprehensive, either through comprehensive schools or separate, specialized schools. The needs of most American youth will be addressed.

ORGANIZATION OF SECONDARY SCHOOLS

Secondary schools are organized using several patterns. One major organizational pattern has been the division of secondary education into junior high schools or middle schools and high schools. This particular format has been implemented in most school districts, except those that have very low enrollments that dictate combining students into one organization.

Secondary schools are also organized by the type of curricular program. Most secondary schools offer three basic types of curricular options: general, academic, and vocational. The general curriculum is designed for students who do not anticipate attending colleges or universities and who plan on entering the job market or technical training after high-school graduation. The academic program focuses on preparing students for higher education programs. Students who choose the academic curriculum most often have definite plans for attending colleges or universities. The third curricular option, vocational education, provides training in vocational areas that are designed to prepare students to enter the job market following high-school graduation. Vocational education programs can be general in nature or job specific. Chapter seven focuses on vocational education programs.

Of the three tracks, students select the academic track most often, with the general track a close second choice. In the spring of 1980, 38 percent of the high-school seniors were in an academic program, 37.2 percent were enrolled in a general program, and the remaining 24.8 percent were taking part in a vocational education program (National Center for Education Statistics 1983).

Another method of organizing secondary schools is through graded or nongraded programs. Nongraded secondary programs provide students with the opportunity to progress at their own rates rather than being tied to grade levels. The concept is based on continuous progress education. Pupils complete courses at their own rate and then progress to other course options (Wood, Nicholson, and Findley 1985).

The more common organizational arrangement for instruction is the graded system. This approach organizes courses around grade levels; students enroll in various courses that are tied to grade levels and continue in the course for a semester or academic year. This is by far the more traditional approach, and is found in the vast majority of secondary schools. While students may be allowed to enroll in courses designed for other grade levels, they usually take courses for their grade. For example, most freshmen enroll in freshman English, general math or algebra, a particular history course such as World History, and general science or biology. Likewise, some courses are primarily geared for upper-level secondary students. Trigonometry, for example, is considered a junior- or senior-level course in most high schools; civics or American government is also geared for upper-level students in most schools.

Secondary schools, therefore, may be organized on several different criteria. Although differences do exist among most secondary schools, the majority follow a traditional model. Most are graded, most districts have junior high schools or middle schools and high schools, and most provide a general, academic, and vocational curriculum track.

CURRICULUM OF SECONDARY SCHOOLS

Secondary schools, like elementary schools, revolve around the curriculum, the sum total of all experiences of students. The curriculum of secondary schools has been debated a great deal. Questions such as the following are continually discussed:

1. Is there a core curriculum that all secondary students should complete?
2. What subjects should be included in a core curriculum at the secondary level?
3. How many units of various subjects should be required of students for graduation?
4. Should curricular requirements be different for students seeking different post-school objectives?
5. Should schools include in their curriculum subjects such as death education, sex education, creation-science, and peace education?
6. What is the role of multicultural education in the secondary curriculum?

Although state departments of education control the curriculum of secondary schools to some degree by imposing minimum graduation requirements, many of these issues are resolved locally by the administration and the school board with considerable input from the constituents of the school district.

Common Curriculum

Most secondary schools require a common curriculum for all students. A common curriculum can be defined as "a study of those consequential ideas, experiences, and traditions common to all of us by virtue of our membership in the human family at a particular moment in history" (Boyer 1984, p. 21). Courses in the common curriculum should include literature, the arts, foreign language, history, civics, science, mathematics, technology, and health (Boyer 1984). Secondary schools require that students complete a certain number of units in many of these subject areas before graduation requirements can be met.

Science. Science education has received a great deal of interest at various times, while at other times it falls out of public and professional attention. Following the launching of the satellite Sputnik by the Soviet Union in the late 1950s, the federal government made a strong effort to improve science education in this country. While the motivation was political, the results were positive for public schools. Curriculum reform, inservice training for teachers, and funds for materials and equipment were made available. Unfortunately, this push in science education did not last. With the Kennedy and Johnson administrations emphasizing educational opportunities for disadvantaged and handicapped students, fewer federal dollars were available for science education.

In the late 1970s and early 1980s, interest again shifted to science education. Critics of public education clamored for more instruction in science for American children and youth. In the post–Sputnik years, back-to-the-basics became a strong movement, but did not include science. Instead it focused on the basic academic skills of reading, writing, and math. The result has been a crisis for science education. The following depicts the state of science education today:

- There is a critical shortage of qualified science teachers.

- Since 1960 the average achievement in science on a variety of tests has shown a steady decline.

- In the elementary school, the average child will spend less than one out of twenty-five instructional hours per week studying science.

- The movement away from science begins in the early grades. About 50 percent of students entering junior high school say that they like science, but only 21 percent say that they like it when they leave.

- For nearly a decade science enrollments in high schools have been decreasing.

- Only one in six high-school juniors or seniors take any science course. Only one in fourteen takes physics.

- Only 13 percent of the general students and 9 percent of the vocational students will have taken three years of high-school science. (Sigda 1983, p. 625)

These facts suggest that science education in the United States is at a low ebb. To alter this trend, several suggestions are being made. First, all students should be required to take science courses each year. Second, content-oriented and process-oriented methods need to be combined. Third, students need to be encouraged to get involved with science courses and reinforced for their efforts. Finally, more and better science teachers must become available (Sigda 1983). With better trained science teachers available, limited funding for science classrooms becomes less important. For example, creative, well-trained science educators can turn regular classrooms into places for science experiments even without high-cost science laboratories (Markle 1984).

Math. Most high schools require students to complete some coursework in math. Too often this is a minimal requirement. Math education, like science education, is in a crisis: students often choose to take only the minimal math requirements in secondary schools; they often elect to take general math rather than algebra or more difficult math subjects when they have the option; math electives are rarely taken by many students; many math teachers only meet minimal teaching qualifications (Stefanich and Dedrick 1985).

Many students do not elect more math and science courses for two basic reasons: (1) courses are perceived as too difficult, and (2) teachers are perceived as unapproachable or poor instructors (Stefanich and Dedrick 1985). Many of the recommendations to improve science education would also be effective in the area of math education. One advantage math education has over science education is that it is included in the back-to-the-basics movement. Math education stands to gain not only from the current reform movements that are resulting from the many national reports of the 1970s and 1980s, but also from the conservative movement that wants to require students to complete more courses in basic subject areas.

Just as science teachers can rely on creativity to make science classes appealing, math teachers can do similar activities to encourage students to enroll in math classes or to motivate students already enrolled in required math classes. Schall (1984) described how teachers could make math classes more fun and more practical. For example, students can learn a variety of math facts and how to apply them simply by using the outdoors as the classroom and natural objects as materials.

Social studies. Social studies could conceivably include the study of everything about human beings and their environments. In practice, however, more traditional definitions are used, which emphasize subjects such as history, civics, geography, psychology, and sociology (Nelson and Michaelis 1980). Social studies is an important area in the secondary school curriculum. "A social studies curriculum that is organized according to its constituent disciplines (e.g., history, economics, geography, and sociology) and that takes the long view of historical perspective can provide students with the background they will need to understand the events of the future" (Spillane and Regnier 1981, p. 731).

Although social studies curricula differ in most schools, some general facts can be concluded regarding social studies in secondary schools:

- The back-to-the-basics movement has emphasized more teaching of U.S. history and government.

- Enrollments in psychology and sociology classes have been increasing.

- Reading and writing skills are being stressed more in social studies classes.

- Current issues, problems, and contemporary events are often included in history classes.

- World history is not taken by many students in secondary schools.

- Geography is taken by students in elementary and middle schools, but rarely in high schools.

- Materials for social studies classes developed through several projects in the 1960s are being used in some schools, but not the majority of schools. (Nelson and Michaelis 1980)

The social studies curricula has been undergoing some reforms during the past several years. In the 1960s and early 1970s, the new social studies curriculum was developed and implemented in some schools. The central aim of the new program was to provide materials that could be used in social studies classes. Only approximately 30 percent of the schools adopted the new approach. Although many teachers view the new social studies curriculum as a failure, several important points were learned from the reform efforts, including the realization that (1) the social studies curriculum should be improved, (2) teachers should be trained in implementing new programs, (3) new programs should be disseminated to schools to enable them to make judgments concerning the programs, and (4) new programs reflect developments in the field (Switzer 1981).

Specialized Curricular Areas

Beyond the basic, common curriculum, schools frequently offer specialized programs for students, depending on their postschool goals. For example, students who are planning on attending college will usually complete extra units in English, mathematics, and science, and students enrolled in a vocational program may only complete the minimum units in the basic curriculum and then complete courses designed for their vocational interest. Chapter seven describes in detail vocational education programs offered by secondary schools.

Several subjects that are not related to common academic pursuits or vocational education are available in some secondary schools. These include sex education, death education, and creation-science.

Sex education. One curricular area that has received a great deal of attention in American schools is sex education. Should schools provide sex education, or is this an area that belongs to parents? A large proportion of adolescents in the United States are sexually active, and an undesirable consequence that frequently results is teenage pregnancy (Rienzo 1981). Over the past decade, there have been major increases in sexual activity, pregnancy, abortions, and out-of-wedlock births for adolescents (Kenney and Orr 1984).

Increased sexual activity and teenage pregnancy provide support for sex education. Research indicates that (1) there is broad support for sex education in the schools and (2) parents support sex education in the schools. The advantages of sex education provided through public schools is that it can reach all children before they become sexually active and it is relatively inexpensive. The task, however, is great. Sex education programs must "modify, in a few hours of classroom instruction, the messages that young people receive every day from their friends, the mass media, and other sources" (Kenney and Orr 1984, p. 494). Although sex education is popular with parents, many schools still face major challenges from some groups when they initiate sex education programs, and these programs are likely to continue to be an optional component of most secondary schools.

For several decades, sex education focused on helping young adolescents understand the physical changes of puberty, the reproduction system, and family responsibilities. This rather simplistic approach to sex education has given way to diverse programs. Today's programs range from short units on menstruation to long, comprehensive courses on family life. Some of the programs begin in kindergarten; others are offered at the secondary level. Objectives for sex education programs are also diverse, including "helping young people feel more comfortable about their sexuality, contributing to a better understanding between the sexes, and, in some cases (albeit relatively few), preventing teenage pregnancies" (Kenney and Orr 1984, p. 492).

Death education. An area that has received much less attention and adoption than sex education but is growing in popularity is death education. Death education is designed to help students come to grips with death and has many benefits:

- The teacher, as well as all of the students, develops his or her own philosophy of life as it relates to death.

- Working through the topic of death will enable each person to perceive the network of people involved in the death of any person.

- Working through the topic will also allow the student to deal with his or her feelings. (Waterman and Lipka 1982, p. 82)

Although death education is still considered taboo in many circles, it is becoming more acceptable and may become an elective in many schools in the future.

Education about the nuclear threat. Another topic that appears to be growing as a curricular area is the nuclear threat. Although not a subject included in many secondary schools, universities have begun to develop courses on the nuclear threat, and these courses have been growing in number and in enrollments. In the future secondary schools will likely begin to educate students about the nuclear threat. Teachers and teacher organizations are beginning to realize that the best way to deal with the nuclear threat is to include the topic in the curriculum. While some believe that the subject should be covered as early as the middle grades, others think that the best time is in high school.

Curricular materials, although slow in being developed, are beginning to be available. Educators for Social Responsibility (ESR) is currently developing such materials for grades K–12 (Elam 1983). The National Education Association has developed "Choices: A Unit on Conflict and Nuclear War," which received a great deal of criticism from many sources, including President Reagan (Salhoz 1983). Although few school boards, state departments of education, and textbook publishers have made moves to include courses and materials on the nuclear threat, the movement appears to be gaining in momentum (Elam 1983). As the superpowers of the world continue to engage in confrontation, topics on the nuclear threat will likely increase in secondary schools.

Creation-science. During the late 1970s and early 1980s, many proponents of the new right advocated the teaching of creation-science alongside evolution. Their concerns centered around children being exposed to only one theory of creation, that of evolution. As a result, many individuals advocated that schools take a more active role in religious instruction and pressed school boards, state departments of education, and state legislatures to mandate equal time to the teaching of creation-science. Arkansas was the first state to pass legislation mandating that creation-science be given equal status to evolution in secondary school curriculum. As many had predicted, the Arkansas law, Act 590, was struck down by the U.S. District Court for the Eighth Circuit as being unconstitutional because it violated the separation of church and state principle (Hahn 1982). A similar law was declared unconstitutional in Louisiana in 1985.

Even though the courts have not supported the teaching of creation-science, many religious conservatives continue to support its teaching in public school programs. Legislation was introduced in fifteen states in 1981 to require that creation-science be given equal time with evolution, with four other states having legislation introduced in 1982. One supporter, George Hahn, stated that those advocating the inclusion of creation-science in public school curricula did so to enable children to see both sides of the issue, not to insert creation-science and delete evolutionism (Hahn 1982). Creationists are opposed by many individuals who view creation-science as a subject that should be dealt with by churches, not publicly supported schools. They argue that creation-science curriculum materials were not supported by any published research in the natural sciences (Cole and Scott 1982). The debate continues; however, as a result of the federal court action that declared the Arkansas law unconstitutional, creation-science probably will not be added to many curricula guides in the future.

Multicultural education. While not a specific subject to be included in secondary curricular options, multicultural education should be a part of every course taught in secondary schools. Berry (1979) indicated the importance of multicultural education in the secondary curriculum by stating that it was a principle that was excluded from the seven Cardinal Principles of 1918 and 1978. He indicated that "the secondary school pupil has a moral responsibility to learn, understand, and respect the values inherent in other races and religions, and to practice behaviors that will insure human dignity and civil rights to males and females of cultural groups different from their own" (Berry 1979, p. 745).

Multicultural education goes far beyond teaching courses labeled "ethnic studies" and "social assimilation." While it does include teaching such courses, it also includes changing schools to provide equal educational opportunities for all children, regardless of ethnic background. Educators interested in making their schools multicultural must evaluate their school environments and curricula to determine to what extent it is monoethnic and Anglo–Centric. Once this determination is made, systematic efforts can be made to implement necessary changes to bring about multicultural education (Banks 1981).

Other curriculum areas. Occasionally various groups will express their support for increased emphasis in certain existing curricular areas. For example, Starr (1979) stated that foreign language is one area that is neglected in the United States and should be given more emphasis in our schools. His reasoning was that the United States was lagging behind other countries in teaching foreign languages, and that we must stop taking the attitude that everybody will learn English, therefore, negating the need to learn other languages.

MacDowell and Clow (1983) expressed the concern that economics education be given more time in secondary schools. They based their rationale on the premises that an understanding of economic concepts had a strong relationship to consumer behavior and that the utilization of resources could be better analyzed with a basic understanding of economics principles.

Curriculum for the future. With the twenty-first century rapidly approaching, secondary schools must determine the needs of its students not for today, but for tomorrow. This requires that the curricula of secondary schools start changing now to meet the demands that high-school graduates will face in the twenty-first century. Harold Shane, a noted futurist, described the predictions made by 135 distinguished scholars about the needs of children for the coming twenty-first century. The following summarizes some of the projected needs of students that need to be addressed by public schools:

1. Students must realize the limitations placed on man by the earth.
2. Students need to understand the need to conserve and the ways to conserve natural resources.
3. The ability to create new life forms brings an awesome responsibility.
4. Students must understand the basic principles of science.

5. Students need to understand the history of the world, not simply the history of the United States and Western Europe.
6. Students must understand and accept the idea of trade-offs, not only economically, but also environmentally.
7. An understanding must be made that human society is a global society.
8. Students must understand that different people learn differently and learn different things in various cultures.
9. More than one language should be learned.
10. Cultural "pluralism" must be learned. (Shane 1981)

The future curriculum of secondary schools cannot be accurately predicted. As the world changes, education curricula must alter to enhance students' chances for success.

Curriculum Development and Revision

The curricula of secondary schools must be in a constant state of change in order for schools to meet the changing needs of students. Several steps must be taken to develop curricula (see table 6–2).

Once the school curriculum is established, curriculum renewal becomes the process. Curriculum renewal is an ongoing process whereby schools update, modify, and alter the curriculum to meet the needs of students. If schools had the same curriculum today as they did in 1920, students would be completing schools with limited skills required for functioning in the late twentieth century. Curriculum renewal requires a collaborative effort. School personnel must cooperate with community members to develop and enhance a curriculum that is responsive to the needs of students (Brickell and Jones 1983).

Extracurricular Activities

In addition to the academic curriculum, most secondary schools provide many extracurricular activities for students. Examples include clubs, band, athletics, dramatics, and school newspaper. The 1984 Gallup Poll revealed that 77 percent of the respon-

TABLE 6–2 Eight Steps of Curriculum Development	
Step One	Identification of School Goals
Step Two	Creation of Subject Goals
Step Three	Creation of Scope and Sequence Charts
Step Four	Identification of Competencies
Step Five	Creation of Compilation of Curriculum Guides
Step Six	Identification of Instructional Objectives
Step Seven	Curriculum Evaluation
Step Eight	Curriculum Revision

Source: J. H. Littrell and G. D. Bailey. *Eight-step model helps systematic curriculum development.* NASSP Bulletin, *September, 1983, p. 1.*

Extracurricular activities provide students with many enjoyable activities.

dents felt that extracurricular activities are either very important or fairly important for young people's educational programs. Although this represents a sizable majority, the number stating that extracurricular activities are very important declined from 45 percent in 1978 to 31 percent in 1984 (Gallup 1984), suggesting a trend away from extracurricular activities toward more rigid academic activities.

One extracurricular activity in particular, competitive athletics, has received a great deal of criticism. Commager (1983) states that high school competitive athletics have, in too many communities, become the focus of the community. Rather than being a means to interest the community in the school, competitive athletics have become the community's source of entertainment. With the recent trend to make schools more academic, many districts have established policies requiring students to pass certain courses or maintain certain grade-point averages to participate in competitive athletics and all other extracurricular activities. For example, the Los Angeles School District passed such a policy in 1982.

The most controversial and comprehensive policy regarding athletics and academic standards was passed by the Texas legislature and went into effect in January 1985. This policy, referred to as the "no pass/no play" rule, resulted from a governor's commission studying education in Texas that recommended numerous measures to improve public education. The "no pass/no play" rule states that any student who does not receive a grade of 70 or above (out of 100) in any course cannot participate in extracurricular activities for the next six-week grading period. Already this rule has been challenged in the courts. In June 1985 the Texas Supreme Court unanimously upheld the rule and stated that a "student's [right] to participate in extracurricular activities does not rise to the same level as the right to free speech and free exercise of religion." The court also supported the right of the state of Texas to regulate extracurricular activities in public schools (Flygare 1985).

While other states have and will likely continue to pass policies regarding participation in extracurricular activities and academic performance, some problems do result from this exclusionary policy toward extracurricular activities:

- Grade inflation by teachers trying to keep students eligible for activities.

- Student enrollment in easier classes to facilitate keeping their grades above the magic level.

- Cheating.

- School personnel who support extracurricular activities may make their classes or grading system easier.

- Social, emotional, and physical development will not be considered a function of the school.

- Many students will drop out of school, because they will be unable to participate in certain activities. (Frith and Clark 1984)

Although the trend appears to be away from extracurricular activities, substantial support still exists for their continued presence (Gallup 1984). However, there does seem to be a movement to restrict participation in these activities to those students who do well in their academic work.

———— HIGHLIGHT ————

Survey Calls Texas' Prep Rule 'Overkill'

AUSTIN (AP)—A national survey says that Texas' controversial no pass, no play rule amounts to "overkill," but that's a finding the state's education commissioner disputes.

The Texas Association of Secondary School Principals asked executives of counterpart associations in other states for details of their laws on eligibility for participation in extracurricular activities, and 43 responded.

"Texas has shown overkill in legislation dealing with no pass, no play," the association concluded Monday.

"Practically all states require a student to pass only three, four or five courses to be eligible to participate in extracurricular activities," it said. "These states take into account extreme condi-

tions not under the control of students that sometimes affect student achievement."

Only Hawaii and the District of Columbia require youngsters to pass all their courses, the survey indicated. Four states leave eligibility decision to local districts, and some California cities have rules as strict as those in Texas.

But state Education Commissioner Bill Kirby downplayed the survey and said the no pass, no play rule—which bars students from extracurricular activities for six weeks after getting a failing grade—is a model other states are adopting.

"I don't know that I would use the word 'overkill.' But I think Texas is way out front in that. Other states are talking about following Texas' lead," he told the Fort Worth Star-Telegram.

The high school principals will be quizzing both Gov. Mark White and former Gov. Bill Clements about it June 13 as they move toward an endorsement in the governor's race.

The association favors reducing the period of ineligibility from six weeks to three weeks after making at least one "F" on a six-week report card.

It also wants a change that would leave intact a student's eligibility if he or she passes all courses at midterm, even though there might be one or more failing grades for the third six weeks.

Harold Massey, executive director of the association, said it is natural to compare Texas with other states "to see whether you are in line or not."

The survey "shows we are out of line. What we have done with no pass-no play is punitive," he said.

Arkansas, a state that recently went through a school reform movement, is toughening its requirement from passing three courses to four. Oklahoma is doing the same. Louisiana and New Mexico require students to pass five courses.

Used by permission of the Associated Press. *Northwest Arkansas Times*, June 3, 1986.

METHODS OF INSTRUCTION

Secondary school teachers use a variety of teaching styles and strategies. These include lectures, classroom discussion, independent study, and individual instruction.

Lectures

Lecturing is the most frequently used method of instruction in secondary schools. In a study of high-school seniors, Wagenaar (1981) found that over 80 percent of the students reported that they were in classes that emphasized lectures frequently. The lecture method has received a great deal of criticism; during the late 1960s and early 1970s, the lecture method almost became doomed because of new teaching techniques and criticisms. However, the lecture method has been retained and is still the major method used in secondary schools (Michel and Weaver 1984).

Some of the criticisms of the lecture method espoused in the past are still a concern. Namely, many teachers who use this method have a lack of sensitivity toward students, are not effective presenters, and are not sufficiently prepared (Michel and Weaver 1984). Several actions can be taken by teachers to meet these concerns and be better lecturers (see table 6–3). What should be remembered is that the lecture method is not necessarily bad. When used properly, it is an effective method of instruction. It does, however, place the responsibility for selecting, organizing, and sequencing information on the teacher, not the student (Gold 1984). Teachers who rely on this instructional method must realize this and be prepared to take appropriate preparatory actions.

Classroom Discussion

The discussion method of instruction is also used extensively in secondary schools. Nearly 60 percent of the seniors studied by Wagenaar (1981) reported that they were in classes that used the discussion method of instruction. Although a popular method, beginning teachers often have difficulty with classroom discussions. They need to learn to ask leading and appropriate questions at the proper time to stimulate the

TABLE 6–3   Actions to Improve Lectures
Improve Sensitivity to Students
Use Humor
Be Organized
Capture Students' Attention
Take Time for Adequate Preparation
Use Examples Frequently

Source: T. A. Michel, and R. L. Weaver, II. 1984. Lecturing: Means for improvement. The Clearing House 57(9), 389–91.

discussion, be good listeners, and know how to respond to students' questions to keep the discussion going (Armstrong and Savage 1983).

One effective method of promoting discussion is to require students to read textbook assignments and base the discussion on the reading selection. Alvermann (1984) studied the use of discussion in middle school social studies classes and

Small group discussions are one teaching method in secondary schools.

determined that very little actual discussion took place. More time was spent on listening and reciting information than on discussions. Also, almost as much time was spent on social, off-task talking as on classroom discussion. Alvermann pointed out that this did not have to be the case. Given proper methods to use discussions, they can be effective in following textbook reading assignments.

Independent Study

The independent study technique can be effective with some children; the key is in determining which children can benefit from this form of instruction. Children who are self-motivated and who work well without close supervision are likely candidates for independent studies. On the other hand, children who require a great deal of structure would not do well with an independent study assignment. After determining which students could benefit from an independent study assignment, teachers must decide (1) what students are to do, (2) what materials are necessary, (3) how grades will be assigned, and (4) activities for students not involved in independent study (Armstrong and Savage 1983).

Independent studies allow some students to venture into activities that would not be possible in large groups. This method of instruction is excellent for gifted students, but can also be effective with students of average academic abilities and students who have learning difficulties. Teachers should be cautious in using the independent study model; it takes a great deal of planning. Teachers cannot assume that this particular model makes teaching easy. Quite the contrary exists. If students are to benefit from an independent study assignment, it must be well planned, monitored, and evaluated.

Individual Instruction

Similar to the independent study method is individual instruction. Individual instruction differs in that students in a class are all studying the same thing, whereas in independent study, individual students study different topics. Individual instruction is important in secondary schools because teachers must teach students with varying abilities. For example, a high school history teacher not only has a majority of students who are functioning at a similar level, but also has students who are academically superior and those who have learning difficulties. Regardless of the abilities of the high achievers or the type of problem experienced by students with difficulties, individual instruction allows teachers to teach to the appropriate level, using the appropriate methods.

Several steps must be followed when individualizing instruction (see table 6–4). These include determining the functioning level of students, establishing objectives, choosing appropriate materials, presenting information, and evaluating students' progress (Post 1984).

Other Instructional Methods

Many other instructional methods are frequently used in secondary schools. Some of these overlap to some degree, but have distinct characteristics. They include:

1. brainstorming
   - promotes discussion of a particular topic
   - ensures that all views are heard

TABLE 6–4   Steps to Individualize Instruction

Step	Actions
Determine Functioning Level	• Use pretest instruments • Use formal and informal assessment
Develop Objectives	• Break objectives into smaller steps • Decrease the amount of work required if students can meet objectives with less work • Allow students to work at their own pace
Choose Appropriate Materials	• Use visual aids for some students • Use games when appropriate • Use props for concrete aids • Use cues, such as color coding • Provide outlines for students • Accommodate different reading levels • Break up work sheets and other assignments to smaller segments
Present Information	• In large group lectures, use visual aids, outlines, and props • Use questioning techniques to encourage discussion in large groups • Make small group selections carefully • Take advantage of the independent study strategy
Evaluating Students	• In formal, written examinations, accommodate for students' reading problems; for example, tape record tests or have them read • Provide immediate feedback for some students on assignments • Keep individual student folders to assess student's work • Consider using a student's product for evaluation

Source: L. M. Post. 1984. *Individualizing instruction in the middle school: Modifications and adaptations in curriculum for the mainstreamed student.* The Clearing House 58*(2), 73–76.*

	• encourages creative problem solving • allows students to apply knowledge
2. case study	• is excellent for presenting new material • helps students understand materials after an intense study • uses debriefing questions to bring closure
3. debate	• class debate, not individual debate, enables the entire class to participate • is excellent for presenting new information • promotes understanding of different points of view
4. project approach	• emphasizes doing • is traditionally used in industrial arts • results in a product
5. role playing	• helps students see things from various perspectives • requires a great deal of planning • requires debriefing to help students bring closure to the process
6. simulation	• places students in real-life situations • is excellent for motivation • enables the application of real knowledge to practical situations

7. teacher demonstration	• has long been used in secondary science classes
	• demonstrates the proper method of accomplishing a task
	• works best when students have an opportunity to perform the task following the demonstration
8. team learning	• allows teachers to present new information in a new manner
	• requires small-group interactions
	• uses teams to attempt to deal with a task or questions
9. telelecture	• uses the telephone to hook up students with lecturer
	• requires a great deal of preparation
	• requires students to have questions prepared to ask the lecturer (Armstrong and Savage 1983)

SCHOOL PHILOSOPHY AND POLICIES

The philosophy and policies of secondary schools greatly affect students, teachers, and parents. Often these are determined by the school board and state department of education. Individual school administrators and teachers, however, must implement the philosophy and policies of the school district. Areas affected by school philosophy and policies include discipline, appearance codes, and student rights.

Discipline

Probably one of the most talked about topics in secondary schools is discipline. How are students to be disciplined? Whose responsibility is discipline? What disciplinary methods are effective? School discipline is consistently noted as a major concern of parents and school personnel (Barth 1980; Polakowski 1984). Respondents in the 16th Annual Gallup Poll on Attitudes Toward Public Schools listed discipline as the major problem of public schools (Gallup 1984).

Discipline in schools is essential if learning is to take place. Critics often say that discipline is too lax, while others may say that discipline is too harsh (Barth 1980). Professional educators are often caught in the middle. Knowing how to maintain discipline is a difficult task, but it can be made easier if certain principles are followed. First, school policies must be made clear to students. The policies must be written down and clearly explained (Lordon 1983). If students are not aware of school rules and the consequences for breaking rules, they should not be held accountable for violating them.

Second, disciplinary standards must be consistent. "Inconsistency in policies and approaches to dealing with discipline problems, in expectations by teachers from one room to another, in interpretation of rules and policies, and in types of punishment used is the most serious detriment to a good school discipline system" (Lordon 1983, p. 59). If one teacher enforces school rules and applies certain consequences to violaters of the rule, other teachers must do the same. Inconsistency creates environments where children will not know what to expect or what the consequences to certain behavior will be.

Rules are only as good as the support they have (Polakowski 1984). If teachers attempt to enforce school rules, they must have administrative support. Nothing defeats teachers' attitudes as much as the belief that they will not be backed up by administrators in disciplinary matters. Likewise, teachers must be supportive of each other and the administrator. If administrators try to enforce school rules and teachers circumvent them, the climate is ripe for disciplinary problems.

Probably the best and most effective disciplinary program is preventive in nature: keep problems from occurring in the first place (Maynard 1983). If the school climate is positive and not overly restrictive, students are less likely to create disciplinary problems. Establishing a positive school climate requires the collaborative efforts of teachers, administrators, and students. Helm (1984) lists the following teacher actions that help in establishing a proper learning atmosphere:

- involve students in learning as soon as class begins

- be positive

- do not look for problems

- vary learning activities

- use a seating chart

- maintain control; do not start yelling

- discipline students in private, not in front of their peers

- ensure that future assignments are understood

- be flexible with learning activities

- do not have a class debate on disciplinary matters

- be prepared for class

- ensure that students understand class rules

- ensure that students understand rules for making up class work

Teachers' philosophy of education, attitude toward children, and self-concept all play a role in establishing a positive classroom atmosphere (Wagner 1983). Poor self-concepts can be strengthened through observing other teachers who do not have discipline problems, attending workshops on discipline, and keeping abreast of the literature on effective school discipline (Helm 1984).

Once school or classroom rules have been broken, teachers and administrators must be prepared to deal with the situation. Several different disciplinary methods may be used. When punishing students for breaking rules, teachers and administrators must consider several things. First, they must ask if the disciplinary action is fair. If students were aware of the rules and consequences for breaking them and the punishment fits the infraction, then the action is probably fair. Second, school personnel should not "make an example" of rule breakers. Finally, adequate records should be maintained. With the public's bent on accountability for educators, and with the courts getting involved in disciplinary cases, teachers and administrators must protect themselves with documentation (Nolte 1985).

Before punishing students for violating rules or policies, school personnel should take certain actions. First, school personnel must meet with the misbehaving student. The beginning of the meeting is critical, because it sets the stage for the entire discussion. School personnel must then gather the facts. Listening to only one side of the story can lead to inappropriate disciplinary methods. After gathering facts, school personnel must decide on the appropriate punishment. Although rules and regulations may be in writing, school personnel should take into consideration any extenuating circumstances that could affect the punishment. Finally, school personnel should follow through. For example, if the school administrator metes out the punishment, contact should be made with the child's teacher concerning actions that were taken (Merrill 1984).

Teachers and administrators in secondary schools have myriad disciplinary actions that can be taken with students. Consequences to misbehavior should be considered on an individual basis. What is effective punishment for one child might not be effective for another, and a critical element in disciplining students is that whatever adversive treatment given to the child is indeed considered punishment by that child (Heitzman 1983). Disciplinary options include those typically thought of, such as detention hall, extra work, reduced privileges, and suspensions, as well as some less popular but effective measures, such as in-school suspension (Disciullo 1984), time out (Engelhardt 1983), and individual behavior management plans (Thomason and Pedersen 1984). Whatever disciplinary approach is used, school personnel should make sure that policies are explicit, that students understand policies, and that consequences are made clear before the rules violation occurs.

Appearance Codes

Appearance codes, namely dealing with dress and hair length, have been challenged in schools during the past several years. Students, especially during the 1970s, began challenging school policies in these areas as being repressive and denying them their right to free expression. The courts have been inconsistent in their rulings on these issues. Some courts have upheld school policies related to dress and appearance of students; other courts have rejected them as being unnecessary. The one principle that has emerged is that schools apparently have the right to impose various dress and appearance standards when they can be shown to be related to the preservation of safety and the orderly functioning of the school program (Armstrong and Savage 1983).

Expulsion and Suspension

Expulsion and suspension have been used as disciplinary measures against students for many years. Students who violate certain rules have been automatically expelled for long periods of time or suspended for a few days. These disciplinary actions have been challenged during past years as excessive. As with dress codes, the courts have at times upheld expulsion and suspension policies, and at times have rejected them. While expulsion and suspension were once common methods of dealing with disruptive students, they are currently used a great deal more cautiously. Suspending and expelling students are now used most often when schools can show that the continued presence of a particular student is dangerous or severely disruptive to the school program. Even under these circumstances, schools must follow due process procedures and allow students to present their side of the issue. Schools that use expulsion and suspension should ensure that students' rights have not been infringed upon (Armstrong and Savage 1983).

Search and Seizure

The right of school officials to search students' lockers and personal areas has been an issue during the past several years. For example, do school personnel have the right to search a student's locker for suspected drugs without the student's permission? Many court cases have dealt with this subject. Although some of the rulings have denied schools the right to search students' property without their permission, other rulings have given schools this authority. The key to these rulings is that the Fourth Amendment to the United States Constitution prohibits unreasonable searches, not all searches. Courts have upheld cases where there was probable cause, in other words, in cases where school officials have evidence to support a belief that a student is guilty of a particular offense (Armstrong and Savage 1983).

After reviewing several search and seizure litigation cases, Sendor (1984) recommended that school officials consider two things. First, evidence should be searched for only if it is related to a student's alleged offense, and second, a school policy for regular, unannounced locker searches should be developed and publicized. While the courts have upheld students' rights to privacy, school officials do have the right to search private areas under appropriate circumstances. Teachers must be familiar with school policies and procedures related to search and seizure.

Other School Policies

In addition to policies on discipline, appearance codes, suspension and expulsion, and search and seizure, schools frequently have policies on topics such as:

- use of school facilities during after-school hours
- field trips/excursions away from school
- grading
- graduation
- school-sponsored social activities

These are merely a few of the types of policies many school districts have. Without policies, school personnel may be at a loss as to what to do in certain circumstances. Policies, developed by the local board of education in compliance with state and federal regulations, enable school personnel to establish and implement guidelines that are necessary for the day-to-day functioning of the school.

PROBLEMS FACING SECONDARY SCHOOLS

Many problems currently face secondary schools in the United States. Examples include school dropouts, discipline, declining academic performance, and general problems facing adolescents, including alcohol and drug abuse, teenage pregnancy, and suicide. Although many of these reflect general problems of society, schools are expected to deal with these problems as they relate to school-age children.

School Dropouts

The dropout rate of American high schools is approximately 28 percent. This figure is arrived at as a result of the 1979–80 graduating class representing approximately 72 percent of its age group (National Center for Education Statistics 1983). This would approximate a national rate. In some areas, the dropout rate is as high as 50 percent (Bottoms and Copa 1983). Although the students who do not graduate may do so for various reasons, a large part is the result of dropouts.

While students drop out of school before they graduate for many reasons, personal problems appear to be the major cause (Mahan and Johnson 1983). Students who are potential dropouts present the following characteristics:

- a record of truancy or excessive absence from class;

- a low level of identification with or participation in school activities;

- low or failing grades in two or more academic classes;

- difficulty in communicating with teachers and other students;

- little interest in classroom work. (Ross 1983, p. 16)

Schools can use these characteristics to identify potential dropouts and intervene to reduce the numbers of dropouts. One program that attempts to do this was initiated in Gateway High School, Aurora, Colorado. This program, called the Experimental Program for Orientation (EXPO), identified sixty students who were considered potential dropouts. Of these sixty, thirty were enrolled in the program (on a volunteer basis) and thirty were considered a control group. The program consisted of mentors being assigned to students to help them with any problems and workshops on study skills, assertiveness, time management, team building, self-image, and decision making. Following one year, the thirty students enrolled in the EXPO program exhibited several characteristics superior to those in the control group: (1) less truancy, (2) higher grade point average, and (3) fewer dropouts (only one student in the EXPO program dropped out, while seven in the control group dropped out). This program, therefore, was considered a huge success.

Many programs have been developed to help prevent students from dropping out of school. Some ideas that can help include (1) providing support programs, (2) providing alternative classes, (3) encouraging cocurricular activities, (4) encouraging positive group interactions, and (5) working with families (Mahan and Johnson 1983). Preventing students from dropping out of school before they complete the regular school program requires a great deal of time and effort from all school personnel and family members.

Boston Civic Leaders Weigh Response to Dropouts

By Blake Rodman

Concerned about Boston's growing dropout rate, local school, business, and community leaders met this month to consider proposals to keep students in school, but rejected such punitive measures as denying dropouts work permits and drivers' licenses.

The meeting came as school officials were preparing to issue a study reporting that 43 percent of the students who began in the city's public high schools in 1981 dropped out before graduation—a higher proportion of the class than finished school.

The report, titled "A Working Document on the Dropout Problem in Boston Public Schools," also states that during the 1984–85 school year more than 16 percent—or 3,498—of Boston's 21,350 public high-school students dropped out.

"There is little doubt that the dropout rate is both high and growing," says the report, which contains a statistical analysis of Boston's problem, a summary of research on why students drop out, and a review of possible intervention programs.

School and city officials say the report—produced by the school district's 8-month-old office of research and development—presents the first complete, authoritative picture of the city's high-school dropout problem and possible strategies for dealing with it.

"It brings bad news, but it does it in a very credible way," said Robert B. Schwartz, director of the Boston Compact, a cooperative program of the city's schools, universities, businesses, and civic groups that cosponsored this month's dropout meeting. Also sponsoring the conference were the Boston Private Industry Council and the Committee for Economic Development.

"Now no one can claim ignorance of the magnitude of the problem," Mr. Schwartz said. "It can no longer be swept under the rug."

Nationwide, approximately one in four teenagers drops out of school.

James S. Catterall, an economist at the University of California at Los Angeles, estimates that as a result of this dropout rate, the economy loses $228 billion in lifetime earnings for each class of students

passing through the nation's schools and $68 billion in tax revenues for all levels of government.

At the meeting on dropouts, about 225 business, education, and community leaders considered dropout-prevention tactics contained in a "working outline" prepared by a special task force of the Boston Compact and presented by the superintendent of schools, Laval S. Wilson.

The draft, titled "Dropout Prevention and Re-Entry Plan," suggests reducing incentives for students to drop out. "Work permits might be linked with continuing school attendance," the outline states.

But it also proposes more punitive measures affecting both students and their families. "When students apply for drivers' licenses or their parents apply for a social service like [Aid to Families with Dependent Children], the school status of teenagers should be monitored," the outline argues.

"What the superintendent wanted to ask is how important is it to us that kids stay in school," Mr. Schwartz said. "Are we prepared to look at some of the possible levers we have available and apply some pressure?"

The underlying question, Mr. Schwartz added, is "how do you create a consistent set of measures that say to kids and their families, 'You may have the legal right to drop out of school at the age of 16, but we want to say to you in the strongest possible terms that we need you to stay in school'? We can no longer afford to lose this number of kids, both in human and economic terms."

But the leaders attending the meeting were unwilling to endorse the more punitive measures suggested in the outline, Mr. Schwartz said.

"There was unanimous resistance to these measures and skepticism about whether they would in fact prove to be effective," he said. "The participants favored positive incentives, carrots rather than sticks."

In a memorandum attached to the outline, Mr. Wilson said he had asked the task force "to develop a draft plan that would highlight not only what the schools can and must do to reduce the dropout rate, but what other key institutions and organizations can do as well."

He said he was presenting the draft to "stimulate discussion and constructive criticism from school and community leaders." A final plan is expected later in the year.

The goal of the task force, as stated in the outline, is to reduce by one-half, from 3,000 to 1,500, the number of students who drop out annually and to double the number of dropouts who return to regular or alternative education. Currently, about 500 return each year.

The draft also recommends these strategies:

- Training teachers to be more effective with academically deficient students.

- Opening a full-time evening high school for teen-agers who must care for children or ill family members, or work to support their families.

- Awarding additional resources to schools that reduce dropout rates.

- Establishing school health centers.

- Providing summer remediation and orientation programs to smooth students' transition from elementary to middle school and from middle to high school.

- Placing community social workers in schools employing too few guidance counselors.

- Sending a letter to parents of middle-school students describing the success current school-system graduates experience in college and the labor market.

Of the 6,136 students who entered Boston high schools as 9th graders in 1981, 43 percent—or 2,640 students—dropped out; 42 percent—or 2,595 students—graduated either last June, finished their studies during the summer, or will finish at the end of this year, according to the dropout report.

Yohel Camayd-Freixas, director of the district's office of research and development and author of the report, said the "cohort dropout rate"—the rate for a class entering high school together—is rising. He noted that the cohort dropout rate for the class that graduated in 1982 was 36 percent, 7 percentage points below the rate of last year's graduating class.

The report cites "increased promotional standards and curricular demands in the face of insufficient supports for 'at-risk' students" and Boston's growing poverty rate as probable causes for the increase.

"When you up the ante with the same level of at-risk students, you will up the number of dropouts," Mr. Camayd-Freixas said, unless the level of support is also increased for those students.

Reprinted with permission from Education Week, Volume V, Number 35, 1986.

Declining Academic Performance

One of the major reasons for the reform reports of the late 1970s and early 1980s was the declining academic performance of students as measured by norm-referenced, standardized tests. Scores on the Scholastic Achievement Test (SAT) are quickly pointed to by critics of education as evidence of declining academic performance. The National Commission on Excellence in Education report, issued in 1983, pointed out that SAT scores have declined steadily from 1963 to 1980 and that science achievement test scores of seventeen-year-olds have declined in testings in 1969, 1973, and 1977. The report further indicated that remedial math courses offered by colleges and universities increased 72 percent between 1975 and 1980 (National Commission on Excellence in Education 1983).

Although some reports indicate that test scores for top students have remained relatively constant, the concern is for the majority of students whose scores have declined. Secondary educators must be concerned about declining test scores. Following the Nation at Risk report and other reform reports of the late 1970s and early 1980s, many state departments of education and state legislatures adopted policies to help reduce this academic decline. Whether some of the measures have a positive, long-term effect remains to be seen. At least for now, college entrance examination scores have begun to increase. Scores on the American College Testing (ACT) Program and SAT have risen in the past few years. This, associated with recent increases in Stanford Achievement Test scores, may signify a reversal of the declining academic performance trend that started in the 1960s (Stedman and Kaestle 1985). Educators, however, must still be aware of the past trends and maintain efforts to improve students' scores.

Problems of Adolescence

For many, the adolescent years are marked by turbulence. During this period, generally thought of as the teenage years, individuals must deal with physical, physiological, and emotional changes. These are the years when children mature into young adults. This period "seems to hold the sweetest and most painful experiences" (Stevens-Long and Cobb 1983, p. 12). Educators who teach adolescents must be aware of their needs and problems. Although most individuals pass through adolescence without major problems, some experience traumatic events that significantly affect their lives.

Alcohol and drug abuse. Alcohol and drug abuse used to be thought of as problems for a small, select segment of the adolescent population. Currently, however, abuses of these substances among American youth is an acknowledged fact.

Alcohol abuse is considered by some as America's number one mental health problem (Stevens-Long and Cobb 1983). That adolescents in the United States are drinking too much is becoming an accepted fact. The negative results of alcohol abuse are many, including

- increased likelihood of accidents, especially auto accidents;

- impaired motor functioning;

- relationship with serious and violent crimes;

- eventual physical degeneration. (Stevens-Long and Cobb 1983)

Drug abuse is defined as the use of drugs contrary to medical and legal regulations and/or norms. Professional and popular literature present data supporting the contention that drug abuse exists in all segments of our society, crossing barriers of race, socioeconomic status, age, and geographic location. Of particular interest are estimates of drug use among high-school students ranging as high as 80 percent (Millman 1978).

Some people postulate that drug abuse is correlated with feelings of rejection and isolation (Bronfenbrenner 1972) and peer pressure (Warner and Swisher 1975). Adolescents are highly susceptible to these feelings and are, therefore, prime candidates for drug abuse. The need to belong to a group, to be accepted, is strong for adolescents who are at a turning point in their life. During the adolescent years individuals turn from parents to peers for acceptance and reinforcement. Sometimes the lure of being accepted tempts adolescents to use drugs to be considered an acceptable group member.

Teenage pregnancy. Approximately 1.2 million adolescents get pregnant each year; nearly half of these pregnancies result in live births, with the remaining pregnancies ending in either spontaneous or induced abortions or maternal death (Anastasiow 1983). Teenage pregnancy, therefore, is a large problem in the United States.

In increasing numbers, pregnant adolescents are opting to give birth and keep their children. This often results in young families with low incomes, low socioeconomic status, and low educational attainment (Stevens-Long and Cobb 1983). The future outlook for these families is bleak.

Children born to teenage mothers have been found to be more susceptible to problems than children born from older mothers. For example, in women under age fifteen, the risk for low birth-weight and premature births increases. These factors have been associated with various disabilities later in life. There also is an increased likelihood for "failure-to-thrive infants, emotional disturbance among preschoolers, and lower academic and more frequent grade retention, particularly among males" (Anastasiow 1983, p. 398).

Teenage pregnancy occurs over one million times each year and can result in difficulties for young families and learning and behavior problems for children later in life. Educators need to be cognizant of the problems resulting from teenage pregnancies and understand the needs of students who must deal with an unwanted pregnancy.

HIGHLIGHT

St. Paul Group Seeking Rescue Plan for City's Troubled Teen-Pregnancy Clinics

Austin C. Wehrwein
Special to Education Week

ST. PAUL—A communitywide emergency task force here is working to devise a private-sector rescue plan for the city's pioneering and nationally acclaimed teen-age-pregnancy program.

Threatened by a budget deficit that could total $761,700 by the new fiscal year, the Maternal Infant Care/Adolescent Health Services Project [MIC] faces the closing of at least one of its four school clinics and curtailed operating hours for the remaining three unless it receives swift cash transfusions from some source, officials say.

A day-care center operated at one of the high schools served by the program would also be affected by budget reductions, the officials add.

Now in its 14th year, the MIC has served as a model for a growing number of similar pregnancy-clinic projects across the nation. Its financial crisis—

due primarily, officials say, to cuts in federal funding and rising costs—comes at a time when increasing public attention to the problem of teenage pregnancy has aroused national concern and made school pregnancy-prevention programs the subject of heated debate in some areas.

The project, which operates clinics at four of the city's six high schools, is run by the St. Paul-Ramsey Medical Center, the combined city-county hospital complex, with an annual operating budget of $1.4 million. Its projected deficit is approximately $311,700 for this year and $450,000 for next year.

Ann Ricketts, a project administrator, described the current situation as "very foggy," but said she was "optimistic that with community support services will be maintained."

The newly formed task force, headed by Leonard Wilkening, head of the Wilder Foundation, is expected to urge that MIC be absorbed by a new private, nonprofit, tax-exempt entity. It would be governed by a board with members from the Wilder Foundation and other private-sector organizations, as well as representatives from the medical center, the city, the county, and the school district.

According to members, the task force envisions a flexible, financially stable overseer organization that could attract substantial support from foundations, individuals, and other private sources, including the United Way. Such an entity would contract with the district and the medical center for pregnancy and related services in the school clinics, they say.

Ms. Ricketts cited Kansas City's Adolescent Resources Corporation as one such arrangement already in existence.

The lion's share of MIC's $1.4-million budget has come from the U.S. Health and Human Services Department through a Title V maternal and child-health block grant and Title XX funds from the Adolescent Pregnancy Project.

But such federal funding was eroding even before the Gramm-Rudman cuts, officials say. Now, they add, the program faces deeper federal cuts, with an operating budget that remains dependent on Washington for about half of its expenditures.

Current foundation support amounts to only $66,000, they say, with money from the state accounting for much of the remaining portion of the budget. The St. Paul School District provides no cash, but Ms. Ricketts estimated the value of the district's "space and overhead" contributions at about $40,000 annually.

A political debate is expected if the proposed new board presses the district for more financial support. The issue will be whether the pregnancy-health clinics meet a "health" or an "educational" need—for example, the reduction of the dropout rate. A related issue will be whether the state, the city, or the county should bear the cost along with the district.

Although the evidence is more anecdotal than statistical, MIC officials claim credit for a dramatic reduction in teen-age pregnancies and for a growing sense of responsibility among sexually active male students. Live births at the schools with clinics, they note, fell from 59 per thousand in the 1976–77 school year to 35 per thousand in 1984–85.

Nationally, 50 percent of the teenage girls who have children before they are 18 never finish high school and 30 percent are pregnant again within two years. But within the clinic schools, where social-work counseling goes hand in hand with medical counseling, the dropout rate is 20 percent and the rate of repeat pregnancies is 2 percent.

Besides family planning—and aid for pregnant girls—MIC provides health and "wellness" services, from immunizations to mental-health counseling.

The medical staff hopes to include information about acquired immune-deficiency syndrome in its program, if the budget permits. One side effect of urging students to use contraceptives as a preventive measure against AIDS, one staff member points out, would be a reduction in pregnancies. Education Week. April 23, 1986. Reprinted with permission.

Suicide. Adolescent suicide in the United States is frightening; it is the leading cause of death among fifteen- to twenty-four-year-olds. Even with these high figures, suicide is still considered a rare occurrence for adolescents (Stevens-Long and Cobb 1983). The number is far too high "because promising young lives are destroyed" (Konopka 1983, p. 391).

Although *every* adolescent suicide is unique, some generalizations can be made about what causes adolescent suicides. These include:

1. Adults generally have a "doomsday" outlook.
2. Adolescents have been taught to think, not simply accept trite explanations.
3. Expectations placed on adolescents are very high.
4. Adolescents are not taught how to live with pain.

5. There is a general lack of warmth and friendship in our society.
6. Young people want close family ties, contrary to the myth that they want no part of families.
7. Prejudice continues to exist toward certain groups of people.
8. Child beating is acceptable to some in our society. (Konopka 1983)

If educators are aware that these causes contribute to teenage suicide, they can take steps to help prevent suicide. First, adults must give adolescents some time. Often adolescents simply need to be listened to and considered as "persons." Second, adults need to indicate that they respect the ideas and personalities of adolescents. Third, adults' ideas, values, and opinions need to be shared with adolescents. Finally, adults should stop assuming that the generation gap is an automatic barrier and not be afraid of showing love (Konopka 1983). These actions are not likely to end adolescent suicides; however, if they are taken by parents, teachers, and other significant adults, they may discourage many adolescents from attempting to take their own lives.

SUMMARY

This chapter focused on secondary education in the United States. Although secondary education was a rather late occurrence, it has grown dramatically during the twentieth century. Secondary education in the United States is organized into high schools and either junior high schools or middle schools. Middle schools are a more modern development than junior high schools and are intended to allow educators to consider the unique needs of early adolescence.

The objectives of secondary education have been and will continue to be debated. Should secondary schools attempt to be all things to all children, or should they focus their efforts only on academic tasks? Secondary schools are organized along several different criteria, including curriculum tracks and vertical organization, or graded versus nongraded.

One major section of the chapter dealt with the curriculum found in secondary schools. Most schools have a common curriculum, consisting of English, math, science, and social studies. In addition, specialized courses are available, such as sex education, death education, and education about nuclear war. Extracurricular activities are also offerred at most secondary schools. With vocational education programs also being available to students in most American secondary schools, they can easily be classified as "comprehensive."

The methods used to instruct secondary students were also discussed. These include lecture, discussion, independent study, and individual instruction. Another section of the chapter focused on the school philosophy and policies, especially as they relate to such issues as discipline, appearance codes, expulsion and suspension, and search and seizure.

The final section of the chapter dealt with problems facing secondary schools in the United States, including (1) school dropouts, (2) declining academic performance, and (3) problems experienced by adolescents, such as drug and alcohol abuse.

Secondary education in the United States is widespread. Although it developed later than elementary education, it has become a world standard as a model for educating the masses. Although problems in secondary education in the United States exist today, educators have to assume that solutions will be found. The resolution of such difficulties will call upon the collective wisdom and skill of the professional and the public.

IN THE FIELD

1. Does the district have middle schools or junior high schools, or a combination of both? How long has the current organizational structure been used?

2. Are there stated objectives for the secondary school and secondary education in the district? If so, are these objectives available to students and teachers?

3. What suggests that the high school is a comprehensive high school?

4. What types of curricula are offered at the high school?

5. What are the required courses for graduation? Have these changed recently? If so, why?

6. Do requirements differ for college-prep students and other students? If so, what is the rationale for the differences?

7. Are special topics, such as sex education, death education, and peace education, included in any courses?

8. What is the primary method of instruction used by teachers?

9. What is the school's policy on discipline, dress codes, and suspension and expulsion?

10. What steps are taken to prevent dropouts?

11. Are there any programs to address adolescent problems such as pregnancy and drug abuse? If so, what is their nature?

12. Are there requirements for participation in extracurricular activities? If so, what are they and are they considered effective?

REFERENCES

Alvermann, D. E. 1984. Using textbook reading assignments to promote classroom discussion. *The Clearing House 58*(2), 70–72.

Anastasiow, N. J. 1983. Adolescent pregnancy and special education. *Exceptional Children 49*(5), 396–401.

Armstrong, D. G., and T. V. Savage. 1983. *Secondary education: An introduction.* New York: Macmillan Publishing Co.

Banks, J. A. 1981. *Multiethnic education: Theory and practice.* Boston: Allyn and Bacon.

Barth, R. S. 1980. Discipline: If you do that again. *Phi Delta Kappan 61*(6), 398–400.

Berry, G. L. 1979. The multicultural principle: Missing from the Seven Cardinal Principles of 1918 and 1978. *Phi Delta Kappan 60*(10), 745.

Bottoms, G., and P. Copa. 1983. A perspective on vocational education today. *Phi Delta Kappan 64*(5), 348–54.

Boyer, E. L. 1984. Clarifying the mission of the American high school. *Educational Leadership 41*(6), 20–22.

Brickell, E. E., and N. T. Jones. 1983. Making curriculum renewal a reality. *NASSP Bulletin*, 83–86.

Bronfenbrenner, U. 1972. Childhood: The roots of alienation. *National Elementary Principal 52*(2), 22–29.

Clark, B. R. 1985. The high school and the university: What went wrong in America, part I. *Phi Delta Kappan 66*(6), 391–97.

Clark, L. H., and I. S. Starr. 1981. *Secondary and middle school teaching methods.* New York: Macmillan Publishing Co.

Cole, H. P., and E. C. Scott. 1982. Creation-science and scientific research. *Phi Delta Kappan 63*(8), 557–58.

Commager, H. S. 1983. A historian looks at the American high school. *American Journal of Education 91*(4), 531–48.

Cuban, L. 1982. Persistent instruction: The high school classroom, 1900–1980. *Phi Delta Kappan 64*(2), 113–18.

Digest of education statistics 1980. Washington, DC: U.S. Government Printing Office and from Historical Statistics of the United States: From Colonial Times to 1970, Part I. 1975. Washington, DC: U.S. Government Printing Office.

Disciullo, M. 1984. In-school suspension: An alternative to unsupervised out-of-school suspension. *The Clearing House 57*(7), 328–30.

Elam, S. M. 1983. Educators and the nuclear threat. *Phi Delta Kappan 64*(8), 533–38.

Engelhardt, L. 1983. This system called for time out on student discipline problems. *The American School Board Journal*, June, 21–24.

Flygare, T. J. 1985. Texas Supreme Court upholds 'no pass/no play' rule. *Phi Delta Kappan 67*(1), 71.

Frith, G. H., and R. Clark. 1984. Extracurricular activities: Academic incentives or nonessential functions? *The Clearing House 57*(7), 325–27.

Gallup, G. H. 1984. The 16th annual Gallup poll of the public's attitudes toward the public school. *Phi Delta Kappan 66*(1), 23–36.

Gold, S. 1984. What's wrong with telling? A veteran teacher re-examines her classroom style. *The Clearing House 57*(7), 331–32.

Gross, R. E. 1978. Seven new cardinal principles. *Phi Delta Kappan 80*, 291–93.

Hahn, G. E. 1982. Creation-science and education. *Phi Delta Kappan 63*(8), 553–55.

Heitzman, A. J. 1983. Discipline and the use of punishment. *Education 104*(1), 17–22.

Helm, D. J. 1984. To discipline or not to discipline. *The Clearing House 57*(7), 333.

Kenney, A. M., and M. T. Orr. 1984. Sex education: An overview of current programs, policies, and research. *Phi Delta Kappan 65*(7), 491–96.

Konopka, G. 1983. Adolescent suicide. *Exceptional Children 49*(5), 390–94.

Lordon, J. F. 1983. Establishing a climate for school discipline: The total perspective. *NASSP Bulletin 67*(62), 58–60.

MacDowell, M. A., and J. Clow. 1983. Integrating economic concepts into consumer education. *NASSP Bulletin*, 39–45.

Mahan, G., and C. Johnson. 1983. Portrait of a dropout: Dealing with academic, social, and emotional problems. *NASSP Bulletin*, April, 80–83.

Markle, S. 1984. Do-it-yourself science labs. *Instructor XCIII*(6), 46–50.

Maynard, B. 1983. Is your discipline policy part of your discipline problem? *The Executive Educator*, 26–27.

Merrill, A. 1984. Humane discipline is possible. *The Clearing House 57*(9), 392–93.

Michel, T. A., and R. L. Weaver. 1984. Lecturing: Means for improvement. *The Clearing House 57*(9), 389–91.

Millman, R. B. 1978. Drug and alcohol abuse. In B. B. Wolman, Ed., *Handbook of treatment of mental disorders in childhood and adolescence.* Englewood Cliffs, NJ: Prentice-Hall, Inc.

National Center for Education Statistics. 1983. *The condition of education.* Washington, DC: U.S. Government Printing Office.

National Commission on Excellence in Education. 1983. A Nation at risk: The imperative for educational reform. Washington, DC: U.S. Government Printing Office.

Nelson, J. L., and J. U. Michaelis. 1980. *Secondary social studies: Instruction, curriculum, evaluation.* Englewood Cliffs, NJ: Prentice-Hall, Inc.

Nolte, M. C. 1985. Use caution in punishing kids who break the rules. *The American School Board Journal 172*(5), 42.

Polakowski, K. 1984. Some ideas on discipline. *The Clearing House 58*(2), 83–84.

Post, L. M. 1984. Individualizing instruction in the middle school: Modifications and adaptions in curriculum for the mainstreamed student. *The Clearing House 58*(2), 73–76.

Rienzo, B. A. 1981. The status of sex education: An overview and recommendations. *Phi Delta Kappan 63*(3), 192–93.

Ross, V. J. 1983. Find potential dropouts early then help them stay in school. *Executive Educator*, June, 16–17.

Salhoz, E., M. Lord, and D. H. McDonald. 1983. Teaching about nuclear war. *Newsweek*, July 18, 78.

Schall, W. E. 1984. Take math outdoors. *Instructor XCIII*(8), 46–49+.

Sendor, B. 1984. Student drug searches: Can you risk the frisk? *The American School Board Journal*, 171(3), 27+.

Shane, H. G. 1981. A curriculum for the new century. *Phi Delta Kappan 62*(5), 351–56.

Sigda, R. B. 1983. The crisis in science education and the realities of science teaching in the classroom. *Phi Delta Kappan 64*(9), 624–27.

Sizer, T. R. 1983. High school reform: The need for engineering. *Phi Delta Kappan 64*(10), 679–83.

Spillane, R. R., and P. Regnier. 1981. Revitalizing the academic curriculum: The case of the social studies. *Phi Delta Kappan 62*(10), 731–32.

Starr, S. F. 1979. International high schools: Their time has come. *Phi Delta Kappan 60*(10), 743–44.

Stedman, L. C. and C. F. Kaestle. 1985. The test score decline is over: Now what? *Phi Delta Kappan 67*(3), 204–10.

Stefanich, G., and C. Dedrick. 1985. Addressing concerns in science and mathematics education: An alternative view. *The Clearing House 58*(6), 274–77.

Stevens-Long, J., and N. J. Cobb. 1983. *Adolescence and early adulthood.* Palo Alto, CA: Mayfield Publishing Co.

Switzer, T. J. 1981. Reflections on the fate of the "new social studies." *Phi Delta Kappan 62*(10), 729–30.

Tanner, D. 1979. Splitting up the school system: Are comprehensive high schools doomed? *Phi Delta Kappan 61*(2), 92–97.

Thomason, J. and J. Pedersen. 1984. Perfect 10: A discipline alternative. *The Clearing House 57*(8), 353–55.

Wagenaar, T. C. 1981. High school seniors' views of Themselves and their schools: A trend analysis. *Phi Delta Kappan 63*(1), 29–32.

Wagner, H. 1983. Discipline in schools is inseparable from teaching. *Education 103*(4), 390–94.

Warner, R. W., and J. D. Swisher. 1975. Alienation and drug abuse: Synonymous? In H. Thornburg, Ed., *Contemporary adolescence: Readings.* Monterey, CA: Brooks/Cole.

Waterman, L., and R. P. Lipka. 1982. Death education: A responsive curriculum. *Kappa Delta Pi Record 18*(3), 81–84.

Wood, C. L., E. W. Nicholson, and D. G. Findley. 1985. *The secondary school principal: Manager and supervisor.* Boston: Allyn and Bacon.

Chapter 7

VOCATIONAL AND CAREER EDUCATION

OBJECTIVES

After reading this chapter, you will be able to

- define vocational education;
- list the purposes of vocational education;
- describe the history of vocational education;
- discuss the current status of vocational education;
- discuss the effectiveness of vocational education;
- describe the relationship between vocational education and the federal government and business;
- define career education;
- list the objectives of career education;
- describe the components of career education;
- discuss the relationship between career education and vocational education.

OUTLINE

ADVANCE ORGANIZERS
INTRODUCTION
VOCATIONAL EDUCATION
    What is Vocational Education?
    Purposes of Vocational Education
    History of Vocational Education
    Current Status of Vocational Education
    Effectiveness of Vocational Education
        Role of the Federal Government
        in Vocational Education
    Role of Business in Vocational Education
    The Reform Movements
        and Vocational Education

Future of Vocational Education
CAREER EDUCATION
    Objectives of Career Education
    Components of Career Education Programs
    Career Education in Elementary Schools
    Career Education in Secondary Schools
RELATIONSHIP BETWEEN VOCATIONAL
    AND CAREER EDUCATION
SUMMARY
IN THE FIELD
REFERENCES

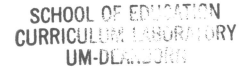

1. What is vocational education?
2. What are some general ideas about vocational education?
3. What are the purposes of vocational education?
4. What federal legislation has had an impact on vocational education?
5. What types of students enroll in vocational education?
6. How effective is vocational education?
7. In what ways does the federal government support vocational education?
8. What is the relationship between business and vocational education?
9. What is career education?
10. What are the objectives of career education?
11. What occurs in career awareness, career exploration, and career preparation?
12. What is the relationship between career education and vocational education?

INTRODUCTION

In addition to the academic curriculum available to students enrolled in public schools in the United States, many schools offer students training referred to as vocational education. All secondary students are not interested in pursuing extensive education or training beyond the twelfth grade. For some students, high-school graduation signals an end to formal, academic education and training. At the approximate age of eighteen years, these students attempt to enter the job market. Unfortunately, without preparation for employment, many of these students will have significant adjustment difficulties.

Two educational models are found in many school districts to facilitate the success of students who terminate their educational experiences upon high-school graduation. Vocational education, which provides specific training to students, and career education, which is an all encompassing K–12 program to prepare students for postschool adjustment, attempt to facilitate postschool adjustment.

VOCATIONAL EDUCATION

Vocational education has been a component in many public schools for several years. Since around World War I, various aspects of vocational education have been in some schools (D'Alonzo 1983). During the past two decades, vocational education has grown significantly (Bottoms and Copa 1983). Marsh and Price (1980) suggest that two of the major reasons for the recent growth in vocational education programs have been the shifting of the economy from an agrarian to an industrialized base and the population shift from rural to urban. Prior to these developments, a large percentage of students lived in rural areas and followed their families into the farming business. Schools were not required to provide specific vocational training, because students did not enter into jobs requiring specific new skills. As a result of the shift of the economy to its current industrialized base, the need for schools to prepare individuals for specific vocations increased. Not only are schools expected to train students in specific skill areas, but they may be severely criticized when students graduate from high school without specific, salable skills.

What is Vocational Education?

Vocational education is probably the least understood area in American education (Bottoms and Copa 1983). Indeed, "the mere mention of vocational education creates varying images and perceptions," (Swanson 1978, p. 87) including:

- Vocational education is only provided in secondary schools (Swanson 1978).

- Vocational education is only on the periphery of the high-school curriculum (Lotto 1985).

- Vocational education only focuses on the needs of low-achieving students.

- Vocational education only attracts students from low socioeconomic classes.

- Vocational education primarily serves the needs of boys.

- Secondary vocational education programs have low status in secondary schools (Lotto 1985).

The aim of vocational education is to prepare students for employment.

Many of these perceptions about vocational education are inaccurate and add to the confusion about vocational education, making it more difficult for schools to provide comprehensive vocational programs.

Vocational education has been defined by many different groups and individuals in many different ways. The definition used by the federal government states that vocational education

> means organized education programs which are directly related to the preparation of individuals for paid or unpaid employment, or for additional preparation for a career requiring other than a baccalaureate or advanced degree; and, for purposes of this paragraph, the term "organized education program" means only (a) instruction related to the occupation or occupations for which the students are in training, or instruction necessary for students to benefit from such training, and (b) the acquisition, maintenance, and repair of instructional supplies, teaching aids, and equipment, and the term "vocational education" does not mean the construction, acquisition, or initial equipment of buildings, or the acquisition or rental of land. (Title 45, U.S. Code of Federal Regulations 1979, p. 166)

Basically, the definition means training directly related to the preparation of students for employment or other training related to employment. The distinction is made between preparation for occupations that do not require a university degree and those that do.

Purposes of Vocational Education

Vocational education programs have many purposes, including:

1. Providing skills and experiences considered valuable by students.
2. Facilitating the mastery of avocational and vocational skills by students.
3. Providing hands-on learning opportunities.
4. Providing a curriculum that is closely related to everyday life needs.
5. Possibly providing an alternative for potential school dropouts. (Lotto 1985)

In addition to these, Weisberg (1983) indicates that supporters of vocational education programs believe that vocational education (1) can help integrate children from the lower economic sector, (2) can help with national economic problems, (3) can provide an appropriate curriculum for the approximately half of the student body not suited for a more academic program, and (4) can help with the broader problems posed by youth, such as crime, gangs, and teenage pregnancy.

Vocational education should incorporate multicultural components. Students in vocational education programs need to be aware that race, cultural background, sex, handicapping conditions, and socioeconomic status should have no bearing on vocational opportunities. The idea that all students, within their physical and intellectual limitations, can enter any vocational area should be stressed.

History of Vocational Education

The history of vocational education in the United States is related to federal involvement in public education. Federal legislation affecting vocational education can be divided into several distinct periods. Prior to 1900, the federal government had limited involvement in education, and therefore passed little legislation related to public education programs. Between 1900 and 1960, the involvement grew substantially, and since 1960 federal involvement has been at an all-time high (Calhoun and Finch 1982).

In the first period of federal involvement, two legislative acts affected vocational education. The first, the Morrill Act of 1862, provided land grants to states for the establishment of agricultural and mechanical colleges. The second Morrill Act, passed in 1890, added to the first by providing funds to support instruction in the agricultural and mechanical colleges (Calhoun and Finch 1982).

Between 1900 and 1960, a great deal of federal legislation was implemented that affected vocational education. The key act was the Smith-Hughes Act of 1917, which provided money to states to support vocational education. Vocational education was affected in two major ways by this legislation: money was provided to states to encourage vocational education programs and standards were established for vocational education. Other acts, including the George-Reed Act of 1929, the George-Ellzey Act of 1934, the George-Dean Act of 1936, and the George-Barden Act of 1946, authorized funds for home economics and agricultural education, distributive education, and trade industry. "These legislative acts illustrate an intermediate state of legislation as the federal government moved toward a total commitment to assisting the states in the development of vocational education" (Calhoun and Finch 1982, p. 35).

Legislation passed since 1960 made the final commitment of the federal government to vocational education. Key legislation included the Vocational Education Act of 1963, Vocational Education Amendments of 1968, and the Education Amendments of 1976 (see table 7–1).

Current Status of Vocational Education

Vocational education is an option available to students in many American secondary schools.

Students. In 1982, 27 percent of all high-school seniors indicated that they were enrolled in a vocational education program, and 75 percent of all 1982 high-school

---

TABLE 7–1   Recent Federal Legislation Affecting Vocational Education

Legislation	Description
Vocational Education Act 1963	• Increased federal support for vocational education • Funds made available for residential vocational schools, vocational work-study programs, and research, demonstration, and training programs
Vocational Education Amendments 1968	• Changed formula for funding programs • Established a National Advisory Council on Vocational Education • Expanded services to meet needs of disadvantaged students • Established procedures to collect and disseminate information
Education Amendments 1976	• Extended and revised the Vocational Education Act of 1963 and the Vocational Education Amendments of 1968 • Granted more flexibility in the use of vocational education funds

Source: Calhoun and Finch, 1982.

graduates completed at least one vocational course (National Center for Education Statistics 1984). In the 1978–79 school year, approximately nineteen million individuals were enrolled in vocational education programs in the United States. More than twelve million, or approximately 63 percent of these students, were enrolled in vocational education programs in public secondary schools. The remaining students were in programs provided by private schools and other organizations (National Center for Education Statistics 1983) (see table 7–2).

Approximately 24.5 percent of 1980 high-school seniors were enrolled in a total vocational education program in the spring of 1980 (National Center for Education Statistics 1983). These students varied in gender, racial/ethnic, background, ability, and socioeconomic status (see table 7–3).

Additional data on students enrolled in vocational education programs indicate that more than four hundred thousand are disabled, most being enrolled in mainstream vocational programs. While the mean achievement scores of vocational education students in reading and math are significantly lower than students enrolled in college-preparatory courses, "the scores of 65 percent of the students in vocational programs are in the same range as the scores of their college-bound counterparts" (Bottoms and Copa 1983, p. 349). The composite of vocational education students would therefore be the following:

- equal chance of being male or female

- greater chance of being from a minority culture

- likely possess low to middle academic achievement

- likely from low to middle socioeconomic families

Location of vocational programs. Currently more than nineteen thousand public institutions in the United States offer some form of vocational education opportunities, including both secondary and postsecondary public schools (see table 7–4).

Types of vocational programs. In the past, vocational education programs primarily consisted of agriculture, wood shop, and possibly industrial arts. Schools currently offer a wide variety of program options in vocational education, classified as general or occupational specific. General vocational education programs provide a founda-

TABLE 7–2 Number of Students Enrolled in Vocational Education

Program	Number of Students	Percentage
Public Secondary Schools	12,513,000	65%
Private Secondary Schools	22,000	1%
Public Noncollegiate Postsecondary	741,000	4%
Private Noncollegiate Postsecondary	989,000	5%
2-Year Institution of Higher Ed.	4,423,000	23%
4-Year Institution of Higher Ed.	309,000	2%
Totals	19,339,000	100%

Source: National Center for Education Statistics, 1983.

TABLE 7–3   Variables of Students Enrolled in Vocational Education
Programs, Spring 1980

Variable	Percentage
Sex	
Male	47%
Female	53%
Racial/Ethnic	
White non-Hispanic	17%
Black non-Hispanic	24%
Hispanic	23%
American Indian/Alaskan	
Native	22%
Asian or Pacific Islander	14%
Ability Level	
Low	54%
Middle	36%
High	10%
Socioeconomic Status	
Low	50%
Middle	35%
High	15%

Source: National Center for Education Statistics, 1983.

tion for career decisions, skills for an occupational area, and generic skills useful in work and daily living, while occupational-specific programs train students for a specific job (Bottoms and Copa 1983). Examples of occupational-specific courses include agriculture, computer programming, masonry, machine shop, automobile mechanics, and welding. Many students were enrolled in these and other occupational-specific courses in the spring of 1980 (see table 7–5).

The number of students enrolled in various occupational-specific training programs reflects the needs of the work force. After analyzing enrollment figures for 1965 and 1980, Bottoms and Copa (1983) concluded that enrollments in the areas of health occupations, occupational home economics, office occupations, technical, and trade and industry had increased substantially while enrollments in agriculture had remained relatively constant. Overall approximately 7.3 million students were enrolled in occupational-specific programs (Weisberg 1983).

Vocational education programs are popular with both students and parents. The 1984 Gallup Poll of the Public's Attitudes Toward the Public Schools revealed that 83 percent of those responding thought that students not planning on attending college should enroll in vocational education courses (Gallup 1984). Vocational education, therefore, is filling a major role in public secondary education and should continue to be an integral part of secondary education in the future.

Effectiveness of Vocational Education

Vocational education is a popular option for many secondary education students. However, the fact that programs are popular with students is not sufficient justifica-

TABLE 7–4   Types of Institutions Offering Vocational Education

Institutional Type	Characteristics	Number
General high school	Usually offers two or three vocational courses, typically in the areas of business and office, agriculture, industrial arts, consumer and homemaking	10,851
Comprehensive high school	A general school offering programs in at least six different vocational subjects (although the majority of students are not enrolled in vocational education programs)	4,878
Vocational high school	A specialized secondary school offering a *full-time* program that combines academic and vocational subjects; all or a majority of the students are enrolled in vocational education programs	225
Area vocational center, secondary	A shared-time facility that provides *only* vocational education instruction to students from throughout a school system or region; these students study academic courses in their regular high schools or in other institutions	1,395
Area vocational school, postsecondary	A *non-degree-granting* institution (or an institution offering a degree that is not recognized by the regional accrediting commission for higher education), which offers instruction only in vocational and technical subjects and whose educational programs are terminal	504
Community college	A two-year, postsecondary, *degree-granting* institution (that may also award certificates and licenses), which offers a comprehensive instructional program in both general and vocational/technical education and a transfer program to institutions of higher education	720
Technical institution	A two-year, postsecondary, *degree-granting* institution, which offers instruction primarily in vocational and technical programs that are focused on immediate job placement	162
Specialized postsecondary school	Usually offers specialized preparation in one occupational area	308
Four-year institution offering two-year programs	A four-year college or university offering two-year degree programs in vocational or technical areas	185
Skill center	Usually a separate institution that specializes in providing vocational education to economically disadvantaged students	70
Total		19,298

Reprinted with permission. G. Bottoms, and P. Copa. 1983. A perspective on vocational education today. Phi Delta Kappan *64(5), 350.*

tion for schools to continue offering vocational education programs. Empirical data are needed to justify expenditures for vocational education. Many of the studies that have attempted to determine the effectiveness of vocational education have been done poorly, with major research methodological problems. Still, the results of many of these studies have proved helpful in trying to determine the effectiveness of vocational education (Weisberg 1983).

Measuring the effectiveness of vocational education is difficult, which probably accounts for the somewhat contradictory research results. In summarizing research to determine the effectiveness of vocational education, Swanson (1978) concluded that graduates from secondary vocational education programs fared better than those from academic programs in several areas, including the time it takes to get a job and accumulated earnings over an eleven-year period following graduation. Bottoms and

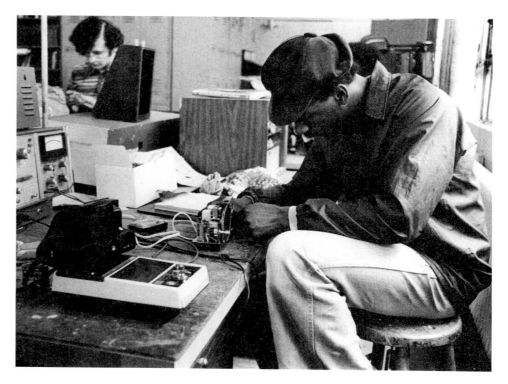

Schools currently offer vocational training in a wide variety of areas such as electronics.

Copa (1983) cited studies that indicated vocational education graduates had a lower unemployment rate than others in their age group, found related employment, and reaped long-term benefits in the job market. On the negative side, Weisberg (1983) reports data that suggest that (1) only limited evidence indicates that vocational education prevents dropouts, (2) vocational education graduates perform no better in the labor market than others, and (3) vocational programs are more related to popularity than labor-market needs.

Data on graduates from vocational programs also present an unclear picture of the effectiveness of vocational education (see table 7–6). For example, the average wage earned by a 1972 high-school graduate from a vocational program was $5.55 per hour compared with $5.50 per hour for graduates from academic programs and $5.29 per hour for graduates from general programs (National Center for Education Statistics 1983).

Results of research are therefore inconclusive; however, vocational education does serve many purposes, and does so very well. Although many believe that vocational education cannot keep up with the changing needs of the labor market, many of the growth jobs of the 1980s and 1990s are those that require more general than specific abilities. Therefore, general vocational education programs would provide adequate training for individuals to enter into these positions (Weisberg 1983). A study conducted by Wilms (1984) determined that 63 percent of the employers participating in the study rated good work habits and positive attitudes as critical

TABLE 7-5   High School Seniors Who Took Vocational Courses Preparing Them for Beginning Job [1], by Sex and Region: Spring 1980

Subject Area				Region [2]			
	Total	Male	Female	Northeast	South	North Central	West
				Percent of Seniors			
Total	87.4	85.3	89.6	84.0	88.0	88.2	89.2
Agriculture	8.3	12.2	4.7	4.1	10.6	9.2	9.3
Auto mechanics	11.2	21.4	1.9	8.1	7.8	14.2	17.4
Commercial arts	16.2	17.6	15.0	14.8	13.8	17.1	21.6
Computer programming operations	12.9	13.7	12.2	15.7	10.2	13.7	12.0
Carpentry	14.8	28.2	2.5	13.3	12.2	17.5	17.8
Electrical	8.6	17.1	.9	7.6	7.6	11.1	8.6
Masonry	3.0	6.0	.2	2.5	3.9	3.2	2.1
Plumbing	2.3	4.6	.2	1.9	2.5	2.8	2.0
Cosmetology/barbering	2.6	.7	4.3	2.4	2.9	2.0	3.5
Drafting	17.4	31.0	4.9	16.7	13.7	20.6	19.5
Electronics	7.8	15.0	1.2	6.8	6.2	9.4	9.8
Home economics, including dietetics and child care	31.9	14.9	47.4	23.0	34.9	34.0	35.0
Machine shop	13.3	25.5	2.1	11.1	11.4	16.9	15.0
Medical dental assisting	4.2	2.3	5.9	3.7	4.1	4.8	4.1
Practical nursing	4.2	1.3	6.9	3.7	4.1	4.6	4.2
Quantity foods occupations	11.6	7.7	15.2	7.7	12.4	13.1	13.4
Sales/merchandising	19.2	16.0	22.1	15.9	19.2	21.0	20.3
Secretarial office work	51.5	29.4	71.4	46.8	53.4	50.4	53.7
Welding	12.1	23.9	1.3	7.8	11.7	15.4	14.0
Other	27.7	31.4	24.4	25.8	25.8	28.8	32.8
Sample size	24,816	11,815	13,001	5,396	8,891	7,812	4,927

[1]   On the student survey, high school seniors were asked to respond to the question, "Have you taken any high school courses in the following areas which have equipped you for a beginning job in that area?" More than one area could be checked.
[2]   The regions correspond to the U.S. Bureau of the Census definitions. See the Definitions of Selected Terms in the Appendix.
Source: National Center for Educational Statistics, 1983.

skills, 23 percent indicated that technical job skills were important, and 14 percent thought that employees should have good linguistic and computational abilities. General work skills, therefore, are judged by employers as critically important for employees, and these skills can easily be incorporated into general vocational education programs.

Mertens (1983) analyzed several studies of the effectiveness of vocational education and concluded the following:

- Short-term effects on earnings are positive for females from business and office programs and negligible for males. Long-term effects are positive for male graduates in the areas of marketing and trade and industry programs.

- Females in trade and industry programs receive higher earnings than those in more traditional, sex-stereotyped roles.

TABLE 7–6 Earnings of and Hours Worked by 1972 High School Graduates in Initial Job
After Completing Formal Schooling, by Sex and High School Program:
1972 to 1979

| | Earnings [1] Weeks, and Hours Worked | | | | |
Program and Sex	Average Hours Worked Per Week	Average Weeks Worked Per Year	Average Hourly Wage	Average Yearly Earnings [2]	Sample Size
All programs:					
Total	38.9	44.7	$ 5.44	$11,085	22,458
Male	41.4	46.2	6.01	12,906	11,139
Female	36.4	43.2	4.88	9,087	11,276
Academic:					
Total	38.9	44.8	5.50	11,311	9,343
Male	41.2	46.1	6.04	13,021	4,766
Female	36.4	43.4	4.90	9,244	4,565
General:					
Total	39.1	44.6	5.29	10,942	7,490
Male	41.7	46.3	5.89	12,786	3,566
Female	36.7	43.1	4.74	9,096	3,901
Vocational:					
Total	38.7	44.5	5.55	10,864	5,625
Male	41.3	45.9	6.09	12,836	2,807
Female	36.2	43.0	5.04	8,812	2,810

[1] *Earnings and hourly wages have been adjusted to 1980 dollars.*
[2] *Average yearly earnings are derived using raw data and would only approximate yearly earnings calculated by multiplying average hours by weeks worked by hourly wage.*
NOTE: Precision of the estimates may be calculated using the sample size and following procedures provided in the Data Sources in the Appendix.
SOURCE: U.S. Department of Education. National Center for Education Statistics, National Longitudinal Study of the High School Class of 1972. First through Fourth Followups: 1972 to 1979, unpublished tabulations (October 1982).

- Students who graduated from vocational programs are less likely to attend college than those from the general curriculum.

The major conclusion arrived at by Mertens following the analyses was that "vocational education is good for some of the people some of the time" (Mertens 1983, p. 361).

One crucial area to consider when determining the effectiveness of vocational education programs is whether employers prefer individuals from a vocational or academic background. In the study conducted by Wilms (1984), 49 percent of the participants indicated that they had no preference, 34 percent preferred individuals who had been enrolled in an academic program, and only 17 percent preferred individuals with a vocational background. These results indicate that employers do not consider vocational education as very important to the potential performance of employees. Therefore, while some studies suggest the unequivocable effectiveness of vocational education programs, others reveal that vocational program graduates do not have an advantage over graduates from other secondary programs, and employers may not even prefer to hire them over graduates from academic programs.

Role of the Federal Government in Vocational Education

Vocational education is supported by tax monies from local, state, and federal coffers. The majority of the support comes from the local level, even though vocational education is commonly thought of as a federal program (Swanson 1978). Vocational programs offered at the secondary level receive their federal support from the Vocational Education Act, which provides approximately $700 million. Postsecondary programs, on the contrary, receive benefits from many other federal programs, including Basic Educational Opportunity Grants, Guaranteed Student Loans, and veteran's benefits (Weisberg 1983). Federal programs such as the Appalachian Regional Development, the Public Works and Economic Development Acts of 1965, the Tennessee Valley Authority, and the Rural Development Act also contribute greatly to vocational education (Bottoms and Copa 1983).

Financial support, however, is only one way the federal government participates in vocational education. It also helps states provide vocational education by "collecting and distributing vital data, conducting useful research, identifying exemplary programs, disseminating information, or offering national seminars that will bring useful, practical new approaches to the attention of our state and local leaders" (Worthington 1984, p. 22). The role of the federal government, therefore, is complex. The executive branch provides the leadership, the legislative branch passes legislation, and the judicial branch rules on cases dealing with vocational education.

Role of Business in Vocational Education

Business has been involved in general education for many years. During the first half of the twentieth century, business was involved in education through business leaders sitting on local boards of education and schools being managed using business models. However, in the 1960s and 1970s, the role of business changed. Issues such as due process, equal educational opportunity, and teacher activism shifted policy decisions away from the previous focus of preparing students for a productive work life. Recently, business has begun to get involved in education once again. Reasons for this renewed involvement include:

- Fewer students will enter the labor market in the future.

- The number of women in the labor market will not increase in the future as quickly as in the past.

- Workers' skills are becoming increasingly complex.

- Improving worker productivity is becoming a key issue.

- Schools have the best opportunity to train individuals on issues related to work. (Timpane 1984)

Business is also doing a great deal of its own training. In one study investigating vocational education and employers, Wilms (1984) found that approximately two-thirds of the employers in the survey did most of their own training, while only 7 percent did no training. Businesses are conducting their own training because (1) the training provided by the business is more relevant to actual job requirements than training conducted by external groups; (2) skills learned can be put to immediate use;

and (3) the training is conducted by individuals within the business who have a thorough knowledge of the job requirements (McQuigg 1980).

Schools need to do a better job of getting involved with businesses in providing vocational education. To do this, schools must open communication with businesses and encourage businesses to get more involved in the schools (Timpane 1984). School personnel must convince businesses that collaboration can be mutually helpful.

If vocational education is to continue to have the success it has had in the past, schools must focus more on the needs of business and industry (Gleason and Harvey 1984). An excellent method is for schools and businesses to develop on-site work opportunities. This approach, called field-based learning, "refers to educational experiences that students have in the workplace or in community service" (Lotto 1985, p. 572). One example where schools and businesses developed on-site work opportunities was in Delaware. The programs, called the Jobs for Delaware Graduates (JDG), operated in eight schools and had 727 seniors participating during the first year. More than 90 percent of the students participating in the program were placed in nearly five thousand jobs that local businesses made available (Wichess 1984).

Besides developing on-site training programs, vocational education programs must have appropriate instructional materials that correspond to industry needs and utilize instructors who understand the needs of local industries (Gleason and Harvey 1984). Educators should also keep in mind the needs of small businesses and industries, not only large employers (Wilms 1984). Small businesses provide many opportunities for on-site training and postschool job placements for students.

HIGHLIGHT

Vo-Tech Meets Demand for Skilled Training

SPRINGDALE—With the increasing demand for more highly-specialized training facilities and a surging emphasis on computer knowledge, vocational institutions are being looked on to do more for local industries, and changes implemented at Northwest Vocational-Technical School in Springdale during the last year are allowing it to do just that.

Not only has the school expanded the curriculum and added one course at the suggestion of local businessmen, but an industry coordination program has been developed in which the school works with local industries to implement new training programs and upgrade existing ones.

Director Jim Taylor says the industry coordination program is "one of the better things we've ever done." The program is headed by Bob Sonner, who became the school's first industry coordinator

in August. Sonner works directly with industry heads in Benton, Madison and Washington counties to develop specialized in-house training programs which fit their needs. In many cases the training programs actually take place at the school. In other instances, Sonner works with representatives to improve existing programs.

Since he began duties, Sonner has completed in-house training programs at Delco Manufacturing in Siloam Springs and is currently working on training programs with Franklin Electric in Siloam Springs and the Crane Company and Union Carbide of Rogers. In addition, Sonner is working with Campbell Soup of Fayetteville, and plans to develop a training program for Superior Industries International, a company which supplies aluminum road wheels to automobile manufacturers. Superior Industries is slated to open in Fayetteville's industrial center in July or August.

Taylor said the program allows the school to work more closely with local businesses and in turn could help the chances for graduate placement.

The industry coordination program, though, isn't the only specially-tailored program to begin during the past year at Northwest Vo-Tech. At the request of several Fayetteville-Springdale retailers, a checker/cashier-training program was added to the curriculum. David Bibb, assistant director of finance with the school, said the response to the checker program was excellent. He said it was the result of a number of requests from retailers who wanted entry-level checkers with better checking skills. According to Taylor, the checker and industry coordination programs are a good example of the school's growing commitment to spread the word about its services and its willingness to try new projects which can be of immediate benefit to local employers.

At the same time, the school has expanded several programs with the addition of a new wing. The $378,000 construction project, completed in July, added about 9,000 square feet of space for nursing, drafting and industrial electronics courses which made room for about 60 more students in the three programs.

The donation in February of about $800,000 worth of computer equipment from Sperry Inc. will allow for the beginning of a computer-aided drafting program which is slated to begin in August.
Published by Northwest Arkansas Times. April 27, 1986.

The Reform Movements and Vocational Education

Chapter one described in detail the reform movements in education that began sweeping the country in the early 1980s. Many vocational education supporters have become somewhat concerned about some trends in these reforms as they are primarily designed to strengthen the academic component of education. This brings out critical questions related to vocational education: how much, what kind, and when?

In response to the many reports on the status of education that were published in the late 1970s and early 1980s, states are beginning to implement wide-ranging reforms. Among them are (1) increased graduation requirements, (2) lengthened school year, (3) lengthened school days, (4) increased required academic courses, and (5) reduced opportunities for enrolling in elective courses. Leaders in some states feel that these types of actions will lead to "an increased student dropout rate and reduced vocational education enrollments," and "students will find it increasingly difficult to fulfill graduation requirements and take a program of vocational education" (Taylor 1984, p. 28).

Requiring more coursework in certain academic subjects may not be a proper solution for some students. To underline this point of view, the National Commission on Secondary Vocational Education, which was appointed by the National Center for Research in Vocational Education at Ohio State University, issued a report titled *The Unfinished Agenda*. The report calls for a balanced curriculum for secondary students, including academic and vocational coursework and supports an even stronger role for vocational education than is currently found (Lotto 1985).

Future of Vocational Education

Vocational education is a popular program option for many students. It goes well beyond its original purposes, especially the focus of simply preparing students for a particular vocation. Although some educators question the role of vocational education in American secondary education, it will likely remain a strong aspect of secondary schools. The reform reports issued in the late 1970s and early 1980s could negatively affect vocational education programs. However, once education and government leaders see the probable negative effects of some of the reforms, vocational education will likely regain its status in secondary education.

For vocational education to remain a strong component of public secondary education in the future, some changes need to be made. These include

- offering more field-based training options;

- responding more to the needs of industry and business;

- ensuring continued and increased support from local, state, and federal sources;

- providing more realistic job training to students.

CAREER EDUCATION

Career education is a concept, or a philosophy, designed to modify existing curricula at both the elementary and secondary level (Marsh and Price 1980). Career education does not require extra teachers, additional courses, expensive materials, or sophisticated equipment; it can be infused into the existing curricula by dedicated, knowledgeable teachers.

Many professionals have defined career education. While not all definitions concur on every aspect, most are similar to the following:

> Career education is the total effort of public education and the community to help all individuals become familiar with the values of a work-oriented society, to integrate these values into their personal value systems, and to implement these values into their lives in such a way that work becomes possible, meaningful, and satisfying to each individual. (Mangum, Becker, Coombs, and Marshall 1975, p. 8)

Career education ideally begins early in the elementary school and continues throughout the public school experience (Cullinan, Epstein, and Lloyd 1983).

Career education was formally introduced in 1971 by former United States Commissioner of Education Sidney Marland. Since that time it has been completely accepted by many, rejected by others, and received by some with a wait-and-see attitude (Brolin and D'Alonzo 1979). As a result career education has been implemented in many different ways by different groups, creating a hodgepodge of career education programs.

A great deal of confusion exists concerning career education. The following is presented in an attempt to capsulize some of the concepts included in career education:

- Goals and objectives of career education do not conflict with those of academic classes.

- Career education is not a separate class.

- Career education is incorporated in each academic discipline.

- Career education is not a narrow concept, antihumanistic, antiliberal, or anti-intellectual.

- Career education includes a focus on values, attitudes, knowledge, and skills related to lifelong careers.
- Everything required for successful careers is included in career education, including communication skills, good physical and mental health, human relations skills, motivation to achieve in work, and knowledge of the economy.
- Career education is not limited to school years; it is lifelong.
- Persons other than school personnel, such as family members, are involved in career education. (Mangum et al. 1975)

Career education, therefore, is not a simplistic, one-shot, one-course approach that is intent on preparing students for a particular job. It is broad, complex, and lifelong. When properly implemented, career education should greatly facilitate vocational adaptability.

Objectives of Career Education

While an overall goal of career education would be to better enable individuals to experience successful employment, there are many other objectives. In 1972, shortly after the concept was introduced at the federal level by Marland, Duane Mattheis, then deputy commissioner for school systems in the Office of Education, suggested the following objectives for career education:

1. Provide students with a more unified curriculum with career relevance.
2. Provide students beginning in elementary school with knowledge concerning career options.
3. Provide students with nonacademic career options without the traditional stigma attached to such options.
4. Provide comprehensive, flexible career preparation programs.
5. Provide opportunities for greater involvement by employers in school programs.
6. Provide students with career counseling that emphasizes realistic career options.
7. Provide opportunities for reentry into the system for those who have left the system.
8. Provide graduating students with necessary skills to either enter into a vocation or additional training.
9. Train students to be critics of the vocational system.
10. Provide opportunities for students to have input into the career education system.
11. Equalize credits provided for college preparatory courses and vocational courses. (Marland 1974)

The objectives of career education could not be reached with a simplistic approach. One course on careers, a work-study program, or a vocational education program alone would not achieve these objectives. A comprehensive career education program that begins in the elementary grades and continues beyond high school is required to meet program objectives.

Components of Career Education Programs

Phelps and Lutz (1978) describe a comprehensive career education program as consisting of three phases: (1) career awareness, (2) career exploration, and (3) career preparation. Phase I, career awareness, attempts to make students aware of the many

Career preparation is the final phase of a comprehensive career education program.

vocational opportunities available and should begin in the elementary grades. A logical place to begin such a program is with the careers of parents of students. Following an examination of parents' careers, Gillet (1980) suggests an exploration of workers who come into the home, such as plumbers; workers in the school environment, such as teachers and cafeteria workers; and workers in the immediate community and beyond. Stories, pictures, role playing, and field trips are just a few of the many different ways career awareness can occur.

Career exploration, Phase II, usually occurs in junior high or middle school and enables students to explore various vocations with hands-on experiences. Several programs have been developed to provide career exploration. These include American Industry, The World of Manufacturing, and Project Feast (Phelps and Lutz 1978). While these programs have been extensively used, teachers can develop their own career exploration programs that might have more local relevance, depending on the type of industry and other vocational opportunities available in the community.

The career exploration phase of the curriculum includes four basic components (see table 7–7).

Phase III, the final phase of a comprehensive career education program, is career preparation. This phase may occur in a postsecondary education setting, an industry,

---

TABLE 7–7   Components of Career Exploration

Component	Activities
1. Career education-educational system relationship	Development in academic areas, such as language and communication, math, science, etc.
2. Prevocational	Industrial arts, home economics, general business, fine arts
3. Vocational education and community relationship	Work experiences, such as Junior Achievement, simulated work experiences, observation of various workers
4. Career education and community relationship	Community youth activities, such as scouting, church groups, part-time employment

Source: Phelps, L. A., and R. Lutz. Career exploration and preparation for the special needs learner. *Boston: Allyn and Bacon, 1977.*

a vocational-technical school, a high school, or the military, to name a few. The type of career preparation activities is directly related to the target career. If an individual wants to become a physician, extensive formal, academic training beyond high school would be required. On the other hand, if a specific factory job were the career target, two weeks of training provided by the company might be the only post–high school career preparation required. The career preparation phase, therefore, is designed to provide the necessary training, formal and/or informal, vocational and/or academic, extensive or minimal, to prepare an individual to perform a specific job.

Too often public school vocational programs only focus on career preparation. High-school students may find that at the tenth grade level they have to decide (1) whether to go into the vocational track, general track, or academic track, and (2) which specific area of vocational training they wish. Options available for students are extremely limited. Minimal vocational training options, coupled with a lack of career awareness and career exploration, often lead to adults who are not vocationally satisfied and who are working at their jobs simply because it was the best job available at the time. Comprehensive career education programs could alleviate much of this discontent.

Career Education in Elementary Schools

Career education programs should begin early in the school years, preferably in the elementary school. Career education in the elementary school is not deciding on a career; it does not address career decision making in any way. The goal of career education at the elementary level is career awareness (Marland 1974).

At the elementary level career education can be infused into most of the existing curriculum. Since reading is a major emphasis area in elementary classrooms, teachers could easily include readings on various careers. In math, careers that use math could be discussed and be the subjects of story problems and math application.

One method frequently used in career awareness activities is the use of occupational clusters, or careers that are related. The United States Office of Education designated fifteen clusters that can be used in career awareness programs:

- agri-business and natural resources

- business and office

- communication and media

- consumer and homemaking education

- construction

- environments

- fine arts and humanities

- health

- hospitality and recreation

- manufacturing

- marine science

- marketing and distribution

- personal services

- public services

- transportation occupations (Phelps and Lutz 1978)

Teachers might develop units based on various career clusters, use reading programs that are categorized by career clusters, or use the clusters in many other modes of instruction. The concept, regardless of how it is implemented, is to make young students understand the relationships among various vocations as well as learn about specific careers.

Teachers can also develop career awareness using (1) jobs within the classroom, (2) school jobs such as administrative messenger, or (3) establishing a business for the classroom (Gillet 1980). These methods can be used in conjunction with other career education approaches or in isolation. Career clusters infused in the curriculum, special activities to help students understand career groups, and school jobs and businesses can be used simultaneously. With such a broad coverage, students can develop a good understanding of various careers.

Career Education in Secondary Schools

Career education at the secondary level should be a continuation of the program initiated in the elementary school. Of the three phases of comprehensive career education programs, career exploration and career preparation are the two activities that occur at the secondary level.

Career exploration begins after career awareness. This phase is usually found in the junior high or middle school and leads directly into the career preparation phase. As with career awareness, career exploration and preparation include many elements in addition to job selection and training. This emphasizes the fact that career education is designed to develop the total person and takes into consideration that to be successful on the job requires more than simple vocational preparation activities.

RELATIONSHIP BETWEEN VOCATIONAL AND CAREER EDUCATION

The relationship between vocational and career education has been confusing to many people. Vocational education is a part of career education. Career education is more encompassing and more general; vocational education is more specific. A basic difference between the two is that vocational education occurs at the secondary or postsecondary level, and career education can be implemented at any level and is considered lifelong (Phelps 1983). Career education and vocational education do have similarities. Both focus on the employment of individuals, both occur in schools and in the community, and both are major components in many school districts (see figure 7–1).

SUMMARY

This chapter focused on vocational and career education. The first section, on vocational education, described the importance of vocational education to American public education. Vocational education is very misunderstood; some educators and parents think that vocational education is a federal program that is only designed for low-income, low-achieving students. Vocational education has many purposes that go beyond this rather simple misunderstanding of vocational education. These purposes were discussed, along with the history of vocational education, which has been very closely related to federal legislation.

One section in the chapter focused on students enrolled in vocational education programs. Approximately nineteen million individuals are enrolled in vocational pro-

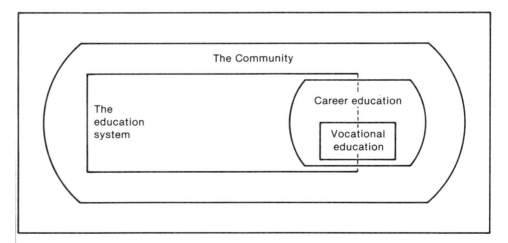

Figure 7-1. *Relationship between career and vocational education. Reprinted by permission. L.A. Phelps. Vocational and career education. In R.M. Smith, J.T. Neisworth, F.M. Hunt, Eds., The exceptional child. New York: McGraw-Hill Book Company, 1983.*

grams, either in public or private secondary schools or a host of other postsecondary programs. Students involved in vocational education have a wide variety of characteristics, ranging from high to low academic achievement, high to low socioeconomic class, and approximately evenly split between males and females. These students are enrolled in one of two types of vocational programs: general or occupational-specific.

Contradictory facts, some supportive of vocational programs and others non-supportive, were brought out. A lack of consensus about the effectiveness of vocational education is probably the result of poor research studies and the difficulty in studying the effects of educational programs. The role of the federal government and private business was discussed. Both of these groups are heavily involved in vocational education programs and probably should remain involved to ensure the continued success of vocational programs.

The final section of the chapter dealt with career education, an all-encompassing educational model geared to better preparing students for the world of work. Unlike vocational education, career education is lifelong, beginning in the elementary grades and extending beyond high school. The three phases of career education—career awareness, career exploration, and career preparation—were discussed. Career education, along with vocational education, could greatly facilitate the positive transition of students from high school to postschool adjustment.

IN THE FIELD

1. Does the school have a vocational education program? If not, is there a special vocational school or program available to the school's students?

2. What vocational education options are available to students?

3. Are students not fully enrolled in a vocational program allowed to take vocational education courses?

4. Does the school have an advisory committee on vocational education?

5. Is career education a component of the school curriculum?

6. Is career education dealt with at the elementary and secondary levels? If so, how?

REFERENCES

Bottoms, G., and P. Copa. 1983. A perspective on vocational education today. *Phi Delta Kappan* 64(5), 348–54.

Brolin, D. E., and B. J. D'Alonzo. 1979. Critical issues in career education for handicapped students. *Exceptional Children* 45(4), 246–53.

Calhoun, C. C., and A. V. Finch. 1982. *Vocational education: concepts, and operations.* Belmont, CA: Wadsworth Publishing Company.

Cullinan, D., M. H. Epstein, and J. W. Lloyd. 1983. *Behavior disorders of children and adolescents.* Englewood Cliffs, NJ: Prentice-Hall, Inc.

D'Alonzo, B. J. 1983. *Educating adolescents with learning and behavior problems.* Rockville, MD: Aspen Systems.

Gallup, G. H. 1984. The 16th annual Gallup poll of the public's attitudes toward the public schools. *Phi Delta Kappan 66*(1), 23–38.

Gillet, P. 1980. Career education in the special elementary education program. *Teaching Exceptional Children 13*(1), 17–21.

Gleason, J. R., and B. M. Harvey. 1984. Excellence begins with curriculum. *VocEd*, May, 42–43.

Lotto, L. S. 1985. The unfinished agenda: Report from the national comission on secondary vocational education. *Phi Delta Kappan 66*(8), 568–73.

McQuigg, B. 1980. The role of education in industry. *Phi Delta Kappan 61*(5), 324–25.

Mangum, G. L., J. W. Becker, G. Coombs, and P. Marshall. 1975. Introduction to career education in the academic classroom. In G. L. Mangum, J. W. Becker, G. Coombs, and P. Marshall, Eds., *Career education in the academic classroom.* Salt Lake City, UT: Olympic Publishing Company.

Marland, S. P., Jr. 1974. *Career education: A proposal for reform.* New York: McGraw-Hill Book Company.

Marsh, G. E., and B. J. Price. 1980. *Methods for teaching the mildly handicapped adolescent.* St. Louis: C. V. Mosby.

Mertens, D. M. 1983. The vocational education graduate in the labor market. *Phi Delta Kappan 64*(5), 360–61.

National Center for Education Statistics. 1983. *The condition of education, 1983 edition.* Washington, DC: U.S. Government Printing Office.

National Center for Education Statistics. 1984. *The condition of education, 1984 edition.* Washington, DC: U.S. Government Printing Office.

Phelps, L. A. 1983. Vocational and career education. In R. M. Smith, J. T. Neisworth, and F. M. Hunt, Eds., *The exceptional child: A functional approach.* New York: McGraw-Hill Book Company.

Phelps, L. A., and R. J. Lutz. 1978. *Career exploration and preparation for the special needs learner.* Boston: Allyn and Bacon.

Swanson, G. I. 1978. Vocational education: Fact and fantasy. *Phi Delta Kappan 60*(2), 87–90.

Taylor, R. E. 1984. An emerging policy for vocational education. *VocEd*, January–February, 27–28.

Timpane, M. 1984. Business has rediscovered the public schools. *Phi Delta Kappan 65*(6), 389–92.

Weisberg, A. 1983. What research has to say about vocational education and the high schools. *Phi Delta Kappan 64*(5), 355–59.

Wichess, S. F. 1984. Jobs for America's graduates: A youth employment program that means business. *The Clearing House 57*(5), 197–200.

Wilms, W. W. 1984. Vocational education and job success: The employer's view. *Phi Delta Kappan 65*(5), 347–50.

Worthington, R. M. 1984. A statement on vocational education. *Vocational Education 59*(4), 22–23.

Chapter 8
SPECIAL EDUCATION

OBJECTIVES

After reading this chapter, you will be able to

- trace the history of treatment and education of handicapped persons to the present;
- outline the major legislative acts that preceded Public Law 94–142;
- describe Public Law 94–142;
- discuss the major litigation cases dealing with special education;
- describe the categorical classification model;
- discuss the benefits of generic classification;
- list the major services used in a traditional service delivery system;
- describe the cascade of service model.

OUTLINE

ADVANCE ORGANIZERS
INTRODUCTION
HISTORY OF TREATMENT
    OF THE HANDICAPPED
    Education and Treatment Prior to 1750
    Education and Training Since 1750
SPECIAL EDUCATION TODAY
    Students Served
    Legislation
    Litigation
MULTICULTURAL SPECIAL EDUCATION
    Multicultural Concerns

Responding to the Multicultural Problem
HANDICAPPED CHILDREN
    Traditional Classification System
    Generic/Noncategorical Model
SPECIAL EDUCATION SERVICES
    Traditional Service Delivery Model
    Current Service Delivery Model
SUMMARY
IN THE FIELD
REFERENCES

ADVANCE ORGANIZERS

1. How were disabled individuals treated prior to 1750?
2. What is the magnitude of special education today?
3. What legislation led to the passage of Public Law 94–142?
4. What are the key components of Public Law 94–142?
5. What court cases are considered landmarks in special education?
6. How did the civil rights movement affect special education?
7. What are the categories used to classify handicapped children using the traditional classification system?
8. What is the definition of "mildly handicapped"?
9. What service options were available using the traditional service delivery system?
10. What options should be available along a continuum of services model?

INTRODUCTION

Special education has been provided for students with disabilities for most of the twentieth century; however, the magnitude of special education has grown dramatically since the 1950s. As a result of legislation and litigation, special education is available to students with disabilities in all public schools in the United States. Disabled children currently receive special education and related services at an unprecedented level. While special education was a small program just a few years ago, it now serves approximately 10.7 percent of the school population (United States Department of Education 1984) and touches all teachers and administrators in a school district. Madeleine Will, assistant secretary for the Office of Special Education and Rehabilitative Services, U.S. Department of Education, noted the recent growth in special education: "The past decade has produced results for students with disabilities that were considered unobtainable and unthinkable only a few years earlier. Little more than a decade ago, many children were left completely out of the nation's school systems" (Will 1984, p. 11).

The impetus of expanded services is the federal government. Federal legislation, funding, and court decisions have brought about increased services for the handicapped. Special education in the 1980s has been shaped a great deal by federal involvement during the 1970s.

Special education used to be limited to educational services provided for handicapped students, primarily mentally retarded students, in a self-contained classroom by a special education teacher. Regular classroom teachers rarely saw these students or their teachers. At present the focus is to provide educational and therapeutic services to all handicapped children in an integrated setting. Children with disabilities are educated with nondisabled children as much of the time as is appropriate. The education of disabled children, therefore, has become a shared responsibility among special education personnel, regular classroom teachers, and school support personnel.

HISTORY OF TREATMENT OF THE HANDICAPPED

Handicapped people have not always been afforded special education and other necessary services. Hundreds of years ago, individuals with disabilities were actually put to death. The treatment and education of disabled individuals has evolved during the past two thousand years to what is currently considered special education, with the most rapid advances in services occurring since the mid-1900s.

Education and Treatment Prior to 1750

Prior to the middle 1700s, the plight of handicapped people was not exceedingly positive. The first written reference to the handicapped appeared in the therapeutic Papyrus of Thebes, an Egyptian papyrus dated 1552 B.C. Other ancient works, including the Bible, Talmud, and Koran, also contained references to the handicapped; however, during this era many handicapped people were forced to beg for survival (Blackhurst and Berdine 1981). In the Greek city states of Sparta and Athens, handicapped individuals were frequently left to die or actually put to death. The philosophy of the time was that individuals unable to take care of themselves should be done away with.

The life for handicapped people improved little during the next several hundred years. A few would be chosen for duty as court "fools," with the responsibility of making people laugh, but the majority, if allowed to live, were destined to a meager life of begging. During the Middle Ages, the church began to provide some of the basic necessities for handicapped people. Although no formal training or education was provided, at least food, water, and shelter were provided.

During the Renaissance and Reformation periods, individuals were caught up in witchcraft, demonology, exorcism, and the persecution of the handicapped. Such persecution was even practiced by religious leaders of the time. "Martin Luther and John Calvin, for example, accused the mentally retarded of being 'filled with Satan', and many were put in chains and thrown into dungeons" (Blackhurst and Berdine 1985, p. 14).

Changes began to occur by the 1600s. A hospital in Paris began treating emotionally disturbed people, a manual alphabet for the deaf was developed, and John Locke differentiated between the mentally retarded and mentally ill (Blackhurst and Berdine 1985). From the beginning of recorded history, individuals have attempted to change the views of the populace toward people with disabilities. These individuals, however, were always frustrated in their attempts at improving the lives of disabled people (Gearheart 1980).

Education and Treatment Since 1750

Itard and the educational movement (1750–1900). The educational era for disabled people started with the work of a French physician named Jean Itard. Itard became personally involved in trying to educate and socialize a boy who had been found in the Aveyron forest in southern France in 1799. The boy, given the name of Victor, had been abandoned for several years and had somehow managed to survive in the wilderness. Itard obtained custody of Victor and attempted to educate him, even though many thought Victor was incurable. The program for Victor was not successful, but it was an attempt to provide educational training to individuals with functional mental retardation, something that had not been attempted before.

Education and treatment in the United States. People with disabilities in colonial America were no better off than their peers in Europe. Mentally retarded people were either kept at home, placed in poorhouses, or auctioned off to bidders who took care of them and received work in return (Blackhurst and Berdine 1985).

As a result of Itard's work, things began to change in the United States in the 1800s. The first residential school for the deaf was established by Thomas Hopkins Gallaudet in 1817 in Connecticut, and Samuel Howe established the first residential school for the blind, the Perkins School for the Blind, in Massachusetts in 1829 (Blackhurst and Berdine 1985). Many other individuals also pushed for increasing services to the disabled. These included Sequin, a colleague of Itard, who immigrated to the United States and did a great deal of work with the mentally retarded (Gearheart 1980), as well as Dorothea Dix, a retired school teacher who campaigned tirelessly for the rights of mentally ill people (Cartwright, Cartwright, and Ward 1981).

Education and training since 1900. Services for disabled children and adults have grown tremendously since the turn of the century. One major action that facilitated improved services was the testing movement. Prior to the development of an individual intelligence test by Binet in 1905, there were no good measures of intelligence or aptitude. As a result of Binet's efforts, the testing movement was launched in which

Public school programs for handicapped children have grown dramatically since 1900.

many assessment instruments were developed that aided in the provision of appropriate services to disabled individuals.

Several other trends occurred during the first part of the twentieth century. These included:

1. An increase in the number of public school classes for the educable mentally retarded.
2. An increase in the number of residential schools for lower functioning mentally retarded, visually impaired, and hearing impaired children.
3. The beginning of classes for the physically handicapped.
4. Establishment of speech therapy services in the public schools.
5. The beginning of classes for the emotionally disturbed (beginning around 1950). (Gearheart 1980)

These trends greatly enhanced the educational and training opportunities for disabled children, but they were only a sign of things to come. During the 1960s and 1970s, legislation and litigation provided disabled children and adults with the right to appropriate educational programs and other services. Public schools and other government agencies began providing services that had previously been denied. The era of full opportunities had arrived.

HIGHLIGHT

Will Is Grilled On Budget 'Cut'

WASHINGTON—Despite its past assurances that funds for the education of the handicapped would be maintained at current levels, the Reagan Administration has proposed what amounts to a cut in the special-education program, Senator Lowell P. Weicker Jr. charged last week.

The Connecticut Republican, who chairs the Appropriations subcommittee that oversees the Education Department, vowed to restore the funds.

"X number of children are going to have their future jeopardized because of budget constraints," Senator Weicker said. "I will not accept that."

But Madeleine C. Will, assistant secretary of education for special education and rehabilitative services, said in testimony before the subcommittee that the Administration's commitment to handicapped children remains "substantial."

States and localities provide the vast majority of funds for education of the handicapped, she said, and the federal reductions will have only a slight impact.

The Administration has proposed $1.14 billion in funding for state grants for education of the handicapped, the largest portion of the $1.3-billion budget proposed for special education. Ms. Will said the proposed budget for state grants would "maintain" funding at last year's level.

But Senator Weicker charged that the amount proposed for the state grants was $104 million less than the funding needed to maintain the current level of services. In addition, he said, the number of students needing assistance may have grown and the per-student cost of services has risen.

Rather than "maintain," Senator Weicker asked Ms. Will, "do you think the word 'cut' should have been used?"

Senator Weicker also criticized Secretary of Education William J. Bennett, whom he quoted as saying that the Administration held special education "safe from any cuts at all."

"There is no evidence through our monitoring efforts," Ms. Will replied, "to suggest that there is an inability to deliver these services."

Senator Weicker also said it was a "disgrace" that the department had not named a director of special education in four years.

Ms. Will said the application process for that position was almost complete.

Education Week. April 23, 1986. Reprinted with permission.

SPECIAL EDUCATION TODAY

Educational and support services provided for disabled children in public schools are more extensive than ever before. The growth of special education has been largely the result of two factors: legislation and litigation.

Students Served

The growth of special education programs has enabled schools to serve many more students. Reporting to Congress in the sixth *Annual Report to Congress*, the Department of Education included the following statements in its 1984 report:

- The number of handicapped children who receive special education and related services continues to grow.

- In the 1982–83 school year, 4,298,327 handicapped children received special education and related services.

- The number of children served in the 1982–83 school year reflected a 1.5 percent increase over the number served the previous year.

- The number of children served in the 1982–83 school year reflected a 16 percent increase since the 1976–77 school year.

- Special education and related services were received by 10.76 percent of the school population during the 1982–83 school year.

- The percentage of children served in special education programs increased from 10.47 percent in 1981–82 to 10.76 percent in 1982–83.

- The number of preschool handicapped children served increased 23 percent from 1976–77 to 1982–83. (United States Department of Education 1984)

Services to handicapped children have become widespread in all states. In 1980 the percentage of school-age children served in special education programs ranged from a low of 5.9 percent in the state of Nevada (the District of Columbia reported serving only 2.7 percent) to a high of 13.5 percent in Delaware. The five states serving the lowest percentage of children in special education were Nevada (5.9 percent), New York (6.0 percent), Hawaii (6.1 percent), and South Dakota and Idaho (6.7 percent each). The states serving the largest percentage included Delaware (13.5 percent), Vermont (11.8 percent), Maryland and Missouri (11.0 percent each), and Nebraska and Tennessee (10.6 percent each) (National Center for Education Statistics 1983).

A wide variety of disabled children are currently being provided with special education and related services. In the fall 1980 school year, learning disabled children represented 3.2 percent of the total school population, followed by speech impaired (2.3 percent), educable and trainable mentally retarded (1.6 percent), and seriously emotionally disturbed (0.5 percent) (National Center for Education Statistics 1983). The number of children served as learning disabled has grown dramatically during the past several years. From the 1976–77 to the 1982–83 school year, the number of children served as learning disabled has grown 119 percent (United States Department of Education 1984).

The 1984 *Annual Report to Congress* reflected an increase in number of students served, but the number of children identified and served through special education is expected to level off soon. With approximately 10 percent of the school population identified as disabled, all teachers and administrators must understand the special needs of disabled students and the legal responsibility of educators to provide these students with appropriate educational services.

Legislation

Federal legislation affecting handicapped children in public schools dates back to 1823, when Public Law 19–8 was passed. This legislation provided a federal land grant to establish an asylum for the deaf in Kentucky (Boston 1977). Other early federal legislation that affected disabled children included:

- P.L. 45–186. In 1879 this legislation was passed to provide $10,000 to the American Printing House for the Blind to produce Braille materials.

- P.L. 66–236. This act, passed in 1920, made civilians eligible for vocational rehabilitation benefits that were provided for World War I veterans.

- P.L. 80–617. In 1948 this bill was passed to eliminate discrimination in hiring physically handicapped persons.

- P.L. 83–531. Passed in 1954, this legislation provided funds for educational research in the area of mental retardation. (Boston 1977)

Since the mid-1950s, more federal legislation has had a significant impact on special education (see table 8–1). These legislative actions culminated with the passage of P.L. 94–142, the Education for All Handicapped Children Act of 1975.

P.L. 94–142. Passed in 1975, Public Law 94–142 has had a profound impact on the education of handicapped children. Support for such a law came from a variety of sources.

Forces leading to the passage of P.L. 94–142. The 1950s and 1960s were the decades for civil rights activities. In 1954, the landmark United States Supreme Court's decision in *Brown v. Board of Education, Topeka, Kansas*, legally eliminated racial discrimination in public education. P.L. 94–142 is an extension of civil rights legislation for racial minorities. "Basically, this Act is Civil Rights as well as educational legislation, and can be fully understood only from that perspective" (Corrigan 1978, p. 10). Following litigated victories by minorities, parents of handicapped children decided to pursue equity through the courts and legislative lobbying.

Legislation	Date	Description
TABLE 8-1		Recent Legislation Dealing with Special Education
PL 85–926	1958	Provided funds for universities to prepare teachers for mentally retarded children
PL 88–164	1963	Provided funds to prepare special education teachers for all types of handicapped students
PL 89–10	1965	Known as the Elementary and Secondary Act, provided funds to schools to assist the disadvantaged and handicapped
PL 89–36	1965	Created the National Institute for the Deaf
PL 89–750	1966	Created the Bureau of Education for the Handicapped and a National Committee on the Handicapped
PL 91–61	1969	Established National Center on Educational Media and Materials for the Handicapped
PL 91–205	1970	Required buildings constructed with federal funds be accessible to the physically handicapped
PL 93–112	1973	Assured rights of the handicapped in employment and educational institutions; also known as Section 504
PL 93–380	1975	Forerunner to PL 94–142; assured due process, nondiscriminatory assessment, and protection of school records

The actions of parent advocacy groups was another force that led to the passage of P.L. 94–142. Parents of handicapped children, who began to lobby state and national legislators and file suit in the courts, began to realize that together they could be a much stronger force than as individuals. Parent groups expanded rapidly and became an important factor in the passage of P.L. 94–142.

The group of parents that has taken a leadership role in the struggle for the rights of the disabled is the National Association for Retarded Citizens (NARC). Beginning in 1950, NARC has worked hard to generate support for appropriate legislation for disabled people. Following the lead of NARC, other parent groups were formed, such as the Association for Children with Learning Disabilities (ACLD), which has also been extremely influential in gaining the passage of federal and state legislation.

Professional associations, like parent groups, also lobbied for strong state and federal legislation to support educational opportunities for disabled children. Probably the one organization that had the greatest impact was the Council for Exceptional Children (CEC), which expanded from 141 chapters in 1950 to 967 in 1980 (Lord 1981). This advocacy group, made up primarily of professionals serving handicapped children in public school programs, played a key role in the development and ultimate passage of P.L. 94–142.

The passage of P.L. 94–142 was also helped along by litigation. Parents of handicapped children began filing suit in the early 1970s to force public schools to provide their children with appropriate educational programs. Courts often ruled in favor of the parents. Litigation victories made legislators aware that the courts would likely mandate certain services unless they were required by legislation.

Purposes of P.L. 94–142. The basic purpose of P.L. 94–142 is to ensure that every handicapped child receives a *free appropriate public education in the least restrictive environment.* The act contains provisions to

1. assure that all handicapped children have available to them a free appropriate public education;

2. assure that the rights of handicapped children and their parents are protected;
3. assist states and localities to provide for the education of handicapped children;
4. address and assure the effectiveness of efforts to educate such children. (A free/ appropriate public education 1977, p. 20)

P.L. 94–142 was no doubt the most comprehensive legislation ever passed by Congress related to special education. It is very broad, complex, and addresses many different areas.

Key component of P.L. 94–142. The component of P.L. 94–142 that has most affected the way handicapped children are educated is the requirement that handicapped children be educated in the least restrictive environment. This mandates that handicapped children are to be educated with their nonhandicapped peers as much of the time as is possible. Although P.L. 94–142 did not include the term *mainstreaming*, most people have interpreted the least-restrictive-environment concept to mean mainstreaming (Biklen 1985).

The writers of P.L. 94–142 envisioned that schools would match children's placements with their individual needs. A continuum of services should be made available, and children should be placed in the appropriate setting along the continuum that corresponds with their needs. The goal is always to move the child toward the least restrictive setting, toward full-time regular classroom placement.

To determine the least restrictive setting for a child, an individual evaluation must be conducted by a trained, qualified individual. Following the evaluation, a committee of professionals, along with the parents of the child, analyze the evaluation results and determine programming needs and the placement that will best meet the child's unique educational needs.

Another component of P.L. 94–142 that has had a significant impact on schools and teachers is the requirement that every handicapped child have an *individual educational program (IEP)*. The legislation makes individualized educational programs a reality for handicapped children by requiring that a written IEP be developed and implemented for every handicapped child served. The phrase *individual educational program* should and does convey some important concepts: (1) the IEP is designed for a single child, not similar children in a group; (2) the IEP should only include elements related to the child's educational program; (3) the IEP is not a plan, but a specific program (Weintraub 1977). Educators should integrate the IEP into actual instruction (Sugai 1985).

At a minimum, IEPs must include a statement concerning the current functioning level of the child, annual goals and short-range objectives, services that will be provided, dates for the services, and an evaluation plan. Although the act makes these specific requirements for IEPs, the implementation of the IEP requirement has been somewhat less than intended by Congress. Scanlon, Arick, and Phelps (1981) conducted a study to determine who participates in the development of IEPs. Results revealed that, except for parents and special education teachers, attendance by administrators and other support staff was very low. P.L. 94–142 calls for involvement from all individuals who are involved in the child's program, and when appropriate, even the child (Gillespie and Turnbull 1983).

Parents, by law, should be extensively involved in developing the IEP. Unfortunately, many parents feel intimidated by professionals and are rarely full participants in the IEP development. To rectify this situation, several strategies should be implemented by the school, such as the appointment of a school employee to act as the advocate for the parent at the IEP meeting. This method of parental support has been found to be very effective (Goldstein and Turnbull 1982). Parental input is so important that teachers should make every effort to ensure that the collaboration with parents is mutually beneficial (Price and Marsh 1985).

P.L. 94–142 also defined the handicapped population. Regulations implementing the act state that handicapped children are those evaluated as being "mentally retarded, hard of hearing, deaf, speech impaired, visually handicapped, seriously emotionally disturbed, orthopedically impaired, other health impaired, deaf-blind, multihandicapped, or as having specific learning disabilities, who because of these impairments need special education and related services" (Federal Register, Vol. 42, No. 163, August 23, 1977, Sec. 121a.5). The definition excludes gifted and talented children, and therefore, does not extend the rights granted by P.L. 94–142 to this group of children.

Still another component of P.L. 94–142 is its requirement for *nondiscriminatory assessment*. Individuals who test children using norm-referenced, standardized test instruments are aware that these tests may often be discriminatory toward some cultural and/or socioeconomic groups. For example, non–Anglo children and children from poor families cannot be expected to do as well on some tests as children who belong to the majority culture, or middle- or upper-class children. In an effort to avoid misclassification and labeling, P.L. 94–142 requires that children be assessed nondiscriminatorily. The act provides guidelines to prevent discriminatory assessment (see table 8–2).

Assuring *due process* rights for parents and children is another major feature of P.L. 94–142. The right to due process, a procedure meant to ensure fair treatment, is a requirement of the Fifth and Fourteenth Amendments to the United States Constitution. "Without a means of challenging the multitude of discriminatory practices that the schools had habitually followed, the children would have found that their right to be included in an educational program and to be treated nondiscriminatorily (to receive a free appropriate education) would have a hollow ring" (Turnbull and Turnbull 1978, p. 1).

TABLE 8–2 Nondiscriminatory Assessment Procedures

- Tests and other evaluation materials must be administered in the child's native language or other mode of communication, be administered by trained personnel, and be validated for the purpose for which they are used.
- Tests and evaluation materials should include areas of academic need, not solely provide a single intelligence quotient (IQ).
- Tests administered to children with various sensory, manual, or speaking skills reflect the child's aptitude, not the child's deficits in sensory, motor, or speaking skills.
- No single procedure is to be used as the sole criterion for determining an appropriate program.
- A multidisciplinary team should be involved in the assessment.
- The child should be assessed in all areas of suspected disability.

Source: Federal Register, *Vol. 42, No. 163, Tuesday, August 23, 1977.*

Due process requirements guaranteed by P.L. 94–142 include the right to examine school records, the right to obtain an independent evaluation, the right to receive prior notice before a change of program, and the right to disagree with and appeal a decision made by the school concerning special education services. This right to appeal provides parents an option to request a due process hearing, conducted by an impartial hearing officer, in which both parties to the disagreement present their side of the conflict (see table 8–3).

Parents and schools have used the due process hearing extensively since P.L. 94–142 was implemented. Smith (1981) conducted a national survey to determine the status of due process hearings. Findings included:

- Thirty-eight states reported that more than 3,500 hearings had been held.

- Placement was the issue most often represented in hearings.

- Parents requested the vast majority of hearings.

- Rulings were in favor of the school the majority of the time.

P.L. 94–142 also requires that handicapped students receive *related services* when these services are required to enable a child to benefit from special education. Services include:

> transportation and such developmental, corrective, and other supportive services as are required to assist a handicapped child to benefit from special education, and includes speech pathology and audiology, psychological services, physical and occupational therapy, recreation, early identification and assessment of disabilities in children, counseling services, and medical services for diagnostic or evaluation purposes. The term also includes school health services, social work services in schools, and parent counseling and training. (Sec. 121a.13)

TABLE 8–3   Due Process Requirements of Public Law 94–142

Requirement	Explanation	Reference
Opportunity to examine records	Parents have a right to inspect and review all educational records.	Sec. 121a.502
Independent evaluation	Parents have a right to obtain an independent evaluation of their child at their expense or the school's expense. The school pays only if it agrees to the evaluation or is required by a hearing officer.	Sec. 121a.503
Prior notice; parental consent	Schools must provide written notice to parents before the school initiates or changes the identification, evaluation, or placement of a child. Consent must be obtained before conducting the evaluation and before initial placement.	Sec. 121a.504
Contents of notice	Parental notice must provide a description of the proposed actions in the written native language of the home. If the communication is not written, oral notification must be given. The notice must be understandable to the parents.	Sec. 121a.505
Impartial due process hearing	A parent or school may initiate a due process hearing if there is a dispute over the identification, evaluation, or placement of the child.	Sec. 121a.506

Source: Final regulations, P.L. 94–142.

The bottom line in determining if a child is eligible to receive a related service is whether the service required is necessary for the child to benefit from special education (Ballard and Zettel 1978). Unfortunately, this is not always clear. For example, when is a medical service diagnostic, and when is it treatment? As physicians become more involved with disabled children (Levine 1982), these questions are likely to surface regularly.

───────────────── HIGHLIGHT ─────────────────

Senate Committee Approves Expansion of P.L. 94–142

By Robert Rothman

WASHINGTON—Over the strong objections of Secretary of Education William J. Bennett, the Republican-controlled Senate Labor and Human Resources Committee last week unanimously approved a bill requiring states to provide education services to handicapped children between the ages of 3 and 5.

The panel also backed the creation of a new grant program for services to infants from birth to age 2.

Approved with little debate, the bill, S 2944, would also extend for three years discretionary programs under the Education of the Handicapped Act that are due to expire Sept. 30. If not renewed before the fall deadline, the programs would get an automatic one-year extension under a different education law.

In a letter to the committee chairman, Senator Orrin G. Hatch, Republican of Utah, Mr. Bennett said mandating aid to 3- to 5-year-old handicapped children would, "be a serious encroachment on the longstanding right of states and local communities to control the education of their children." Current law mandates aid to those ages 5 through 17.

In addition, he wrote, the program for infants would be "unduly prescriptive, burdensome, and costly."

Spokesmen for the Council of Chief State School Officers and the National Association of State Directors of Special Education do not oppose the committee bill, which was sponsored by Senator Lowell P. Weicker Jr., Republican of Connecticut; however, they said they will seek further changes when the House considers it.

In response to one of Mr. Bennett's concerns, also voiced by state officials, the committee amended the bill to delay implementing the new programs for three years rather than two, as originally proposed. Mr. Bennett said two years is too short a period of time for states to be prepared to provide the new services.

In addition, under the committee bill, the mandate for services to children in the 3 to 5 age range would not take effect if the Congress appropriates less than $1.3 billion for P.L. 94–142, or Part B of the Education of the Handicapped Act. According to committee aides, several senators were concerned that if the funds dipped below that level, the amount provided per child would be too low to be effective. The current appropriation for P.L. 94–142 is $1.2 billion.

The bill would also require states, in providing services for 3- to 5-year-old handicapped children, to include developmentally delayed children, and would include as handicapped infants those with acquired, as well as congenital, conditions requiring early intervention.

Currently, 10 states and territories provide services to handicapped children from birth, according to the committee staff. In addition, aides said, one state provides services from age 2, 14 states and territories provide them from age 3, and 4 provide them from age 4.

Mandating services for children ages 3 to 5 would cost an additional $100 million, the aides say, and the bill authorizes another $100 million for the infant-grant program.

The full Senate is not expected to consider the bill before June. There is no comparable measure in the House.

Reprinted with permission from Education Week, Volume V, Number 36, 1986.

Litigation

A force equal to legislation in shaping special education services has been litigation. Parents of handicapped children realized in the early 1970s that one method to obtain services for their children was through the courts. Certainly, racial minority groups had established the precedent in the 1950s and 1960s for access to equal opportunities through litigation.

Litigation in education. Prior to the 1950s, the courts did not play a major role in education. This changed, however, with the landmark decision by the United States Supreme Court in the *Brown v. Board of Education, Topeka, Kansas*, decision in 1954. During the past ten years, court cases involving most aspects of education have been heard at all levels of the court structure. "Topics of litigation have included students' rights to free expression, compulsory attendance and mandatory curriculum offerings, school finance reform, employment practices, student discipline, educational malpractice, sex discrimination, collective bargaining, employees' rights to privacy, desegregation, and the rights of handicapped and non-English-speaking students" (McCarthy and Cambron 1981, p. 13).

Litigation in special education. Since the mid-1970s, litigation in special education has been extensive. In a study of civil rights cases involving students, Marvell, Galfo, and Rockwell (1981) found that approximately 46 percent of the cases involved special education issues. As early as 1974, Laski (1974) noted that "Handicapped persons are in court. They are in courtrooms throughout the land asserting their rights under the U.S. Constitution, federal and state statutes, including their right to services from the public sector. In increasing numbers, they are finding the judicial branch of government an effective forum to secure rights long denied" (p. 15).

Literally hundreds of court cases have dealt with special education. A few are recognized as landmark decisions that have had a significant impact on schools and handicapped students.

Pennsylvania Association for Retarded Citizens (PARC) v. Pennsylvania (F. Supp. 279, E.D. Pa. Order Injunction and Consent Agreement, 1972). Known as the PARC case, this suit is considered the landmark right-to-education case in special education. The suit was filed in 1971 by the Pennsylvania Association for Retarded Citizens (PARC) and thirteen mentally retarded children on behalf of all mentally retarded children being denied an education in public schools. The action challenged Pennsylvania laws that denied educational programs to mentally retarded children because they were considered "uneducable." Expert testimony presented was so convincing that both parties entered into a consent decree with the state of Pennsylvania acknowledging its responsibility to provide appropriate public education to all children (Laski 1974).

Mills v. Board of Education of the District of Columbia (348 F.Supp. 866, D.D.C., 1972). As in the PARC case, this case was brought by parents who were attempting to gain educational services from public schools for their handicapped children. The court's ruling extended the rights to education beyond the mentally retarded category to all handicapped children and specifically indicated that the poor could not be subject to discrimination.

Diana v. State Board of Education (C–70 37 R.F.P., Jan. 7, 1970 and June 18, 1973). This case dealt with the right to fair classification and placement. Parents of Spanish-speaking children filed suit to challenge the classification of their children as mentally retarded. The court's ruling was that minority children, specifically Mexican-American and Chinese, were to be tested in their native languages and that all children in California should be reassessed to determine if inappropriate placements had been made due to discriminatory assessment practices.

Armstrong v. Kline. A landmark decision related to extended year programming resulted from this case. The parents of three severely handicapped students filed suit in 1978 challenging Pennsylvania's law prohibiting funds for educational programs for handicapped children beyond 180 days per year. The parents claimed that this law was contradictory to P.L. 94–142, which indicated that a handicapped child's IEP should determine the program, not a state law refusing certain services (Stotland and Mancuso 1981). In June 1979 the court ruled in favor of the parents, stating that some handicapped children may legitimately require extended year programming. The court was quick to point out that this in no way mandated summer programming for all handicapped children, but only for those who truly needed continuous services during the summer months.

Board of Education of the Hendrick Hudson Central School District Board of Education v. Rowley. This case, known simply as the Rowley case, was the first case that dealt with P.L. 94–142 that was ruled on by the United States Supreme Court. In this case, the parents of a deaf child wanted the local school district to provide the services of a sign language interpreter in all of the child's academic classes. The school refused, and its decision was upheld by the New York State Commissioner of Education. At this point the Rowleys filed suit in federal court. The federal district court, and the appeals court, ruled in favor of the Rowleys, stating that the denial of a sign language interpreter in effect denied the child the right to a free, appropriate education.

The United States Supreme Court, to the surprise of many special education advocates, reversed the lower courts' decisions. In doing so, the Court ruled that the intent of Congress in P.L. 94–142 was to guarantee access to public education, not equality of educational opportunity (Heaney 1984).

MULTICULTURAL SPECIAL EDUCATION

Multicultural considerations must be made in special education. Many children identi-fied as disabled and referred for special education are from minority cultural groups. Black children and Mexican-American children form the nucleus of this group. In addition, many children served in special education programs are from poor homes, which also causes multicultural considerations.

Multicultural Concerns

Several concerns related to racial and cultural minority children in special education have been noted, including

1. overrepresentation of minority children in special classes, especially MR classes;
2. discriminatory assessment procedures;
3. stigmatizing labels;
4. negative teacher attitudes toward the potential of minority children. (Jones and Wilderson 1976)

Studies have substantiated that more children from racial and cultural minorities are in special education classrooms than would be expected based on prevalence estimates. This is particularly true in classes for the mentally retarded (Jones and Wilderson 1976). The primary reason for the overrepresentation probably is discriminatory assessment procedures.

Professionals recognize that many of the norm-referenced tests used to determine eligibility for special education are biased against certain minority groups. Test designers are working to develop tests that are culturally fair. Unfair testing may bring out overidentification of minority children for special education, placement of children in slow tracks, and may impede minority children from entering postsecondary educational programs (Samuda 1976).

Responding to the Multicultural Problem

Public Law 94–142 has attempted to address some of the problems and concerns of multicultural special education. One of its strong requirements is that schools must use nondiscriminatory assessment practices in determining eligibility for special education. One method of eliminating some of the bias found in assessment instruments is to test the child in the native language of the home. This at least gives the child the opportunity to listen to questions and provide responses in his or her primary language. As long as some tests are used that are inherently discriminatory, totally nondiscriminatory assessment will not be possible. That attention has been focused on discriminatory assessment procedures has greatly facilitated the efforts to correct the situation.

Other problems related to racial and cultural minority students and special education should be resolved by following the due process requirements of P.L. 94–142 (Abeson 1976). Total parental involvement in the decision process, parental permissions, notifications, and the right to due process hearings should help in limiting problems associated with multicultural special education.

Requiring that all handicapped children served in special education have an individualized educational program (IEP) should also reduce some of the concerns related to multicultural special education. No longer should students be placed in particular classes or tracks because of minority status. Every child should be evaluated, and based on an individual's strengths and weaknesses, programs should be developed to provide appropriate educational programming. The policy advances made by all handicapped children during the past several years should have a positive effect on minority children in special education programs (Abeson 1976).

HANDICAPPED CHILDREN

Special education is for handicapped children, or children with disabilities. To determine if a child is eligible for special education services, the child must exhibit one of several different handicapping conditions. The final regulations implementing P.L. 94–142 list eight handicapping categories, including mental retardation, learning disabilities, seriously emotional disturbance, orthopedic handicaps, visual impairment, hearing impairment, speech impaired, and other health impaired (Federal Register, Vol. 42, No. 163, August 23, 1977). Each category is designed to group children with similar disabilities and needs.

Traditional Classification System

Classifying children into specific disabling categories, such as noted in P.L. 94–142, has been the traditional method of classifying handicapped children. The major reason for this tradition has been that various groups of disabled children have come to the attention of educators at different times. For example, learning disabilities is a relatively new category, having only been recognized during the past ten to fifteen

The eligibility of children for special education is determined after a comprehensive assessment has been conducted.

years. Since many state statutes, as well as P.L. 94–142, recognize special education eligibility by children fitting into one of several categories of disabilities, all educators should be aware of the different categorical groups.

Mental retardation. Children classified as mentally retarded have been served in special education classes in some public schools for many years. The generally accepted definition of mental retardation was published by the American Association on Mental Deficiency (AAMD):

> Mental retardation refers to significantly subaverage general intellectual functioning existing concurrently with deficits in adaptive behavior, and manifested during the developmental period. (Grossman 1973, p. 11)

The definition is not very understandable unless various conditions are explained. In general terms, the AAMD says that individuals can be classified as mentally retarded if they have an intelligence test score of seventy or below, have deficits in the ability to adapt, and have had the condition since before the age of eighteen (Grossman 1973).

Within the category of mental retardation there have been numerous subcategories; the model that is used most often was published by the AAMD. It contains four different groups: mild, moderate, severe, and profound (see table 8–4).

Learning disabilities. The newest category used to classify handicapped children is learning disabilities. Until 1960 there were no classes for learning disabilities in public schools; however, since the 1970s, this category has grown into one of the largest being served. The report to Congress submitted by the Department of Education in 1984 indicated that learning disabilities is the largest, single category of handicapped children currently served in public school programs (U.S. Department of Education 1984).

TABLE 8–4 Characteristics of Categories of Mental Retardation

Category	Characteristics
Mild	• IQ 55–70 • Possible academic achievement to third-grade level • Capable of living independently as adults • Potential for employment good
Moderate	• IQ 35–55 • Possible academic achievement to first-grade level • Capable of employment in sheltered workshop • Capable of sheltered living
Severe	• IQ 20–35 • Communication difficulties • Possible physical disabilities • Need supervised living • Possible ability to work in sheltered environment
Profound	• IQ 0–20 • Communication difficulties • Possible physical disabilities • Need supervised living

One of the problems of learning disabilities is a lack of agreement on a definition. The definition issued by the federal government in 1977 has been adopted by most states for use in determining eligibility for special education.

> Specific learning disability means a disorder in one or more of the basic psychological processes involved in understanding or in using language, spoken or written, which may manifest itself in an imperfect ability to listen, think, speak, read, write, spell, or to do mathematical calculations. The term includes such conditions as perceptual handicaps, brain injury, minimal brain dysfunction, dyslexia, and developmental aphasia. The term does not include children who have learning problems which are primarily the result of visual, hearing, or motor handicaps, or mental retardation, or of environmental, cultural, or economic disadvantage. (Federal Register 1977, p. 42478)

Basically, a learning disabled person is one who has average or above average intelligence, but who has trouble in academic areas that cannot be explained. With such a nebulous definition, the category has been abused, with many more children being classified as learning disabled than should be.

Characteristics associated with learning disabilities include

- average or above average intelligence
- academic deficit area(s)
- hyperactivity
- perceptual-motor problems
- impulsivity
- emotional swings
- attention disorders
- disorders of speech and hearing

Learning disabilities is a little understood category. School districts vary considerably in their interpretation of eligibility requirements for the learning disability category. Children classified as learning disabled in one school district might be deemed nonhandicapped in a neighboring district. Suffice it to say that the learning disability category is one that creates a great deal of disagreement among professionals and parents.

Emotional disturbance/behavior disorders. This category is plagued, as are several others, by problems with definitions and characteristics. The term *emotional disturbance* had many forerunners, including lunacy, psychosis, neurosis, and schizophrenia, to name a few. The social stigma associated with a condition of mental aberration is "craziness," and historically "crazy" people have had a difficult time receiving appropriate services. P.L. 94–142 uses the term *seriously emotionally disturbed* (SED) to describe these children and defines the category as follows:

> The term means a condition exhibiting one or more of the following characteristics over a long period of time and to a marked degree, which adversely affects educational performance:
>
> (A) An inability to learn which cannot be explained by intellectual, sensory, or health factors;

(B) An inability to build or maintain satisfactory interpersonal relationships with peers and teachers;

(C) Inappropriate types of behavior or feelings under normal circumstances;

(D) A general pervasive mood of unhappiness or depression; or

(E) A tendency to develop physical symptoms or fears associated with personal or school problems.

The term includes children who are medically diagnosed as schizophrenic or autistic. The term does not include children who are socially maladjusted, unless it is determined that they are seriously emotionally disturbed. (Federal Register, Vol. 42, No. 163, August 23, 1977, p. 42478)

Slightly different from emotional disturbance is the category of behavior disorders. P.L. 94–142 does not include such a handicapping category, but some states use this nomenclature rather than SED, or in addition to SED. Succinctly defined, a behavior disorder is a deviation from age-appropriate behavior which significantly interferes with the child's growth and development and/or the lives of others (Kirk 1972.). The behavior disorder category, therefore, is less severe than the ED or SED category called for in P.L. 94–142.

As with other disabilities, there are many different methods of subclassifying emotionally disturbed children. Quay (1975) divided emotional disturbance into conduct, personality, and immaturity problems. Conduct disorders included striking other children and being disobedient, personality problems included withdrawing and being shy, and immaturity problems included passivity, short attention spans, and clumsiness.

Hearing impairment. Hearing impairment is a familiar disability to most people. Most individuals know of someone, perhaps an older person, who has difficulty hearing. It is a disability that is common in older individuals, but also occurs in school-age children. Individuals are classified as hearing impaired if they have a decibel (dB) loss as measured by an audiometer. There are two categories of hearing impairment: hard of hearing and deaf. Persons with dB losses of 25 to 90 are considered hard of hearing, while individuals with a loss of 90 or greater are classified as deaf.

Educators have adopted more functional definitions that allow them to discern certain hearing abilities from the label. Most schools have accepted the definition of hearing impairment for educational purposes reported by Moores (1978) that was adopted by the Conference of Executives of American Schools for the Deaf. According to the definition, a deaf person is one whose hearing is disabled to an extent that precludes the understanding of speech through the ear alone, with or without assistance of an amplification device. A hard of hearing person is one whose hearing is disabled to such an extent that speech is difficult to understand through the ear alone, with or without a hearing aid.

Visual impairment. Like hearing impairment, visual impairment is a disability that is frequently found in the population. Many people wear glasses; without them they might have a severe visual problem. Older individuals frequently find themselves losing their vision. However, the category of visual impairment used in special education is for school-age children whose disability cannot be corrected with glasses.

There are two major groups of visually impaired individuals: blind and partially sighted. Individuals are classified as legally blind if they have a visual acuity of $^{20}/_{200}$ or less in the better eye with best correction, or if they have a field restriction of 20 degrees or less. Partially sighted persons are those with a visual acuity of $^{20}/_{70}$ to $^{20}/_{200}$ in the better eye with best correction. These definitions, considered legal or medical definitions, may be useless to educators.

School personnel have adopted more functional definitions for use with children who experience visual problems. Children are classified as educationally blind when they cannot read print and are classified as partially sighted, or low vision, if they have visual problems but are able to read print. These more functional definitions alert educators to the functional ability of students regarding their abilities to see letters.

Physically handicapped. This group of children is extremely heterogeneous. Because of the wide variety of disabilities included in the category it is virtually impossible to define. For example, children who would be labeled physically handicapped could include those with spina bifida, cerebral palsy, amputations, muscular dystrophy, or general paralysis. P.L. 94–142 uses the category *orthopedically impaired* and defines it as

> a severe orthopedic impairment which adversely affects a child's educational performance. The term includes impairments caused by congenital anomaly (e.g. clubfoot, absence of some member, etc.), impairments caused by disease (e.g. poliomyelitis, bone tuberculosis, etc.), and impairments from other causes (e.g. cerebral palsy, amputations, and fractures or bruns which cause contractures). (Federal Register, Vol. 42, No. 163, August 23, 1977, p. 42478)

Other health impaired. Another category that consists of many different disabilities is *other health impaired.* The federal definition states that children are placed in this category if they have limited attention, vitality, or stamina that results from one of several conditions, including diabetes, asthma, epilepsy, lead poisoning, or a heart condition (Federal Register, Vol. 42, No. 163, August 23, 1977).

Speech and language disorders. A succinct definition of all communication disorders that has been widely accepted is that a person has a communication disorder if his or her speech differs from the speech of others to the extent that it calls attention to itself, interferes with the message that is intended, or causes distress to the speaker or listener (Van Riper 1978). There are three general categories of communication disorders: nonverbal, language disordered, and speech impaired. Nonverbal children are those who, for a variety of reasons, do not have speech and language ability. This may be due to brain damage, emotional problems, or as a result of severe mental retardation. Many children are erroneously regarded as nonverbal who have receptive and inner language ability but who are unable to use expressive language. They are certainly not nonverbal. Another relatively small group of children have problems of dysfluency, usually characterized as stuttering, or voice disorders. The majority of children with speech disorders have articulation problems such as omissions, substitutions, or distortions of sounds. Most such conditions occur during the elementary school years and yield readily to remediation. Ordinarily the regular classroom teacher will have little difficulty managing and supporting such children.

Generic/Noncategorical Model

Although the different disability categories are still used in many states and school districts, there is a trend to implement a new classification model. Some professionals in special education believe that categorical labels have little practical usefulness (Smith and Neisworth 1975; Lilly 1979; Hallahan and Kauffman 1978; Marsh, Price, and Smith 1983; Smith, Price, and Marsh 1986). Specific criticisms of the categorical model include:

1. The categories are educationally irrelevant.
2. Categorical groupings overlap.
3. Categories label children as "defective," implying that the cause of the educational or developmental deficiency lies only within the child.
4. Special educational instructional materials and strategies are not category-specific.
5. Preparation of teachers along traditional categorical lines results in redundancy of coursework and barriers within the profession.
6. Patterns of funding for special education have perpetuated the categorical approach. (Smith and Neisworth 1975, pp. 8–9)

One primary reason to move toward the noncategorical or generic model to serve handicapped children is that categorical descriptions of mildly handicapped children are meaningless in a system that is gravitating rapidly toward the inclusion of additional groups of handicapped persons and the inclusion of new services for handicapped persons. The "mild" conditions that emerged in the field during the past several years, namely the mildly or educable mentally retarded, the learning disabled, and the mildly emotionally disturbed/behaviorally disordered, compose the largest number of children who are regarded as handicapped (Smith, Price, and Marsh 1986). Hallahan and Kauffman (1978) note that these categories overlap in all dimensions—psychologically, educationally, and behaviorally. Lilly (1979) totally abandons the categories and refers simply to exceptional children as those who require special services of a substantive nature and degree to assure optimum learning and educational development.

This rationale is opposed by traditional special educators who prefer the strict categorical approach to special education. However valid some of the arguments presented by this group, the trend is clearly toward the noncategorical approach. One major reason for this trend is the current emphasis on delivering services to handicapped children in public schools using the resource room model. Handicapped children are less likely to be segregated into separate classrooms and are more likely to be mainstreamed into regular classrooms at least a portion of each school day.

Mildly handicapped is therefore a new category for handicapped children. Children will no longer be considered seriously handicapped simply because of a categorical label. As a result of the noncategorical model, labels will be more functional and less stigmatizing. Only a relative minority of handicapped children will be considered severely handicapped: those mentally retarded at the low end of the intellectual continuum and those severely emotionally disturbed children who may be dangerous to themselves or others. Others, including the physically handicapped, health impaired, and vision and hearing impaired, will be considered mildly handicapped and attend regular classrooms in increasing numbers.

The following summary points stress the important issues related to the mildly handicapped category:

1. The similarities among handicapped students of various categories are greater than their differences. Characteristics associated with one condition or another overlap significantly, and materials useful for one diagnostic category are also appropriate for another. In the same vein the differences among children labeled within one category are greater than their similarities. Characteristics are significant only as they are applied to a particular student.

2. Teaching should be based on what the student can and cannot do, on what the curricular sequence should be in response to specific, individual objectives, and on what the teacher should or should not do to improve change and learning in the student.

3. Instructional methods and materials should be selected to meet the needs and characteristics of an individual learner rather than those that seem to be appropriate for a label or certain type of group assignment deemed appropriate for children who share certain theoretical characteristics. (Marsh, Price, and Smith 1983, p. 9)

The trend is away from categorical labels to noncategorical/generic classification. The following definition of the mildly handicapped was developed by Smith, Price, and Marsh (1986):

The term mildly handicapped refers to the large group of students who differ from nonhandicapped students in cognitive-academic, sensoriphysical, and socioemotional characteristics to such an extent that special education and related services are required, but not to the degree that segregated special class placement is essential. These are children who violate the norms of the school in some way: deviation from norms of behavior, academic expectations, acquisition of standard English in spoken and written forms, motivation and aspirations for achievement, or exceeding the school's traditional resources to provide instruction.

SPECIAL EDUCATION SERVICES

The philosophical underpinnings of serving handicapped children is *normalization*. As a result of litigation, legislation, and advocacy, handicapped children are being provided a free, appropriate education in the mainstream. While the normalization movement started in the Scandinavian countries (Nirje 1969), the changes that have occurred most specifically in America and Canada are unique within the cultural contexts of each country.

One result of normalization has been mainstreaming. P.L. 94–142 requires that handicapped children be educated in the least restrictive setting. This requires that each handicapped child be evaluated and a decision made concerning the child's least restrictive setting. Some mildly handicapped children may be able to benefit from regular classroom placement several hours daily, while others may not be able to benefit from any regular classroom placement. The mainstreaming movement differs significantly from the more traditional service delivery system that was used extensively in special education prior to the passage of P.L. 94–142.

Traditional Service Delivery Model

Following the pressures exerted by parents in the early 1950s, some schools began providing educational services to some handicapped children. The services were provided using categorical groupings and physical segregation.

Categorical grouping. The delivery of special education services has been, until the late 1970s, exclusively along categorical lines—that is by category of handicapping condition. Mentally retarded children, learning disabled children, emotionally disturbed/behaviorally disordered children, and physically handicapped children were grouped by label for special education. The training of teachers, certification standards for teachers, and funding patterns to support special education were all based on categories. Professionals have been concerned that categorical labels applied to children are damaging in many ways, including self-esteem and expectations of teachers and peers.

Self-contained classes. For most of the history of special education, children were classified by category and segregated from their nonhandicapped peers in self-contained special education classrooms. Students remained in the same classroom with the same teacher for the entire school day. This model has become a major point of contention in special education. Johnson (1983) noted that self-contained services were attacked as a result of the civil rights movement and high national productivity and affluence. The efficacy of such placement has been seriously questioned as well as the discriminatory nature of such programming for any class of student, no matter how defined.

Special schools. Another model used extensively in the past was to use public funds to operate a segregated facility for all handicapped children in a school district. In essence, this is not different from the self-contained classroom except that it is much more blatant as a form of segregation. While special schools for handicapped children still exist, the number of children served in such settings has been greatly reduced.

Institutional settings. Still another service option using the categorical approach is institutional, which was an early method of intervention for all handicapped individuals. The current trend is toward *deinstitutionalization*, moving individuals from institutions into community programs. This is a major component of the normalization philosophy and has greatly reduced the institutional population in the United States (Scheerenberger 1976).

Current Service Delivery Model

The traditional model of providing educational services to handicapped children has changed during the past several years. Now, rather than providing most special education in self-contained programs, the majority of schools educate handicapped children using the resource room model (Friend and McNutt 1984). Several factors led to the adoption of the resource room model.

Efficacy studies. Probably the single, most important development that encouraged the adoption of the resource room model was a group of studies published that questioned the efficacy of self-contained special education programs. In the professional literature, the research became known as *efficacy studies*, or a comparison of the performance of educable mentally retarded children in self-contained and regular classrooms (Yoshida 1984).

The most famous and perhaps influential attack on traditional, segregated special education services came from Dunn (1968), who criticized the practice of special education for mentally retarded children and called for a reexamination of the procedures employed in schools to educate handicapped children. His article, "Special Education for the Mildly Retarded—Is Much of it Justifiable?" created the atmosphere for change. Later, Dunn (1973) outlined a series of negative conclusions about the effectiveness of traditional special education classes:

1. As a group, mildly retarded pupils make as much or more progress in regular classes as their counterparts in special classes.
2. Mentally retarded children do not work up to their mental age capacity whether they are in regular classrooms or special classes.
3. Special class children do not achieve academically above randomly selected regular class-placed mentally retarded children.
4. Mentally retarded students with higher IQs develop a dislike for special class placement and an increase in their feelings of self-derogation about such placement.
5. Low IQ children who make the best progress in the regular grades are those who come from ethnic minorities and who are adjusted and accepted in their communities.

On the whole, Dunn was of the opinion that the effectiveness of special, segregated or self-contained classes could not be demonstrated. He recommended that such classes be eliminated. Other voices that joined Dunn included Blatt (1960), Johnson (1962), Fisher (1967), Johnson (1969), Christopolos and Renz (1969), Jansen, Ahm, Jensen, and Leerskov (1970). Still other professionals stood firm and defended special class placement for many mentally retarded children. Kolstoe (1976), one of the leading defenders of self-contained placement, has continued to argue in support of special classes.

Johnson (1983) suggested that all programs that segregate handicapped children are now considered bad, regardless of their true quality. Regardless of the concern about the dismantling of a large portion of self-contained classrooms, the tide turned. Normalization and mainstreaming have spread effectively throughout the school systems and are undeniably civil rights trends. Whether the efficacy studies were good research is of little consequence now, because they played an important part in the professional deliberations that helped to usher in the mainstreaming movement and to alter conceptualizations of handicapping conditions that are now referred to as mild conditions. P.L. 94–142 mandated that handicapped children be served in the least restrictive setting. For many children now considered mildly handicapped, this means regular classroom placement for a large portion of the school day.

Continuum of services model. P.L. 94–142 calls for a continuum of educational services, because it requires schools to provide appropriate educational services on an individual basis. As a result, schools must be prepared to provide educational services in a variety of settings, with the placement decision of each child depending on unique characteristics, strengths, and weaknesses.

The model that closely parallels the requirements of P.L. 94–142 is Deno's (1970) Cascade of Services. This model has been incorporated into federal and state guidelines and laws, and forms the basis for implementing the least restrictive environment requirement (Peterson, Zabel, Smith, and White 1983). The Cascade of Services Model

- aids conceptualization of a continuum of services (Podemski, Price, Smith, and Marsh 1984);

- presents a base of service options for exceptional students (Merulla and McKinnon 1982);

- focuses on aspects of placement other than physical and mechanical (Reid and Hresko 1981);

- emphasizes appropriate assignment of special education students in order that they advance toward eventual regular class placement (Cegelka and Prehm 1982).

The model consists of seven levels, ranging from full-time placement in a regular classroom to full-time placement in an institution (see figure 8–1).

Level I, full-time regular classroom. Level I represents the least restrictive setting possible. For some mildly handicapped children, accommodations made by regular classroom teachers are sufficient to circumvent manifested disabilities. These accommodations could consist of changing seating arrangements, reading tests orally, and giving extra time for assignments, to name a few.

Level I	Regular classroom with or without supportive services
Level II	Regular classroom plus supportive services
Level III	Part-time special class (Resource room)
Level IV	Full-time special class (Self-contained room)
Level V	Special stations (Segregated schools)
Level VI	Homebound
Level VII	Hospital or residential setting

Figure 8-1. *Cascade of Services. Adapted from E. Deno, Special education is developmental capital,* Exceptional Children, *1970, 37, 229-37.*

Level II, full-time regular classroom with assistance. Level II enables children to be placed full-time in regular classrooms, and at the same time receive special, supportive services. One of the strategies subsumed under this arrangement is the itinerant teacher model similar to the model that schools have used for several years to provide speech therapy services to students. Other types of special services using this model include mobility training for visually impaired students. The itinerant teacher, who would go into regular classrooms to provide support for disabled students, is the primary support person when using this model.

Gearheart and Weishahn (1980) state that the itinerant model is not as practical as the resource room model for some types of disabled children, because it does not provide daily services. For other children who do not require daily intervention, however, the itinerant model works well.

Level III, part-time special class. Level III is the most popular service model used today (Smith, Price, and Marsh 1986). The resource room is the special education setting where level III is implemented. Students are placed in regular classrooms and attend the resource room part of the day to receive intensive assistance in problem areas from special education teachers. The resource room model is a bridge between total special education placement and total regular classroom placement. Two needs led to the development of the resource room model: (1) provide more direct services to more handicapped children, and (2) provide regular classroom teachers with support services (Mandell and Gold 1984).

Resource rooms can be of several types, as indicated by Wiederholt, Hammill, and Brown (1978) (see table 8–5). Although there are differences, there are also many commonalities among resource rooms:

1. The student divides the day between the resource room and the regular classroom.
2. Resource room scheduling is usually done, so that only small groups of students are in the resource room at any one time.
3. Instruction is almost totally individualized and centers around the goals and objectives of the IEP for each student.

TABLE 8–5   Types of Resource Rooms

Type	Description
Categorical	The children who attend are from one area of exceptionality.
Cross-Categorical	Children are assigned according to instructional level not label.
Noncategorical	Children in this model may or may not be labeled handicapped, but they do have mild or moderate learning and/or behavior problems.
Specific Skill Program	Teachers usually work on a specific skill area, typically with nonlabeled children who need assistance.
Itinerant Resource Teacher	Services are provided to more than one district, with the teacher serving part-time in each district.

Adapted from: Wiederholt, J. L., Hammill, D. and Brown, V. The resource teacher: A guide to effective practices. Boston: Allyn and Bacon, 1978.

4. The focus of instruction may include remediation of the student's basic skills or assistance in passing regular class subjects, an approach termed *accommodation*.
5. The teacher should be a certified special educator with experience and training in management of a resource room.
6. Successful resource room programs require extensive interaction and cooperation between the special education program and the regular classes in the building. (Marsh and Price 1980)

Resource rooms are the most popular service model used in special education. A recent study determined that all fifty states, plus the District of Columbia, serve at least some of their handicapped children in resource rooms (Friend and McNutt 1984). While resource rooms and mainstreaming programs are the rule, some are more successful than others. Salend (1984) suggests that six factors contribute heavily to the success of mainstreaming programs: (1) developing criteria for mainstreaming, (2) preparing handicapped students, (3) preparing nonhandicapped students, (4) promoting communication among educators, (5) evaluating student progress, and (6) providing in-service training.

The majority of handicapped children are served in resource rooms.

TABLE 8–6 Summary of Possible Advantages and Disadvantages of the Self-Contained Classroom Model

Advantages

1. Full-time interaction with the teacher may allow more scheduling flexibility.

2. Students are able to spend more time in small groups with peers, which may foster friendships.

3. Parents may form closer relationships with one teacher than when dealing with several teachers.

4. Grouping for instruction may be easier to accomplish.

5. It may be easier for one teacher to assume complete responsibility for the student's performance.

Disadvantages

1. The student's opportunities to interact with peers and other adults are restricted.

2. Teachers may be isolated from other staff members.

3. There is limited opportunity for special education students to have experiences with students of other ability levels.

Adapted from: Cegelka, P. T. and Prehm, H. J. Mental Retardation From Categories to People. Columbus, OH: Charles Merrill Publishing Co., 1982.

Level IV, full-time special class. Full-time placement in special classes was the most popular service model for special education before P.L. 94–142 emphasized serving handicapped children in regular classrooms as much as possible. In the self-contained model, one special education teacher has the primary responsibility for the entire educational program of students placed in the classroom. Students remain in the self-contained room all day every day, with the possible exception of attending music or other nonacademic classes, having lunch with nonhandicapped students, and attending assemblies.

From 1950 to 1970, the self-contained special classroom became the preferred organizational strategy for educating special education students served in public school programs (Reynolds 1973). Although displaced in popularity by the resource room model, the self-contained approach has some advantages (see table 8–6).

Levels V through VII. These lower levels of the Cascade of Services Model are inappropriate for most mildly handicapped children. They are primarily reserved for more severely handicapped children, such as severely and profoundly mentally retarded, seriously emotionally disturbed, autistic, and medically fragile students. However, when determining appropriate placements for these more severely handicapped children, schools are still required by P.L. 94–142 to determine the least restrictive placement.

SUMMARY

This chapter focused on special education. The beginning section discussed the history of treatment of disabled persons. Handicapped people were treated badly for much of history, even being persecuted and killed during various historical periods.

Benevolent treatment for the disabled began around 1600; however, services were not truly expanded until the twentieth century.

Currently in the United States more than four million students are served in special education programs in public schools. The number has grown tremendously during the past decade. Federal legislation and litigation have primarily been responsible for the growth. Since the mid-1950s a great deal of federal legislation has been passed that has had an impact on special education. The one piece of legislation that had the most impact was Public Law 94–142, the Education for All Handicapped Children Act. The key components of this act were discussed, as well as actions that led up to its passage.

The final section of the chapter was a discussion on traditional and current categorizing of disabled people and services provided. The traditional classification system used with disabled individuals placed individuals into categories such as mental retardation, learning disabilities, and visual impairment. The discussion then moved to focus on the current classification model, generic or noncategorical classification.

Finally, services provided to disabled students in special education were discussed. The traditional method of delivering services to this population, segregating students into self-contained classrooms, has given way to mainstreaming students into regular classrooms. Using this model, known as the resource room model, students leave the regular classrooms and go to the resource room for specialized instruction. The pros and cons of this current model of service delivery were discussed.

IN THE FIELD

1. Does the school have a special education program?

2. Is the special education categorical or noncategorical?

3. How many resource rooms are in the school? How many self-contained rooms?

4. What did you observe to indicate the relationship between regular classroom teachers and special education teachers?

5. What administrative actions indicate support for the special education program?

6. Approximately what percentage of the school's students receive special education?

7. Are there any variations for special education students relative to pass/fail and graduation requirements?

8. Can special education students participate in extracurricular activities? If so, which activities?

REFERENCES

A free appropriate public education. 1977. *AMICUS 2*(3), 20.

Abeson, A. 1976. Legal forces and pressures. In R. L. Jones, Ed., *Mainstreaming and the minority child.* Minneapolis, MN: Leadership Training Institute.

Ballard, J., and J. J. Zettel. 1978. Fiscal arrangements of public law 94–142. *Exceptional Children 44*(5), 333–37.

Biklen, D. P. 1985. Mainstreaming: From compliance to quality. *Journal of Learning Disabilities 18*(1), 58–61.

Blackhurst, A. E., and W. H. Berdine. 1985. Basic concepts of special education. In A. E. Blackhurst, and W. H. Berdine, Eds., *An introduction to special education.* Boston: Little, Brown and Company.

Blackhurst, A. E., and W. H. Berdine. 1981. Basic concepts of special education. In A. E. Blackhurst, and W. H. Berdine, Eds., *An introduction to special education.* Boston: Little, Brown and Company.

Blatt, B. 1960. Some persistently recurring assumptions concerning the mentally subnormal. *Training School Bulletin 57*, 48–59.

Board of Education of the Hendrick Hudson Central School District Westchester County v. Rowley ex rel. Rowley, 458 U.S. 176 (1982).

Boston, B. O. 1977. *Education policy and the Education for All Handicapped Children Act (P.L. 94–142).* Washington, DC: Institute for Educational Leadership, The George Washington University.

Cartwright, G. P., C. A. Cartwright, and M. E. Ward. 1981. *Educating special learners.* Belmont, CA: Wadsworth Publishing Company.

Cegelka, P. T., and H. J. Prehm. 1982. *Mental retardation: From categories to people.* Columbus, OH: Charles Merrill Publishing Co.

Christoplos, F. and P. Renz. 1969. A critical examination of special education programs. *Journal of Special Education 3*, 371–79.

Corrigan, D. 1978. Political and moral contexts that produced P.L. 94–142. *Journal of Teacher Education 29*, 10–14.

Deno, E. 1970. Special education as developmental capital. *Exceptional Children 37*, 229–37.

Dunn, L. M. 1968. Special education for the mildly retarded: Is much of it justified? *Exceptional Children 35*, 5–22.

Dunn, L. 1973. *Exceptional children in the schools: Special education in transition.* New York: Holt, Rinehart, and Winston.

Fisher, H. K. 1967. What is special education? *Special Education in Canada 41*, 9–16.

Federal Register 1977. Washington D.C.: U.S. Government Printing Office. *42*(163) August 23, 1977.

Friend, M., and G. McNutt. 1984. Resource room programs: Where are we now? *Exceptional Children 51*(2), 150–55.

Gearheart, B. R. 1980. *Special education for the 80s.* St. Louis: C. V. Mosby.

Gearheart, B. R., and M. W. Weishahn. 1980. The handicapped student in the regular classroom. St. Louis: C. V. Mosby.

Gillespie, E. B., and A. P. Turnbull. 1983. Involving students in the planning process. *Teaching Exceptional Children 61*(1), 27–29.

Goldstein, S., and A. P. Turnbull. 1982. Strategies to increase parent participation in IEP conferences. *Exceptional Children 48*(4), 360–61.

Grossman, H. J. (Ed.). 1973. Manual on terminology and classification in mental retardation. Washington, D.C.: American Association on Mental Deficiency.

Hallahan, D. B. and J. W. Kauffman. 1978. *Exceptional children.* Englewood Cliffs, N. J.: Prentice-Hall.

Heaney, J. P. 1984. A free appropriate public education: Has the Supreme Court misinterpreted Congressional intent? *Exceptional Children 50*(5), 456–62.

Jansen, M. J., P. E. Ahm, and A. Leerskov. 1970. Is special education necessary? Can this program possibly be reduced? *Journal of Learning Disabilities 3*(9), 11–16.

Johnson, G. O. 1962. Special education for the mentally retarded—A paradox. *Exceptional Children 29*, 62–69.

Johnson, G. O. 1983. Inconsistencies in programming. *Education and Training of the Mentally Retarded 18*(2), 101–102.

Johnson, J. L. 1969. Special education in the inner city: A challenge for the future or another means of cooling the markout? *Journal of Special Education 3*, 241–51.

Jones, R. L., and F. B. Wilderson. 1976. Mainstreaming and the minority child: An overview of issues and a perspective. In R. L. Jones, Ed., *Mainstreaming and the minority child*. Minneapolis, MN: Leadership Training Institute.

Kirk, S. A. 1972. *Educating exceptional children*. Boston: Houghton-Mifflin Company.

Kolstoe, O. P. 1976. *Teaching educable mentally retarded children*. New York: Hole, Rinehart, and Winston.

Laski, F. 1974. Civil rights victories for the handicapped—I. *The Record 1*(5), 15–20.

Levine, M. D. 1982. The child with school problems: An analysis of physician participation. *Exceptional Children 48*(4), 296–304.

Lilly, S. 1979. *Children with exceptional needs: A survey of special education*. New York: Holt, Rinehart, and Winston.

Lord, F. E. 1981. The attainment of professional stature, 1950–1980, part I. *Exceptional Children 47*(6), 438–52.

McCarthy, M. M. and N. H. Cambron. 1981. *Public school law: Teachers' and students' rights*. Boston: Allyn and Bacon.

Mandell, C. J. and V. Gold. 1984. *Teaching handicapped students*. St. Paul: West Publishing Company.

Marsh, G. E., and B. J. Price. 1980. *Methods for teaching the mildly handicapped adolescent*. St. Louis: C. V. Mosby.

Marsh, G. E., B. J. Price, and T. E. C. Smith. 1983. *Teaching mildly handicapped children: Methods and materials*. St. Louis: C. V. Mosby.

Marvell, T. A. Galfo, and J. Rockwell. 1981. *Student litigation: A compilation and analysis of civil cases involving students 1977–1981*. Williamsburg, VA: National Center for State Courts.

Merulla, E., and A. McKinnon. 1982. "Stuck" on Deno's cascade. *Journal of Learning Disabilities 15*, 94–96.

Moores, D. F. 1978. *Educating the deaf: Psychology, principles, and practices*. Boston: Houghton Mifflin Co.

National Center for Education Statistics. 1983. *The condition of education, 1983 edition*. Washington, D.C.: U.S. Government Printing Office.

Nirje, B. 1969. The normalization principle and its human management implications. In R. B. Kugel and W. Wolfensberger (Eds.). *Changing patterns in residential services for the mentally retarded*. Washington, D.C.: U.S. Government Printing Office.

Peterson, R. L., R. H. Zabel, C. R. Smith, and M. A. White. 1983. Cascade of services model and emotionally disabled students. *Exceptional Children 49*, 404–10.

Podemski, R. S., B. J. Price, T. E. C. Smith, and G. E. Marsh. 1984. *Comprehensive special education administration*. Rockville, MD: Aspen Systems.

Price, B. J., and G. E. Marsh. 1985. Practical suggestions for planning and conducting parent conferences. *Teaching Exceptional Children 17*(4), 274–78.

Quay, H. C. 1975. Classifications in the treatment of delinquency and anti-social behavior. In H. Hobbs, Ed., *Issues in the classification of children. Vol. I*. San Francisco: Jossey-Bass.

Reid, D. K., and W. P. Hresko. 1981. *A cognitive approach to learning disabilities*. New York: McGraw-Hill Book Company.

Reynolds, M. C. 1973. Changing roles of special education personnel. Paper presented to University Council on Education Administration, 1973.

Salend, S. J. 1984. Factors contributing to the development of successful mainstreaming programs. *Exceptional Children 50*(5) 409–16.

Samuda, R. J. 1976. Problems and issues in assessment of minority group children. In R. L. Jones, Ed., *Mainstreaming and the minority child*. Minneapolis, MN: Leadership Training Institute.

Scanlon, C. A., J. Arick, and N. Phelps. 1981. Participation in the development of the IEP: Parents' perspective. *Exceptional Children 47*(5), 373–74.

Scheerenberger, R. C. 1976. *Deinstitutionalization and institutional reform*. Springfield, IL: Charles C. Thomas.

Smith, R. M. and J. T. Neisworth. 1975. *The exceptional child: A functional approach*. New York: McGraw-Hill.

Smith, T. E. C. 1981. Status of due process hearings. *Exceptional Children 48*(3), 232–36.

Smith, T. E. C., B. J. Price, and G. E. Marsh. 1986. *Mildly handicapped children and adults*. St. Paul: West Publishing Co.

Stotland, J. F. and E. Mancuso. 1981. U.S. Court of Appeals decision regarding *Armstrong v. Kline*: The 180 day rule. *Exceptional Children 47*(4), 266–70.

Sugai, G. 1985. Case study: Designing instruction from IEPs. *Teaching Exceptional Children 17*(3), 233–39.

Turnbull, R. H., and A. P. Turnbull. 1978. Procedural due process and the education of handicapped children. *Focus on Exceptional Children 9*(9), 1–12.

United States Department of Education. 1984. Sixth annual report to Congress on the implementation of public law 94–142: The education for all handicapped children act. *Exceptional Children 51*(3), 199–202.

Van Riper, C. 1978. *Speech correction: Principles and methods.* 6th ed. Englewood Cliffs, N. J.: Prentice-Hall.

Wiederholt, J. L., D. D. Hammill, and V. Brown. 1978. *The resource room teacher: A guide to effective practices.* Boston: Allyn and Bacon.

Weintraub, F. J. 1977. Understanding the individualized education program (IEP). *Amicus 2*(3), 26–31.

Will, M. C. 1984. Let us pause and reflect—but not too long. *Exceptional Children 51*(1), 11–16.

Yoshida, R. K. Perspectives on research. *Mental retardation: Topics of today—Issues of tommorow.* Edited by E. L. Meyen. Lancaster, Pa.: Lancaster Press.

Chapter 9
EDUCATIONAL ADMINISTRATION

OBJECTIVES

After reading this chapter, you will be able to

- describe a typical administrative hierarcy in a public school district;
- list the responsibilities of the local school board;
- discuss the history of local boards of education;
- describe the roles of the district superintendent;
- list various assistants found at the district level;
- discuss the roles of the principal;
- describe the role of disciplinarian;
- discuss the ways principals evaluate personnel and programs;
- list groups that hold expectations for the principal;
- describe the various career options for school administrators;
- discuss how to become a school administrator.

OUTLINE

ADVANCE ORGANIZERS
INTRODUCTION
ADMINISTRATIVE HIERARCHY
LOCAL BOARD OF EDUCATION
    Powers and Responsibilities of Boards
PROFESSIONAL ADMINISTRATIVE STAFF
    Districtwide Administrative Staff
    Building-Level Administrative Staff

CAREERS IN ADMINISTRATION
    How to Become an Administrator
    Benefits of School Administration
SUMMARY
IN THE FIELD
REFERENCES

1. What is an administrative hierarchy?
2. How did local control of public schools evolve?
3. What are the specific responsibilities of local boards of education?
4. What is the relationship between the superintendent and the board of education?
5. In what roles do superintendents become involved?
6. What roles do assistant central office staff fill?
7. What are the primary roles of school principals?
8. What are the major management responsibilities of principals?
9. How do principals influence the school climate?
10. How does a typical principal spend a day?
11. What expectations do various groups have for principals?
12. What career opportunities are there for school administrators?
13. How can you become a school administrator?

INTRODUCTION ⎯⎯⎯⎯⎯⎯⎯⎯⎯⎯⎯⎯⎯

Schools, like businesses, social organizations, and institutions, must have leaders. In schools leaders are called school administrators. Without administrators schools would have no direction; they would be leaderless institutions functioning in a haphazard fashion without any common purpose or goals. School administrators definitely perform a vital role in public education. As more emphasis is placed on effective schools, the role of school administrators will become even more critical.

ADMINISTRATIVE HIERARCHY

Public schools are administered by an administrative hierarchy that, while differing from school to school, most often fits a similar pattern. At the top of the hierarchy is the local school board, a group of constituents. The local board hires the school superintendent, who is the chief local school officer; the superintendent in turn employs other central office administrative staff as well as building principals. Each level of the hierarchy serves a specific purpose involving the administration of the public schools (see figure 9–1). School administrators are for the most part bound by the chain of command that is established in the hierarchy (Brieschke 1985).

LOCAL BOARD OF EDUCATION

In the 1981–82 school year, there were 15,538 local school districts operating in the United States (National Center for Education Statistics 1983). Most of these districts are administered by a local school board that is either elected or appointed. In the majority of districts, school board members are elected.

Local control of education by lay persons began in the New England colonies. The Massachusetts School Ordinance of 1642 delegated the responsibility for education to the "townsmen." This trend was reinforced with the Massachusetts School

		Board of Education		
		Superintendent		
	Central Office Staff			
Principal Elementary #1	Principal Elementary #2	Principal Elementary #3	Principal Junior High	Principal High School

Figure 9-1. *Typical organizational chart of a middle-sized school district.*

Ordinance of 1647 and in subsequent amendments passed in 1671 and 1683. Even stronger than the Massachussetts laws were the Connecticut Laws of 1650. These laws were specific in the description of duties and responsibilities of individuals selected to oversee the schools (Campbell, Cunningham, Nystrand, and Usdan 1980).

The laws enacted in the New England colonies directing the public to control the schools became the pattern throughout the rest of the country. Not until 1721 in Boston, however, were individuals responsible for overseeing the schools set apart from the local governmental structure of the community (Campbell et al. 1980). Following this lead, other states and communities started separating the administration of schools from local governments.

Powers and Responsibilities of Boards

Today the powers and responsibilities of local school boards are established by state statutes. State laws dictate the size of boards, terms of office, methods to fill vacancies, meeting requirements, and the duties of board members.

Specific duties frequently cited include

- designing and constructing buildings
- staffing schools with appropriate staff
- determining which students will be served at various schools
- enforcing state and federal laws
- abiding by court decisions
- transporting students (Campbell et al. 1980)

Local boards also have some discretionary powers. For example, they may exceed various state requirements for graduation, teacher qualifications, or course offerings; they may pay teachers more than the state mandated minimum salary; they may set salaries in states without minimum teachers' salaries; or they may elect to offer a wide variety of extracurricular activities or none at all. Therefore, while local boards of education are obligated by state law to accomplish certain activities, many decisions can be made at the local level that are not bound by state or federal statutes or litigation decisions.

Specific responsibilities of local boards of education include the following:

- To delegate to the superintendent responsibility for all administrative functions, except those specifically reserved through board policy for the board chairperson. Those reserved areas might include: conducting board meetings and public hearings, approving the agenda and minutes and other activities incidental to, and associated with, serving as presiding officer of the board.

- To support the superintendent fully in all decisions that conform to professional standards and board policy.

- To hold the superintendent responsible for the administration of the school through regular constructive written and oral evaluations of the superintendent's work. Effective evaluation is an ongoing effort and should be linked to goals established by the board with the assistance of the superintendent.

- To provide the superintendent with a comprehensive employment contract.

- To give the superintendent the benefit of the board's counsel in matters related to individual board members' expertise, familiarity with the local school system, and community interests.

- To hold all board meetings with the superintendent or a designee present.

- To consult with the superintendent on all matters, as they arise, that concern the school system and on which the board may take action.

- To develop a plan for board-superintendent communications.

- To channel communications with school employees that require action through the superintendent, and to refer all applications, complaints, and other communications, oral or written, first to the superintendent in order to assure that the district processes such communications in an effective, coordinated fashion and is responsive to students and patrons.

- To take action on matters only after hearing the recommendations of the superintendent.

- To establish a policy on the effective management of complaints.

- To provide the superintendent with sufficient administrative help, especially in the area of monitoring teaching and learning. (Roles and Relationships: School Boards and Superintendents 1980, pp. 3–4)

Local boards of education comprise community members who are either elected by the local citizenry or appointed by elected officials and have the responsibilities of operating the local school district. With the assistance of local school administrators, boards "establish policy, consider relevant state and federal guidelines, and seek appropriate information before making important decisions..." (Podemski, Price, Smith, and Marsh 1984, p. 3).

The individuals who make up local school boards vary from wealthy to poor, educated to uneducated, interested in the schools to interested in self-advancement. While school board members represent all segments of the community, they are most often from higher educated, upper-middle-class groups. The latest survey of school board members published in *The American School Board Journal* describes the typical school board member as "a white man in his forties who's married and has children attending public school in the system he serves. Armed with at least a college degree, he holds a professional or managerial position and earns a family income of between $40,000 and $50,000. He was elected—not appointed—to his position on the school board, and he has served his community in that capacity for six years" (Alvey, Underwood, and Fortune 1986, p. 26) The majority of board members in 1985 were male (63.9%) and white (93.5%) (Alvey, Underwood, and Fortune 1986). Approximately ninety thousand Americans serve on local boards of education. That number alone reveals the interest of our citizenry in the quality of education in this country.

PROFESSIONAL ADMINISTRATIVE STAFF

Public schools are administered by a host of professional staff, with the superintendent being the chief school officer hired by the local school board. Responsible to the superintendent are many other professionals involved in school administration, including central office staff, principals, and assistant principals.

Districtwide Administrative Staff

Administrative staff that oversee all activities within the district are housed in the central office. These include the superintendent and any assistant administrators who may be employed to assist the superintendent in carrying out districtwide activities.

Superintendents. Superintendents are the chief executive school officers in local school districts. They are hired by the board of education and normally serve at the pleasure of the board. Consequently, superintendents are responsible to their boards for all of the activities within the school district.

The duties and responsibilities of superintendents vary among districts as a result of the size of the district, the financial condition of the district, and the expectations of the local school board and community members. However, most superintendents perform certain functions regardless of the district in which they serve. Examples of these duties include (1) maintaining relationships with the board, (2) organizing staff, (3) maintaining positive relationships among the community, and (4) ensuring that all legal requirements are met by the district (see table 9–1). In 1980 the American Association of School Administrators published *Roles and Relationships: School Boards and Superintendents*. Specific responsibilities of the superintendent included the following:

1. To serve as the board's chief executive officer and advisor.
2. To serve as the school system's educational leader.
3. To keep the board informed about school operations and programs.
4. To keep the community informed about board policies, programs, and district procedures.
5. To interpret the needs of the school system to the board.
6. To present and recommend policy options along with specific recommendations to the board when circumstances require the board to adopt new policies or revise existing policies.

TABLE 9–1   Roles of School Superintendents

Role	Description
Maintain relations with board	Keeps in contact with board
	Informs board of staffing decisions
	Advises board on policy decisions
	Informs board of school activities
	Informs board of the needs of the schools
Educational Leader	Stays informed about educational practices
	Facilitates staff development
	Secures necessary teaching materials and equipment
	Encourages educational innovations
Maintain positive relations with the community	Disseminates information about school programs
	Forms community advisory groups
	Informs parents about school activities
	Facilitates contacts between school staff and community

7. To develop and inform the board of administrative procedures needed to implement board policy.
8. To provide leadership for the district's educational programs.
9. To develop an adequate program of school-community relations.
10. To manage the district's day-to-day operations.
11. To evaluate personnel and keep the board informed about evaluations. (Roles and Relationships: School Boards and Superintendents 1980, p. 5)

The district superintendent, therefore, is a key individual in the functioning of any local school district. The individual occupying this position "is obviously the most important member of the administrative team at the district level..." (Gorton 1983, p. 121). This person must give information and counsel to a host of groups, including other administrators, board members, teachers, parents, and students (Doremus 1985). There are approximately fourteen thousand superintendents in the United States. The majority of superintendents are employed in districts with between 300 and 2,999 students, have a master's degree or higher, and are males (Knezevich 1971) (see table 9–2).

Central office staff. In large school districts, the superintendent is assisted by one or more assistant superintendents. In smaller districts, all central office functions are carried out by the superintendent. Large districts, however, require so many actions by the central office that assistant superintendents and other administrative staff are necessary. There are approximately fifty thousand administrative staff in school districts that assist the superintendent in carrying out central office duties. These individuals, primarily assistant superintendents, directors, or supervisors, carry many different titles, including

- assistant superintendent
- assistant superintendent for business
- assistant superintendent for personnel
- assistant superintendent for pupil services

TABLE 9-2   Characteristics of School Superintendents

Characteristic	Mean
Age	48.1 years
Entry age—first superintendency	36.7 years
Classroom teaching experience	7.4 years
Years in first superintendency	6.4 years
Total years as superintendent	11.6
Number with Master's degree as highest degree	65.7%
Number with Doctorates	15.4%
Hours per work week	56.1
Number who would select superintendency as vocation again	71.4%

Source: Knezevich 1971.

- administrative assistant
- director of elementary education
- director of secondary education
- director of curriculum
- director of special education
- director of adult education
- director of instructional materials
- director of audiovisual education
- director of publications and information
- director of planning
- director of research
- director of evaluation
- director of finance
- director of buildings and grounds
- director of health services
- director of cafeteria services
- director of transportation
- elementary supervisor
- primary supervisor
- music supervisor
- art supervisor
- physical education supervisor

- mathematics consultant

- science consultant

- foreign language consultant (Campbell et al. 1980, pp. 251–52)

Most school districts do not employ all of these administrative staff; however, in large school districts all of these positions, plus others, may be filled. The number and variety of administrative staff in the central office varies, primarily as a result of district size and financial condition.

The duties performed by central staff administrators are determined by their specific roles. For example, in a small district there may only be one assistant superintendent. This individual may be assigned the responsibilities for transportation, food services, and the curriculum. In larger districts, these duties may be divided among several central office staff members.

Building-Level Administrative Staff

At the building level, principals are the key administrators. Many schools also employ assistant principals, department heads, and supervisors to assist the principal in carrying out the administrative duties found at the building level.

Principals. Similar to superintendents, who oversee the operations of the entire district, principals are responsible for all activities that occur within their school building. Simply stated, "the school principal is a primary force in making a school work" (Caputo 1980, p. 25) The roles expected of principals have expanded dramatically during the past twenty years. For example, prior to the passage of Public Law 94–142 in 1975, principals had little to do with special education programs. One teacher may have had fifteen students in a self-contained setting. As a result of P.L. 94–142, however, principals must spend a great deal of time with special education activities. One study indicated that principals spend an average of 15 percent of their time on activities related to special education, a major shift from pre–P.L. 94–142 (Raske 1979).

Federal legislation, therefore, often places extra burdens on the principal. Other factors that have affected the roles of principals include demographic changes, the economy, collective bargaining, influence of state and federal governments, and the news media (Gorton 1983) (see table 9–3). Certainly the role of school principals has changed dramatically from the days when the principal teacher was the school's administrator. No longer can schools simply promote male teachers or athletic coaches who have been with the district for many years into the job of principal. The position is currently far too complex and requires many different skills.

Roles of principals. Principals are expected to perform many varied roles in today's schools, including manager, instructional leader, disciplinarian, human relations facilitator, evaluator, and conflict manager (Gorton 1983). The roles of the principal can also be organized by (1) the learning environment, (2) the learning needs of children, (3) the instructional program, (4) staff development, (5) community resources, (6) building management, and (7) financial management (Klopf, Scheldon, and Brennan 1982). In small, rural schools the roles of principals often go beyond expectation. Wilkens (1983), in detailing his activities as a principal in such a school,

---

TABLE 9–3   Factors Affecting the Role of Principals

Factor	Impact
Demographic Changes	Decline in school enrollments Increase in school enrollments Difficulty in estimating future enrollments Changes in tax base
State of Economy	Unemployment and reduced tax base Tax revolt movement Difficulty in passing millage increases
Collective Bargaining	Adversarial relationship between principals and teachers Collective decision making Teacher assignment difficulties Forced reallocation of school budgets
Federal and State Government	Legislation mandating actions Funds for certain programs Regulations and paperwork Court imposed activities
News Media	Negative publicity Positive publicity Generalizations resulting from media coverage

---

Source: Gorton 1983.

revealed that his roles included working on school buses, herding cows from the playground, looking for a child's first lost tooth on the playground, and "discussing" a child's discipline problems with an irate, aggressive father. Although the principal's role as instructional leader is considered by many to be the primary role, without expertise and leadership in the noninstructional activities, the school would have a difficult time functioning.

A major function of the principal is to manage all aspects of the school, including the instructional program, school plant, food services, transportation, pupil and personnel services, and budget. With all these different areas to manage, principals need to be well skilled in management.

As part of management responsibilities, "the school administrator is expected to procure, organize, and coordinate both physical and human resources so that the goals of the organization can be attained effectively" (Gorton 1983, p. 72). In other words, management of all school resources should be geared toward the accomplishment of the school goals.

The principal as instructional leader is another role that is frequently mentioned when discussing what principals do. Instructional leadership includes "those actions that a principal takes, or delegates to others, to promote growth in student learning" (De Bevoise 1984, p. 15). The principal should be heavily involved in the curriculum of the school and the instructional process. A few of the responsibilities related to this role are to

- ensure that the curriculum of the school meets state and district guidelines;

- ensure that the curriculum meets the needs of students;

The instructional leadership role includes being aware of what takes place in classrooms.

- ensure that teachers are qualified to teach the level of students in their classes;

- ensure that teachers are qualified to teach the subjects they are assigned;

- resolve conflicts among staff related to the instructional program;

- keep abreast of current curricular trends and developments that might be appropriate for adoption by the school.

Howell (1981) suggests that there are seven leadership tasks related to instructional leadership, including supervision of teachers, teacher evaluation, staff development, scheduling, planning, selection of instructional materials, and student evaluation. Many teachers actually look to the principal for guidance related to teaching. Too often principals get overly involved in activities such as management and discipline, and the instructional program may suffer as a result. Principals should, however, make a strong effort to get into classrooms and stay involved in the instructional program of the school. Principals simply need to spend more time out of their offices with teachers and students than most principals do (Taylor 1978).

De Bevoise (1984) analyzed research related to the principal as an instructional leader. The following are highlights from the analysis:

- Principals cannot exercise instructional leadership in a vacuum. They need support from teachers, students, parents, and the community.

- Common leadership functions that must be fulfilled in all schools include communicating the purpose of the school, monitoring performance, rewarding good work, and providing staff development. Whether these functions must be carried out by the principal depends upon the composition of the teaching staff and the organization of the school district.

- While previous studies have generally concentrated on only one facet of instructional leadership—such as personal traits, leadership styles, management behaviors, or organizational contexts—current studies tend to address the interrelationships among these factors.

- The personal characteristics of the principal cannot be ignored when studying what constitutes effective instructional leadership. However, studies of personal characteristics and leadership styles are of limited use out of context.

- The desirable characteristics of effective principals have not been convincingly correlated with student achievement. (De Bevoise 1984, p. 18)

Although many different activities occupy the principal's time each school day, principals must return to the instructional leadership role, the role that actually began the profession. Although the responsibilities for scheduling, record keeping, and staff development must be addressed by principals, realizing that these functions are secondary to instructional leadership in facilitating the school's instructional goals may help keep principals more involved in the instructional program (Pinero 1982).

School discipline has been the major concern expressed by many Americans during the past several years (Polakowski 1984). In the opinion of many, especially parents and students, a primary role of the principal is that of disciplinarian. The role of disciplinarian is time consuming for many principals. Principals often reject this role because of its negative perception, because the disciplinarian is the one who punishes students (Gorton 1983). Regardless of the desire of principals to be removed from implementing punishment, adequate discipline must be maintained in schools if the goals and objectives of the school are to be met. The instructional program, student and teacher morale, and community support can all be negatively affected by schools without adequate discipline. Since the principal is the chief administrative officer of the school, the ultimate responsibility for discipline belongs to that office.

Principals must establish a positive climate for good discipline. To do so, they must view discipline from the total school perspective, not merely isolated cases of inappropriate behavior. Lordon (1983) suggests that principals determine (1) the commitment of the school staff for out-of-class discipline, (2) the clarity of school policies, (3) the attitudes of teachers about discipline, (4) consistency of disciplinary policies in the school, and (5) the clarity of supervision policies. By looking at these areas, principals are in a better position to implement a consistent, well-founded school discipline policy.

Establishing an effective discipline program can be facilitated if students are taught to be successful, have the opportunity to be responsible for their actions, and are encouraged to establish positive social relationships. Principals should also examine chronic discipline problems to determine if other actions would be more successful (Maynard 1983). Disciplining the same child for the same infraction day in and day out obviously means that something is not working. Principals must understand that all disciplinary measures will not be successful with all children and try different measures when standard procedures are not successful. Three features should be included in any effective discipline program:

- a philosophy of discipline clearly stated in the student handbook;

- visible authority figures;

- suitable punishments and consistent application of school rules. (Fellmy 1983, p. 68)

Principals do spend a great deal of their time on discipline. However, if the school's discipline program is adequate, excessive amounts of the principal's time on disciplinary matters can be eliminated.

Principals must also perform the role of facilitator of human relations. To do this, the principal must exhibit good human relations skills, as well as foster such skills in the school staff. Staff morale and the climate of the school are related to the human relations skills of the principal and staff (Gorton 1983). If conflicts arise among staff, if overall staff morale is low, or if the school climate or environment is not healthy, the goals and objectives of the school could be negatively impacted. Therefore, administrators must be able to recognize these negative forces and intervene to create a positive environment.

Another primary role of the school principal is evaluation. With the wave of emphasis on accountability, parents, students, and professionals are demanding that proof be provided of the the effectiveness of the school program. This requires principals to evaluate programs, personnel, and in some cases, even students (Gorton 1983).

HIGHLIGHT

Austin Agrees to New Evaluations for Teachers

By David Davies
Gazette Staff

Faced with complaints from about a third of the teachers in the North Little Rock School District concerning their yearly job evaluations, Dr. Joe Austin, District superintendent, agreed Tuesday that all evaluations would be redone.

Dr. Austin announced the decision at a meeting Tuesday of the School Board. Earlier Tuesday, a committee of principals and teachers and head-ed by Board member Larry Lazenby had recommended that job evaluations be redone.

Dr. Austin had formed the committee last week in response to grievances filed May 19 by about 200 teachers. The teachers complained they had been ranked unfairly in the middle of the District's nine-point rating system. Representatives of the North Little Rock Classroom Teachers Association had said most teachers were getting 5's and 6's when they deserved better evaluations, and had asked that the evaluations be redone.

District officials did not know Tuesday how many teachers had been evaluated so far this year nor how many had been evaluated in the middle of the evaluation scale.

Lazenby said he did not know whether a disproportionate number of teachers had been ranked in the middle of the scale. He said the committee would meet again after evaluations are redone and determine whether there was a "distribution like you would expect."

Before the evaluations are redone, Dr. Austin said, administrators will meet with principals to discuss the evaluation procedure and tell them "they are free to use that scale at any point." He acknowledged that "teachers perceived that we put some kind of lid" on the scale, but denied the allegation he had told principals to give most teachers 5's and 6's.

"We're going to make doggone sure [principals] understand the directions that we give" concerning the evaluations, Dr. Austin said.

Principals will not be asked to again observe teachers in the classroom, Dr. Austin said, but instead will be instructed to meet individually with all teachers and re-evaluate them using the notes they took in previous classroom visits.

Sue Perry, a teacher at Ole Main High School who headed a committee established by teachers on the evaluation complaints, thanked the administration for its action, and her remarks were followed by applause from teachers at the meeting. The applause prompted Murry Witcher, Board president, to quip, "Boy, we needed that."

Perry asked the Board to appoint a committee of teachers elected by their colleagues to make recommendations about the evaluation system, but the Board took no action.

The teacher evaluation system, established this school year, was drafted by a group of teachers and administrators. The new evaluation system replaced a system in which teachers were ranked in one of three categories. Dr. Austin said earlier that the old evaluation system unfairly ranked teachers at the higher end of the scale.

The new evaluation system ranks teachers from 1 to 9 in five categories: Instruction, classroom management, knowledge of subject content, planning and communications and human relations.

According to the District's system, a score of 8 or 9 in a category constitutes "exceptional performance," 6 or 7 "commendable performance," 4 or 5 "professionally competent," 2 or 3 an "area of concern" and 1 "unacceptable performance."
Arkansas Gazette, May 28, 1986. Permission to reprint by *Arkansas Gazette.*

Program evaluation is a multifaceted activity. There are many different evaluation models, including the discrepancy evaluation model (DEM); context, input, process, product model (CIPP); program evaluation review technique (PERT); and formative and summative model (Podemski, Price, Smith, and Marsh 1984) (see table 9–4). Regardless of the model used, the principal must do several things to carry out the evaluation function, including

- determining who should be involved in the evaluation;

- establishing evaluation criteria;

- selecting methods of evaluation;

- collecting data;

- analyzing data;

- drawing conclusions and developing recommendations;

- reporting findings;

- implementing recommendations. (Gorton 1983, p. 74)

Personnel evaluation is a major responsibility of the principal. Principals are expected to determine which staff are doing a good job and which ones need counseling and possibly termination. While principals have always been expected to evaluate teachers, in the past this has been less formal and less frequent than it will be in the future (McDaniel 1982). With the current trend of investigating merit pay plans and increased demands for accountability, personnel evaluation will become much more critical.

As with program evaluation, there are many different approaches to personnel evaluation. Haefele (1980) summarized the ones most often used as (1) performance of students on standardized tests; (2) gains students make during the school year, as determined by standardized tests; (3) test scores of students compared among classes; (4) informal observations of the teacher; (5) systematic observation of the teacher by the principal or supervisor; (6) systematic observation of the teacher by peers; (7) students' ratings of the teacher; (8) scores earned on the National Teacher Examination (NTE); (9) students' performance on a predetermined set of teaching objectives; (10) scores on the Teacher Perceiver Interview (TPI); (11) teacher responses to written descriptions or films of classroom problems; and (12) attainment of goals predetermined by the teacher and principal or supervisor. Although there are many criticisms to each evaluation approach, Haefele (1980) believes that the last method, having teachers and administrators develop goals and objectives and measuring teacher performance against those goals and objectives, is the best method.

Through evaluation, principals can determine strengths and weaknesses in the instructional program and in personnel. If weaknesses exist, principals may need to

TABLE 9–4 Models for Program Evaluation	
Model	*Description*
Discrepancy Evaluation Model (DEM)	• Develops standards • Compares results with standards • Necessary adjustments made to respond to any discrepancies
Context, Input, Process, Product Model (CIPP)	• Determines needs of programs • Determines resources required for programs • Provides ongoing monitoring of program components • Determines the attainment of goals and objectives previously established
Program Evaluation Review Technique (PERT)	• Develops a chart that includes all activities and timelines necessary to reach goals and objectives • Enables ongoing monitoring of program relative to projections in chart • Enables program modifications if necessary
Formative and Summative Evaluation	• Monitors program during its process • Measures results or products

Source: Podemski, Price, Smith, and Marsh, 1984.

As change agents, principals must encourage teachers to develop new skills such as educational uses of the computer.

intervene with program modifications or personnel counseling in the case of inadequate performance by staff. Ongoing evaluation enables principals to be aware of the success of the school's programs and provide additional support to certain aspects of the program that may need improvement.

The final role included by Gorton (1983) is that of conflict mediator. Conflicts may develop as a result of student disruptions, teacher militancy, or demands by some community members for greater involvement in the operation of the school. Regardless of the source of conflict, school principals must intercede to reduce conflicts. When conflicts exist, the entire school operation can be disrupted, greatly impeding the attainment of school goals and objectives. "When one views the turmoil surrounding education today, it is clear that the role of conflict mediator is an essential one for the school administrator" (Gorton 1983, p. 75).

Principals have roles and responsibilities other than those delineated by Gorton (1983). These include acting as a change agent or innovator and working with the community in community relations. The role of change agent is one that many principals relish. This role gives principals the opportunity to assume a leadership role in instigating changes in the school. The changes may be in the areas of instruction, curriculum, personnel policies, discipline, or any other area. Principals set the tone or atmosphere in their buildings. If principals are supportive and encouraging of change and innovation, changes and innovations are more likely to occur than if principals are nonsupportive (Sivage 1982; Mechling 1983). Mechling (1983) discusses the role played by principals in improving science programs. He states that "in schools where the climate is open—where the principal leads in curriculum and instruction, stays close to his staff, and recognizes that improvement needs careful spadework—the seeds for change are already there" (Mechling 1983, pp. 16–17).

Principals who want to facilitate change rather than maintain the status quo need to do several things (Sivage 1982). First, they must create the climate for change and encourage collaboration among staff. Second, they must delegate responsibilities for change efforts to teachers. Innovations managed by teachers are often more success-ful than activities dominated by principals. Third, principals must reward individuals who invest time in the change efforts and are willing to try new things. Fourth, social support for individuals involved in innovations must be provided. Fifth, ample oppor-tunities must be provided for communication among school staff so that everyone knows what is going on. Finally, the processes involved in communication, problem solving, and decision making must be strengthened. Maintaining the status quo is relatively easy compared with developing and implementing innovations; however, if schools are to improve, changes are often necessary.

Principals also must perform a major role related to community relations. Al-though the "neighborhood school" may not be as common as it once was in this country, the community that is located near a school is vital to the success of the school. Principals must help foster this support. Gaining and maintaining active community support is difficult. The first group that should be involved is parents. Parents who are involved in the school operations provide principals with much needed political support. More important, however, parents who are involved in decision making in the school are more likely to support those decisions than if they were simply imposed upon them (Jenkins 1981).

Jenkins (1981) presented a model for parent involvement in urban schools that was effective in gaining parental support. The model should be effective in rural and suburban schools as well. There are five levels to the model:

Level 1: Entry. Efforts are made to get parents interested in the school pro-grams. Assemblies, information dissemination, and home visits are examples of activities.

Level 2: Getting Involved. Parents become directly involved with the education-al program of their children. An example would be to have parents listen to their children read for twenty minutes each night.

Level 3: Curriculum Participation. This requires more parent involvement; an example would be to invite parents to participate in a workshop that focuses on the instructional program.

Level 4: Self-Assertion. This level includes a workshop where parents learn how to deal with their child's self-concept and how to intervene with prob-lems.

Level 5: Decision Making. Parents get directly involved in the school's decision making.

Expectations of principals. Principals are expected to do many different things for different groups of people, such as teachers, students, central administration person-nel, state departments of education, and the local community (see figure 9–2).

Specifically, students expect principals to have a personal relationship with them. This is the most important, ardent expectation expressed by students in several

At the Building Level	At the District Level
1. Teachers and other members of the faculty 2. Other administrative personnel in the school 3. Students 4. Clerical and maintenance staff	1. The superintendent 2. Central office administrative/ supervisory staff 3. The school board 4. Administrators in other schools

Local and State Groups

1. Parents 2. Parents' organizations 3. Social, labor, and business organizations	4. State department of public instruction 5. Professional organizations 6. Accreditation agencies

Figure 9-2. *Groups with expectations of principals. Reprinted with permission. R.A. Gorton.* School Administration and supervision. *Dubuque, IA: William C. Brown Company Publishers, 1983.*

studies (Gorton 1983). Students also want fewer rules and rules that are more reasonable. As students get older, they are more interested in textbook review, scheduling, and the evaluation of teachers (Taylor 1978). Different students expect different things from their principals. Academically inclined students may be in favor of principals supporting higher academic standards, providing higher level courses, and holding less academic students responsible for their poor performance. Students whose primary interest is athletics will likely have different expectations of their principals. They will want the principal to be understanding of their travel and practice requirements, encourage teachers to be flexible in homework assignments, and generally support school athletics.

Another reference group whose expectations are as important to the principal as students are teachers. Because of the central role teachers play in the educational process, principals must attend to the expectations teachers have of them. After reviewing several studies, Gorton (1983) determined three major expectations held by teachers for principals:

1. The school administrator should support the teachers in the building on issues and problems of student discipline.
2. The school administrator should treat teachers as professional colleagues, not subordinates.
3. The school administrator should provide opportunities for teachers to participate in decision making, especially when dealing with decisions that directly affect teachers.

Still another important group that holds expectations of principals is parents. Parents in the community may be able to exert a great deal of power over the principal through the school board and superintendent. Although many parents have minimal expectations of their principals, others have rather high expectations and may be very verbal when these expectations are not met. Generalizing about the expectations of parents is difficult, because they are such a diverse group. Some are educated, others not; some have high-paying jobs, others may be on welfare; and some have a very high, specific interest in the schools, while others may not care.

Some expectations of principals expressed by parents include (1) instructional leadership, (2) collaboration with parents, and (3) interest in children (Gorton 1983). These expectations are broad, but consist of most of the specific expectations that could be voiced by parents. While not having to respond to all of the expectations held by parents, principals definitely need to be aware of these expectations and attempt to meet those that have a positive effect on the school.

Principals must also adhere to the expectations of their superiors, namely the superintendent and school board. Although the principal in most districts is hired by the superintendent in conjunction with the board, principals must be aware of the expectations held by both groups. Some expectations held by the principals' superiors would include

- carrying out school policy;
- maintaining a positive relationship with community members;
- providing instructional leadership;
- maintaining student discipline;
- maintaining staff morale;
- effectively managing the school.

Principals, therefore, are expected to do different things by a host of groups. Although principals cannot always meet the expectations of everyone, they must at least determine the feasibility of meeting the expectations, the impact on the school and on their personal life if the expectations are not met, and the importance of the expectations to the goals and objectives of the school. Principals cannot be all things to all people; they must make decisions related to which expectations are in the best interests of the school.

Typical day of principals. As has been described, principals have many different roles and functions and are expected to please many groups. All of these tasks appear to be overwhelming. Howell (1981) studied the ways principals spend their days by having fourteen middle school and junior high principals record their activities every fifteen minutes on a particular day. The results indicted that paperwork was the major activity performed, taking up approximately 33 percent of the principals' time. Other activities included parent conferences (13.5 percent), personnel conferences (13.5 percent), discipline (9 percent), scheduling (9 percent), cafeteria duties (9 percent), supervision (7.5 percent), and instructional leadership (2.5 percent). Less time was spent on instructional leadership than any other major activity, a finding not inconsistent with other studies.

Principals, therefore, are burdened with many responsibilities that take away time that could be used in the instructional program. Although these times are probably representative of many principals at all levels, principals in effective schools likely spend more time related to the curriculum and instruction.

Effective principals. Principals, like other employees, can either be effective or ineffective. Shoemaker and Fraser (1981) reviewed several studies that investigated effective schools and found that principals can have a major impact on the effectiveness of schools. In general the findings indicated that in those schools considered "high achieving," principals were strong leaders, had high expectations, and were oriented to cognitive goals. Effective principals are those "who have learned to lead within that work structure, to identify and use the discretionary authority they have, and to expand their discretionary powers within the larger organization" (Manasse 1982, p. 15). Although principals can become bogged down with a variety of tasks not directly associated with instruction, when they do get involved in their instructional leadership role, positive gains can result in the achieving level of the school.

Assistant principals. Some schools employ assistant principals to help principals carry out their many and varied responsibilities. Assistant principals perform many activities, depending on the wishes of the principal. Marsh (1981) described the many different roles he performed while serving as an assistant principal for several different principals. These included assisting the principal with duties associated with (1) the lunchroom, (2) transportation, (3) books and supplies, (4) bicentennial program planning, (5) assemblies, fire drills, and special events, (6) policy-making decisions, and (7) curriculum. Marsh (1981) pointed out that his role as an assistant principal varied considerably from one principal to the next. Some principals had openly

Assistant principals perform many varied roles in the school, sometimes even cafeteria supervisor.

involved him in most school activities, while others had severely restricted his activities.

When used effectively, assistant principals can prove a valuable resource to the principal. If not properly used, assistant principals can be more of a burden than an asset. Principals need to learn how to best utilize assistant principals to relieve some of their work load while increasing the efficiency of the school.

CAREERS IN ADMINISTRATION

Educational administration is a career for many individuals. As previously indicated, approximately sixty-four thousand superintendents and other central office staff serve in public school programs. Added to this number are principals and assistant principals. With approximately eighty-five thousand elementary and secondary schools in this country, it could be estimated that there are eighty-five thousand principals. Although not every school employs a principal, the great majority do. Therefore, there may be approximately 150,000 positions in administration in American public schools.

How to Become an Administrator

Most school administrators start out as classroom teachers. This seems to be the best way to become a school administrator. Most states have specific certification requirements for administrators that go beyond the requirements for a teaching certificate. These certificates are usually job specific; that is, there is a state-issued elementary principal certificate, secondary principal certificate, supervisor certificate, and superintendent certificate. The requirements for these certificates vary from state to state, but they usually include college coursework at the graduate level and years of experience as a teacher. Some states (e.g., Michigan) do not yet require a specific license for administrators.

Individuals interested in becoming a school administrator should write the state department of education in the state where the certificate is desired. The request should generally be addressed to the state certification office.

Benefits of School Administration

School administrators receive many benefits, including

- higher salaries than teachers;
- management responsibilities;
- opportunities for advancement in administration;
- leadership opportunities.

Although not substantially more, administrators do earn higher salaries than teachers. The Educational Research Service and the National Association of Secondary School Principals conducted a study to determine the salaries paid to administrative personnel in 1,217 school districts. The results indicated that the lowest salary paid to a school principal was $13,556, and the highest salary was $63,024. The mean salary earned by a secondary principal was $32,520, $30,260 for a junior high

TABLE 9-5   Salaries of Principals 1983-84: Mean & Median of Minimum Salaries Scheduled*

	Enrollment Stratum				
	25,000 or more	*10,000 to 24,999*	*2,500 to 9,999*	*300 to 2,499*	*Total: All Systems Reporting*
Senior High Principals					
No. Systems Reporting	128	211	208	62	609
Mean	32,960	33,193	32,710	28,689	32,520
Median	32,804	34,303	32,913	29,066	32,760
Range: Low	18,574	15,510	13,556	18,750	13,556
High	63,024	49,427	52,000	39,608	63,024
Junior High and Middle School Principals					
No. Systems Reporting	125	207	205	62	599
Mean	30,330	30,503	30,608	28,154	30,260
Median	30,469	31,443	31,163	28,000	30,538
Range: Low	16,864	15,510	13,556	19,200	13,556
High	51,873	45,151	50,000	38,550	51,873
Elementary School Principals					
No. Systems Reporting	128	211	223	78	640
Mean	28,163	28,250	28,387	27,540	28,194
Median	27,916	28,526	28,685	27,492	28,230
Range: Low	15,044	15,510	13,556	17,093	13,556
High	47,740	39,000	47,000	43,209	47,740

* *Using enrollment of the school district as a comparative factor.*
Reprinted with permission. Administrative Information Report. *National Association of Secondary School Principals and Education Research Services, 1984.*

TABLE 9-6   Salaries of Assistant Principals: Mean & Median of Minimum Salaries Scheduled*

	Enrollment Stratum				
	25,000 or more	*10,000 to 24,999*	*2,500 to 9,999*	*300 to 2,499*	*Total: All Systems Reporting*
Senior High Assistant Principals					
No. Systems Reporting	128	214	208	45	595
Mean	26,814	27,533	27,527	24,753	27,166
Median	26,448	28,333	28,099	25,144	27,258
Range: Low	15,898	14,314	13,556	15,650	13,556
High	49,111	42,726	47,000	35,276	49,111
Junior High and Middle School Assistant Principals					
No. Systems Reporting	120	204	188	24	536
Mean	25,487	25,822	26,498	24,728	25,935
Median	25,470	26,386	27,389	25,156	26,168
Range: Low	15,393	14,041	13,556	15,456	13,556
High	49,000	38,340	47,000	35,559	49,000

* *Using enrollment of the school district as a comparative factor.*
Reprinted with permission. Administrative Information Report. *National Association of Secondary School Principals and Educational Research Service, 1984.*

TABLE 9–7   Profile of Fringe Benefits Currently Available to Elementary School and Middle School Principals

Type of Benefit	All Reporting Systems	Type of Benefit	All Reporting Systems
Percent providing vacation leave	73.1	Mean monthly benefit/limit	$ 1,477
Percent providing sick leave	99.0		14.9
Specified number days per year	96.4	Percent providing group life insurance	76.3
Provided as needed*	3.6	Fully paid*	69.5
Unlimited accumulation of unused leave days allowed*	44.7	Mean percent of premium paid if less than full	67%
Sick leave counts towards retirement service*	36.0	Mean face value/maximum value of policy	$25,236
Percent providing personal/emergency leave	90.8	Percent providing severance pay	36.0
Charged in whole or part to sick leave*	34.3	Percent with tuition reimbursement provisions	22.8
Percent providing sabbatical leave	55.9	Convention attendance:	
Mean number of leave days		Percent paying at least part of cost	80.2
Vacation leave—		Percent providing professional leave to attend	69.9
Minimum number of days credited per year	12	Percent paying at least part of professional dues	37.2
Maximum (or fixed) number of days credited per year	19	Percent providing transportation expenses	95.5
Maximum accumulation	30	Mileage allowance*	83.1
Sick leave—		Annual allowance*	2.6
Days credited per year	13	Monthly allowance*	5.6
Maximum accumulation	133	Both mileage and annual allowance*	1.4
Personal/Emergency leave—		Mean mileage allowance**	$ .18
Days allowed per year	4	Mean annual allowance**	$ 625
Percent providing insurance:		Mean monthly allowance	$ 76
Group hospitalization	95.1	Percent paying at least part of the cost of physical exam	22.4
Family coverage*	70.5		
Fully paid*	47.9	Percent providing professional liability insurance	71.3
Medical/surgical	93.0		
Family coverage*	70.8	Percent with retirement plans:	
Fully paid*	48.2	State retirement system	96.8
Major medical	93.9	Local retirement system	1.9
Family coverage*	71.5	Social security coverage	53.4
Fully paid*	48.4	Tax-sheltered annuity plan	77.5
Dental	50.6	Early retirement option	39.7
Family coverage*	67.7		
Fully paid*	51.7		
Vision care	15.4		
Family coverage*	54.8		
Fully paid*	43.5		
Prescription drugs	42.6		
Family coverage*	64.9		
Fully paid*	43.0		
Percent providing income protection insurance	30.3		
Mean percent of salary covered	66%		
	24.0		

Note: Tabulations of family group insurance coverage do not include school systems that provide such coverage under "cafeteria plan" arrangements.

* Percents based on only those respondents providing the benefit specified above.

** Includes data from school systems reporting both mileage and annual allowances.

School salaries, 1981: An NAESP/ERS research report. Principal 61(4), 46–50. Reprinted with permission, Educational Research Service.

principal, and $28,194 for an elementary school principal (Administrative Information Report 1984). Secondary principals receive higher salaries than those in junior high and elementary schools; the size of the district was not a major factor except in very small districts (see table 9–5).

Salaries for assistant principals were also determined by the ERS study. The lowest salary paid to an assistant principal was $13,556; the highest salary paid was $49,111. The mean salary received by assistant principals was $25,935 (Administrative Information Report 1984) (see table 9–6).

In addition to salaries, school administrators usually receive a variety of fringe benefits, some of which are not available for the district's teaching staff. Examples of fringe benefits include vacation leave, insurance, severance pay, travel expenses, professional liability insurance, retirement plans, and housing (see table 9–7).

SUMMARY

This chapter focused on educational administration. The beginning section discussed the administrative hierarchy found in schools. Although differing to some degree among districts, the administration hierarchy of public schools is fairly similar. At the top is the local school board. The board has powers that have been established by state statutes. Superintendents are hired by the board to carry out board policy, and they in turn employ principals and other professional administrative staff to carry out the functions of the school.

The local board of education is most often an elected body of lay persons from the community. Boards have legislated, specific powers, such as building buildings, and discretionary powers, such as establishing policies that go beyond the state minimum requirements for graduation. Local boards must work closely with the superintendent, since that individual is the chief administrative school official.

Superintendents have many responsibilities, but the most important one is to advise the board and serve as the school district's educational leader. Superintendents are key individuals in the effectiveness of the school district and must respond to the wishes of many groups, including the board, staff, and parents. In some districts, superintendents have the assistance of other central office administrators. The number of these assistants is usually determined by the size and wealth of the school district.

At the building level, principals are the chief administrative officers. They oversee the entire operation of their particular school and are expected to perform a variety of jobs. These include instructional leader, manager, disciplinarian, facilitator of human relations, conflict manager, evaluator, and change agent. Each of these roles was thoroughly discussed in the chapter.

In performing these many and varied roles, principals must consider the expectations of many groups. The superintendent and central office administrative staff, teachers, parents, students, and community members all have expectations of the principal. Principals spend their days doing a host of different jobs, and research has determined that too often principals are bogged down with paperwork and other administrative chores at the expense of the instructional leadership role. Still, there are many effective principals. For the most part, effective principals do get involved in the school's instructional program and juggle other duties in an appropriate priority.

The final section of the chapter focused on how to become a school administrator and the benefits of school administration. In most states, the prerequisite for becoming a school superintendent or principal is to be qualified or certified by the state department of education or state department of public instruction. This usually requires various degrees and a certain number of college credits in administration coursework. Salaries and fringe benefits for administrators usually surpass those for teachers. Therefore, for individuals so inclined, school administration is a rewarding vocation.

IN THE FIELD

1. Is the local board of education in the district elected or appointed? How many individuals make up the board and what are their terms?

2. Who makes up the local board of education?

3. Does the board have a set of board and district policies? If so, are they accessible to students and teachers?

4. What are included in local district policies?

5. Is there a list of duties and responsibilities for the local superintendent?

6. What other central administrative staff are there in addition to the superintendent? What are their duties?

7. Are there any assistant principals in your building? If so, what are their specific duties and responsibilities?

8. What activities of the principal suggest that he/she is an effective administrator?

9. What different roles does the principal fulfill?

10. What are some of the expectations of teachers and students of the principal?

11. How does the school principal spend a typical day?

REFERENCES

Administrative Information Report. 1984. Reston, Virginia: *Salary report #1: Principals and assistant principals.* National Association of Secondary School Principals.

Alvey, D. T., K. E. Underwood, and J. C. Fortune. 1986. Our annual look at who you are and what's got you worried. *American School Board Journal 173*(1), 23–27.

Brieschke, P. A. 1985. Principals in schools: Insubordination in discretionary decision making. *The Educational Forum 49*(2), 157–69.

Campbell, R. F., L. L. Cunningham, R. O. Nystrand, and M. D. Usdan. 1980. *The organization and control of American schools.* Columbus, OH: Charles E. Merrill Publishing Co.

Caputo, E. M. 1980. Freedom, order, and school-based management: One principal's story. *Principal 60*(2), 25–27.

De Bevoise, W. 1984. Synthesis of research on the principal as instructional leader. *Educational Leadership 41*(5), 14–20.

Doremus, R. R. 1985. The superintendent as teacher. *Educational Leadership 42*(5), 82–84.

Fellmy, W. 1983. Keys to effective discipline: Making rules simple, clear, and visible. *National Association of Secondary School Principals Bulletin 67*(462), 68–70.

Gorton, R. A. 1983. *School administration and supervision.* Dubuque, IA: William C. Brown Company Publishers.

Haefele, D. L. 1980. How to evaluate thee, teacher—Let me count the ways. *Phi Delta Kappan 61*(5), 349–52.

Howell, B. 1981. Profile of the principalship. *Educational Leadership 38*(4), 333–36.

Jenkins, P. W. 1981. Building parent participation in urban schools. *Principal, 61*(2), 21–23.

Klopf, G. J., E. Scheldon, and K. Brennan. 1982. The essentials of effectiveness: A job description for principals. *Principal 61*(4), 35–38.

Knezevich, S. J., Ed. 1971. *The American school superintendent.* Arlington, Virginia: American Association of School Administrators.

Lordon, J. F. 1983. Establishing a climate for school discipline: The total perspective. *National Association of Secondary School Principals Bulletin 67*(462), 58–60.

McDaniel, T. R. 1982. What's your PQ (principalship quotient)? A quiz on improving instruction. *Phi Delta Kappan 63*(7), 464–68.

Manasse, A. L. 1982. Effective principals: Effective at what? *Principal 61*(4), 10–15.

Marsh, L. 1981. Nobody knows the principals I've seen. *Educational Leadership 38*(7), 542–43.

Maynard, B. 1983. Is your discipline policy part of your discipline problem? *The Executive Educator 5*(3), 26–27.

Mechling, K. R. 1983. Taking charge: How principals can improve school science programs. *Principal 62*(3), 16–21.

National Center for Education Statistics. 1983. *The condition of education.* Washington, DC: National Center for Education Statistics.

Pinero, U. C. 1982. Wanted: Strong instructional leaders. *Principal 61*(4), 16–19.

Podemski, R. S., B. J. Price, T. E. C. Smith, and G. E. Marsh. 1984. *Comprehensive administration of special education.* Rockville, MD: Aspen Systems.

Polakowski, K. 1984. Some ideas on discipline. *The Clearing House 58*(2), 83–84.

Raske, D. C. 1979. The role of general school administrators responsible for special education programs. *Exceptional Children 45*(8), 645–46.

Roles and relationships: School boards/superintendents. 1981. Arlington, Virginia: American Association of School Administrators.

School Salaries. 1981. An NAESP/ERS research report. *Principal 61*(4), 46–50.

Shoemaker, J., and H. W. Fraser. 1981. What principals can do: Some implications from studies of effective schooling. *Phi Delta Kappan 63*(3), 178–82.

Sivage, C. R. 1982. Oiling the gears: How the principal helps, or hinders, change. *Principal 61*(4), 20–23.

Taylor, R. G. 1978. If I were boss . . . *Education 99*(1), 8–9.

Wilkens, E. R. 1983. Lives of a rural principal. *Principal 62*(5), 27–29.

Chapter 10
SCHOOL FINANCE *

OBJECTIVES

After reading this chapter, you will be able to

- define taxes;
- classify types of taxes;
- discuss tax shifting;
- list various tax sources;
- trace the development of school finance;
- describe local tax support for public schools;
- discuss the property tax and the issue of equity;
- discuss the methods in which states support public education;
- describe federal support for education and the future of such support.

OUTLINE

ADVANCE ORGANIZERS
INTRODUCTION
TAXES
    Classification of Taxes
    Tax Shifting
    Tax Sources
THE DEVELOPMENT OF SCHOOL FINANCE
    School Finance During Colonial America
    School Finance After the Colonial Period
LOCAL SUPPORT FOR SCHOOLS
    Property Tax

STATE AID FOR EDUCATION
    Minimum Foundation Programs
FEDERAL SUPPORT OF EDUCATION
    Formula Grants
    Discretionary Funds
    The Future of Federal Aid
SUMMARY
IN THE FIELD
REFERENCES

Dr. Martin Schoppmeyer of the University of Arkansas is the author of this chapter.

1. What are taxes?
2. What benefits do taxpayers receive from education?
3. What is a progressive, proportional, and regressive tax?
4. What is tax shifting?
5. Where do taxes come from?
6. How did public support for schools develop?
7. How are property taxes used to support public schools?
8. What are the issues in equitable school finance?
9. What is a minimum foundation program?
10. How does the federal government support public education?
11. What is the future of federal support for public education?

INTRODUCTION

Schools, like any other organization, require money with which to operate. Funds must be available to establish and maintain an up-to-date educational program, pay salaries, purchase supplies and equipment, provide transportation, maintain buildings and grounds, construct new buildings, contract for some services, and provide staff development. Without funding for these activities, schools would not be able to provide appropriate educational programs for students, the basic purpose of public schools. As with any other public enterprise, the chief source of these funds is taxes. Schools receive tax dollars from local, state, and federal governmental levels.

HIGHLIGHT

SCHOOL FUNDING UP 8.7%
N.H. Leads With Increase of 45%

By Richard Benedetto
USA Today

The push to continue improving the USA's schools has triggered a $6 billion gain in state education spending for fiscal 1986.

Support for elementary and secondary schools jumped 8.7 percent, to $71.3 billion, according to the National Conference of State Legislatures. Overall state spending grew only 6.7 percent.

The increase for education was nearly 10 percent in 1985.

For fiscal 1986, 26 states posted higher increases than the 8.7 percent average, and 22 were lower. Only Nebraska and Alaska had decreases.

"While we're generally pleased with the increases, some states are still inadequate and have a long way to go," said Keith Geiger of the National Education Association.

Big gainers:

- New Hampshire—up 45 percent; revised local aid formula to put more money into less-wealthy school districts.

- Illinois—up 16.8 percent; $90 million to raise teacher salaries, improve reading programs and aid pre-schoolers.

- Virginia—up 15 percent; boosted spending by $296 per pupil and created five regional high-tech high schools.

- Nevada—up 25 percent; raised teacher salaries 11 percent, provided funds to improve curriculum.

USA Today. April 6, 1985. Copyright, 1985.
USA Today. Reprinted with permission.

TAXES

A tax is a payment to a government to pay for various services. The definition of taxes has not changed over the years, and can still be considered "a compulsory contribution from the person to the government to defray the expenses incurred in the common interest of all with reference to special benefits conferred" (Seligman 1925, p. 432).

Schools receive tax money because public education is a matter of common interest. However, a relationship does not exist between the payment of a tax for education and the receipt of any direct benefit. The recipients of a public education are children, who pay no taxes; the taxpayer is an adult with or without children to be educated. No special benefits are received from the tax by the taxpayer. However, taxpayers benefit indirectly from publicly supported education programs by

- increasing the level of education in the community;

- attracting industry and additional tax base to the community as a result of having a sound educational program;

- increasing the earning power of local students thereby increasing the tax base.

Classification of Taxes

Taxes can be classified in a number of ways. One important method is in terms of the effect of the tax upon the taxpayers. When related to the taxpayer's income, a given tax may be termed progressive, proportional, or regressive. A progressive tax is one where a person with a higher income pays a greater proportion of that income than an individual with a lower income. The federal and state income taxes are the closest approximation of progressive taxation, because individuals with different incomes pay a different percentage of their taxable income (see table 10–1). However, various deductions and shelters detract from the progressive nature of the income tax.

A proportional tax requires the same percentage of each person's income to be paid in taxes. A sales tax is an example, assuming that all income is spent in a manner subject to taxation. Persons who save or invest part of their income and do not spend it lower the proportion of it which is taxed. Hence, the sales tax has certain regressive tendencies.

A regressive tax is one where a person with a lower income pays proportionally more in taxes than someone with a higher income. The property tax, which is based

---

TABLE 10-1   Federal Tax Rates

Schedule X Single Taxpayers

Use this Schedule if you Checked Filing Status Box 1 on Form 1040—

If the amount on Form 1040, line 37 is:		Enter on Form 1040, line 38	of the amount over—
Over—	But not over—		
$ 0	$2,300	-0-	
2,300	3,400	11%	$2,300
3,400	4,400	$121 + 12%	3,400
4,400	6,500	241 + 14%	4,400
6,500	8,500	535 + 15%	6,500
8,500	10,800	835 + 16%	8,500
10,800	12,900	1,203 + 18%	10,800
12,900	15,000	1,581 + 20%	12,900
15,000	18,200	2,001 + 23%	15,000
18,200	23,500	2,737 + 26%	18,200
23,500	28,800	4,115 + 30%	23,500
28,800	34,100	5,705 + 34%	28,800
34,100	41,500	7,507 + 38%	34,100
41,500	55,300	10,319 + 42%	41,500
55,300	81,800	16,115 + 48%	55,300
81,800	—	28,835 + 50%	81,800

Source: *Federal Income Tax Forms and Instructions 1984. United States Department of the Treasury.*

on the assessed value of a house, may be an example of a regressive tax. Two families occupying houses of the same value may have different incomes, yet pay the same amount in property tax. Since the property tax bears no necessary relationship to income, it is often termed a regressive tax (Johns, Morphet, and Alexander 1983). On the other hand, persons with a lower income are more likely to take advantage of local services paid for with the property taxes, such as parks and public schools, while the higher income earner may well choose private schools and country clubs. This tends to decrease the regressive nature of the property tax.

Tax Shifting

A second important aspect of taxes is what is termed shifting, which means simply having someone else pay the tax for you. An example of tax shifting would be a landlord who receives an increase in property taxes and passes the increase to tenants through raised rents. A utility that must pay increased property taxes could raise electric rates to shift the added tax burden to the consumer.

Too often the consumer is the victim of tax shifting. The price of a loaf of bread includes part of the tax burden of the farmer, the miller, the baker, and the retail store. Consumers cannot avoid having to pay for the extra tax burden placed on businesses and providers of services.

Tax Sources

Each level of government—local, state, and federal—theoretically may be able to tax the same things; however, this is generally not the case. The levels of government usually rely on different taxes as their primary sources of revenue. For the federal government, these sources are primarily individual and corporate income taxes. Many states also tax income, but for the most part states depend upon sales taxes, severance taxes, exise taxes on alcohol and tobacco, and where legal, pari-mutuel betting and lotteries for their revenues. Local governments often have sales taxes, but their basic revenue source is from property taxes.

Local governments are prohibited from taxing states or the federal government on federal and state land and property within city limits. To compensate local governments for this loss of revenue, the federal government and many states make payments in lieu of taxation to local governmental units. Property such as military bases, parks, forest and grazing lands, wildlife areas, wilderness areas, and governmental buildings are examples of these kinds of properties.

THE DEVELOPMENT OF SCHOOL FINANCE

Prior to the settlement of North America, the support of schools with tax funds was unknown in western Europe. Not until Prussia began the practice in the early eighteenth century did any European nation have public tax supported schools (Butts 1955). On this side of the Atlantic, the Massachusetts Bay Colony enacted the "olde deluder Satan" law of 1647. Not only did this act create tax supported schools, but it set an unfortunate pattern of permitting communities to evade their responsibilities by paying a fine rather than operating a school. Some towns found it cheaper to pay the penalty rather than operate a school (Good and Teller 1973).

Therefore, the idea of spending tax funds to support public education, but only as little as possible, took root and still exists today. The latest Gallup Poll on attitudes toward the public schools revealed that, although people are dissatisfied with public schools, the majority would not vote a tax increase to improve them (Gallup 1985). Only 38 percent of the individuals polled indicated that they would support increased taxes to support public schools. Fifty-two percent indicated that they were against raising taxes, while 10 percent had no opinion. In the 1984 survey, 41 percent indicated that they were in favor of raising taxes for education, which indicates a negative trend in public opinion for financing educational programs. Too many people want quality education programs but do not want to pay the price necessary to provide adequate support.

School Finance During Colonial America

All of the New England colonies with the exception of Rhode Island enacted versions of the "olde deluder" law in the seventeenth century (Good and Teller 1973). In the Middle and Southern colonies, private and church supported schools were the rule. These, like the private schools in New England, depended upon charity and tuition payments. The most famous method of tuition was called the rate bill. This, similar to what some private schools practice today, often provided for a lesser tuition charge for the second or additional child. Public tax support of schools in the Middle and Southern colonies was not present in colonial America.

School Finance After the Colonial Period

Shortly after the end of the revolutionary war, the Continental Congress passed the Northwest Ordinances of 1785 and 1787. These laws granted section sixteen of every township in the Northwest Territory, later extended to all new territory added to the Union, for the use of education. This meant that the land could be used for a school location, it could be rented and the payment used to support a school, or it could be sold and the proceeds invested with the interest earned used for operating a school. The "Permanent School Fund" created by the latter option became the basis for school funding in the early days of the Republic. Aided by lotteries, gifts, and donations, schools were started in the new states, as well as the older states where public education had fallen on bad times due to the waning influence of the Puritan church. In some communities, tax funds were spent on education; however, they were not legally required to do so and the practice was very limited.

The leadership of Thomas Jefferson and Horace Mann in the early nineteenth century made tax supported schools more acceptable and accessible. However, "despite the advocacy of Jefferson and many others, tax supported public education did not generally become available in the Middle Atlantic and Midwestern states until after 1830 and in the Southern states until the last quarter of the nineteenth century" (Johns, Morphet, and Alexander 1983, p. 235).

Battles over statewide referendums to use tax funds to support public schools were fought in New York and Pennsylvania. Finally, the United States Supreme Court in 1874 approved that taxes could be spent on high schools (Good and Teller 1973).

By 1900 the principle of tax supported schools was firmly established and the stigma associated with attending "charity schools" supported by tax money had been removed. This attitude enabled the expansion of public schools in this country. Had this change of attitude not occurred, publicly supported education would not have become the foundation of the American educational system.

The turn of the century also marked the final chapter of passage of compulsory school attendance legislation. Prior to 1900 thirty-two states had such laws; by 1920 all states had adopted them (Good 1956). In 1900 only 8 percent of the fourteen- to seventeen-year-old group was enrolled in public high schools (Johns, Morphet, and Alexander 1983). This number expanded dramatically, largely at the secondary school level, following the passage of compulsory schools laws. Since secondary education programs are more costly than elementary programs, added pressure was placed on local, state, and even national authorities for additional funding for schools. Although federal aid to higher education existed as early as 1862, the beginning of the twentieth century marks the start of federal aid for public elementary and secondary schools, in the form of the Smith-Hughes Act and expanded state programs of aid to local districts. Current methods of financing schools are rooted in the developments of this era.

LOCAL SUPPORT FOR SCHOOLS

Historically, the primary source of funding for public schools has been local taxation. Recently, however, this has been changing. States currently provide a larger share of support due largely to initiatives that have placed limits on property taxes, such as Proposition 13 in California and Proposition 2½ in Massachusetts. The property tax is still the backbone of local taxation, and therefore, a major source of funds for public education. Such a tax is imposed on real estate and may also be applied to personal property, both tangible, such as automobiles, and intangible, such as bank accounts, stocks, and bonds.

Property Tax

Each county within a state normally administers the property tax. Several officials are involved. The county assessor determines the value of the property to be taxed. This can be done on several different bases such as actual cash value, fair market value, or use value. Two different assessors can determine two different values even using the same method. As a result, most counties have Equalization Boards, which review assessments when they are challenged by the property owner. The board has the final decision as to the assessment.

Another factor adds confusion to property assessment. Many states use what are termed assessment ratios where the taxable assessment is a legally set percentage of

The county tax office is a key component in educational finance.

the real value. Thus, a $100,000 home would be assessed at only $40,000 if the assessment ratio is set at 40 percent.

The property tax collector's role is rather self-evident. This official has the responsibility of collecting taxes and enforcing penalties for nonpayment, which consists of selling tax deeds to the property upon which taxes have not been paid. In some states the property owner has a grace period of several years to redeem (i.e., purchase) these deeds plus accumulated interest. If this is not done, the deeds against the title, or liens, make it difficult to sell. In either case, the tax is ultimately collected.

The county also has a treasurer or other official acting in such a capacity whose function is to distribute the tax revenues among the various taxing authorities within the county. For example, if there is more than one school district in the county, each receives the funds that it is due from the property assessments within its district boundaries.

Tax rate. In most states, the tax rate on property is expressed as millage. A *mill is a tenth of a cent or a thousandth of a dollar.* Hence, millage rates can be expressed as either twenty mills or twenty dollars per thousand. Millage rates are at least partly set by elections. The voters determine the level of millage that they want to pay, which can be a problem with property tax income since this is the only form of taxation that requires a popular vote. An antitax mood cannot be taken out on federal or state taxes directly, but can have an impact on local millage elections. Quite often local millage increases fail, which can be very harmful to school building programs and other activities in the district. School officials cannot easily convince taxpayers that they should vote to increase their taxes, especially when many of those taxpayers do not even have school-age children. Teachers should be aware of the system used in their states.

School buildings. Although the idea of statewide authorities issuing school construction bonds to fund new school buildings is growing, construction of most new school buildings is the responsibility of local boards of education. If the district cannot build a new school from existing local funds, it must borrow the money by selling bonds. To sell the bonds, a millage amount sufficient to pay interest and retire the bonds within a set time frame, normally a twenty-year period, must be passed. To achieve this, the community must be made well aware of the need. If not, the millage increase may be defeated and no new buildings will be available. School administrators are responsible for selling the need for this tax increase to fund new construction.

State assessments. In most states railroad and utility properties, along with carriers such as aircraft and large trucks, are assessed by a state agency. This provides a standard method of assessment of these kinds of property within a state. Each county, school district, or other taxing authority is credited with the amount of the assessment that lies within its borders. Therefore, school districts receive a fair share of taxes paid by utilities and carriers.

Differences in wealth. Differences in the wealth of local school districts obviously exist. Some will have more taxable property than others. In some districts the value of the property may be much higher than in other districts. For example, some suburbs, primarily populated by young, upwardly mobile professionals, the so-called YUPPIES which the media discuss so frequently, will likely have houses with a much higher average value than found in older, established cities with mostly older dwellings.

Districts with more money may or may not have more children to educate. When one district has far more taxable wealth per pupil than another, it can afford to provide a superior education at the same level of tax effort than another district with less valued taxable property. A district may even be able to do this at a lower tax rate.

The child in the poorer district may not have the same educational opportunity as the child in the wealthier district. Wealthier districts can pay higher teacher salaries, and therefore, possibly attract better-qualified staff. They can also purchase state-of-the-art equipment, such as computer equipment, which can only enhance educational opportunities. This situation raises the issue of equity, which has been the concern of state aid programs for several decades; recently the courts have become involved with this issue.

———— HIGHLIGHT ————

Momentum Grows for Change in School Funding

By Scott Van Laningham
Gazette Staff

Finding a way other than property taxes to fund public education picked up momentum Thursday among state legislators, frustrated over the difficulties of ensuring equity statewide in property tax assessments.

The legislative Joint Revenue and Taxation Committee was reviewing the implementation of Amendment 59, which was designed to prevent large property tax increases after the court-ordered statewide property reappraisal, when legislators turned their attention to looking for other ways to fund public education.

Marvin Russell, administrator of the state Assessment Co-ordination Division, reported to legislators that a preliminary review has shown that some counties that underwent reassessment five years ago already have slipped in assessments below 20 percent of market value, the condition that prompted the lawsuit and court-ordered reassessment.

Russell said the Division has developed a new manual to assist assessors, but the manual itself came under fire from officials from Garland County.

Ish Beame, chairman of the Garland County Equalization Board, and William Windell, chief deputy in the Garland County assessor's office, told the Committee that use of the new manual could re-

sult in a property tax increase of 15 percent to 20 percent in Garland County.

Windell said the county would need to recheck the assessments of about 35,000 parcels of land by August to comply with Division guidelines and the county couldn't do that without additional staff members.

State Representative Charles R. Moore of Luxora said quorum courts always would be reluctant to add staff members to assessors' offices because the additional staff could find additional property to add to tax books and update assessments, in effect resulting in property tax increases. "I think it's time we seriously considered, at least study, getting away from funding schools with property taxes, real property especially," Moore said.

Representative John E. Miller of Melbourne said he had been advocating the same thing for years and a proposal to study doing that will go before the Legislative Council today. He said he had been convinced of the need "for devising a new system to support the operations of schools" before Amendment 59 was adopted.

Miller also said that despite the criticism of Amendment 59, the measure was "doing what it was designed to do," prevent "confiscating people's property" through higher taxes stemming from court-ordered reassessment.

Several legislators nodded in agreement with Moore and Miller as they called for a new system to fund public education, which now receives about 80 percent of property taxes. A proposed constitutional amendment to change the system was sponsored in the last legislative session by state Senator Clarence Bell of Parkin but failed to get enough support to get out of committee.

Miller, however, said he didn't think a constitutional amendment was needed and the legislature could develop another source of funding for public schools. He suggested the system might include allowing school districts to use property taxes to finance construction of buildings while the state provided another source of operating and maintenance funds.

The Committee took no formal action on the proposal but adopted a resolution calling for a legislative committee to review the assessment manuals developed by Russell's office. Russell said the manual hasn't been submitted to the State Agencies Committee, which reviews rules and regulations promulgated by state agencies, because the manual was only a guideline and not a rule or regulation.

Beame, however, noted that if the Division uses the manual and finds that a county's assessments have dropped below 18 percent of market value, the state will withhold from the county a portion of state turnback funds.
Arkansas Gazette. January, 17, 1986. Permission for reprint by Arkansas Gazette.

Equity in financing. Equity refers to many things in school finance. One example is equity for taxpayers. Should taxpayers in one school district be required to pay a much higher rate of taxation than taxpayers in another district to maintain the same level of public education? More important, should children receive a less-adequate education in one district than children in another district merely because one district has lower assessments per child and, therefore, fewer dollars to spend on school programs? The question is: Do children have a right to access the same quality program regardless of where they live in a state?

This issue has been debated for years. State aid programs have tried unsuccessfully to provide adequate solutions to the equity problem. The issue finally found its way to court in California in the case of *Serrano v. Priest*. In this case, the California Supreme Court declared that the school finance plan violated the California constitution, because it denied equal treatment of the law as the education of the child in question was comparatively underfinanced. In its ruling, the court stated that the California financing plan "as presently constituted is not necessary to the attainment of any compelling state interest. Since it does not withstand the requisite 'strict scrutiny,' it denies to the plaintiffs and others similarly situated the equal protection of the laws" (Benson 1975, p. 85). A similar case, *Robinson v. Cahill* arose in New Jersey. The New Jersey Supreme Court stated that equal educational opportunity must exist throughout the state.

Finally, a case involving equitable school financing reached the United States Supreme Court. In this case, *San Antonio Independent School District v. Rodriquez* the Court declared that since education was not a right guaranteed by the United States Constitution that relief would have to be sought at the state level. In making its decision, the Court indicated that "its decision should not be interpreted as placing a 'judicial imprimatur' upon the status quo. But the ultimate solution, said the Court, should come from the lawmakers in each of the states" (Campbell, Cunningham, Nystrand, and Usdan 1980, p. 41). As a result, more cases have been brought in state courts seeking equity. The supreme courts of Connecticut, Washington, West Virginia, and Arkansas have declared that equity was not being achieved under their state aid formulas. On the other hand, the courts in Arizona, Michigan, Ohio, Maryland, and Georgia have held that the inequities found in their states were acceptable. Equal access to an education is still an unsettled issue. State finance plans have to provide at least an approximation of equal educational opportunities. In the meantime, courts have not ceased to speak on the topic; additional cases will likely be filed involving equitable school financing before the issue is settled.

STATE AID FOR EDUCATION

During the latter nineteenth century, states recognized the need for funding local schools at a higher level than many local districts could afford. State aid began as an equal amount per pupil whenever they lived within the state's boundaries. This system was termed a flat grant, because it did not consider differences in local wealth.

By the 1920s state laws began to recognize the need to equalize educational opportunity through the equalization of funding. The New York legislature, in attempting to equalize school financing in that state, exacted the Strayer-Haig formula. The concept behind this approach was for the state to rank all of its school districts from top to bottom in terms of their expenditures. Then a district would be selected and districts spending less than the amount expended by the selected district would receive state aid sufficient to bring it up to the level of the selected district.

This approach, although sound, led to several abuses. It did not consider the cost of educating children in different districts, and it did not look at the matter of local district effort. A district could be spending fewer dollars than the optimal district, because it had improperly lowered property assessments or tax rates. Although corrective actions were taken to alleviate some of these abuses, states continued to seek other solutions.

Minimum Foundation Programs

The concept of the Minimum Foundation Program was developed in the 1940s as a solution to equalizing school finance. This idea was based on the state's guarantee that every child receive an educational program funded at an average minimal level. Wealthier, or higher taxing districts, could go beyond this minimum amount with local effort. Districts funding programs above the minimal level were termed "lighthouse" districts, because they set a pattern that other districts could model. This idea, adopted in several states, required the state to calculate the district's wealth. In the states where local assessment practices were questionable, an index of taxpaying ability was used. This index, using alternative measures of wealth rather than property assessments, was translated into a calculated tax base for the district, which then had to raise an appropriate amount of local tax revenues to receive state aid. Alternative measures included personal income, sales tax receipts, auto license fees, the value of farm products, and the preparation of nonfarm equipment.

Utilization of these measures meant that an underassessed district would receive a higher calculated wealth index and be forced to raise its tax rate. An overassessed district, on the other hand, might have a lower-than-average millage rate.

How minimum foundation aid works. Minimum foundation aid works as follows: Each district's wealth is determined either by the use of actual assessment data or by a calculated tax base. Each district must levy a statewide millage on that base. Then the cost of educating children in the district is determined. The funds raised, or supposedly raised, by the local district are subtracted from the cost of education, and the difference is made up by state aid. Individual states have developed numerous variations to this concept. However, most are based on the same concept.

Only one state has solved the problem of equity in funding. This is Hawaii, which has only one school district and all funding is on a statewide basis. Of the states with multiple school districts, Utah has come closest to solving the funding problem. In Utah, if a school district charges the required statewide millage and produces more revenue than it costs to run its schools, the excess funds are returned to the state, which can then distribute the funds to schools in other districts.

Costs of educational programs. The calculation of the cost of education for minimum foundation requires the recognition that the education of some children costs more than others. Some states have class size limits on primary grades. Vocational education, special education, science and computer literacy programs, and education for gifted children will require added funding. The method generally used to calculate these cost differences is called *weighting*.

Weighting. Weights are cost factors assigned to represent the average added cost of education for certain groups of students. They are expressed as percentages of costs for regular students. Weights can be calculated in two general ways: as teacher units and as weighted pupils.

Teacher units. Teacher-unit weighting is expressed as a proportion of regular units. Assuming that a state has defined a teaching unit as twenty-five children, then a primary unit could be twenty students, a vocational class fifteen, and some special education classes ten or fewer students. The student population is totalled by category, regular students are divided by twenty-five, and the other categories are divided by the assigned numbers. The total number of units are then multiplied by whatever number of dollars the state has determined will be spent per teacher unit.

Weighted pupils. The weighted-pupil approach works in a parallel fashion to teacher units. A regular child is weighted as 1.00. Assigning weights of 1.25 to a primary child, 1.65 to a child in vocational education, and 2.50 to a child in special education generates approximately the same amount of cost as using the teacher-unit method. The total number of weighted children is then multiplied by the dollar amount that the state has determined should be expended for each child.

Drawbacks to minimum foundation plans. Although they are the most commonly used state funding method, minimum foundation programs are not without drawbacks. One, which became evident soon after the programs were started, is that although minimum foundation programs were enacted to ensure funding at a minimum level, the "minimum" became the standard in most districts. Rather than becoming the true minimum to be exceeded, the minimum became the standard to be attained. The result is that minimum foundation programs have not led to equity, because the expenditures of wealthy districts cannot be restricted. They can and do vastly exceed the minimum or guaranteed amount. This creates a highly inequitable situation, because children in one of the select districts will have a higher quality program available than the average child in the state due purely to the accident of residence. Therefore, efforts to enact equitable educational opportunities for all children in a state should continue.

FEDERAL SUPPORT OF EDUCATION

Federal aid to public education did not begin until the twentieth century. Prior to that time, federal interests were directed almost totally toward higher education, with the exception of the Northwest Ordinances. During the nineteenth century, Congress created the military and naval academies and passed the Morrill Acts, which gave land grants and operating funds to states for the operation of colleges and universities. As a result, each state has at least one land grant university.

Federal involvement in precollegiate education began with the Smith-Hughes Act of 1917. This law provided for vocational education in secondary schools for agriculture, home economics, trade, and industrial education. Boards were created at both state and federal levels to oversee the distribution of these funds, which had to be matched by the states (Butts 1955).

Federal involvement in public education increased through programs such as school lunches, the Civilian Conservation Corps (CCC), and the National Youth Administration (NYA), which were developed during the depression of the 1930s. While these programs did not provide direct aid to the instructional process, they did have a positive effect on the public schools.

Federal funds have long been used in such programs as school lunches.

The late 1950s and early 1960s saw the establishment of large-scale federal aid to public education through the National Science Foundation (NSF), the National Defense Education Act of 1958 (NDEA), and the Elementary and Secondary Education Act of 1965 (ESEA). These actions, which were taken primarily in response to advances in science by the Soviet Union, set the trend for direct federal aid to public education. Other legislation passed by Congress during this period provided for Teacher Corps, Education Professions Development, Bilingual Education, Education for the Handicapped, and a flurry of other programs. Many of these programs were combined in 1981 by the Educational Consolidation and Improvement Act. By 1980 the annual total dollar figure of these programs for elementary and secondary schools was in excess of seven billion dollars (Johns, Morphet, and Alexander 1983).

Unlike state aid to education, federal aid is not concerned with equity. Rather, it is concerned with special problems. Federal aid is categorical; it can only be spent for those purposes specified in the authorizing legislation, regardless of the school district's needs. It is distributed in two ways, by formula and by discretion. Formulas determine the division of most federal money, yet in general, more programs have been funded by discretionary means.

Formula Grants

Formula funding is based on the number of children eligible for a particular funded program. This total is then multiplied by a dollar amount, which may vary from state to state. The best example of this is Chapter I of the Educational Consolidation and Improvement Act, which is still well known by its previous designation as Title I of ESEA. This, which is the largest federal aid program for public education, distributes well over three billion dollars each year to school districts. The number of children living below the poverty level is calculated to determine how much of these funds a given school district will receive. Then the state expenditure per pupil, but no less than 80 percent or more than 120 percent of the national average expenditure, is calculated (Ginsburg, Noell, and Rosenthal 1985). The number of eligible children in each county is then multiplied by a portion of the expenditure figure, and the funds are distributed to the states where the amounts to be received by individual districts are determined.

Chapter II funds are calculated on the basis of the same dollar amounts for each child enrolled in a particular program. States, at their option, may vary the dollars expended per pupil within the state to favor urban or rural schools. Funds must be spent within a specific category, however, as defined by federal law.

Discretionary Funds

Although in recent years the amount of discretionary funding from the federal government has decreased, it still continues. Unlike formula funds, applications must be made for discretionary funds. The applicant, a local school district or state educational agency, must demonstrate a need for the program and outline in detail its plans for carrying out the program. These applications are competitive, and only a certain number receive funding. Information concerning these programs is published in the *Federal Register*, which is printed daily. The *Federal Register* contains new and altered regulations covering all federally funded programs, including education. Requests for proposals (RFPs) also appear in a second publication, the *Commerce and*

Business Daily. Such reports, or RFPs, solicit programs that provide a service to the Department of Education or to certain groups of children.

Categorical aid. Federal aid to public education must be spent only on federally defined categories and cannot be used to supplant state or local funding; it can only supplement them. For example, if a state requires a program in bilingual education, the school district cannot totally support such a program from federal funds. Federal dollars might be used to enlarge or supplement the program, but not to provide the basic instruction. This situation has led many to believe that federal aid should become more general. Recently, the combination of many categories into Chapter II of ECIA in 1981, which is known as a block grant, has met with considerable approval. This approach allows greater state and local discretion in the use of federal funds.

The federal government has had only one noncategorical aid program for education, Impact Aid. Originally contained in the Lanham Act, which was passed at the beginning of World War II, the concept was to give money for buildings and operations to school districts severely affected by defense activities. A small, rural school district would not be able to absorb children from a new army post or an urban school would not be able to take in the children of workers at new defense plants by relying totally on local and state funds. In time the building aid became Public Law 815, and the operating aid became Public Law 874. Districts qualify for these funds on the basis of the number of children living on federal property and the number of children whose parents are federal employees. In recent years the highest concentration of the latter variety of students is in the Washington, D.C., suburbs. As a result, every president since Dwight Eisenhower has tried to eliminate the program. However, the funding is so popular with schools that receive the funds because of its flexibility that Congress has continued the funding. In recent years, the appropriations for these programs have been severely restricted, and the programs may soon be terminated.

The Future of Federal Aid

With school enrollments beginning to increase as a result of children of the baby-boom generation, aid to education will become a major political issue. In addition, as the education of the handicapped and other special groups continues to be recognized as a responsibility of schools, costs will continue to escalate. These facts, combined with the atmosphere to improve public education in the United States, make it likely that federal aid to education will continue and may possibly increase. The nature of the aid, however, may change. The Reagan administration has pushed hard for block grants rather than the categorical aid that has been the rule. Whether more aid is moved to the block category remains to be seen; however, substantial reduction in federal aid to education is unlikely.

SUMMARY

This chapter investigated school finance. Public education must be funded through local, state, and federal governments. Taxes are the source for these funds. Taxes used for educational purposes come from income taxes, primarily at the federal and state levels, sales taxes at the state level, and local property taxes at the local level.

A major problem discussed in the chapter dealt with equity in school financing. This has long been a controversial issue. Should children who reside in a school district with limited funds be provided an inferior education? Should districts with ample wealth, due to a broad tax base, be able to offer their school children educational opportunities that far exceed the norm? Efforts have been made to resolve these issues with little positive results. Unequal school finance still remains. Not only have states and local districts attempted to solve this problem, but recently the federal government, through the courts, has been involved.

One section of the chapter focused on the ways states have attempted to deal with the equity issue and with court cases testing the existing system. State funding programs such as minimum foundation, which were developed to guarantee that every child receives an opportunity to at least a minimally quality education, have been implemented nationally. However, the issue still remains; school finance remains inequitable in most states.

The final section of the chapter discussed the role of the federal government in funding public educational programs. Federal involvement with precollegiate education is relatively new. The aid, which is mostly categorical in nature, has grown from a small beginning to several billion dollars annually. With the trend to improve education and the increasing student population in public schools, federal financing will likely continue. The nature of the future funding, however, remains to be seen.

IN THE FIELD

1. What percent of the school district's budget is from local taxes?

2. What percent of the school district's budget is from the state?

3. What percent of the school district's budget is from federal funds?

4. Have the percentages of budget money from these three sources changed during the past five years? If so, what is the trend?

5. What is the current millage rate for the school district?

6. When was the last election to increase the local millage?

7. Is another millage increase needed during the next three years?

8. What attempts have been made in the state to equalize school financing among districts?

9. What is the minimum foundation program like in the state?

REFERENCES

Benson, C. S. 1975. *Education finance in the coming decade.* Bloomington, Indiana: Phi Delta Kappa Foundation.

Butts, R. F. 1955. *A cultural history of western education.* New York: McGraw-Hill Book Company.

Campbell, R. F., L. L. Cunningham, R. O. Nystrand, and M. D. Usdan. 1980. *The organization and control of American schools* (4th Ed.). Columbus, Ohio: Charles E. Merrill Publishing Co.

Gallup. 1985. The 17th annual Gallup poll of the public's attitudes toward the public schools. *Phi Delta Kappan 67*(1), 35–47.

Ginsburg, A. L., J. Noell, and A. S. Rosenthal. 1985. Is the federal "chapter I" education formula equitable? *Journal of Education Finance 10*(3), 360–74.

Good, H. G. 1956. *A history of American education.* New York: Macmillan Publishing Co.

Good, H. G., and J. D. Teller. 1973. *A history of American education.* 3d ed. New York: Macmillan Publishing Co.

Johns, R. L., E. L. Morphet, and K. Alexander. 1983. *The economics and financing of education.* 4th ed. Englewood Cliffs, NJ: Prentice-Hall, Inc.

Robinson v. Cahill (62 NJ 473, 303 A.2nd 273).

San Antonio Independent School District v. Rodriquez (411 US 1).

Seligman, E. R. A. 1925. *Essays in taxation.* 10th ed. New York: Macmillan Publishing Co.

Serrano v. Priest (487 P.2nd 1241).

Chapter 11

EDUCATIONAL PSYCHOLOGY *

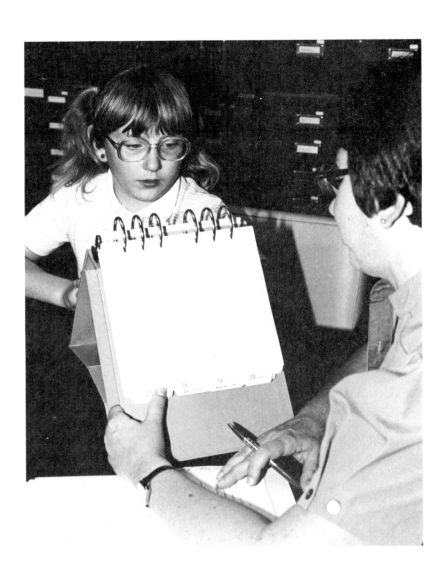

OBJECTIVES

After reading this chapter, you will be able to

- discuss the general principles of human development;
- discuss the key concepts of Piaget's theory;
- list the cognitive states of development identified by Piaget;
- discuss language development;
- describe the components of moral development;
- describe behaviorism as a learning theory;
- discuss operant conditioning;
- discuss cognitive learning theory;
- understand motivation and motivational theory;
- describe the major necessary components of measurement.

OUTLINE

ADVANCE ORGANIZERS
INTRODUCTION
HUMAN DEVELOPMENT
    The Development of Thinking
    The Development of Language
    The Development of Morality
PRINCIPLES OF LEARNING
    Behavioral Theorists

Cognitive Theorists
Eclectic Theorists
MOTIVATION
MEASUREMENT AND EVALUATION
SUMMARY
IN THE FIELD
REFERENCES

Dr. Max W. Lewis and Dr. Arleen C. Lewis of the University of Arkansas are the authors of this chapter.

1. What is the purpose of educational psychology?
2. What is human development?
3. What general principles apply to human development?
4. What are the key concepts of Piagetian theory?
5. What are the stages of cognitive development according to Piaget?
6. What occurs during the stage of concrete operations?
7. How is language developed?
8. What are the three levels of moral development?
9. What are the major differences between the behaviorists and cognitive learning theorists?
10. What are the major components of behaviorism?
11. What are the major components of cognitive insight theory?
12. What is motivation?
13. What is Maslow's theory of needs?
14. What are some considerations in selecting measurement instruments?

INTRODUCTION

Teaching is a complex profession, relying heavily on the skills and personal qualities of the individual involved. The expectations placed upon teachers by parents, students, administrators, and the community at large are extremely high. A number of related fields can greatly assist the teacher in preparing to meet these challenges. Educational psychology is one such area. Stated simply, the purpose of educational psychology is to assist teachers in understanding the processes whereby learning takes place. This is done by focusing on those areas of psychology that deal with the ways in which individuals develop and learn. As teachers come to better understand the processes of development and learning, they are better prepared to provide methods of instruction that meet the individual needs of children and young adults in the classroom.

Educational psychology has taken several areas of general psychology and applied them directly to the classroom. In addition to learning and development, these include principles of motivation, evaluation, and measurement. Principles of motivation help the teacher to involve the student in the learning process. Through a thorough understanding of evaluation and measurement, teachers learn to set objectives, assess individual differences, and evaluate the outcomes of the educational process.

HUMAN DEVELOPMENT

Development refers to the changes that take place in human beings through the life span. While all human development can best be understood as an interaction between the effects of heredity and environment (Weisfeld 1982), psychologists have long debated the relative importance of each for understanding human characteristics such as intelligence. This becomes a question of practical concern for the teacher. After all, teachers seek to affect the development of children and young adults by helping them acquire the cognitive and social skills they will need to function productively. Are there certain aspects of development that teachers can most easily affect? Are there critical times in a child's development that are best for learning specific tasks? The more knowledge a teacher has about development and learning, the better prepared he or she will be to respond to these questions.

Most theorists recognize certain general principles that apply to development.

1. *Development tends to be orderly.* This means that individuals can be expected to acquire skills in a certain order. Children usually crawl before they walk and walk before they run or skip.
2. *Individuals will develop at different rates.* Some children are naturally more coordinated than others or somewhat more mature in their social relationships.
3. *Development moves from the general to the specific.* For example, children will develop the gross motor skills used in arm movements before they will develop the fine motor skills required for movement of the fingers.

The Development of Thinking

To discuss the development of cognition or the processes of thinking without discussing the work of Jean Piaget is impossible. He is second only to Sigmund Freud

Human development is a very complex process.

in terms of the number of references that appear to his work in the psychological literature (Endler, Rushton, and Roediger 1978). Piaget's skills in observation were highly developed and much of his theory of cognition originated from the careful observations he made of children, including his own. He noticed that when children of different ages were presented with the same problem to solve, they would often approach the task in different ways, seeming actually to understand the task differently. Having been trained as a biologist, Piaget began to wonder about the possible interaction between the experience of the child and the development of the child's brain and cognitive abilities. This led to the development of his theory of cognition and publication of a number of books and articles describing his views (Piaget 1952, 1960, 1970).

Piaget believed that humans could be expected to demonstrate considerable consistency in their overall developmental processes, since they are genetically similar and share many of the same environmental experiences. He argued that children could therefore be expected to pass through certain predictable cognitive developmental stages. Piaget described four discrete stages, which will be discussed in detail in the following sections.

Key concepts of Piagetian theory. Because his theory concerning the development of cognitive process was unique, Piaget used a number of terms in specific ways that must be defined prior to a discussion of his developmental stages.

Schema. This term refers to the cognitive framework that individuals develop for understanding and organizing experiences. The term as used by Piaget is similar to the way in which many other theorists use the term. Piaget believed that as the brain matures and the child obtains additional experience, these schemata gradually become more complex. These differences in schemata in part account for the qualitative differences in thinking between children and adults.

Adaptation. Changes in the schemata of the child are part of the process of adaptation. Piaget believed that from birth individuals seek ways of adjusting to their environment in more effective ways. He believed that we do this through the processes of *assimilation* and *accommodation*. Assimilation is the act of taking experiences and making sense of them in terms of current schemata or cognitive categories. For example, a child might see a horse for the first time and be told that the animal is called a horse. Shortly thereafter, the child sees a cow and calls it a horse. In this case the child has assimilated the cow into the schema for horse. Accommodation is the process of modifying existing schemata in response to experience or new information. In the previous example the child might be corrected by a parent or another person who could tell the child the new animal is a cow and point out the differences between horses and cows. This process of accommodation then allows the schema to develop further.

The processes of accommodation and assimilation are strongly related. People understand events because of their ability to assimilate new information, and they mature intellectually because of their ability to accommodate their existing cognitive categories. In this way people continually *adapt* to their environment.

Equilibration. Piaget believed that individuals possess an innate drive to maintain a state of balance between their existing schemata and experience. Therefore, when a person encounters information that cannot easily be assimilated into an existing schema, a state of disequilibrium results. Accommodation or the modification of the schema would be one process that would allow for the restoration of balance. In any event equilibration provides a kind of energy that propels a child upward through the stages of cognitive development (Block 1982).

Piaget's stages of cognitive development. Piaget identified four stages of cognitive development (see table 11–1). Although age levels are associated with each stage, these ages are only approximations. A child's cognitive developmental level cannot be determined from the child's age alone. Teachers will have children in the classroom who may vary according to their developmental stage even though they are all the same age. Depending on the age group, they may also differ significantly from the way the teacher thinks.

Children pass through all of the stages in a prescribed order, and they do not skip stages. However, as children move from one stage to the next higher stage, they often exhibit behaviors associated with both. Children continue to have available the ways of dealing with the environment that were used in previous stages.

The sensorimotor stage. The period from birth to approximately two years of age encompasses the sensorimotor period. The name reflects the importance of sensory functioning for infants and young children. Infants interact with the world through their senses—touch, taste, smell, sight, and sound. The primary cognitive growth that takes place during this period is the development of what Piaget called *object permanence.*

Adults are fully aware that objects and people continue to exist when they are removed from sight. This book has the same form and substance whether a person holds it or leaves it under the bed. Mick Jagger is somewhere right this moment even though he may not be seen at this moment. Adults are able to represent the object and the person in their minds. They have object permanence and, therefore, are able to think about things they cannot see or touch. In the experience of the infant, this is not so. In the initial part of the sensorimotor stage, objects are literally "out of sight, out of mind." Gradually the infant does come to develop object permanence, and thereby the basis for thought as it is known.

During the sensorimotor stage, the infant moves from behavior dominated by reflex actions to goal-directed actions. A young infant will spend long periods of

---

TABLE 11–1   Piaget's Stages of Cognitive Development

Stage	Typical Age	Principal Characteristics
Sensorimotor	0–2 years	Child develops object permanence and beginnings of goal-directed behavior.
Preoperational	2–7 years	Child begins to develop ability to think in symbols, but has difficulty taking perspective of others or solving problems logically.
Concrete Operational	7–11 years	Child is able to solve concrete problems and think logically. Reversibility is present and child understands conservation, seriation, and classification.
Formal Operational	11–15 years	Young adult is able to use logical thinking to solve abstract problems.

time in repetitive actions such as kicking or moving the arms in a circular fashion. Gradually the infant's focus moves away from its own body and begins to reach out for objects in the environment. Such behavior becomes more organized until the infant reaches a level where he or she can reach for, grasp, and then manipulate an object such as a rattle or bottle. During the sensorimotor stage then, the development of object permanence and the beginnings of goal-directed actions can be observed.

The preoperational stage. The preoperational period typically encompasses ages two through seven. Mature intellectual activity requires the ability to carry out actions mentally or to perform what Piaget called *operations*. The performance of mental operations depends on the ability to symbolize. People cannot think through a problem until they are able to form concepts and attach labels to objects and ideas in their minds. The primary activity of the preoperational stage is the development of the ability to symbolize in preparation for performing mental operations; hence, the name *preoperational*.

Piaget described the various modes of preoperational thinking in great detail. The common theme for children in the preoperational stage is their tendency to classify objects according to limited criteria or to draw inferences about relationships between objects based upon a *single* attribute. When young children classify objects, they commonly place a pencil and a comb in the same category, because "they both go in mama's purse." In another example a child might conclude that images on television are alive because they move.

Piaget described the thinking processes of preoperational children as *intuitive*, because they tend to be based on what the child senses rather than on what is rational. Additionally, preoperational children are *egocentric* for they believe that others experience the world and its events in the same way they do. For example, if a person sits across the table from a child who is looking at the pictures in a book, the child will believe that the person sees the image exactly as he or she does—right side up!

In summary, the preoperational stage is concerned with development of the ability to mentally symbolize, or form concepts for, objects in the environment. Children at this stage have great difficulty taking the perspective of others and are not yet capable of logical thought in solving problems.

The concrete operational stage. The concrete operational period covers the ages of approximately seven to eleven. The significant aspects of this stage are the child's acquired ability to perform certain mental or cognitive operations and thereby think logically. *Reversibility* is necessary to be able to transform information in one's head. Piaget placed a great emphasis on the importance of reversibility in thinking. As children move into the concrete operational stage, they learn that reversing a sequence of actions will return an object to its original state. For example, adding three and then subtracting it returns the original value. Adults think forward and backward in an orderly sequence all of the time. Children are not able to do this until they reach the stage of concrete operations.

Operations that children are able to perform when they reach the developmental level of concrete operations include *conservation, seriation*, and *classification*. Conservation is the understanding that the quantity of an object remains constant in spite of changes in appearance. For example, when water is poured from a short, fat

There is disagreement concerning when adolescents reach the formal operational thought stage.

glass into a tall, thin glass, the child who is able to conserve understands that the amount of water remains the same.

Seriation is the process of understanding serial position. The child who has mastered this task is able to order objects according to a single dimension such as weight, quantity, or height. Accordingly the child also understands that if A is bigger than B, and B is bigger than C, then A is bigger than C.

Classification is the ability to focus upon a single characteristic and group objects according to that characteristic. Subclasses of objects consequently become salient groupings.

The ability of the child to perform conservation, seriation, and classification are evidence that the child has developed the basis for logical thought.

The formal operational stage. Formal operational thought typically occurs between the ages of eleven and fifteen. The child acquires the ability to think logically about *abstract* problems. This may be thought of as the beginning of "scientific thought." Students are now able to mentally generate alternatives and hypotheses that are not tied to the students' concrete experiences.

Some disagreement does exist about the ages at which young people acquire formal operational thought or even if everyone can be expected to in all areas. Kohlberg and Gilligan (1971) found that only about 30 to 50 percent of the adolescents they studied were able to perform formal operational tasks.

Classroom applications. The work of Piaget is an excellent example of the ways in which educational psychology facilitates the work of the teacher. Descriptions of the thinking processes of the child and young adult suggest many ways of improving the quality of instruction. Activities in the classroom must be developmentally appropriate for the young people in the classroom. For example, unless a child has truly grasped the operation of seriation, he or she will not be able to grasp math concepts.

Research on aspects of Piaget's theory has been conducted by a wide variety of individuals over the years. Whether the formal research will document all aspects of Piaget's theory remains to be seen. Certainly his observations were accurate. On the other hand, Piaget's explanations of why developmental changes take place are not as clear (Dworetzky 1984). No doubt future research will continue to provide us with information on this important aspect of human development.

The Development of Language

The development of language is closely related in importance to the development of thinking. Whatever the situation may be, teachers must work with the language skills of their students. Language is intrinsically related to the acquisition of cognitive abilities. The process of thinking is tied directly to the acquisition of symbols and operations for mentally manipulating those symbols.

Considerable disagreement exists about the mechanisms for the development of language in human beings. Infants and children clearly do pass through a similar sequence in the acquisition of language. Infants make sounds from the moment they are born—cooing, crying, and eventually babbling. Interestingly, the initial sounds made by babies are not related to the sounds they hear around them. Babies throughout the world tend to make the same general sounds. The sounds that are not related to the language the child will speak gradually drop out. While theorists and researchers are still uncertain about how this happens, the selective attention of parents to sounds that make up their language is an important factor (Thain, Casto, and Peterson 1980).

Around the ages of eight to twelve months, children form their first words. These words are usually tied to objects and people in the child's environment. After children have learned some words, they will begin to put the words together. These two-word "sentences" usually appear around the age of two and increase rapidly in complexity, so that the average four- or five-year-old is able to utter complex sentences.

Language is not simply a matter of putting words together. It is a system of complex rules for linking words in accord with the structure of the language. These rules for joining words are called syntax. Noam Chomsky (1965), a well-known theorist in this area, has suggested that children actually have an innate capacity for acquiring language.

Language development includes much more than putting words together.

Tremendous individual differences are found in the language skills of children. Factors associated with these differences include the sex of the child, the parents' educational and occupational levels, and the child's experience with language.

Knowledge about the sequence of language development in children coupled with an understanding of the mechanisms that affect language development will help teachers construct verbal instructions and written materials targeted to the appropriate level of the child. Teachers must attend to the large variation in language competence that is likely to exist among children.

The Development of Morality

Much of the discussion thus far has focused on aspects of development that emphasize cognition. However, even Piaget (1981) with his lifelong commitment to the study of the development of the thinking processes maintained that affective processes must also be given attention. The affective processes, which include our feelings, emotions, attitudes, and values, go hand in hand with cognition in the psychological development of the child. Krathwohl, Bloom, and Masia (1964) published a well-known book that classified effective goals into a taxonomy for use in education. Nevertheless, the affective goals of education have received little attention compared with cognitive goals.

Parents and teachers seek to encourage a number of prosocial behaviors in children. These include sharing, cooperation, empathy (the ability to understand the feelings of another person), and altruism. Parents and teachers are also concerned that children learn self-control and establish a system of values that is consistent with the community and family systems. With affective development, as with cognitive development, the ability of the teacher to have an impact on the child will rest on the teacher's understanding of the development of such concepts as morality.

Lawrence Kohlberg (1963, 1975) has elaborated a theory of morality based on the work of Piaget. He describes three levels of moral thought that incorporate six stages of moral development (see table 11–2). The three levels of moral development are the preconventional, the conventional, and the postconventional. Kohlberg classifies moral thought and determines a child's developmental stage by presenting the child or young adult with a moral dilemma. Such problems have no right or wrong answers, but require the children to reach a conclusion on their own. The child's *reasoning* about what determines right or wrong in the situation is the basis for the scoring.

Preconventional thought. Moral decisions at this level are based on the child's conception of the immediate effects of the decision on him- or herself. In Stage I, right or wrong is determined by the physical consequences of an act ("It is wrong if I get spanked"). In Stage II, satisfaction of one's personal needs determines right and wrong ("I will share my cookie and mommie will give me another").

Conventional thought. At this level the child has internalized a set of moral values based on the beliefs of parents and others. While the child now has a code for evaluating behavior, the guidelines really come from outside rather than a total understanding of moral concepts. In Stage III, behavior is governed by the belief that what pleases or helps others is good ("I will put my toys away because that will make daddy happy"). In Stage IV, right and wrong are determined by a need to maintain the social order and conform to rules ("I always raise my hand before I leave my desk").

Postconventional thought. Decisions about right and wrong at this level are based on the values of justice and equity. The values are internalized and shape the nature of ethical and moral decisions. Stage V behavior is governed by the relationship of personal values to societal values. The importance of consensus is emphasized ("Perhaps the time has come to talk about changing this law"). In Stage VI, right is determined by conscience and recognition of the need for respect of human dignity ("I will not participate in an activity that could result in the loss of human life").

TABLE 11–2   Kohlberg's Stages of Moral Development

Level of Thought		Stage of Development
1. Preconventional	I.	Punishment and Obedience (physical consequences)
	II.	Instrumental Relativist (personal satisfaction)
2. Conventional	III.	Interpersonal Concordance (pleasing to others)
	IV.	Maintenance of Social Order (obey the law)
3. Postconventional	V.	Social Contract, Legalistic (societal values, consensus)
	VI.	Universal Ethical Principles (justice and equity)

Ages are not attached to the stages in the same way they are for cognitive development, as the approximate ages at which children progress through the stages is related to cognitive development. For example, a person cannot be expected to reach Level 3 of moral reasoning until that person is capable of formal operational thought. Many adults make moral decisions at Level 2, and everyone regresses to earlier levels in special situations.

A distinction must also be made between thinking and behavior. A student who is capable of making a Stage V decision will not always do so when presented with an actual situation.

What are the implications of all of this for teachers? First, teachers must expect that students will respond to ethical dilemmas or questions of conduct in relationship to their personal level of moral development. This will vary from student to student and in some cases from situation to situation. Rigid emphasis on conformity to rules will tend to fixate students' thinking at lower levels. On the other hand, if a student has not advanced beyond Stage II or III, discussions of general ethical principles will make no sense to that student. Daily events in the classroom, such as violations of rules, cheating, or conflicts between students, can become a springboard for discussions that encourage moral development.

PRINCIPLES OF LEARNING

The concept of learning is so basic to teachers it seems almost unnecessary to offer a formal definition. Teachers, students, administrators, and the general public seem to share the same meaning for the term and understand the teacher's role in facilitating the process. This consensus, however, quickly evaporates when an attempt is made to define learning in a precise manner. Differences of opinion about the nature of learning, how it is best facilitated, and how it is measured are at the core of contemporary educational debates.

Biggee (1982) has described three general families of learning theorists: mental discipline, behaviorism, and cognitive insight. The oldest theories of learning assumed that learning took place as a result of exercising the mind to develop or train its natural powers. This view of learning originated in the golden age of ancient Greece among the philosophers Socrates, Plato, and Aristotle, and may have been a result of the discovery that the inherent beauty and strength of the body could be developed through repetitive, strenuous exercise. Perhaps the Greeks believed that the ideal of mind could be developed in the same manner as the ideal of body. Socrates drank his cup of hemlock rather than recant his beliefs about the natural talents of the mind and the value of the Socratic method of releasing them.

The mental discipline view of learning has not held up well under scientific scrutiny. While components of this perspective still exist among current theories, the concept has been largely discredited by research focusing on repetitive mental exercises and their effects on general abilities or intellectual development (Biggee 1982).

Contemporary psychological debates about learning have pitted behavioral and cognitive theorists against one another. Just as the mental discipline viewpoint grew out of Greek philosophy, behaviorism and cognitive insight theories also have their philosophical roots. Cognitive theories are rooted in rationalism as championed by Immanuel Kant and René Descartes. These philosophers believed that reason and logic were the keys to unraveling the confusions and contradictions of the world. The life of the mind and its interpretations of the world were thought to be as important as the physical properties of the world. Cognitive psychologists study the manner in which individuals gather, organize, and integrate information with previous knowledge to develop a more complex and adaptive cognitive system. They study the mental processes and intellectual structures involved in learning.

Behavioral theories are based on the work of the British empiricist philosophers such as John Locke, David Hume, and John Stuart Mill. The empiricists argued that the only source of knowledge is sensory experience, that people learn by seeing, smelling, hearing, tasting, and feeling. Sensory experiences become linked to objects or behaviors through association as they occur together in time and/or space (Hilgard and Bauer 1975). Traditional behavioral psychologists study only those phenomena that can be measured empirically (verifiable by direct observation, not logic or reason) and can be replicated (reproduced under specific conditions). They contend that mental processes cannot be observed and are therefore inappropriate for scientific study.

Most contemporary theories of learning can be placed along a continuum between strict behavioral and strict cognitive theories (see figure 11–1).

Behavioral Theorists

Ivan Pavlov. Pavlov was a Russian physiologist who won a Nobel prize for his research on digestion. As a part of his work, he studied the salivation and digestion of dogs. One day he noticed that when the dogs heard his footsteps, they would begin to salivate. He hypothesized that his footsteps had become associated with the food he brought. Pavlov became fascinated with the phenomenon. From a strictly physiological perspective, salivating to a sound did not make much sense.

During the 1890s Pavlov investigated the phenomenon using strict experimental procedures. He paired the presentation of a sound with the introduction of powdered meat into the mouth of a dog. He found that after several repetitions the dog would salivate to the sound alone. Pavlov reported his work in *Conditioned Reflexes*, which was translated into English by Anrep in 1927.

Pavlov delineated several important principles of learning. The first was the principle of *classical conditioning*, which was used to explain the manner in which the tone came to elicit salivation by association with the food (see figure 11–2).

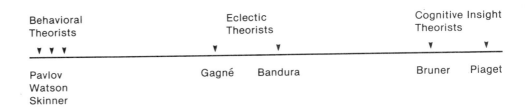

Figure 11–1. The Behavioral Cognitive Continuum.

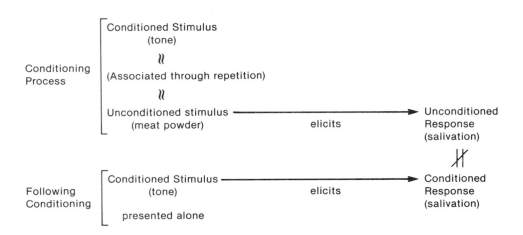

Figure 11–2. Classical Conditioning Paradigm.

The conditioned response (CR) is distinguished from the unconditioned response (UR) even though both involve salivation, because the CR and UR are similar to one another but not equal. The CR is an abbreviated response that Pavlov discovered could differ in intensity, duration, and/or completeness.

If the tone is presented many times without the meat powder, Pavlov found that the CR faded away. He called this principle *experimental extinction*. The CR must be paired or reinforced by the unconditioned stimulus (US) to condition and maintain the CR. This is called the principle of *reinforcement*.

If a new tone that is similar to the tone used as the conditioned stimulus (CS) is presented, salivation is likely to occur. This is the principle of *stimulus generalization*. However, if only the CS is followed by the US (meat powder), the new tone will not elicit the CR (salivation). This is called the principle of *stimulus discrimination*.

John Watson. John Watson was the father of behavioral psychology. His publication of *Behaviorism* in 1924 was heralded as one of the most important scientific works in the history of science (Hall 1982). Watson was indeed an original and free thinker. He sought to move the field of psychology away from its roots in philosophy toward a scientific method that did not rely on introspection. Introspection was a technique used by many psychologists who hoped to discover basic psychological and perceptual processes through the self-reports of subjects concerning their internal experience. Watson was appalled by the lack of scientific rigor in such an enterprise. He sought a more empirical approach and was one of the first psychologists to reject the study of internal processes and focus entirely on observable behavior.

Watson asserted that all behavior was elicited by stimuli in the environment. He believed that he could train any child to become a scientist, a millionaire, a pauper, or a criminal by controlling the child's environment.

Watson's most famous experiment was conducted with an eleven-month-old boy known as Little Albert (Watson and Rayner 1920). Watson conditioned a fearful, emotional reaction to a previously neutral stimulus. He began by introducing Albert to a white rat. Albert initially showed no fear of the rat. Watson found that Albert did react with fear and crying if startled by a loud gong, so every time Little Albert touched the rat, Watson startled him with the gong. Soon the rat alone elicited the fear reaction. The fearful response was generalized to many similar stimuli such as a rabbit, a dog, white cotton, and even a Santa Claus mask. Watson used a classical conditioning model to condition a phobia, or a fearful response. The phobia was generalized, so that a previously calm infant became quite fearful.

B. F. Skinner. Skinner is the modern heir to the behavioral tradition. He first gained widespread recognition with the publication of *The Behavior of Organisms* in 1938. Most of his research has been conducted with rats and pigeons. However, Skinner claimed that the species studied does not matter, because the laws of behaviorism apply to all species.

Skinner has been called a radical behaviorist because of his strict denial of mental processes or any form of self-determinism. In recent years Skinner has been less radical in his public statements and more interested in social issues such as aging and nuclear threat. Whether he still holds the fundamentalist behavioral opinions that made him both famous and infamous is not clear.

Skinner's primary contribution to learning is the model of *operant conditioning*. Major limitations of the classical conditioning model are the automatic nature of the responses studied and the emphasis on the stimulus as the cause of behavior.

Skinner was interested in more complicated behaviors and in what followed a response as well as what preceded it. He used a Skinner box to train rats and pigeons (see figure 11–3). The training began with *shaping*. Any behavior that brought the rat closer to the lever was reinforced by releasing a food pellet into the goal box. Through a process of *successive approximations*, the rat eventually approached the lever, touched it, and finally pressed it down. Consequently only depressions of the lever were reinforced by release of the food pellet. This type of learning was called operant conditioning, because the rat learned to operate upon (rather than react to) the environment to obtain a reinforcer. The basis of operant conditioning is the *law of effect*. This law states that the presentation of a reinforcer increases the likelihood that the preceding behavior will recur.

A rat can also learn to press the bar only under specific conditions. For example, the rat might only be reinforced for pressing the lever when the light is on. The light is called a *discriminative stimulus*. A discriminative stimulus is one that precedes a response and distinguishes between when a response will be reinforced and when it will not.

If all responses are not reinforced, the behavior will be extinguished. The length of time that it takes for extinction is a function of the *reinforcement schedule*. The rat can be reinforced for pressing the bar a specific number of times or for a certain period of time. For example, the rat may be reinforced each time it presses the lever for ten seconds (*fixed interval schedule*). If the time the rat is required to press the bar varies, it is a *variable interval schedule* of reinforcement.

If the average amount of time required for reinforcement under a variable interval schedule is equal to the amount of time for a fixed interval schedule, the rat's rate of lever pressing will be about equal over a long period of time. However, if reinforcement is discontinued, the variable interval schedule will be much harder to extinguish. The same relationship holds for *fixed ratio* (e.g., reinforce every fifth

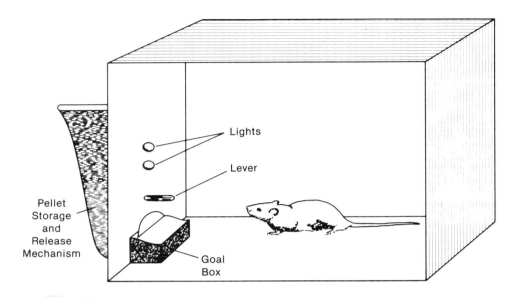

Figure 11–3. The Skinner Box.

response) and *variable ratio* (e.g., reinforce an average of every fifth response) *schedules*. A tremendous amount of effort per response can be obtained by *stretching the ratio*. This means requiring continually larger numbers of responses in order to receive reinforcement.

Many tasks require several steps to complete, such as a child getting a chair to reach a key to open a drawer to get candy. Skinner taught his animals lengthy sequences by using *behavioral chaining*. He began by shaping a behavior (e.g., pressing a lever). Next he shaped another behavior that allowed lever pressing (e.g., lifting a cover on the lever). Such a chain can be extended by requiring more and more prerequisite behaviors.

A reinforcer is any stimulus that affects the occurrence of a response. Many different reinforcers satisfy basic physiological needs (e.g., food, water, sex, sensory stimulation). These are called *primary reinforcers*. Many things in the environment take on reinforcing properties, because they are associated with primary reinforcers. Money has no value as a primary reinforcer, yet it is so closely associated with many primary reinforcers that it can be used to affect behavior. Such reinforcers are called *secondary reinforcers*. Unpleasant stimuli (e.g., electric shock) can also be used. *Punishment* is the application of a noxious stimulus after a behavior occurs (e.g., shock the rat for pressing the bar). *Avoidance* is when a behavior is used to prevent a noxious stiumlus (e.g., the rat will not be shocked as long as he continues to press the bar).

Classroom applications. Classical conditioning has not been widely applied to the classroom because of the focus on reflexive and innate behaviors. The most frequent application has been in the area of treating negative, emotional reactions such as school phobias or test anxiety. The best-established approach is an extinction procedure called *systematic desensitization* (Wolpe 1961). The physiological reaction is extinguished by associating it with an incompatible response such as a state of relaxation.

The operant conditioning model has been applied more frequently to the classroom. Skinner has written a book specifically for teachers in which he describes how the principles of operant conditioning can be applied to teaching. The book, *The Technology of Teaching* (1968), describes the appropriate role of the teacher as an environmental technologist. The teacher's job is to arrange the environment so that desired behaviors are reinforced. Skinner believes that this can be accomplished by controlling the school environment as closely as the rat's environment is controlled in the Skinner box. He champions the superiority of teaching machines and programmed instruction, because they offer greater control and consistency. Issues such as citizenship, motivation, ethics, and self-control are described as too vague. Skinner contends such abstractions should be redefined in terms of the concrete behaviors we wish to teach and then those behaviors conditioned using the operant conditioning model.

Skinner's primary contribution to education comes from his work and ideas about reinforcement. The educational system is filled with examples where undesirable behaviors are reinforced and desirable behaviors are ignored. The study-hall teacher may spend many minutes interacting with noisy students while the studious ones receive no attention for concentrated effort. A student may be suspended for failure to attend school. Teachers may reward quantity or mediocrity when they intend to teach excellence.

The following example shows how a number of behavioral principles may be applied in the classroom. A teacher had a student who was quite immature and who wanted immediate and continual attention. The assignment for the period was to sketch a drawing. The student hurriedly drew a rough sketch and turned it in to the teacher. The student continued to hang around the teacher's desk. Finally the teacher resorted to praising the work of the student and asking him to work on another drawing in an effort to get him to leave her desk. This contingency quickly resulted in a series of interactions during which the student would rush to his desk, scribble a drawing, and return to the teacher's desk for attention. By the end of the class period, the teacher had a case of the "nerves" and an extensive collection of bad art.

She decided that she was inadvertently reinforcing quantity of production and attention-getting behavior, and decided instead to reward effort and quality. During the next period, she repeated the assignment. The student was soon at her desk with a primitive effort. This time she pointed out the potential for the sketch and suggested ways in which the student could continue to make improvements. Whenever the student returned, she commented on improvements and suggested further efforts. This student still took a disproportionate amount of the teacher's time during the period, but much less so than the previous day. The end result was a fairly good drawing and a teacher who felt that she had been instrumental in guiding learning for an otherwise troublesome student.

Cognitive Theorists

Jean Piaget. The most widely read and researched cognitive developmental theory of learning is that developed by Piaget. The basic cognitive structures, operations, and stages involved in learning have been outlined in a previous part of this chapter.

Briefly Piaget was concerned with the development of mental systems or structures, the "unmeasurables" attacked by the behaviorists. Piaget relied heavily on the processes of biological maturation to account for the development of cognitive structures. These developing structures interact with the physical and social environment to bring about developmental change.

Jerome Bruner. Bruner is an American psychologist who has done extensive work in the areas of learning and human development. As a cognitive structuralist, he has elaborated many of the ideas proposed by Piaget. His best-known work is *Beyond the Information Giver: Studies in the Psychology of Knowing* (Bruner and Anglin 1973). As the title suggests, Bruner is concerned with how people select, retain, and intellectually process information so as to draw general insights, concepts, or principles from concrete information. For Bruner these insights or principles have an existence beyond the individual student. The school teaches models, principles, and strategies to students who in turn use them as mental problem-solving tools and then pass them on to the next generation.

Bruner does not see mental processes or models as physical realities, but as highly abstracted representations of the real world. They may be compared to a blueprint for a house. The blueprint is not a house and cannot serve as shelter. However, the blueprint is an abstraction of a house that can be used to construct useful, elegant, and convenient shelter.

Bruner's main contribution to education is his book *The Process of Education* (1960). Hilgard and Bauer (1975) describe Bruner's instructional theory as having four themes.

1. The learner is an active agent rather than passive or merely receptive.
2. An effective teacher should harness this predisposition and structure lessons so that the pupil can use current cognitive structures to learn the new mental tools being offered.
3. The sequencing of learning tasks is important.
4. The learner should be rewarded. However, the learner should also be encouraged to develop a self-directed reward system in which self-satisfaction and a sense of accomplishment are more important than external rewards.

Bruner's ties to Piaget can be seen in his description of representational systems and their changes as the cognitive system develops. Bruner (1964) describes three developmental levels of representation. He believes children move from one stage to the next, slowly substituting new skills for old skills. Children retain some of the mental skills from the previous stage, but rely more and more heavily on the newer skills because of their greater efficiency.

Enactive representation. This is the earliest form of symbolization. The infant represents his or her world in terms of the physical movements he or she uses to interact with the environment. The bottle or nipple is represented by sucking, the rattle by shaking the hand, and the teddy bear by hugging or cuddling. Infants are able to remember these objects by their enactments. An infant who might otherwise lose track of a bottle while reaching for a puppy can maintain a representation of the bottle for a few seconds with a sucking action.

Iconic representation. This is the representation of the world through mental imagery. The young child may remember how to get a cookie by preserving an image of sliding a chair to the cabinet and climbing up to reach the cookie jar. The use of imagery allows for imagination and mental problem solving. The child may visualize several solutions to a problem and anticipate the possibilities for success or failure.

Symbolic representation. This is the most abstract form of mental process. It may be called verbal learning and problem solving. Experiences and mental tools are converted to language and voiced internally or with the spoken word as rules, principles, laws, steps in a strategy, or thought. Language is the most flexible form of representation. It allows conceptualization and categorization so that objects, events, strategies, and problems can be mentally sorted. Even categories can be categorized to allow rapid and flexible sorting and strategy searching.

Classroom applications. The cognitive insight approach to learning is more congruent with the background of most teachers than behaviorism. Teachers learn their trade in an educational environment that stresses techniques for developing mental skills and generalized problem-solving strategies. However, classroom prescriptions from the cognitive perspective can be more difficult than from the behavioral perspective. Behaviorists posit general laws of learning that supposedly apply across species as well as across individuals. Conversely, cognitive interventions are individually oriented. They involve an analysis of what is to be learned and the status of the child. Is the child ready? What prerequisite skills does the child have? What teaching strategies would build the child's existing knowledge and skills? In what sequence should new skills be introduced?

The unique contribution of cognitive theories comes primarily from their developmental emphasis. The concepts of readiness, acquisition of prerequisite skills, and teaching new content or strategies using what the child already knows are all applications of cognitive developmental theory. Heuristic devices, statements of theory, teaching problem-solving steps or strategies, and developing systems of self-validation or reward all assume some form of internal mental process that can be developed through teaching. The emphasis is on thought or logic rather than association or reinforcement as in the behavioral approaches.

Eclectic Theorists

An eclectic theory is one which draws from several theories to form a hybrid point of view. What eclectic theories lose in terms of philosophical purity or consistency they usually gain in practicality.

Robert Gagné. Gagné is usually classified as a cognitive behaviorist, a term filled with contradiction for loyal members of either school. Gagné's book *The Conditions of Learning* (1977) is his best-known and most consistent work. He explains the apparent contradiction in "cognitive behaviorism" by defining the mental process as a form of human behavior. He is not, however, as concerned with mental processes as with their influences on performance of the tasks to which they are applied.

Gagné may more appropriately be called an instructional or teaching theorist. He focuses on the skill to be mastered and the instructional demands of teaching the skill. He rejects general learning theories as distractors to the task of teaching (Wittrock 1978), claiming that they divert attention away from the specific instructional requirements of the task at hand. He believes that there are several types of learning, all of which require different instructional strategies. Gagné (1977) has defined eight categories of learning to guide the teacher in developing strategies for each type.

Signal learning: Classical conditioning as defined by Pavlov.

Stimulus response learning: Discrimination of correct or incorrect responses. Similar to discriminative stimulus learning tasks in Skinner's operant conditioning.

Behavioral chaining: Linking of two or more stimulus response units. Similar to chaining in operant conditioning.

Verbal association: Behavioral chaining involving verbal content. Learning to name objects is an example of verbal association.

Multiple discrimination learning: Learning to respond differently to a group of similar stimuli. Distinguishing between the letters of the alphabet is an example.

Concept learning: Learning a common response to a general class of stimuli. For example, learning to handle sharp objects with care.

Rule learning: Putting two or more concepts together to form a higher order rule or super concept. For example, putting the concepts of distance and time together to define a formula to compute speed.

Problem solving: Thinking by applying the seven previous types of learning to novel situations. The learning of problem-solving strategies.

Gagné believes that subject content requires different types of learning and teaching at different levels. Math may begin with the verbal association task of learning the names for numbers and proceed through the eight levels of learning to problem-solving tasks at the college algebra level. The teacher must carefully diagnose which type of learning is involved with the target skill, ensure the prerequisite intellectual skills have been mastered by the student, stimulate activation of these skills, arrange the learning environment so the old skills will lead to mastery of the new skills, and provide evaluation and feedback.

Albert Bandura. Bandura is a social learning theorist who studies the ability of human beings to learn through the process of observation (Bandura 1971). Bandura argues that a simple behavioral approach does not account for the complexity of human learning. Daily skills such as driving a car or giving a speech would require such complicated contingencies of reinforcement and chaining of responses as to be impossible. He argues that most human learning takes place through a process of modeling and imitation. An observer watches other people's behavior, notes the consequences of their actions (reward, punishment, or being ignored), anticipates the consequences of his or her own imitation based on those consequences, and then decides to imitate or not based on his or her anticipation of the consequences to him- or herself. Rewarding or punishing a model's behavior affects the likelihood that the observer will imitate, but it does not affect the learning of the behavior. That is, the behavior may be learned but not exhibited because punishment is anticipated.

Teachers are seen as effective models for learning. They should establish themselves as high status models, model desired behaviors and skills, and then encourage imitation through reinforcement. Teachers may reinforce themselves (statements of self-praise or satisfaction for a job well done) as well as students who imitate their actions. Both types of reinforcement affect an observer's appraisal of consequences for imitative behavior and thereby increase the likelihood of imitation.

MOTIVATION

Anyone who has spent time in a school building has heard the statement, "That student just isn't motivated." The implication of the statement is that the student is not interested in learning or pursuing the goals of the classroom. A more appropriate statement on the part of the teacher might be something like, "I just haven't found a way to really involve Billy in learning math." After all, Billy is motivated. He is just motivated to write notes rather than work his assignments, or tease the other children rather than participate cooperatively in the group.

The motivation of students is critical in the teaching/learning process.

Motivation is a psychological concept related to energy or drive. What are the variables that will account for two people with similar abilities performing differently in the same situation? This is one of the questions the psychology of motivation seeks to answer.

Abraham Maslow (1968) developed a theory of needs in an effort to understand the factors that motivate behavior. He postulated that human beings have seven general needs, which he classified into a hierarchy.

1. Survival
2. Safety
3. Belonging
4. Self-esteem
5. Intellectual achievement
6. Aesthetic appreciation
7. Self-actualization

Maslow believed that when the more basic needs are unmet, people's physical and psychological energies are channeled into those unmet needs. Maslow's theory of needs has been criticized by many, but he has made an important contribution by suggesting that human beings are motivated by a variety of things, some of which will clearly take precedence over others. Children who come to school without breakfast, who are neglected psychologically at home, or who do not feel secure or self-confident cannot be expected to approach spelling with the same enthusiasm as children who are physically and psychologically secure.

The experiences that children have in the classroom have also been determined to affect motivation. Children who have had a series of failure experiences will begin to avoid learning situations. For some children, this fear of failure is so strong that they will choose to misbehave and risk being labeled troublemakers rather than risk being labeled stupid. This is unfortunate for the experience of learning is itself a powerful motivator for increased effort in the classroom. Children can get into a vicious cycle where they actively avoid the very process that could bring new enthusiasm into schoolwork for them.

The performance of students in the classroom is also related to the expectations of teachers. In a one famous study, Rosenthal and Jacobson (1968) concluded that when teachers are made to believe that certain students have "special" potential in the classroom, those students will in fact outperform the other students in the group. While the original research has been criticized on methodological grounds, it did start a debate that led to a number of more recent studies.

Cornbleth, David, and Button (1974) found that teachers ask a greater number of difficult questions and give more time to respond to students who are expected to be high achievers by teachers. Teachers need to stay informed about the progress of research efforts in this area.

Motivation can also be affected by the type and pattern of reinforcement. Teachers need to be vigilant about which classroom behaviors are reinforced. The teacher should analyze reward contingencies whenever inappropriate behavior increases and productive behavior decreases. The timing of rewards is important; they should be as immediate as possible. Feedback about performance loses its meaning when it is delayed, especially for the young child. Not every desirable action has to be rewarded; however, consistency is important. Children become confused and unmotivated when an action is rewarded one time and punished another.

The psychology of motivation can make important contributions to the teaching field. The following are of some of the kinds of information that can be used to improve motivation:

1. Be aware that children and young adults are motivated by a variety of needs. Sometimes involving a student requires taking a new approach.
2. Be aware of the emotional responses of children to events in the classroom. When children appear upset or fearful, there are always reasons.
3. Don't be overly influenced by information on students from cumulative records or other teachers. They never present the total picture.
4. Remember that the experience of learning itself has been shown to be a powerful motivator for future learning. Find areas in which every child can be successful.
5. Be aware of the classroom behaviors that are rewarded. A teacher can easily motivate the wrong behaviors inadvertently.

MEASUREMENT AND EVALUATION

Measurement and evaluation activities in education are intended to provide information on the products of teaching. Goal setting is the process of determining the general direction or desired outcomes of education. Different groups can have different and often contradictory goals for education. Teachers must clarify their own personal philosophy of education, so that they can clearly define the goals to which they aspire.

Objectives are the means by which progress toward goals is measured. Goals are general statements that provide the overall direction for educational programs. Objectives are more specific statements and should be easily measurable. For example, progress toward the goal of appreciation of twentieth century literature may be measured by an objective such as "The student will be able to describe the plot, setting, major themes, and characters in F. Scott Fitzgerald's *The Great Gatsby* as measured by the instructor's rating of a short essay." Instructional objectives are important because they enable a teacher to judge if he or she is moving in the direction of his or her goals at an acceptable rate. Mager's (1962) *Preparing Instructional Objectives* is an excellent resource for teachers learning to write objectives.

Once goals and objectives are clarified, teachers can begin to measure and evaluate their progress. This can be either a formal or an informal process. The teacher may simply monitor the number and percentage of students achieving the desired level of performance on the instructional objectives. Or the teacher may choose to use more formal measurements such as commercially prepared standardized tests.

An important decision in selecting a test is whether to choose a norm-referenced or criterion-referenced test. A norm-referenced test is one that compares the student's performance with that of other students. This may take the form of a commercial test that compares the student with a national sample. It could also include an essay test that the teacher grades by rank ordering the essay answers. A criterion-referenced test is one that evaluates attainment of a competence. For example, the

281

instructional objective for twentieth century literature cited above is written in a criterion-referenced form. The student either achieves the criterion for success or fails.

For tests to be considered sound and appropriate for educational use, they must be consistent and they must be valid. Consistency is important in order to establish confidence in the test. Few forms of meaningful measurement are perfectly consistent. For example, every time a person steps on his or her bathroom scale, he or she gets a slightly different reading. If the scale only varies by a few ounces, it is useful in estimating weight. If a person were to step on the scale ten times in ten minutes and get results that varied by ten or fifteen pounds, the scale would lose its usefulness. The same principle holds for educational tests. If scores vary a great deal for no apparent reason, then those tests cannot be relied on.

Validity has to do with how well a test measures what it is supposed to measure. A test can be extremely consistent but not valid. For example, people used to believe that the bumps on the head were an indication of special abilities or personality characteristics. A bump in one place was supposed to mean acute eyesight; a bump in another, a sense of humor. A whole system of measurement called phrenology developed around this belief. Phrenologists were able to make consistent measures of the bumps and draw elaborate maps that were supposed to illustrate special abilities or tendencies. However, the measurements and maps were not valid, because they did not measure the characteristics that they were purported to measure.

Tests are a powerful educational tool. Like most powerful tools, they are subject to abuse and misuse. Teachers have a high level of responsibility in their selection, use, and interpretation. They must select or construct good tests that measure what they are supposed to measure. They must use the tests for the purposes for which the tests were designed. They must be careful to interpret the tests within their limits and be cautious that differences due to cultural or economic factors are not interpreted as differences in ability or achievement. Familiarity with test and measurement work within the field of educational psychology can assist the teacher in appropriate measurement and evaluation activities.

SUMMARY

The purpose of educational psychology is to take the principles of general psychology and apply them to the classroom and instruction. This chapter discussed several areas of psychology that have direct application to the teaching profession. These included development, learning, motivation, and measurement and evaluation.

The general principles of development were reviewed, and the development of thinking, language, and morality were described. The work of Jean Piaget was given special emphasis in the discussion of the development of thinking. Key concepts of his theory include schema, adaptation, and equilibration. The four stages of cognitive development—sensorimotor, preoperational, concrete operational, and formal operational—were defined and examples were given for each.

The sequence of language development in children and the mechanisms that can affect it were also discussed. Emphasis was placed on the impact that language skills have on all areas of learning inside and outside of the classroom.

The section on the development of morality reviewed the work of Lawrence Kohlberg. The levels of moral development, including preconventional, conventional, and postconventional, were defined and the six stages of moral development were described.

The review of the principles of learning was divided into three parts according to general theoretical orientation. This included the behaviorist approaches, the cognitive insight approaches, and the eclectic approaches. The discussion of the behaviorists focused on the work of Ivan Pavlov, who developed the principle of classical conditioning; John Watson, the father of behaviorism; and B. F. Skinner, who developed the model of operant conditioning.

The section on cognitive insight theorists focused on Jerome Bruner and his developmental levels of representation. The section on eclectic theorists reviewed the works of Robert Gagné and Albert Bandura.

The principle of motivation was defined and discussed as it relates to the classroom. Abraham Maslow's theory of needs was reviewed, and methods of motivating children were suggested.

The chapter concluded by discussing measurement and evaluation in education. These areas are concerned with determining the products of education. Goals and objectives were defined and their differences were described. Testing was also discussed, and the important principles of test development, reliability, and validity were defined.

IN THE FIELD

1. Is there any reference to Piaget's theories in the classroom(s)? If so, what?

2. What kind of language development activities are used?

3. Is there any values clarification or other moral education? If so, how is it implemented?

4. Is behaviorism used in the classroom(s)? If so, give some examples of its use.

5. Would you say the teachers you observe are primarily behaviorists or cognitive theorists? Why do you think so?

6. Are there any classroom applications of cognitive theories? If so, what are they?

7. How are students motivated in the classrooms? Give some specific examples.

8. Do classroom teachers perform formal as well as informal measurement of students? If so, how do they perform these activities?

REFERENCES

Bandura, A. 1971. *Social learning theory.* New York: General Learning Press.

Biggee, M. L. 1982. *Learning theories for teachers.* 4th ed. New York: Harper & Row Publishers.

Block, J. 1982. Assimilation, accommodation, and the dynamics of personality development. *Child Development 53*(2), 281–95.

Bruner, J., and I. M. Anglin. 1973. *Beyond the information given: Studies in the psychology of knowing.* New York: Norton.

Bruner, J. S. 1964. The course of cognitive growth. *American Psychologist 19*(1), 1–15.

Bruner, J. S. 1960. *The process of education.* Cambridge, MA: Harvard University Press.

Cornbleth, C., O. L. David, Jr., and C. Button. 1974. Expectations for pupil achievement and teacher pupil interaction. *Social Education 38*(1), 54–58.

Chomsky, N. 1965. Aspects of a theory of syntax. Cambridge, MA: M.I.T. Press.

Dworetzky, J. 1984. *Introduction to child development.* St. Paul, MN: West Publishing Company.

Endler, N. S., J. P. Rushton, and H. L. Roediger. 1978. Productivity and scholarly impact (citations) of British, Canadian, and U.S. Departments of Psychology (1975). *American Psychologist 33*(2), 1064–82.

Gagné, R. M. 1977. *The conditions of learning.* 3d ed. New York: Holt, Rinehart & Winston.

Hall, J. F. 1982. *An invitation to learning and memory.* Boston: Allyn and Bacon.

Hilgard, E. R., and G. H. Bauer. 1975. *Theories of learning.* 4th ed. Englewood Cliffs, NJ: Prentice-Hall, Inc.

Kohlberg, L. 1975. The cognitive-developmental approach to moral education. *Phi Delta Kappan 56*(10), 670–77.

Kohlberg, L. 1963. The development of children's orientations toward moral order: Sequence in the development of moral thought. *Vita Humana 6*(1), 11–33.

Kohlberg, L., and C. Gilligan. 1971. The adolescent as a philosopher: The discovery of the self in a postconventional world. *Daedalus 100*(4), 1051–86.

Krathwohl, D. R., B. S. Bloom, and B. B. Masia. 1964. *Taxonomy of educational objectives. Handbook II. Affective domain.* New York: David McKay.

Mager, R. F. 1962. *Preparing instructional objectives.* Palo Alto, CA: Fearon Publishers.

Maslow, A. H. 1968. *Toward a psychology of being.* 2d ed. Princeton, NJ: Van Nostrand.

Pavlov, I. P. 1927. *Conditioned reflexes.* Translated by G. V. Anrep. New York: Dover Publications.

Piaget, J. 1952. *The origins of intelligence in children.* New York: International Universities Press.

Piaget, J. 1960. *The child's conception of the world.* London: Routledge.

Piaget, J. 1970. Piaget's theory. In *Carmichael's manual of child psychology.* Vol. 1, 3d ed., P. H. Mussen, ed. New York: John Wiley and Sons.

Piaget, J. 1981. *Intelligence and affectivity: Their relationship during child development.* Palo Alto, CA: Annual Reviews, Inc.

Rosenthal R., and L. Jacobson. 1968. *Pygmalion in the classroom: Teacher expectations and pupil's intellectual development.* New York: Holt, Rinehart & Winston.

Skinner, B. F. 1938. *The behavior of organisms.* New York: Appleton-Century-Crofts.

Skinner, B. F. 1968. *The technology of teaching.* New York: Appleton-Century-Crofts.

Thain, W., G. Casto, and A. Peterson. 1980. *Normal and handicapped children.* Littleton, MA: PSG Publishing.

Watson, J. B. 1924. *Behaviorism.* New York: Norton.

Watson, J. B., and R. Rayner. 1920. Conditioned emotional reactions. *Journal of Experimental Psychology 3*(1), 1–14.

Weisfeld, G. E. 1982. The nature-nurture issue and the integrating concept of function. In *Handbook of developmental psychology.* B. B. Wolman, ed. 208–29. Englewood Cliffs, NJ: Prentice-Hall, Inc.

Wittrock, M. C. 1978. The cognitive movement in instruction. *Educational Psychologist, 13*(1), 15–29.

Wolpe, J. 1961. The systematic desensitization treatment of neurosis. *Journal of Nervous and Mental Disease 132*(3), 189–203.

Chapter 12
CAREERS IN EDUCATION

OBJECTIVES

After reading this chapter, you will be able to

- describe the early role of teachers in American public education;

- discuss teaching as a profession;

- list characteristics of good teachers;

- discuss the status of teaching, including supply and demand, salaries, and other benefits;

- describe some of the shortcomings of teaching;

- list educational occupations other than teaching.

OUTLINE

ADVANCE ORGANIZERS
INTRODUCTION
TEACHING AS A PROFESSION
    Early Status of Teaching as a Profession
    Current Status of Teaching as a Profession
CHARACTERISTICS OF TEACHERS
    General Characteristics
    Characteristics of Good Teachers
STATUS OF TEACHING
    Supply and Demand
    Salaries
    Other Benefits
SHORTCOMINGS IN TEACHING
    Burnout

Low Job Status
Low Salaries
Actions from Reform Movements
OTHER EDUCATION PROFESSIONS
    Educational Administration
    School Counseling
    Social Work
    School Health
    Other Professional Support Personnel
TEACHING: SUMMATION
SUMMARY
IN THE FIELD
REFERENCES

1. What was the nature of teaching in colonial America?
2. How many teachers are currently employed in public schools?
3. What benefits do teacher organizations provide?
4. What are some characteristics of good teachers?
5. What is the supply and demand for teachers?
6. What are some potential shortcomings of teaching?
7. What other professional opportunities are there in public education?

INTRODUCTION

Many different professional opportunities exist in education, including classroom teaching, administration, and a host of support positions such as counselors, therapists, social workers, dietitians, and health personnel. Of these various positions, teaching is the one that is considered the cornerstone of education.

Teaching is a noble profession; it requires an ability to impart knowledge, provide leadership, instill values, and help prepare young individuals for the future. Teaching is definitely an awesome responsibility (Newbrough 1983). Teachers posses great power; they affect students not only during the short periods of instruction in classrooms, but beyond. "The profession of the teacher is a high calling, for along with the parents, teachers more than any other group in society fashion the world they will not live to see" (Perkin 1979, p. 658).

Great teachers never die. Plato and Aristotle live because of their teaching. Teachers leave behind scores of former students who carry on with ideas, values, and abilities imparted to them (Robinson and Brower 1982).

Teachers, like education in general, have come under a great deal of criticism during the 1980s. They have been labeled lazy, incompetent, uncaring, unmotivated, and products of poor training. However, teachers do make a difference in their students (Ornstein 1984), and if education is to continue to be the mainstay of our culture, really good, inspiring teachers need to be applauded for their unselfish efforts in the face of the challenges confronting public education (Dedrick and Raschke 1984).

The jobs of teachers have been made difficult during the past thirty years by external forces. These include:

1. Racial desegregation, which started with the 1954 landmark court case, *Brown v. Board of Education*.
2. The panic to catch up with the Soviet Union after the launching of Sputnik in 1957.
3. Criticisms in the 1960s by groups opposed to the overemphasis on traditional education.
4. New requirements imposed by the Elementary and Secondary Education Act of 1965.
5. The back-to-the-basics movement in the 1970s.
6. The role of social problem solver thrust upon the schools in the late 1970s.

7. Federal and state legislation mandating that schools provide appropriate educational programs for all children including those with disabilities, e.g., P.L. 94–142. (Dedrick and Raschke 1984)

These actions have made the teaching profession responsible for much more than merely instructing children in various subject areas. In light of these demands placed on teachers by society, the performances of teachers have been, for the most part, extremely good. However, where there is a public there are critics, and teachers have been on the receiving end of some criticism about education for the past several years. The cover story of a recent edition of *Newsweek* magazine reflected this criticism with the headline "Why Teachers Fail" (Williams, Howard, McDonald, and Michael 1984, p. 64–70).

HIGHLIGHT

Kean Says Teachers Key to Reform

PHILADELPHIA (AP)—Gov. Thomas Kean of New Jersey, the new chairman of the Education Commission of the States, says teachers "are the key to reform."

"It is the teachers themselves who are the great untapped source of creativity for renewing our schools and they know it," Kean said Friday.

"If we can find productive ways to release that creativity, we can sustain the progress of the last three years. And teaching in the process can become a respected profession."

The New Jersey Republican succeeded Gov. Charles Robb of Virginia as head of the nationwide compact formed 20 years ago to develop policies to upgrade education from kindergarten through college.

The commission elected Arkansas Gov. Bill Clinton as chairman-elect.

Kean pledged to return to the classroom "to listen to the best ideas about improving education and then do something about them."

"If we are to continue our success with the reform of teaching, we need to get the view from the classroom (and) states must renew their commitment to effective teaching," he said.

Kean said he intended to focus on creating a renaissance in teaching and on inspiring effective state action to improve undergraduate education.

Noting the nation faces a teacher shortage, Kean called on state leaders to create conditions that will attract 1 million people to the profession in the next five years. Kean said his first task will be a state-by-state survey to identify all efforts now under way to strengthen teaching.

"I would like to use that survey to elicit two carefully focused commentaries on what we have done together," he said. "First, we should go to the scholarly community (and ask) what do they say we should do next.

"Then let's take our survey to a national panel of outstanding teachers. What is the view from the classroom on our efforts? The objective of these activities will be to strengthen and encourage teachers as professionals."

Northwest Arkansas Times. July 28, 1985. Used by Permission of The Associated Press.

Despite the criticisms, people are still interested in becoming teachers, and veteran teachers are continuing in the profession. People are attracted to teaching for many reasons, some of which are characterized by the following statements: "I am a teacher because of teachers" (Yerger 1983, p. 44), and "The major satisfaction of being a teacher lies, for me, in the knowledge that I have made a difference in the lives of children" (Freeman 1979, p. 255).

TEACHING AS A PROFESSION

Whether teaching is a profession has long been debated. Medicine, law, and other vocational areas have been considered professions since their beginning. Teaching, on the other hand, has only begun to emerge as a profession. Many people still argue that teaching is more of a craft than a true profession.

Early Status of Teaching as a Profession

Historically, the roles of teachers have changed dramatically. In colonial America, for example, the qualifications of individual teachers varied considerably. Some teachers, especially of lower schools for the masses, "were often poorly educated and possessed, at best, only a rudimentary knowledge of the basic skills of reading, writing, and arithmetic. Some of them were bond-servants; others were students of the ministry or the law who kept school to support themselves until they were able to enter their preferred profession" (Gutek 1970, p. 131–32). In parochial schools, whichever church supported the school selected the teacher. The teacher's religion was considered more important than academic and teaching abilities (Gutek 1970).

The Latin grammar school had better qualified teachers. Since the role of these schools was to prepare students in the areas of Latin and Greek, teachers had to be better educated. Not until the common school movement, however, was serious attention paid to teacher education (Gutek 1970), and even as late as the 1860s, teachers in some locations were minimally prepared. Bullough (1982) described teachers who taught in Utah in the late 1860s. The typical teacher of the time was "female, poorly educated, religiously motivated, hard working, in need of extra income and committed to education as a vehicle for 'uplifting' young heathens" (Bullough 1982, p. 199).

Teaching during the early years of this country was not a profession at all. Rather it was a job held by individuals with various backgrounds and with various purposes. Some were individuals who taught while receiving training for more respected professions, while others were women who taught because they needed extra money. Most of the teachers in early America had no training in teaching and limited basic academic training and abilities.

Current Status of Teaching as a Profession

Today teachers make up an educated, diverse group of individuals. Approximately 2.1 million teachers are employed in public schools in the United States, and another 280,000 working in private schools (National Center for Education Statistics 1983). The number of teachers is overwhelming. Public education is the largest, single employer in the United States. The question of whether teaching is a profession still troubles individuals who choose to enter, and then remain, in the teaching vocation. Is education a profession, or is it simply a job viewed as being at the level of blue-collar labor?

Teaching, a profession. Many education majors, and possibly beginning teachers, do not care whether teaching is classified as a profession or some other level of employment. Within the educational community, however, the issue is of vital importance. Reasons educators care about the perception of education include status, salary, and benefits. If teaching is considered a profession by the public, a certain amount of status will be associated with the position. Likewise, as a profession, teachers should be in a better position to demand higher salaries and better benefits than if teaching is simply viewed as a run-of-the-mill occupation. As a profession, educators are in better positions to seek gains for the overall quality of education.

Levels of jobs. There are basically three levels of jobs in the United States labor market: professions, semiprofessions, and occupations. Professions emerge from crafts, which use trial and error to learn knowledge. In their later stages of development, *professions* have a distinctive body of knowledge that was developed through research and analysis (Smith 1985).

Ryan and Cooper (1980) list several characteristics of professions:

1. A profession renders a unique service to society not provided by any other group.
2. Intellectual skills are required to provide services.
3. Long periods of training are required for professionals.
4. Individual and group autonomy in decision making are part of a profession.
5. Individual members of a profession must accept responsibility for their own behaviors.
6. Practitioners in a profession emphasize the service over individual rewards.
7. Professions police their own membership.
8. A code of ethics is practiced in a profession.

Using these criteria, is teaching a profession? Some answer affirmatively; others argue that teaching has not yet reached the level of self-confidence to be considered a true profession. The answer to some of the questions would be a definite affirmative, and others would be a qualified or negative. Education, therefore, is viewed as a profession by some and as less by others. The final conclusion is probably that education is an emerging profession (Johnson, Collins, Dupuis, and Johansen 1982), one that should evolve into a full profession as the body of knowledge related to teaching is further advanced.

One thing that must occur if teaching is to be advanced as a profession is to change the attitudes of teachers. Too often teachers consider their jobs as vocational insurance, a job they can always get if they cannot find a more suitable and financially rewarding position. This attitude does not convey professionalism. Teachers must convey to their students the professional aspects of teaching and the commitment required by teachers to improve the quality of education. "Teaching cannot survive as a pseudo-profession..." (Marczely 1985, p. 703).

Teaching and the labor movement. One growing practice of teachers that has eroded the professionalism of teaching in the minds of some is the active involvement of educators in unions. The National Education Association (NEA) and American Federation of Teachers (AFT) are the largest teacher organizations and are increasingly acting similar to labor unions. Teacher unions are here for the foreseeable future (Finn 1985).

Membership in teacher organizations makes teaching one of the most unionized occupations in the United States, especially among so-called white-collar workers (Finn 1985). There is nothing wrong with professional associations, one of which the NEA considers itself. Physicians and lawyers, for example, both have their associations in the American Medical Association and the American Bar Association. What primarily makes teacher organizations different from these two groups is that teacher organizations engage in collective bargaining and, at times, resort to strike actions. Although physicians and other noted professionals have engaged in strikes, their status as professionals has not been questioned by society.

Teacher organizations do provide benefits to their members besides collective bargaining, such as

- a sense of belonging to a professional group;

- group insurance benefits;

- group liability insurance;

- cut-rate tours and excursions;

- the enhancement of the profession.

This last benefit is one of the most beneficial for education. Through professional organizations such as the NEA and AFT, teachers and other members can exert their influence on state and federal policy as it relates to education. Unorganized teachers could not have such an impact. One way of promoting the profession is through the publication and dissemination of materials. The NEA, at one time, was the largest producer of educational materials in the United States (Elam 1981).

Whether teacher organizations have promoted education as a profession or created a unionized atmosphere that makes it more difficult for the public to accept education as a profession is inconclusive. For those who believe that teachers should teach and not worry about their own personal gains, teacher organizations have obviously hurt professionalism. On the other hand, many people consider teachers well within their rights to form groups and lobby for both personal improvement and the improvement of education. For these people, militant teacher organizations have enhanced the image of education as a profession.

CHARACTERISTICS OF TEACHERS

What are teachers like? Are they mostly male or female? Do they stay in the profession long, or do they burn out and "retire" after only a brief fling at teaching? Do they have bachelor's or graduate degrees? These are only a few of the questions that could be asked about characteristics of teachers. Like most professions, individuals engaged in teaching represent a broad-based group; no one type of person enters the teaching profession.

General Characteristics

Teachers represent all types of Americans. Of the bachelor's degree recipients in education in May 1981, the majority were white and female (see table 12–1). However, other racial groups and males were highly represented. The mean number of years taught by public school teachers in 1981 was twelve, compared with eleven in 1961, and eight each in 1966, 1971, and 1976 (National Center for Education Statistics 1983).

In 1980 the National Education Association studied the characteristics of 2,165 practicing teachers. Although the findings revealed the heterogeneity of public school teachers, the following profile resulted: classroom teacher, bachelor's degree, thirteen years of experience, earning approximately $15,500 annually, white, female, and satisfied with their job (NEA Survey Investigates 1980).

Characteristics of Good Teachers

Ask various people what they feel a good teacher is and you will receive a wide range of responses. Some would likely include the following:

- Good teachers love children.

- Good teachers set proper examples for children.

- Good teachers provide knowledge to children.

- Good teachers have community-acceptable morals.

- Good teachers motivate children to learn.

TABLE 12–1 Sex and Racial/Ethnic Distribution of Recent Bachelor's Degree Recipients, Those Newly Qualified to Teach, and Those Teaching Full-Time: May 1981

Characteristic	All Recent Bachelor's Recipients		Recent Bachelor's Recipients Newly Qualified to Teach		Recent Bachelor's Recipients Teaching Full-Time	
	Number	Percentage Distribution	Number	Percentage Distribution	Number	Percentage Distribution
Total	905,700	100.0	132,200	100.0	79,800	100.0
Male	454,700	50.2	36,600	27.7	18,200	22.8
Female	451,100	49.8	95,600	72.3	61,600	77.2
Total	905,700	100.0	132,200	100.0	79,800	100.0
White, non-Hispanic	824,200	91.0	119,800	90.7	73,000	91.6
Black, non-Hispanic	47,100	5.2	8,400	6.4	4,000	5.0
Hispanic	15,400	1.7	2,300	1.7	1,900	2.4
Asian or Pacific Islander	16,300	1.8	1,300	1.0	600	.7
American Indian or Alaskan Native	2,700	.3	300	.2	200	.3
Sample size		7,576		3,207		2,048

NOTE: Data exclude bachelor's recipients from U.S. Service Schools. They also do not include deceased graduates and graduates living at foreign addresses at the time of the survey. Data only approximate the number of bachelor's recipients in 1979–80, reported elsewhere. Precision of the estimates may be calculated using the approximate coefficients of variation provided in the Data Sources in the Appendix.

SOURCE: U.S. Department of Education, National Center for Education Statistics, Recent College Graduates Survey, 1981, unpublished tabulations (September 1982).

Good teachers display a number of characteristics, including providing knowledge to students.

- Good teachers know they are not in it for financial rewards.

- Good teachers work well with parents.

- Good teachers keep children under control.

Some people agree with some of these statements while disagreeing with others. The key is that there is no general consensus about what is a good teacher; everyone has an opinion on the issue.

In general most Americans think that good teachers are working in our public schools. Gallup (1984) found that 50 percent of the sample surveyed said they would give teachers either an A or a B rating related to their performances. Another 31 percent graded teachers a C. Only 3 percent indicated that teachers would receive a failing grade. Although people disagree over what makes a good teacher, a majority of Americans surveyed by Gallup (1984) would rate teachers either an A, B, or C on their job performance.

Teachers themselves also think they are doing a good job. In the Gallup Poll of Teachers' Attitudes Toward the Public Schools, Gallup (1985) found that 59 percent of the teachers surveyed felt that public school teachers made a more significant contribution to society than any other profession. Only 29 percent of the general population agreed with this assessment.

A great deal of literature has been written to describe good teaching. Teaching has been described as an art form by several professionals (Pellicer 1984, Gage

1984). Good teaching, when viewed as an art, involves much more than providing information to students. "It requires improvisation, spontaneity, the handling of a vast array of considerations of form, style, pace, rhythm, and appropriateness in ways so complex that even computers must lose the way, just as they cannot achieve what a mother does with a 5-year-old" (Gage 1984, p. 88).

To be a good teacher, individuals must understand the many different ways students learn and that there is no single, best teaching method for all children (Marczely 1985). Unfortunately, some teachers feel that their primary role is information dissemination and that information can be disseminated in the same way to all students. These are not good teachers. They may provide valuable learning experiences for some students, but the learning experiences could be much more beneficial for all students if teachers simply realized that learning is different for most students. Taking this basic premise into consideration and altering styles for different students helps make good teachers.

Pellicer (1984) summarized several points related to effective teaching:

• Presenting cues. Students need cues to learn. Cues help students understand what is to be learned as well as what is expected of them. Examples of cueing include

Teachers need to understand child growth and development.

communicating learning objectives early in the class, summarizing important ideas covered, and providing signals to students when important information is presented.

- Providing reinforcement. Students need reinforcement, which is nothing more than actions that make certain behaviors more likely to be repeated. Examples of reinforcement include praise, encouragement, and recognition of positive attitudes.

- Providing feedback. Students must have feedback to use as a guide. Examples are verbal and written affirmations of correctness and grades.

- Enabling students to actively participate. Active participation means students are paying attention to the learning process. This may be through reading, writing, or other motor activities, or it may simply be listening.

- Knowing learning objectives and teaching to these objectives.

- Monitoring and adjusting lessons. By paying attention to progress of students, teachers can alter their instructional modes to better accommodate some students.

- Knowing the subject matter. Teachers need to have an excellent knowledge of the subject matter to be effective teachers.

- Providing instruction in group settings. Research suggests that group activities are more beneficial to students than individual activities.

These are not the only qualities of good teachers. They also need to understand child and adolescent development and psychology, have a working knowledge of educational psychology, understand learning theory, and be able to organize classroom activities. They also need to be genuine, warm, empathetic, and caring. When teachers have a genuine affection for students, their instruction will reflect this relationship; teachers who want and expect their students to learn will be more successful than those who have lower expectations.

STATUS OF TEACHING

A great deal is happening in public education today. The entire public education structure is being attacked by critics; teacher education is being described as being inadequate and attracting inferior students to the profession, and dollars needed to support public education continue to shrink. Despite the problems found in public education, teaching is still considered an exciting and rewarding career. Hundreds of thousands of outstanding teachers provide appropriate learning experiences for children and youth; many top high-school students make decisions annually that result in their choosing teaching as a career. Although under fire from many angles, teaching is still considered an excellent vocational choice.

Supply and Demand

All prospective teachers are concerned whether jobs will be available after graduation. The number of teaching jobs has declined over the past decade as public school enrollments have dropped. As the number of job opportunities have declined, fewer students have chosen to enter teacher training programs. This has resulted in a sharp reduction in the number of graduates with teaching credentials, which in turn has created teacher shortages in many different fields.

In 1971 an estimated 314,000 new teachers graduated from universities for which only 163,000 job openings existed. This ratio has changed dramatically over the past five years. In 1985 a projected 691,000 students graduated from teacher education programs for an estimated 670,000 jobs. The projected figures for 1990 indicate approximately 986,000 graduates for 983,000 teaching jobs (see table 12–2).

The ratio of new graduates and available jobs has changed dramatically in favor of graduates over the past years. In certain teaching fields, severe teacher shortages exist. Also, several new fields have greatly expanded during the past ten years creating

TABLE 12–2 Estimated Supply of New Teacher Graduates Compared to Estimated Total Demand for Additional Teachers: Fall 1971 to 1990

Fall of Year	Estimated Supply of New Teacher Graduates [1] in Thousands	Estimated Demand for Additional Teachers, in Thousands	Supply as Percent of Demand
1971	314	163	192.6
1972	317	189	167.7
1973	313	180	173.9
1974	279	178	156.7
1975	238	186	128.0
1971–1975	1,461	896	163.1
1976	222	150	148.0
1977	194	181	107.2
1978	181	140	129.3
1979	163	126	129.4
1980	144	152	94.7
1976–1980	904	749	120.7
Projected [2]			
1981	141	99	142.4
1982	139	108	128.7
1983	138	146	94.5
1984	138	142	97.2
1985	135	175	77.1
1981–1985	691	670	103.1
1986	156	187	83.4
1987	177	192	92.2
1988	197	189	104.2
1989	218	198	110.1
1990	238	217	109.7
1986–1990	986	983	100.3

[1] *Estimates for 1971 through 1980 are from National Education Association, Teacher Supply and Demand in Public Schools, 1980–81.*

[2] *For methodological details, see Volume II of Projections of Education Statistics to 1990–91.*

SOURCE: U.S. Department of Education, National Center for Education Statistics, Projections of Education Statistics to 1990–91, Volume I, 1982, and unpublished tabulations (December 1982).

many teaching positions and creating a great demand. As a result, the number of prospective teachers completing degree requirements in various fields has changed during the 1980s.

An example of a new field that has expanded and created new job opportunities is special education. In 1970–71 a total of 8,360 students graduated with special education certification. In 1980–81, this figure had risen to 13,950, an increase of approximately 67 percent. Other teaching fields where severe shortages exist are science and math. Unlike special education, however, education majors in science and math have decreased substantially in recent years. In 1970–71 there were 2,217 graduates from math education programs; by 1980–81 the number had dropped to a mere 798. In science education the number of graduates dropped from 891 to 597 during the same period (National Center for Education Statistics 1983). In science and math the jobs are available, but students interested in these areas are able to make substantially more money in private business and industry than in public schools. Therefore, college students interested in science and math choose to major in the College of Arts and Sciences and secure jobs that are more financially rewarding.

The National Center for Education Statistics (1983) showed the following changes in the number of graduates from several certification areas from 1970–71 to 1980–81:

- Elementary education   −57 percent
- Secondary education (total)   −16 percent
- Pre-elementary school   +41 percent
- Special education   +67 percent
- Reading   +440 percent
- Art education   −58 percent
- Music education   −27 percent
- Physical education   −23 percent

These figures reflect new job opportunities in areas like preschool, special education, and reading. They may also reflect job opportunities in areas with a severe decrease in the number of graduates, because students choose not to enter into teacher training in areas where there are few job opportunities. Therefore, although the number of graduates in a particular teaching field has declined steadily during the past several years, an abundance of jobs may well be found in those areas because of the shortage created by the reduction in enrollment. Prospective teachers should determine the long-range prospects for positions in their desired teaching area.

The need for teachers, in addition to varying by teaching field, also varies by region of the country. Some areas of the country have a high teacher demand, while other areas continue to be saturated with more teachers than jobs (see table 12–3). Even in the regions with a high teacher demand, job availabilities fluctuate. For example, in a state with an overall teacher surplus, rural areas may still reflect a high demand for certain teaching areas.

Small schools have a particular problem securing teachers for some disciplines. In 1946 the United States had more than one hundred thousand districts; this number now stands at approximately sixteen thousand. Still, small districts make up the bulk of school units. Seventy-five percent of all students in the United States attend schools in districts with fewer than twenty-five hundred students, while 54 percent are enrolled in districts with fewer than one thousand students (Dunathan 1980).

TABLE 12-3   Teacher Supply/Demand by Field and Region

Region / Field	Alaska	Hawaii	1	2	3	4	5	6
Agriculture	3.00	3.00	3.50	2.50	2.67	3.33	3.67	3.00
Art	2.00	2.00	1.60	1.29	1.60	2.43	3.13	2.00
Bilingual Ed.	3.00	4.00	4.50	4.14	3.75	4.25	4.29	4.67
Business	3.00	3.00	2.80	3.50	3.33	3.29	3.00	3.25
Computer Programming	3.00	—	4.40	4.50	4.00	4.17	4.50	4.75
Counselor-Elem.	2.00	4.00	4.50	2.43	3.10	3.67	2.86	2.50
Counselor-Sec.	4.00	4.00	4.50	2.57	3.10	3.83	2.71	2.50
Data Processing	3.00	3.00	4.60	4.33	4.00	4.20	4.20	4.50
Driver Ed.	3.00	3.00	3.20	2.00	3.00	2.20	2.57	2.67
Elem.-Primary	3.00	2.00	2.40	3.29	2.67	2.00	3.25	3.00
Elem.-Intermediate	3.00	2.00	2.40	3.29	2.67	2.00	3.25	2.60
English	4.00	4.00	3.10	3.14	2.79	3.29	3.75	3.25
Health Education	2.00	2.00	1.40	1.50	2.80	2.67	2.13	1.33
Home Economics	4.00	3.00	3.33	4.00	3.13	2.60	2.50	2.50
Industrial Arts	3.00	4.00	3.67	3.80	2.88	3.00	4.00	4.00
Journalism	3.00	3.00	1.75	3.33	3.33	3.50	2.63	1.75
Language, Mod.-French	3.00	3.00	3.25	2.57	3.50	3.57	3.57	4.50
Language, Mod.-German	3.00	3.00	3.00	2.43	3.60	3.57	3.14	4.00
Language, Mod.-Spanish	3.00	3.00	3.60	2.71	3.40	3.43	3.75	5.00
Library Science	4.00	4.00	3.00	3.00	3.50	3.86	4.00	3.75
Math	3.00	4.00	4.80	4.86	4.29	4.43	5.00	4.60
Music-Instrumental	5.00	3.00	4.20	3.29	3.50	3.71	3.38	3.00
Music-Vocal	4.00	2.00	4.00	2.71	3.50	3.14	4.57	2.50
Physical Education	2.00	2.00	1.20	1.67	1.42	1.33	1.88	2.00
Psychologist (school)	4.00	—	4.00	3.50	3.38	4.20	3.60	3.75
Science-Biology	3.00	4.00	3.20	3.29	3.25	3.29	3.88	3.80
Science-Chemistry	4.00	4.00	4.20	4.43	4.08	4.14	4.63	4.60
Science-Earth	2.00	4.00	3.60	3.43	3.40	3.50	4.00	4.00
Science-General	3.00	4.00	3.40	3.29	3.50	3.29	3.83	3.75
Science-Physics	4.00	4.00	4.40	4.43	4.42	4.71	4.43	4.50
Social Science	3.00	2.00	1.40	2.00	2.40	2.00	2.57	1.75
Social Worker (school)	—	—	2.67	2.67	3.50	3.00	2.40	1.00
Speech	2.00	2.00	2.20	2.80	3.13	2.86	2.75	2.33
Special-ED/PSA	4.00	3.00	4.40	4.20	4.60	4.00	4.14	4.20
Special-Gifted	5.00	3.00	3.25	3.67	4.13	4.50	4.00	4.33
Special-LD	4.00	4.00	3.60	4.00	4.60	4.14	3.63	4.40
Special-MR	4.00	3.00	3.80	4.00	4.60	3.43	3.57	4.00
Special-Multi. Handi.	4.00	4.00	4.00	4.00	4.60	4.17	4.00	4.00
Special-Reading	4.00	3.00	3.80	3.14	3.75	3.17	3.71	3.75
Speech Path./Audio.	3.00	—	3.38	3.67	4.67	4.00	4.20	4.50
COMPOSITE	3.20	3.17	3.34	3.24	3.42	3.40	3.50	3.49

Regions are coded as follows: Alaska, Hawaii, 1-Northwest, 2-West, 3-Rocky Mountain, 4-Great Plains/Midwest, 5-South Central, 6-Southeast, 7-Great Lakes, 8-Middle Atlantic, 9-Northeast. Alaska and Hawaii are not included in the Continental United States totals.

5 = Considerable Shortage, 4 = Some Shortage, 3 = Balanced, 2 = Some Surplus, 1 = Considerable Surplus

From October, 1984 survey of Teacher Placement Officers, James N. Akin, Kansas State University
Reprinted with permission. J.N. Akin, 1986, 21–22.

7	8	9	Continental United States							
			1985	1984	1983	1982	1981	1980	1976	
3.50	2.66	—	3.11	3.44	4.02	4.36	4.46	4.73	4.06	Ag.
1.83	2.00	2.00	2.04	1.89	1.92	1.84	2.00	2.45	2.14	Art
4.75	3.50	3.50	4.12	4.04	3.83	4.13	4.10	4.21	—	Bil. Ed.
3.50	4.00	3.00	3.32	3.11	3.24	3.47	3.50	3.80	3.10	Bus.
4.67	4.29	4.00	4.37	4.34	—	—	—	—	—	Comp. Prog.
3.67	2.50	2.83	3.05	2.80	3.03	2.72	3.05	3.38	3.15	Couns.-El.
4.00	2.50	2.67	3.08	2.67	2.83	2.79	3.13	3.76	2.69	Couns.-Sec.
4.33	4.25	4.00	4.30	4.18	4.36	3.86	4.35	—	—	Data Proc.
2.80	2.50	2.67	2.65	2.61	2.94	2.77	2.87	2.98	2.44	Dr. Ed.
1.83	2.50	2.00	2.57	2.13	2.11	2.02	2.24	2.77	2.78	El.-Prim.
2.33	2.50	1.50	2.53	2.20	2.11	2.26	2.56	2.84	1.90	El.-Inter.
3.33	2.88	2.60	3.14	3.13	2.90	3.21	3.37	3.51	2.05	English
2.00	2.25	2.00	2.08	1.90	1.76	1.90	2.24	2.17	2.27	Health Ed.
2.67	2.67	2.33	2.79	2.43	2.44	2.43	2.54	2.85	2.62	Home Ec.
3.00	4.33	4.25	3.65	3.50	3.96	4.36	4.72	4.77	4.22	Ind. Arts
3.33	2.80	2.00	2.74	2.60	2.63	2.61	2.77	2.98	2.86	Journ.
4.00	3.00	2.20	3.31	3.00	2.59	2.49	2.58	2.68	2.15	French
3.33	3.00	2.20	3.11	3.08	2.51	2.48	2.58	2.70	2.03	German
4.17	3.13	2.40	3.43	3.18	2.77	2.68	2.95	3.34	2.47	Spanish
3.50	3.00	3.00	3.49	3.30	3.09	3.12	3.31	3.58	—	Libr. Sci.
5.00	4.88	4.50	4.71	4.78	4.75	4.81	4.79	4.80	3.86	Math
3.50	2.17	2.83	3.29	3.25	2.97	3.28	3.33	3.65	3.03	Instr.
3.33	2.17	2.50	3.19	3.00	2.89	2.95	3.06	3.32	3.00	Vocal
2.00	2.38	1.60	1.75	1.61	1.54	1.72	1.80	1.82	1.74	P.E.
3.83	3.67	3.00	3.65	2.98	3.19	3.56	3.70	3.87	3.09	Psych.
3.67	3.75	4.20	3.58	3.40	4.10	3.66	3.89	3.50	2.97	Biol.
4.67	4.50	4.50	4.42	4.25	4.30	3.13	4.42	4.18	3.72	Chem.
3.50	4.13	4.60	3.79	3.70	3.80	3.89	4.08	3.64	3.44	Earth
3.83	3.88	4.20	3.65	3.65	—	—	4.31	4.10	—	General
4.83	4.63	4.80	4.57	4.45	4.46	4.41	4.56	4.28	4.04	Physics
2.17	2.14	2.60	2.17	1.91	1.75	2.11	2.05	1.98	1.51	Soc. Sci.
3.40	2.75	3.00	2.81	2.33	2.27	2.34	—	—	—	Soc. Wrk.
3.17	3.29	3.67	2.91	2.70	2.51	2.76	2.65	2.50	2.46	Speech
3.83	4.00	2.80	4.02	3.84	4.08	3.98	4.22	4.36	3.42	ED/PSA
4.25	3.50	3.00	3.85	3.74	3.80	3.81	4.10	4.33	3.85	Gifted
4.83	4.00	2.50	3.95	3.98	4.09	4.20	4.47	4.48	4.00	LD
3.33	4.33	3.00	3.76	3.55	3.71	3.84	4.14	4.23	2.87	MR
3.60	4.00	3.00	3.94	3.77	3.82	3.93	4.13	3.87	—	MH
3.50	3.50	2.50	3.39	3.48	3.39	3.73	4.21	2.23	3.96	Reading
4.33	3.83	3.75	4.01	3.83	3.62	3.95	4.27	4.17	3.68	Sp./Aud.
3.52	3.31	2.97	3.36	3.19	3.14	3.20	3.39	—	—	COMP.

These small districts have major problems with teacher shortages. Smaller districts have a higher turnover rate than larger districts, get fewer applicants for vacant jobs, get no fully qualified applicants for jobs such as science and math, and have a high percentage of teachers who were born and raised in the community (Dunathan 1980). The problems created by teacher shortages nationwide is thus compounded for small districts.

Salaries

An obvious area of interest for future teachers is the salaries teachers earn. The 1984 Gallup Poll of the Public's Attitudes Toward the Public Schools revealed that 44 percent of the respondents thought that teachers' salaries were too low (Gallup 1984a). The attitude poll of teachers indicated that 90 percent of all teachers surveyed felt that salaries were too low (Gallup 1985). While historically the pay for teachers has been low in comparison to other college-degree areas, the salaries paid to teachers have begun to improve. One reason for this improvement was the reform reports of the late 1970s and early 80s said that better teachers need to be attracted to the classrooms and good teachers need to be convinced to stay in the classrooms.

New teachers who received bachelor's degrees in May 1981 earned an average beginning salary of $11,200. When compared with other areas, and an overall average of $15,300, this is indeed one of the lowest salaries for degreed persons (see table 12–4).

In a 1980 survey the National Education Association determined the following related to salaries of teachers (NEA Survey Investigates 1980):

- mean salary: $15,589
- mean salary for elementary teachers: $15,041
- mean salary for secondary teachers: $16,297
- mean salary for male teachers: $16,976
- mean salary for female teachers: $14,913
- mean salaries in Northeast: $16,975
- mean salaries in Southeast: $13,351
- mean salaries in Middle states: $15,726
- mean salaries in Western states $16,404
- mean salaries in cities: $16,879
- mean salaries in suburbs: $17,168
- mean salaries in small towns/rural: $13,921

Teachers' salaries are low; however, many states have initiated education reforms that include better pay for teachers. Teachers' salaries have increased during the past several years. For example, the mean salary for classroom teachers in 1983–84 was $22,039 (Salaries stay close to inflation 1984); this amount had increased to $23,587 in the 1984–85 school year (Salary increases around 7 percent 1985).

Teachers' salaries generally rise based on degree and number of years of experience. A teacher with a bachelor's degree and no experience would start at the bottom of the district's salary schedule. That teacher would move up the schedule with step increases each year, and would possibly move over on the schedule if additional hours and/or degrees are earned (see table 12–5).

TABLE 12–4   Occupational Distribution and Average Annual Salaries of Recent Bachelor's Degree Recipients Working Full-Time: February 1978 and May 1981

	1976–77 Recipients in February 1978		1979–80 Recipients in May 1981	
Occupation	Employed Full-Time	Average Annual Salary [1] in Constant (1981) Dollars	Employed Full-Time	Average Annual Salary [1] in Constant (1981) Dollars
Total	610,600	$16,000	632,500	$15,300
Business	123,200	17,800	151,600	16,400
Education	100,400	[2] 13,100	88,800	[2] 11,200
Engineering	36,700	22,400	51,200	22,900
Health professional	43,400	17,700	42,600	17,400
Public affairs	22,300	12,100	28,100	11,800
Biological and physical sciences	7,400	16,800	9,600	15,400
Fine arts	10,800	15,300	15,100	18,700
Social sciences and psychology	6,200	17,200	2,100	15,900
Research	3,600	12,700	10,500	13,400
Communications	11,200	13,600	8,300	13,000
Computer science	12,000	20,400	21,400	19,800
Technical	27,800	14,600	25,000	14,700
Other professional	9,200	16,600	10,900	14,500
Sales	44,300	17,400	58,400	16,300
Clerical and secretarial	76,000	13,100	61,300	11,400
Crafts and operatives	33,000	17,500	16,800	15,900
Other nonprofessional	41,700	15,400	30,900	12,000
Occupation not reported	1,400	17,500	—	—

[1] *Reported salaries of full-time workers under $3,000 in 1978 and $4,200 in 1981 were excluded from the tabulations.*
[2] *Most educators work 9- to 10-month contracts. Their salaries when adjusted for a 12-month period averaged $16,300 in February 1978 and $14,000 in May 1981 in constant (1981) dollars.*
NOTE: Data exclude bachelor's recipients from U.S. Service Schools. Also do not include deceased graduates and graduates living at foreign addresses at the time of the survey. Precision of the estimates may be calculated using the approximate coefficients of variation provided in the Data Sources in the Appendix.
SOURCE: U.S. Department of Education, National Center for Education Statistics, Recent College Graduates Survey, 1978 and 1981, unpublished tabulations (December 1982).

Other Benefits

In addition to salaries, teachers normally receive a package of additional benefits provided by the school district. Normally these benefits include

- participation in a teacher retirement plan;
- health and dental insurance;
- disability insurance and sick leave;
- professional liability insurance and personal days;
- tenure;
- legal insurance.

TABLE 12-5   Sample Salary Schedule

Step	Years of Experience	Salary
B/0	1	18,300
B/1	2	18,300
B/2	3	18,300
B/3	4	18,300
M/0	1	18,300
B/4	5	18,300
M/1	2	18,300
M/2	3	18,300
B/5	6	18,300
B/3	4	18,303
B/6	7	19,000
M/4	5	19,000
B/7	8	19,615
M/5	6	19,745
B/8	8	20,380
M/6	7	20,562
B/9	10	21,228
M/7	8	21,500
B/10	11	22,138
M/8	7	22,320
B/10+	12	23,083
M/9	10	23,251
B/11	13	23,551
B/11+	14	24,200
M/10	9	24,211
B/12	15–16–17	24,497
B/12+	18–19	25,039
M/10	12	25,181
B/13	20–21	25,493
M/11	13	25,715
B/13+	22–23	26,095
M/11+	14	26,195
B/14	24+	26,580
M/12	15–16–17	26,668
M/12+	18–19	27,124
M/13	20–21	27,740
M/13+	22–23	28,216
M/14	24+	28,785

B/ = Bachelor's Degree/Step
M/ = Master's Degree/Step

The exact benefit package will differ among school districts. In some districts, teacher associations actually bargain for certain benefits. In other districts, teacher bargaining is limited, and the school administration and school board determine the benefits package.

A DAY
IN THE LIFE
OF A TEACHER

Rosie Weidlmann is a member of a 5th and 6th grade teaching team. Her day begins before the arrival of students and includes such activities as reviewing lesson plans and notes, duplicating and preparing materials, and writing assignments and announcements on the blackboard. After the homeroom students arrive, she greets them and orients them to the activities of the day.

Photography by Arleen Casto Lewis

Teaching comprises the major part of Ms. Weidemann's day and includes group instruction as well as individual support and discipline. She also provides supervision for daily activities at the school, such as lunch.

During free periods, Ms. Weidemann takes advantage of the time to grade papers, to consult with counselors, administrators, and other classroom teachers concerning the performance of students, or to relax and have a quick lunch.

The afternoon includes more instructional time and then Ms. Weidemann says goodbye to the students. Parents conferences often take place after school, while her evenings are spent preparing lesson plans for the next day.

SHORTCOMINGS IN TEACHING

Teaching is an excellent profession. Good teachers who enjoy their positions are hard to convince that they should be doing something different. Dedicated, *career* teachers are likely to stay in the profession for their entire working lifetime. However, the teaching profession does have pitfalls. Some of these include burnout, low job status, low salaries, and some of the results from the current reform movement.

Burnout

Burnout can be defined as losing the edge, losing the desire to be the best, losing the ability to reap rewards. Teachers can and do burn out. Many excellent teachers enter the profession with enthusiasm only to retire to some other job in a few years. The number of teachers who experience job burnout is growing. In 1962 more than 25 percent of all teachers in the United States had twenty or more years of experience. In 1976 this number had been reduced by one-half (Walsh 1979).

The causes of teacher burnout include physical assaults, harassment by the administration, paperwork, and isolation. Pressures can result in high absenteeism, alcohol abuse, and ultimately leaving the profession (Walsh 1979). These factors occur even though teaching has many advantages. Salaries, although low, are improving; working days are short; job security is high in districts where tenure is awarded; vacations are long and frequent; and good fringe benefits are provided (Bardo 1979).

Teachers must be aware that they are vulnerable to burnout. They need to be aware of the characteristics that sense the beginnings of burnout and be prepared to deal with them before getting too despaired. Although school administrators are not ultimately responsible, they should be cognizant of the burnout problem and initiate steps to keep good teachers from leaving the profession.

While more money may not be available to entice teachers to stay in teaching, administrators can do several things to reduce the chances of burnout among their teachers. These include:

- Provide rewards other than financial, such as travel money to professional conferences.

- Reduce class sizes. Although this may not be possible on a permanent basis, teachers could receive lower student/teacher ratios on a rotating basis.

- Rotate unpopular classes among all teachers.

- Reduce paperwork to a bare minimum.

- Reduce extra duties, such as lunchroom, hall monitors, and playground monitors. While administrators must staff these roles, they could use aides and other staff (depending on state law).

- Provide opportunities for good in-service training that is developed with teacher input.

Low Job Status

Teachers are often looked upon by the public as unprofessionals who are incapable of earning a living in any other vocation. In the Gallup Poll of Teachers' Attitudes

Teachers must be aware of burnout and be prepared to deal with its characteristics.

Toward the Public Schools (Gallup 1985), only 1 percent of the teachers surveyed felt that teaching was regarded as the highest status profession in the community. Although 19 percent of the general public rated the teaching profession as highest in the community, this figure still reflects a fairly low status.

Job status is an intangible; it is something that is difficult to improve. However, it is a real issue for teachers. Individuals in any profession like to feel that their jobs are viewed as important and with a certain amount of prestige. That teachers and the general public have low opinions of teaching can only add to teacher burnout.

'Why Do We Have Such a Bad Image?'

The crisis in education, teachers say, is not what is coming out of the classroom, but what is going in. They list unimaginative, overbearing school administrations and competition for students' attention from television and rock music heroes who ridicule education. Most troubling, however, is their increasing suspicion that society does not value teachers.

"The students have such apathy," says Julie Riegel, an elementary school teacher in Ypsilanti, Mich. "That's coming from the parents. We are working so hard. I think we're doing a great job. But we are not important enough to people out there. Why aren't we? Every parent should spend a day with us in the classroom."

David Sutherland teaches elementary school in Scotts Valley, Calif. "If we as a country don't think that the most important thing is to pass down our values and perpetuate the culture, then that culture is threatened." Sutherland—and many of the teachers PARADE talked with and polled—felt that parents were "significantly responsible" for the fact that the school system is not allowed to get "the business of teaching done." Sutherland, 36, has been teaching for 13 years. "Before we can get down to reading and writing," he says, "we must teach self-discipline, concentration, honesty, integrity—values that should have been brought from home."

Teachers understand the rising expectations from society, and they accept the challenge to improve, but they feel they are not getting the support they need. "As the level of professionalism increases," says Sutherland, "the level of frustration also increases. The best teachers are looking elsewhere."

"I don't think the public understands how hard we are working," says Betty Williams, who has been teaching elementary school in Kirkland, Wash., for 22 years. "They are always hearing about the strikes. But for my 9 o'clock to 3 o'clock day, I work 7 to 5. There's no break with kids. I'm always working on weekends and through the summers. You just give so much time and energy. It's intense. Teach-

ers care. Why do we have such a bad image?"

Teachers, say teachers, are as good as ever. What makes a good teacher? Betty Williams says: "You have to love the profession." Brenda Wilson, a third-grade teacher in Syracuse, N.Y., talks about "those indescribable moments when you walk into a classroom and see what progress the kids are making." Julie Riegel agrees: "It is really exciting to watch a child latch on to something." "A good teacher," says Virginia Smit, a high school art teacher, "is a flexible, caring individual." "And a secure individual," adds Jane Cohen, Smit's colleague at Livingston High School in New York City.

Most of all, good teachers believe in their students. "They are a lot brighter than they were 10 years ago," says Diane Landures, who's been teaching for 16 years—at present in Salt Lake City. "You would be stunned by what an 8-year-old or a 9-year-old knows. The children are our future, but when people ask me what I do for a living and I say 'teach'—they say, 'You're kidding!' There is such scorn."

The lack of respect bothers Ed Amaral, a high school math teacher in Hanover, Mass. "I don't want to blame the parents, I'm a parent myself. But society has changed in the 20 years since I started teaching. We grab more things—VCRs, stereos, TVs. We abuse the kids emotionally. What I mean is that we don't demand enough of them. Maybe we have all forgotten the hard work we put into this country after World War II to get where we are today."

Amaral, however, sees much of the recent criticism of education as a positive thing. "I've been in the business long enough to see the pendulum beginning to swing back now to education as the key to a successful future. I think a lot of parents are looking for more quality and are more concerned. They see the competitive world that their children are facing, and they want them prepared as well as possible. That's good news for teachers." Parade Magazine. December 1, 1985. From an article "A report card from our teachers" by Marguerite Michaels. Reprinted with permission.

Low Salaries

The problems of teachers' salaries have already been discussed. Male teachers, who are expected to be the major income earners in the majority of American families, have a difficult time justifying teaching when they could make more money in many other jobs. Likewise, women teachers, as a result of the equal-pay/equal-opportunity movement for women, could earn substantially more money in many other vocations.

The reform movements of the 1970s and 1980s provided some improvement in salaries for teachers. Still, a large gap exists between what teachers earn and what individuals in many other professions earn. While the gap may be shrinking, to improve teachers' salaries to a level that can attract and hold many individuals who could make major contributions to education will take many years.

Actions from Reform Movements

The educational reforms that were initiated in the late 1970s and early 1980s were viewed by most teachers as very positive. Better pay for teachers, higher standards for students, and a stronger commitment from states for education were all needed. However, several suggested actions from these reform proposals were received negatively by teachers.

Merit pay. Many of the reform reports suggested that teachers be paid using a merit-pay system, paying teachers not merely on years of experience and levels of training. This appears to be an excellent proposal. Certainly, good teachers who go the extra mile should be rewarded. The problem for many teachers is not the concept but how the concept will be implemented.

Many teachers view merit pay as a means for administrators to reward their pets, while punishing other teachers. Some teachers are concerned that merit-pay increases will be given to teachers based on criteria that have little to do with effective teaching. Since the products of effective teaching are difficult to identify and measure, basing teachers' pay raises on merit would be difficult.

Teacher testing. Some of the reform reports indicated that teachers should be tested, with incompetent teachers being weeded out. Again, the idea is sound. The problem arises when deciding how to measure competent teaching. Paper-and-pencil tests are unlikely to ascertain effective instruction. While some would agree that new teachers should be tested to confirm their cognitive abilities, the testing of veteran teachers has met with stiff opposition. Arkansas, which enacted the first law mandating the competency testing of all teachers, has been a battleground between the state and the NEA and its state affiliate.

Despite the many negatives in the teaching profession, prospective teachers should not allow these negatives to change their wanting to be teachers. Teaching is a profession that gives life not only to the students in classrooms, but also to the teachers who teach them and to society in the future. While not perfect, teaching enables individuals to make their mark and help prepare future leaders and citizens of the world. Teachers do make a difference.

OTHER EDUCATION PROFESSIONS

In addition to teaching, education offers many other professional opportunities, including administration, counseling, social work, school health, and support personnel. While these positions all require professional training in Colleges of Education, major differences exist in the training curricula, job expectations, and job benefits.

Educational Administration

All schools have status leaders called administrators. These include superintendents and assistant superintendents in the central administration, building principals and assistant principals, and supervisors. Chapter nine discussed administration as a career.

School Counseling

School counselors are employed and active in most secondary schools and in increasing numbers in elementary schools. Most states require specific certification to be a

School counselors provide personal and career counseling and other support services to students.

school counselor. Most often this encompasses graduate training beyond an undergraduate degree in education. Most states also require that school counselors have some classroom teaching experience.

The roles of school counselors vary from school to school. However, in general they are available to provide counseling to students, assessment of educational and psychological needs, scheduling, and career guidance.

Social Work

Although not as common as school counselors, school social workers are found in many districts, especially in larger schools. To become a school social worker, individuals must possess training in social work. Most states do not have separate social-work certification. Licensure by professional associations is usually the primary eligibility criterion.

School social workers act as a liaison between the school and the family. In situations where students have problems, such as having disabilities, being victims of child abuse, or being delinquent, school social workers attempt to alleviate these problems by working with the parents, child, and various social agencies.

School Health

Most school districts employ certain health personnel. Primarily, these are school nurses. School nurses in most states require no additional certification, licensure, or training than for any regular nursing position. This means that school nurses must successfully complete approved nursing programs and receive professional licensure.

School nurses perform a multitude of duties, including vision and hearing screening, information dissemination, and probably the most important, administering to the health needs of students. Although not regarded as the top of the career ladder for nurses, school nurses do have several advantages over nurses in other settings, including shorter hours, long vacations, and less stressful activities.

Other Professional Support Personnel

Schools often employ many individuals for support roles within the school environment. These include physical and occupational therapists for physically handicapped students, school psychologists for counseling and assessment activities, and speech therapists for speech-impaired children. All these individuals are vitally important for the day-to-day functioning of the school. Although often serving in less visible roles than teachers and administrators, these support staff are critical to the success of the school.

TEACHING: SUMMATION

Teaching is the critical profession in the American education system. Teachers are in daily contact with students and lead them into learning activities. They identify students with special needs, individualize instruction as much as possible for all students, act as counselors, and frequently fill the role of parent-on-the-scene.

Without teachers, public education in the United States would not have achieved its applauded status around the world. Although critics like to say that American public schools, their teachers, and their students are substandard compared with some other industrialized nations, the public education system in the United States in very sound. A major reason for this is the quality and dedication of its teachers.

Teachers have to be dedicated. They have to overlook the low status the profession has in some circles, the low pay, the stress, and the criticisms voiced daily by some parents and others. For the most part, schools are doing an excellent job, and teachers should get the credit. The dedication of teachers is exemplified by the Educator's Oath, which is taken by new graduates from the teacher education program at Michigan State University. The oath is as follows:

> I hereby affirm my dedication to the profession of education. With this affirmation I embrace the obligations of professional educators to improve the general welfare, to advance human understanding and competence, and to bring honor to the endeavors of teaching and learning. I accept these obligations for myself and will be vigilant and responsible in supporting their acceptance by my colleagues.
>
> I will be always mindful of my responsibility to increase the intelligence of students through the disciplined pursuit of knowledge. I will be steadfast in this commitment, even when weary and tempted to abdicate such responsibility or blame failure on obstacles that make the task difficult. I will be persistent in my commitment to foster respect for a life of learning and respect for all students.
>
> To perform faithfully these professional duties, I promise to work always to better understand my content, my instructional practice, and the students who come under my tutelage. I promise to seek and support policies that promote quality in teaching and learning and to provide all engaged in education the opportunity to achieve excellence. I promise to emulate personally the qualities I wish to foster, and to hold and forever honor a democratic way of life that cannot exist without disciplined, cultivated, and free minds.
>
> I recognize that at times my endeavors will offend privilege and status, that I will be opposed by bias and defenders of inequality, and that I will have to confront arguments that seek to discourage my efforts and diminish my hope. But I will remain faithful to the belief that these endeavors and the pursuit of these goals make me worthy of my profession, and my profession worthy of a free people.
>
> In the presence of this gathering, I bind myself to this oath. (Lanier and Cusick 1985, p. 712)

SUMMARY

This chapter has dealt with careers in education. The primary focus was on teaching as a career. The teaching profession has come under a great deal of pressure and attack during recent years. Some of the reasons include desegregation, education for handicapped students, accountability, and the reform movements of the 1970s and 1980s.

Teaching, is it a profession or is it simply a vocation? This issue was discussed in detail, emphasizing the historical place of teaching and the current professional status of teaching. The role played by teacher organizations in the perception of teaching as a profession was also discussed.

Another topic included was the status of teaching. The demand for teachers dropped significantly during the 1970s and resulted in fewer college students majoring in education. This in turn created a situation of teacher shortages in many different fields and several regions of the country, particularly in rural areas.

The final section of the chapter dealt with shortcomings in the teaching profession. Specific items discussed were teacher burnout, low job status, low salaries, and suggested reforms from the reform movement. Also discussed were other career options in education, including administration, school health, counseling, and support activities. In conclusion, teachers are critical in the public education system in the United States, teaching is a rewarding profession, and many of the criticisms of the educational system are unfounded.

IN THE FIELD

1. What do teachers in your school think make their jobs the most difficult?

2. What intangible benefits do teachers in your school feel they receive?

3. Do teachers consider themselves professionals or simply workers? Why do they feel this way?

4. Are the teachers organized into a teachers' organization? If so, is the organization associated with either the NEA or AFT? If not, how is it organized?

5. What do teachers think make good teachers?

6. What actions did you observe that you consider good teaching practices?

7. Does the district have difficulty in hiring teachers who are fully certified in all areas? If so, what specialty areas?

8. What is the current salary schedule for the district? Has the schedule changed much during the past five years?

9. Is teacher testing required in your state? If so, what is the nature of the test that is required? What are the attitudes of teachers in the district concerning teacher testing?

10. What staff are employed in the district/school other than teachers and administrators?

REFERENCES

Bardo, P. 1979. The pain of teacher burnout: A case history. *Phi Delta Kappan* 61(4), 252–53.

Bullough, R. V., Jr. 1982. Teachers and teaching in the nineteenth century: St. George, Utah. *Journal of Curriculum Theorizing* 4(2), 199–206.

Dedrick, C., and D. Raschke. 1984. Plaudits for educators. *Educational Forum* 48(4), 489–95.

Dunathan, A. T. 1980. Teacher shortage: Big problems for small schools. *Phi Delta Kappan* 62(3), 205–206.

Elam, S. M. 1981. The National Education Association: Political powerhouse or paper tiger? *Phi Delta Kappan 63*(3), 169–74.

Finn, C. E., Jr. 1985. Teacher unions and school quality: Potential allies or inevitable foes? *Phi Delta Kappan 66*(5), 331–37.

Freeman, J. 1979. The joy of teaching: Another case history. *Phi Delta Kappan 61*(4), 254–56.

Gage, N. L. 1984. What do we know about teaching effectiveness? *Phi Delta Kappan 66*(2), 87–93.

Gallup, G. H. 1984. The 16th annual Gallup poll of the public's attitudes toward the public schools. *Phi Delta Kappan 66*(1), 23–38.

Gallup, A. 1985. The Gallup poll of teachers' attitudes toward the public schools part 2. *Phi Delta Kappan 66*(5), 323–30.

Gutek, G. 1970. *An historical introduction to American education.* New York: Thomas Y. Crowell Company.

Johnson, J. A., H. W. Collins, V. L. Dupuis, and J. H. Johansen. 1982. *Introduction to the foundations of American education.* 5th ed. Boston: Allyn and Bacon.

Lanier, J., and P. Cusick. 1985. An oath for professional educators. *Phi Delta Kappan 66*(10), 711–12.

Marczely, B. 1985. Teacher education: A view from the front lines. *Phi Delta Kappan 66*(10), 702–706.

National Center for Education Statistics. 1983. *The condition of education 1983 edition.* Washington, DC: Department of Education.

NEA survey investigates teacher attitudes, practices. 1980. *Phi Delta Kappan 62*(1), 49–50.

Newbrough, A. 1983. Twelve steps towards revitalization for teachers. *Education 103*(3), 270–73.

Ornstein, A. C. 1984. A difference teachers make: How much? *Educational Forum 49*(1), 109–17.

Pellicer, L. O. 1984. Effective teaching: Science or magic? *The Clearing House 58*(2), 53–56.

Perkin, J. R. C. 1979. The teacher as the key. *Phi Delta Kappan 60*(9), 655–58.

Robinson, T. E., and W. A. Brower. 1982. Teachers and their survivors. *Phi Delta Kappan 63*(10), 722+.

Ryan, K. and J. M. Cooper. 1980. *Those who can, teach.* Boston: Houghton Mifflin Co.

Salaries stay close to inflation. 1984. *Education USA.* April 9, 252.

Salary increases around 7 percent. 1985. *Education USA.* March 11, 219.

Smith, B. O. 1980. Research bases for teacher education. *Phi Delta Kappan 66*(10), 685–90.

Walsh, D. 1979. Classroom stress and teacher burnout. *Phi Delta Kappan 61*(4), 252.

Williams, D. A., P. King, D. Shirley, and S. Steptoe. 1983. The merits of merit pay. *Newsweek*, June 27, 1983, 61–62.

Chapter 13
TEACHER PREPARATION

OBJECTIVES

After reading this chapter, you will be able to

- provide factual data concerning the status of teacher education;
- discuss some of the current criticisms about teacher education;
- describe actions being recommended and taken to reform teacher education;
- describe how teachers are certified and recertified;
- discuss alternative certification programs.

OUTLINE

ADVANCE ORGANIZERS
INTRODUCTION
TEACHER EDUCATION
    Status of Teacher Education
    Criticisms of Teacher Education
    Reforms in Teacher Education
TEACHER CERTIFICATION

    Traditional Certification Programs
    Alternative Certification Programs
TEACHER EDUCATION: CONCLUSIONS
SUMMARY
IN THE FIELD
REFERENCES

1. What is the status of teacher education?
2. What are the major criticisms of teacher education?
3. How have universities responded to criticisms related to teacher training?
4. How are teachers certified in most states?
5. What is alternative certification and what is its status?

INTRODUCTION

To become a teacher or other professional in the educational vocation, certain training is required. This is similar to other professions, such as medicine, law, and business, which require that certain skills and competencies be acquired before entering into the profession. Educational professionals believe that certain prerequisites must be met before someone can be a teacher.

TEACHER EDUCATION

Teacher training is a vital component of the public education system in the United States (Gage 1984). During the past fifty years, significant contributions have been made by teacher education institutions. In the 1930s the average teacher, especially in rural areas, had two or fewer years of college; many only had a high-school diploma. Currently, teachers must have a minimum of a bachelor's degree, and approximately one-third have a master's degree or higher. Today's teachers have a much broader academic background, a better understanding of child growth and development, and more knowledge about teaching methods than at any previous time in the history of American education (Smith 1980). Much of this improvement is the result of teacher education programs.

Status of Teacher Education

Approximately fourteen hundred institutions of higher education offer teacher education programs in the United States (Smith 1980). This equates to nearly 70 percent of all four-year colleges and universities in the country (Clark 1984). Forty percent of the institutions are private colleges with enrollments of fewer than one thousand students, and the remaining 60 percent are state-operated universities (Smith 1980).

Despite the large number of teacher education programs, the enrollment in these programs has declined sharply since 1970. In 1969, 24 percent of all college-bound students in the United States planned to major in teacher education. This number had dropped to less than 5 percent in 1982 (Weaver 1984a) (see figure 13–1). From 1970 to 1983 the number of students graduating from teacher education programs dropped from 314,000 to under 120,000 (Ranbom 1984).

The most recent Gallup Poll on Attitudes Toward Public Education revealed that the percentage of parents who favor their daughters entering the teaching profession was 50 percent, while the percentage of parents who favored their sons being teachers was slightly fewer than 46 percent (Gallup 1984a). This compares with 43 percent

Percent indicating teaching
as probable career

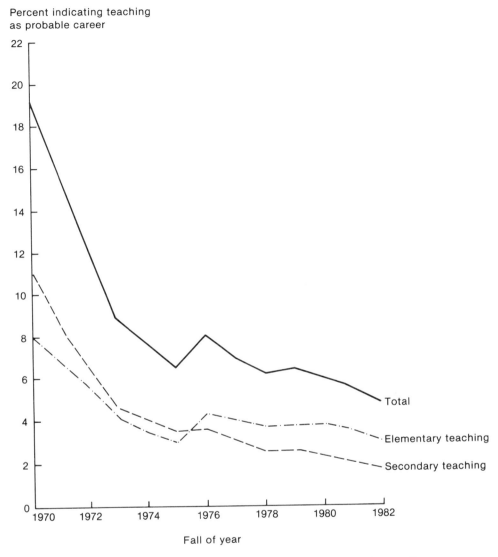

Fall of year

Figure 13-1. *College Freshmen Indicating Teaching as a Probable Career. Source:
National Center for Education Statistics, 1983.*

of the teachers surveyed in a Gallup poll of teachers' attitudes toward the public
schools favoring a daughter entering the teaching profession, and only 31 percent
favoring a son becoming a teacher (Gallup 1985). In 1969, 75 percent of parents
indicated that they would like a son or daughter to enter the teaching profession
(Gallup 1984a).

Why have the numbers of interested students dropped so significantly during the
past fifteen years? The answer to this question is complex. One obvious reason for the

fewer number of education majors is the lack of jobs available. In the 1960s teaching jobs were taken by approximately 25 percent of all college graduates. When the market became oversupplied with qualified teachers at the end of the 1960s, graduates from liberal arts programs who could become certified with minimal additional training found that no jobs were available. The result was that fewer students chose to major in teacher education because the jobs were simply not available (Weaver 1984b).

Criticisms of Teacher Education

Another reason for the declining number of students majoring in education during the past decade is the criticisms launched against teacher education programs. Teacher education in the 1980s is under attack from all sides (Ishler 1984; Clark 1984; Ohanian 1985; Marczely 1985; and Berliner 1984). Politicians, students, parents, and the general public have all accused teacher education programs of being the primary problem with American public education. Many problem areas have been enunciated. Among those most commonly emphasized include:

1. Admission standards are so low that anyone can enroll in teacher education.
2. Education majors take too much coursework on "how to teach" and not enough coursework on "what to teach."
3. The general education program for prospective teachers is less rigorous than that required of other majors.
4. Anyone who gains admission to a teacher education program will undoubtedly graduate, because the academic standards are so low. (Ishler 1984, p. 121)

Other criticisms include the overall quality of education majors, poor abilities of teacher education faculty, and the lack of general education courses taken by education majors.

Quality of education majors. Teacher education programs have traditionally attracted students who are not as academically talented as those who choose to major in other areas. For example, high-school seniors who planned to major in education in 1982 averaged thirty-two points below the national average on the Scholastic Aptitude Test (SAT) on the verbal subtest and forty-eight points below the national average on the math subtest (Schoolteaching Profession in Crisis 1983). Clark (1984) stated that teacher education majors have consistently come from the bottom third of their high school graduating classes. A study conducted by the New Jersey Department of Education determined that "In 1982 the Scholastic Aptitude Test (SAT) scores of New Jersey high school graduates who planned to major in education were lower than those of graduates who planned to major in 22 of 24 fields of study at the college level" (Cooperman and Klagholz 1985, p. 692). The National Center for Education Statistics (1983) has summarized the average vocabulary, reading, and math test scores of college-bound seniors and their intended field of study (see table 13–1). Certainly, the questionable academic competence of teachers has added to the public's loss of confidence in public education (Marker 1984).

Inadequate curriculum. Another criticism voiced by many critics of teacher education is that education majors take too many education courses, especially "methods" courses (Raimo 1983). The basic training program in most colleges of education has changed little during the past fifty years. "The sequence of courses established in the

TABLE 13–1   Average Vocabulary, Reading, and Mathematics Test Scores of College-Bound [1] Seniors, by Sex and Intended Field of Study: Spring 1972 and 1980

Field	Male		Female	
	1972 Seniors	*1980 Seniors*	*1972 Seniors*	*1980 Seniors*
Vocabulary Test (15 Point Maximum)				
Education:				
Average score	6.50	6.20	8.05	6.59
Standard error	.32	.35	.18	.20
Other field:				
Average score	8.19	7.43	8.49	7.31
Standard error	.09	.07	.10	.08
Reading Test (20 Point Maximum)				
Education:				
Average score	10.59	9.69	11.88	9.99
Standard error	.35	.52	.21	.27
Other field:				
Average score	12.03	11.16	12.35	10.84
Standard error	.10	.09	.11	.09
Mathematics Test (19 Point Maximum)[2]				
Education:				
Average score	12.03	10.90	11.96	10.20
Standard error	.36	.44	.22	.24
Other field:				
Average score	13.95	12.88	12.85	11.36
Standard error	.08	.08	.10	.09
Sample size:				
Education	267	172	692	595
Other field	3,754	5,195	3,256	5,297

[1] *College-bound seniors include those who indicated that they expected either to attain some college in the future or to be enrolled in college for academic or vocational training in the year following high school.*

[2] *Caution should be exercised in interpreting change in mathematics scores because scores were based on 19 common items out of 25 items. Differences in levels of difficulty of the other 6 items may have affected time in which to complete the 19 common items.*

NOTE: Precision of the estimates may be calculated using the standard error following procedures provided in the Data Sources in the Appendix.

SOURCE: U.S. Department of Education, National Center for Education Statistics, Education Attracts Fewer Academically High Achieving Young Women, Bulletin, December 1982, and National Longitudinal Study of the High School Class of 1972 and High School and Beyond Study, unpublished tabulations (September 1982).

Thirties—introduction to education followed by social foundations, educational psychology, methods courses, and practice teaching—remains substantially unchanged today" (Smith 1980, p. 89). During these fifty years, a great deal of knowledge has been obtained related to teaching. Unfortunately, much of that knowledge has not been used to change the training program for teacher education majors.

Ishler (1984) found that colleges of education require vastly different course requirements for graduation in education. The range of professional education courses required for elementary education majors ranged from twelve to seventy-eight credit hours, with a mean of thirty hours. Nineteen percent of the training programs required more than fifty semester hours of professional education courses. For secondary education majors, the range was from twelve to forty-seven hours, with a mean of twenty-eight hours; 36 percent required more than thirty semester hours for graduation.

The facts do support the criticism that education majors are required to take a large portion of their coursework in education. Still another criticism related to coursework is the nature of the education courses that are required. Some of the criticisms include:

- Courses are irrelevant and too theoretical (Gage 1984);

- Courses contain too much information about learners and learning and not enough about teachers and teaching (Gage 1984);

- Courses are full of mechanical activities such as lesson planning and deplete in the areas of personal and developmental characteristics of students (Clabaugh, Feden, and Vogel 1984);

- Courses concentrate on developing too many materials and providing students with too many cookbook ideas and ignore showing future teachers how to find their own solutions to problems (Ohanian 1985);

- Courses focus to much on the subject matter to be taught when students may already know more than their education professors (Gage 1984).

Clark (1984) states that secondary education majors miss out on a concentrated period of study in the teaching field, opportunities for socialization with peers, and chances for practice in a variety of settings. Elementary education majors suffer as a result of their not having a major in any subject area and limited practicum experiences (Clark 1984).

These criticisms are not all well founded; however, many teacher education professors would agree, at least to some degree, with some of the points made. Consumers of teacher education programs tend to view their programs much more positively than the critics. In the Gallup Poll of Teachers' Attitudes Toward the Public Schools, 82 percent of the teachers surveyed gave their teacher training programs a C or better, with 49 percent rating their programs as either A or B (Gallup 1984b). The voices of critics, therefore, should not be accepted as reality. As a result of the national reform reports of the late 1970s and early 1980s, critics looked for reasons for the state of public education. Teacher education happened to be one of the targets for this blame. This is not to say that teacher education could not be significantly improved, it could.

—————————— HIGHLIGHT ——————————

TEST TIME FOR TEACHERS
A new report calls for overhauling the profession

Jennet Conant
with Pat Wingert in Washington
and Renee Michael in New York

The message is clear enough: what you don't pay for, you don't get. A new report, "A Nation Prepared: Teachers for the 21st Century," poses the problem facing America's ailing school systems in straightforward economic terms. Unless the country is willing to shoulder the expense of completely overhauling public education, "the cost of not doing so will be a steady erosion in the American standard of living." The key to reform, according to the 14-member task force of the Carnegie Forum on Education and the Economy, is to lure quality teachers into the classroom with higher standards and better pay. "We need to establish in the minds of teachers and the public that teaching is a profession," says Ernest Boyer, president of the Carnegie Foundation. "Like law or medicine, we may need national boards."

The 77-page report, made public last week, proposes the creation of a National Board for Professional Teaching Standards by June 1987. The board would set minimum standards of competence and provide certification for public elementary- and high-school teachers who met them—eventually tying teacher salaries to their competence. Significantly, despite widespread teacher opposition to competence testing, both Albert Shanker of the American Federation of Teachers and (with reservations) Mary Hatwood Futrell of the National Education Association endorsed the report. In exchange for their agreement that student instructors would undergo the test—optional for teachers already working—the report suggests administrative changes that would give teachers more power. The report also recommends abolishing the undergraduate education major.

'No way': The Carnegie report was greeted with enthusiasm by educators and political leaders who believe that the creation of a national standard is the surest way to improve the quality of teaching. William J. Bennett, secretary of education, praised the report, adding that he favors national certification to "evaluate all teachers in school." But critics suggest that the costs of the Carnegie plan could prove prohibitive. The report says that an inflation-adjusted increase of only 2.8 percent annually over 10 years would be sufficient. But with the average high-school teacher earning less than $23,000 a year (chart), "raising salaries by only 25 percent would come to billions of dollars," says Myron Liberman, an education professor at Ohio University and author of a book on school reform called "Beyond Public Education." Any increase in teachers' salaries would probably have to come from state and local taxes. And, says Liberman, "there's just no way that's going to happen."

The chief flaw in the Carnegie plan may be that it proposes a national solution to essentially local problems—at a time when federal funds for education are decreasing. Supporters say the next step is to sell the plan to the states and counties, which bear the brunt of the cost of the nation's schools. "The public has to understand that we can't have good ideas on the cheap," says Boyer. No doubt: but the task force has yet to establish that its ideas will be as good in execution as they are in conception.

Newsweek. May 26, 1986. Reprinted with permission.

Reforms in Teacher Education

Colleges of education around the country are currently engaged in major revisions of their training programs to better meet the needs of students. Some of the changes proposed by critics and professionals include (1) improving the quality of teacher education majors, (2) revising the training curriculum, (3) increasing funding for teacher education, and (4) developing alternative certification requirements. Many of these recommendations are currently being implemented.

Improving the quality of teacher education majors. One of the easiest reforms to implement in teacher education focuses on improving the quality of students majoring in education (Clark 1984). Most professionals agree that more selection criteria and better screening procedures need to be developed concerning requirements for admission into teacher education. The issue is what criteria and what procedures should be adopted (Draba and Steinkellner 1977).

Methods used to increase admission requirements have varied considerably. In some states, legislatures or state departments of education have mandated changes; in other states, individual universities have taken their own steps to change admission requirements. Where states have mandated universal standards, test scores are most often used as the key entrance requirement. Nine of the fourteen southern states

Teacher education programs are implementing reforms to counter recent criticisms.

(Alabama, Florida, Kentucky, Louisiana, North Carolina, South Carolina, Tennessee, Texas, and Virginia) now require minimum test scores to enter teacher education programs. Universites most often use a student's grade point average (GPA) as the primary admission requirement. In these universities, the trend has been to raise the minimum GPAs required for admission into teacher education (Marker 1984). Ishler (1984) studied admission and graduation requirements in 103 institutions training teachers and found that the GPA required for admission into teacher education programs ranged from 2.0 to 3.0. Forty-six percent of the institutions in the study indicated that a GPA of 2.0 was required, 23 percent required a GPA of 2.1 to 2.25, 27 percent required a GPA of 2.5, and 3 percent required a 3.0 GPA.

Improving the training curriculum. Most would agree that some improvement could be made in the teacher training curriculum. However, like admission requirements, there is not a consensus as to what should be included in the curriculum. Suggestions range from making the curriculum more practical to increasing the length of teacher training programs from four to five years.

Teacher education professors cannot agree on a common curriculum for teacher education majors. A comprehensive list of "professional domains" students should be exposed to includes

- different instructional approaches, including use of existing and emerging media;

- the relationship between diverse characteristics of learners and instructional strategies;

- curriculum models and theories, especially in subjects for which a given teacher will be responsible;

- small-group processes;

- professional responsibilities and obligations;

- consultation skills to work with other professionals, including knowledge of their roles and of the organization and administration of schools;

- parent/professional relations (including community relations);

- a capacity for inquiry and design to meet the specific needs of individual learners, including diagnosis, instructional and curricular design, and evaluation skills;

- classroom and behavior management;

- self-awareness, or the ability to be in touch with oneself. (Gideonse 1982, p. 16)

Ohanian (1985) adds that the coursework in education should be geared toward helping prospective teachers develop their own ways of solving problems rather than providing them with long lists of how-to's. Marczely (1985) described this as putting "academic fiber" in college of education courses.

Another critical area in the teacher education curriculum is hands-on experience. Most often called student teaching, this course offers students opportunities to practice what they have learned in classes. The average number of credit hours earned in student teaching by education majors is twelve (Ishler 1984). Two common concerns related to student teaching are that (1) students have to wait until the end of their coursework to student teach and (2) one semester of hands-on experience is not sufficient. Buchanan (1982) suggests that students get into classrooms after they have completed only twelve hours of education courses. By having this early experience, students would be able to relate their coursework to actual experiences and also find out early in their program if they really like teaching.

Some university training programs require more field experience than student teaching. For example, in a program developed at Oregon State University and Western Oregon State College, students enroll in three different field experiences. In addition to the normal student teaching, education majors enroll in an introductory field experience early in their programs and finally complete a senior-year practicum where they are involved in a school improvement project with a cooperating local school district (Barr 1984).

HIGHLIGHT

COMPETENCY TESTING OF TEXAS EDUCATORS UPHELD
Decision says requirement in line with public school reforms, clears way for examining 210,000

AUSTIN, Tex. (AP)—Requiring Texas teachers to take a reading and writing test in order to hold their jobs is legal and in line with major public school reforms, a judge ruled Monday.

The decision by State District Judge Harley Clark gave the Texas Education Agency the go-ahead for competency testing of 210,000 public school administrators and teachers March 10.

Those who fail and do not pass a make-up exam in June will lose their teaching certificates.

The Texas State Teachers Association had challenged the TEA plans, saying school boards should decide whether a teacher is competent.

The TSTA had no immediate comment on the decision but said it would have a statement later.

The Texas Classroom Teachers Association, which was not part of the suit, said it was not surprised at Judge Clark's decision.

"Although we were opposed in principle to the so-called 'competency test,' we felt from the beginning that an effort to fight it would be ill-fated and would falsely raise the hopes of teachers," TCTA President Thomasine Sparks of Kingsville said.

"I am confident that 95 percent of our teachers will pass this test," Commissioner of Education W. N.

Kirby said. "Only a very few do not have adequate reading and writing skills to teach our children.

"Once this test is behind us, we will have shown the citizens of Texas that we have highly qualified people in our classrooms."

Judge Clark made a three-part ruling on the TSTA challenge that the teacher testing, a part of the 1984 school reform act, was unconstitutional and should be cancelled.

The judge ruled the law mandating the test was constitutional and said the State Board of Education had acted properly in implementing the test. Judge Clark also said the testing should proceed without delay.

The Teachers Examination of Current Administrators and Teachers was part of the school reforms mandated by the 1984 special session of the legislature in order to upgrade Texas schools.

"If a teacher cannot read or write, there is a recourse," Robert Chanin, attorney for the National Education Association, argued for the TSTA in a February 21 hearing. "It is the responsibility of the employing school board to determine whether their teachers can read and write."

Chanin said the teaching certificate was a "lifetime license" and it was unfair for the state to change the rules.

Assistant Attorney General Kevin O'Hanlon said the test was aimed at protecting the "students, whose lives and future careers are at stake."

"We are attempting to accord a preference to those teachers who can read and write before we turn them loose on the children of Texas," Hanlon told the court.

Kirby said Monday he realized the morale of Texas educators was suffering and that some teachers "feel the public cares little about them."

"We must use this test as a turning point to reverse those morale problems by generating renewed public support for teachers and public confidence in our education system," Kirby said. Arkansas Gazette. March 4, 1986. Reprinted by permission of the Associated Press.

Implementing exit criteria. In addition to implementing better screening of students at the beginning of teacher education programs, many colleges of education have begun to require teachers to pass exit examinations such as the National Teachers Examination (NTE). By 1984 seventeen states had statutes requiring new teachers to be tested. These states were Arizona, Arkansas, California, Colorado, Connecticut, Florida, Indiana, Kansas (effective 1986), Mississippi, Nebraska, New Jersey, North Carolina, Rhode Island, Tennessee, Texas, Virginia, and Wyoming. Eight additional states require testing as a result of state department of education action (Lines 1985). Al-

Several states are requiring teachers to take competency tests before initial certification.

though some of the states develop their own tests, most use the NTE. Of the fifteen states that used exit tests in 1982, eight required the NTE (Kauchak 1984). Three states, Florida, Georgia, and Alabama, have indicated that universities would be placed on probation if the majority of their graduates cannot pass these tests (Williams, Howard, McDonald and Michael 1984).

Testing new teachers is a controversial issue. The National Education Association, long opposed teacher testing, only recently reversed its opposition to teacher testing. The American Federation of Teachers has a long-term record of support for teacher testing. The AFT president, Albert Shanker, has even called for a national teacher's test (Williams and Howard 1984, p. 53). In addition to testing new teachers, some states have passed, or are considering passing, testing requirements for veteran teachers. In 1983, the Arkansas legislature passed legislation requiring all teachers to take a one-time teacher competency test. The test was administered for the first time during the spring of 1985. As could be expected, the test was challenged by the NEA and many Arkansas teachers.

Expanding teacher education programs to five years. For many years, some critics of teacher training have encouraged colleges and universities to expand teacher training to a five-year curriculum. Their rationale has been that good, competent teachers cannot be trained in a four-year period. Several universities have responded and have developed five-year training programs, including the University of Kansas and the University of Florida.

The program at the University of Kansas requires students to complete sixty hours of general education coursework spread through language arts, the humanities, behavioral sciences, social sciences, natural sciences, and mathematics. Forty semester hours are required in the student's teaching field. At the end of the first four years, students are granted a bachelor's degree and allowed to enroll in the fifth year if they meet certain requirements, such as a 3.0 grade point average for regular admission. The fifth year includes student teaching for a semester, a practicum assignment, and graduate coursework (Scannell 1984).

Florida's program, called PROTEACH, requires 166 credit hours for elementary education majors and 160 credit hours for secondary education majors. The college of education awards the bachelor's degree to elementary education majors, and the college of liberal arts and sciences awards the degree to secondary education majors. The fifth year of the program results in the student earning a master's degree and focuses on coursework and field experiences (Smith, Carroll, and Fry 1984).

Increasing funds. Most colleges of education receive their funding from the university central administration based on the cost of all undergraduate training programs (Clark 1984). This is normally accomplished using a formula to fund college programs based on the full time equivalent (FTE) model. The more students that enroll in courses and generate student credit hours, the more funds are received by that particular college. During times of decreasing public school enrollments due to the population decline of school-age children, fewer teachers are needed. This in turn means that fewer college students choose to major in education because there are limited jobs available. As a result, colleges of education have found themselves having to provide better, more quality programs with continuously decreasing funds (Watts 1982).

Funding colleges of education using the FTE model is inappropriate. Teacher training programs must train competent, well-qualified teachers, or the entire public education system breaks down (Watts 1982). A vicious cycle results when teacher training programs in universities receive fewer dollars to provide programs. The reduced level of funding may result in several outcomes, including

1. reduction in teacher education faculty;
2. reduction in training programs with low enrollments;
3. larger class sizes;
4. fewer stipends for graduate students, which in turn also creates larger classes.

Reduction in teacher education faculty. This result from a reduction in funds can have a critical impact. If colleges of education are required to reduce faculty, the individuals most likely affected would be younger, untenured faculty members. Unfortunately, these individuals may be the ones with new ideas vitally needed by the college. Regardless of the faculty who lose jobs as a result of faculty cutbacks, the result would undoubtedly affect the morale of all remaining faculty.

Reduction in training programs with low enrollments. Often colleges of education must eliminate entire training programs. If this is required to meet the restrictions of a reduced budget, the programs that are most likely to be eliminated are those with low student enrollments. Colleges of education administrators must make these types of decisions because future funding is most likely related to student enrollments. Often low-enrollment programs are greatly needed by the state to meet the demands of providing appropriate programs for all students in the schools. The result is that no graduates are trained and certified in areas of great need, which creates a gap in public school programs.

One common criticism of public secondary education is the lack of science and math courses available for students. Few prospective teachers major in these areas because individuals who are interested in science and math most often enroll in the college of liberal arts, as this better prepares them to enter a more lucrative vocation after graduation. If colleges of education cut back on teacher training programs for science and math teachers, the end result is a furthering of the current shortage crisis.

The FTE funding model may not work for colleges of education. Watts (1982) suggested funding teacher education programs using a program budgeting model rather than using the FTE model. Programs would be judged on their merits, not on the basis of the amount of money brought into the university through enrollment figures.

TEACHER CERTIFICATION

Although some states are beginning to implement alternate certification programs, most states continue to certify teachers using a traditional model. Students who enroll in colleges of education with state-approved teacher education programs and successfully complete the requirements for degrees in those training programs are eligible for state certification.

Traditional Certification Programs

Colleges of education vary considerably in their requirements for graduation. However, all closely follow the state department of education requirements for teacher certification. Although the certification requirements vary from state to state, there are many similarities. For example, most require that all individuals have a bachelor's degree before they can be certified. Most states also require that students earn a minimal number of credit hours in various courses, including general education courses, professional education courses, courses in the student's teaching field, and student teaching.

Ishler (1984) conducted a study to determine admission and graduation requirements for teacher education. The results from 103 teacher training programs that are members of the Association of Colleges and Schools of Education in State Universities and Land Grant Colleges and Affiliated Private Universities revealed major differences in degree requirements (see table 13–2).

Weible and Dumas (1982) studied the fifty states to determine the certification standards in secondary education (see tables 13–3 and 13–4). The range in requirements is great in many areas, meaning that students majoring in secondary education in one state may complete a significantly different program of study than those in another state.

In addition to state requirements for initial teacher certification, forty states have requirements for recertification. Recertification requirements have typically focused on teachers earning a certain number of graduate hours during a specified period of time. However, an emerging trend is to allow teachers to meet recertification requirements by participating in in-service activities planned and provided by the local school district. Twenty-nine states, 58 percent, either have or plan to implement such options. The requirements for recertification vary considerably from state to state in such areas as (1) recertification period, (2) semester hours required, and (3) whether the recertification requirements can be met through district-planned activities (Hanes and Rowls 1984) (see table 13–5).

TABLE 13-2   Graduation/Certification Requirements

	No. of Credit Hours Required	
Areas	Elementary	Secondary
Content Areas	12–38 X= 29	24–66 X= 35
Student Teaching	6–19 X= 12	5–15 X= 9
Professional Education	12–78 X= 30	12–47 X= 28
Cumulative GPA	2.0–3.0 X= 2.25	2.0–3.0 X= 2.25
GPA in Content Areas	2.0–3.0 X= 2.25	2.0–3.0 X= 2.25
GPA in Professional Education Courses	2.0–3.0 X= 2.25	2.0–3.0 X= 2.25

Source: R.E. Ishler. Requirements for admission to and graduation from teacher education. Phi Delta Kappan 66(2) (1984): 121–22.

TABLE 13-3   Secondary Teacher Certification Standards in General
Education

	Number of Semester Hours	
Discipline	*Range*	*Mean*
History/Social Science	2–12	9
Natural Science	0–12	5
Mathematics	0–6	2
English Composition	0–12	6
Humanities	0–15	6
Oral Communication	0–3	1
Health/PE	0–6	2

Source: *T. Weible and W. Dumas. Secondary teacher certification standards in fifty states.* Journal of Teacher Education, *1982, 22–23.*

Alternative Certification Programs

Some states have responded to the call for educational reform through alternative certification for teachers. With teacher shortages being severe in some areas, for example, science and math, and emerging criticisms of traditional teacher education programs, states have opted to initiate alternative methods to certify teachers other than through traditional college of education degree programs.

TABLE 13-4   Secondary Teacher Certification Standards in Professional
Education

Course/Competency Area	*Percent Requiring*
Reading in Content Area	54
Educational Psychology	97
Social Foundations	69
Org./Admin. of Schools	31
Early Field Experiences	38
Exceptional Child/Mainstreaming	36
Tests and Evaluation	38
Multi-Cultural Education	31
General Teaching Methods	74
Special Methods	59
Educational Media	23
Student Teaching	100

Reprinted with permission. *T. Weible and W. Dumas. Secondary teacher certification standards in fifty states.* Journal of Teacher Education 32(4), 23.

TABLE 13-5 Recertification Requirements

	Recertification Required?	Recertification Period (In Years)	Semester Hour Recertification Requirement	Recertification via District-Planned Activities?	Recertification Solely via District-Planned Activities?	% Recertification Credit Allowed via District Activities
Alabama	yes	8–12*	6–9*	yes*	yes*	NA
Alaska	yes	5	6	yes	no	50%
Arizona	yes	6	5	no	NA	NA
Arkansas	yes	6–10*	6	no	NA	NA
California	yes	5(pending)	24(pending)	yes	no	pending
Colorado	yes	5	6	yes	no	66%
Connecticut	no	—	—	—	—	—
Delaware	no†	—	—	no†	—	—
Florida	yes	5	6	yes	yes	NA
Georgia	yes	5–10*	6	yes	yes	NA
Hawaii	no	—	—	—	—	—
Idaho	no	—	—	—	—	—
Illinois	no	—	—	—	—	—
Indiana	yes	5–10*	12–M.S.**	no	NA	NA
Iowa	yes	6–10*	6	yes	no	50%
Kansas	yes	3–5*	6–8*	yes	yes‡	50%
Kentucky	yes	10	30–M.S.*	yes	no	33%
Louisiana	no	—	—	—	—	—
Maine	yes	5	6	yes	yes	NA
Maryland	yes	5–10*	6	yes	yes §	50%
Massachusetts	no	—	—	—	—	—
Michigan	yes	6	18**	no	—	—
Minnesota	yes	5	9	yes	yes	NA
Mississippi	yes	5–10*	6	yes	no	50%
Missouri	no	—	—	—	—	—
Montana	yes	5*	4*	yes	yes	NA
Nebraska	yes	3	6	no	NA	NA
Nevada	yes	5–6*	6	yes	yes	NA
New Hampshire	yes	3	3	yes	yes	NA
New Jersey	no	—	—	—	—	—
New Mexico	yes	4–10*	8	yes	no	50%
New York	no	—	—	—	—	—
North Carolina	yes	5	6	yes	yes	NA
North Dakota	yes	5	4	no	NA	NA
Ohio	yes	4–8*	6–18*	no	NA	NA
Oklahoma	yes	5	8	no	NA	NA
Oregon	yes	3–5*	9–24*	yes	yes	NA
Pennsylvania	yes	6*	24**	yes	yes	NA
Rhode Island	yes	3–5*	6–M.S.*/**	yes	no	33%–50%*
South Carolina	yes	5	6	yes	yes	NA
South Dakota	yes	5	6	yes	no	50%
Tennessee	yes	10	6	no	NA	NA
Texas	yes	3–5*	6*/**	yes	pending	pending
Utah	yes	5	6	yes	yes	NA
Vermont	yes	5	6	yes	yes	NA
Virginia	yes	5	6	yes	no	50%
Washington	yes	4**	10*	no	NA	NA
West Virginia	yes	3–5*	6	no	NA	NA
Wisconsin	pending	5	6	yes	yes	NA
Wyoming	yes	5–10*	5–10*	yes	yes	NA

NA = not applicable
* Contingent on candidate's years of successful teaching experience, certificate level, and/or highest degree attained.
** One to several renewals are allowed, leading toward permanent certificate.
† Recertification is required only after dormant period; district alternative to recertification is allowed.
†† District alternative to recertification is sole option for recertification of teachers with master's degrees and beyond.
§ District alternative to recertification is sole option for first renewal only.
Reprinted with permission. Hanes and Rowls, 1984.

The state of New Jersey responded to shortages in various teaching fields in 1982 with a long-term study related to alternative ways to certify teachers. The result was that in 1985 local school districts in New Jersey started to offer the first district-administered training programs leading to teacher certification in the United States (Cooperman and Klagholz 1985).

The New Jersey plan was developed to replace emergency certification, which had been used since 1942 to staff teaching positions in certain fields with teacher shortages. Most often these positions were in science or math. The plan works the following way:

1. Districts must submit a plan to train teachers at the local level and be approved by the New Jersey Department of Education.
2. Plans should include two hundred hours of instruction, eighty of which must be completed before the certification candidate takes charge of the classroom.
3. Supervision is provided for the teacher during the first year. (Cooperman and Klagholz 1985)

In addition, individuals who want to receive certification through the alternative route must have a bachelor's degree, pass a competency test in the teaching area, have a minimum of thirty semester hours in the teaching field, and be approved by the school district following an interview (Cooperman and Klagholz 1985).

TEACHER EDUCATION: CONCLUSIONS

Teacher education in the United States is currently under a great deal of criticism. Among the charges are that students who enroll in colleges of education are of poor quality, the teacher education curriculum is irrelevant, and funds are insufficient to adequately prepare teachers.

Colleges of education have responded. New, tougher admission requirements have been implemented in many universities, training curricula are being scrutinized, and professors in teacher education are being encouraged to engage in relevant research to provide empirical bases for teacher education.

Some of the criticism is the result of critics looking for a scapegoat for the perceived poor status of public education in the United States. Some of the criticisms are valid and require immediate action on the part of teacher education professors. As a result of some needed changes resulting from the current critical atmosphere, teacher education programs will improve in quality, with the end result being better teachers to staff public schools. Clark (1984) suggests four major actions that can be taken by college of education faculty to counteract much of the criticism and improve teacher education training:

- Establish a better relationship between research on teaching and teaching effectiveness and teacher education;
- Recommit to research and scholarly activities;
- Expand research to include policy development;
- Develop new teacher training programs that are based on empirical data, not simply tradition.

SUMMARY

This chapter focused on teacher education. Teacher education has come under a great deal of criticism lately, with critics emphasizing the low quality of teacher education students and the teacher education curriculum. Current reforms in teacher education were presented, along with the implications of these reforms. Reforms specified include improving the quality of teacher education students, revamping the teacher education curriculum, implementing exit criteria for certification, increasing funding for teacher education, and improving the quality of teacher education faculty.

Teacher certification was also discussed, focusing on traditional approaches and alternative programs.

IN THE FIELD

1. Have enrollment figures in the college of education where you attend bottomed out? What is the current trend in enrollment? What factors attribute to this trend?

2. Do you agree with some of the stated criticisms of teacher education? What factors in the teacher education program at your university do you consider good? What factors do you consider bad?

3. Has your college of education initiated any reforms in the teacher education program during the past five years? If so, what are they?

4. Does your college of education faculty feel as though the college receives its fair share of funding compared with other academic units on campus? If not, why?

5. What are the state certification requirements in your area of emphasis? Have these changed during the past five years, or are they expected to change in the near future?

6. Does your state have alternative certification programs? If so, whay are they? Do college of education faculty members support such alternative programs?

REFERENCES

Barr, R. D. 1984. New ideas for teacher education. *Phi Delta Kappan 66*(2), 127–29.

Berliner, D. C. 1984. Making the right changes in preservice teacher education. *Phi Delta Kappan 66*(2), 94–96.

Buchanan, R. 1982. Out in the field. *Phi Delta Kappan 63*(7), 458–59.

Clabaugh, G. K., P. D. Feden, and R. Vogel. 1984. Revolutionizing teacher education: Training developmentally oriented teachers. *Phi Delta Kappan 65*(9), 615–16.

Clark, D. L. 1984. Better teachers for the year 2000: A proposal for the structural reform of teacher education. *Phi Delta Kappan 66*(2), 116–20.

Cooperman, S., and L. Klagholz. 1985. New Jersey's alternate route to certification. *Phi Delta Kappan 66*(10), 691–95.

Draba, R. E. and L. L. Steinkellner. 1977. Screening applicants for teacher training. *Educational Forum, 42*(1), 101–10.

Gage, N. L. 1984. What do we know about teaching effectiveness? *Phi Delta Kappan 66*(2), 87–93.

Gallup, G. H. 1984a. The 16th annual Gallup poll of the public's attitudes toward the public schools. *Phi Delta Kappan 66*(1), 23–38.

Gallup, A. 1984b. The Gallup poll of teachers' attitudes toward the public schools. *Phi Delta Kappan 66*(2), 97–107.

Gallup, A. 1985. The Gallup poll of teachers' attitudes toward the public schools part 2. *Phi Delta Kappan 66*(5), 323–30.

Gideonse, H. D. 1982. The necessary revolution in teacher education. *Phi Delta Kappan 64*(1), 15–18.

Hanes, M. L., and M. D. Rowls. 1984. Teacher recertification: A survey of the states. *Phi Delta Kappan 66*(2), 123–26.

Ishler, R. E. 1984. Requirements for admission to and graduation from teacher education. *Phi Delta Kappan 66*(2), 121–22.

Kauchak, D. 1984. Testing teachers in Louisiana: A closer look. *Phi Delta Kappan 65*(9), 626–28.

Lines, P. M. 1985. Testing the teacher: Are there legal pitfalls? *Phi Delta Kappan 66*(9), 618–22.

Marczely, B. 1985. Teacher education: A view from the front lines. *Phi Delta Kappan 66*(10), 702–706.

Marker, G. W. 1984. The new crisis: Teacher education responds. *Educational Horizons 62*(6), 55–59.

National Center for Education Statistics. 1983. *The condition of education 1983 edition*. Washington, DC: Department of Education.

Ohanian, S. 1985. On stir-and-serve recipes for teaching. *Phi Delta Kappan 66*(10), 696–701.

Raimo, A. M. 1983. Methods courses are still a vital component in teacher education. *Kappa Delta Pi Record 19*(2), 42–44.

Ranbom, S. 1984. Nation's largest schools of education see hints of enrollment 'turnaround'. *Education Week 3*(34), 1+. May 16, 1984.

Scannell, D. P. 1984. The extended teacher education program at the University of Kansas. *Phi Delta Kappan 66*(2), 130–33.

Schoolteaching profession in "crisis," new Carnegie analysis finds. 1983. *Chronicle of Higher Education*, August 31, 1983, 6.

Smith, B. O. 1980. Pedagogical education: How about reform? *Phi Delta Kappan 62*(2), 87–89.

Smith, D. C., R. G. Carroll, and B. Fry. 1984. PROTEACH: Professional teacher preparation at the University of Florida. *Phi Delta Kappan 66*(2), 134–35.

Watts D. 1982. Pupils or perish: Teacher education's catch-22. *Record 19*(1), 6–9.

Weaver, W. T. 1984a. Solving the problem of teacher quality, part 1. *Phi Delta Kappan 66*(2), 108–15.

Weaver, W. T. 1984b. Solving the problem of teacher quality, part 2. *Phi Delta Kappan 66*(3), 185–88.

Weible, T., and W. Dumas. 1982. Secondary teacher certification standards in fifty states. *Journal of Teacher Education 33*(4), 22–23.

Williams, D. A., and L. Howard. The NEA in a cross fire. *Newsweek*, June 13, 1984, 53.

Williams, D. A., L. Howard, D. H. McDonald, and R. Michael. Why teachers fail. Newsweek, September 24, 1984, 64–70.

Chapter 14
EDUCATIONAL TECHNOLOGY

OBJECTIVES

After reading this chapter, you will be able to

- describe instructional television;
- list advantages and disadvantages of instructional television;
- describe the use of closed-circuit television in schools;
- indicate the usage of audiovisual kits;
- describe the uses of computers in education;
- discuss computer-assisted instruction;
- list barriers to implementing computer-assisted instruction;
- discuss other technologies of instruction;
- describe some needed new directions in educational technology.

OUTLINE

ADVANCE ORGANIZERS
INTRODUCTION
INSTRUCTIONAL TELEVISION
CLOSED–CIRCUIT TELEVISION
AUDIOVISUAL KITS
VIDEOCASSETTE TECHNOLOGY
COMPUTERS
    Computers in Education

Uses of Computers in Education
Teacher Training in Computers
OTHER EDUCATIONAL TECHNOLOGIES
EDUCATIONAL TECHNOLOGY: NEEDED
    DIRECTIONS
SUMMARY
IN THE FIELD
REFERENCES

ADVANCE ORGANIZERS

1. What is instructional television?
2. How much is instructional television used today?
3. What are some advantages and disadvantages to instructional television?
4. How can closed-circuit television be used in instruction?
5. What is the usage of audiovisual kits in schools?
6. What are some advantages and disadvantages of audiovisual kits?
7. What is the history of using computers in education?
8. What is computer-assisted instruction?
9. What are some advantages and disadvantages to computer-assisted instruction?
10. What barriers block the implementation of computer-assisted instruction?
11. How can software be evaluated?
12. What new directions does educational technology need?

INTRODUCTION

Today the world is in a technological revolution. New technologies are being developed every day. Beginning with radios in the early 1900s, moving to televisions in the 1950s, and finally microcomputers in the 1980s, technological advances have heavily affected the everyday life of most Americans.

Technology in education has long been an interest of professional educators. How can the latest technology be implemented to assist in the learning process? What is the most cost-efficient method of teaching children using technology? How can technological advances complement teachers in classrooms? These are but a few of the many questions asked by educators relative to technology and education.

Educational technology has long been associated with the audiovisual movement (Chan 1984). Today educational technology is primarily associated with computers, especially microcomputers. Educational technology, however, is much more than either audiovisual materials or computers. Educational technology includes the use of a broad range of different resources, emphasizes individual learning, and uses a systems approach (Chan 1984). Technology of instruction can be defined "as the application of our scientific knowledge about human learning to the practical tasks of teaching and learning." (Heinich, Molenda, and Russell 1982, p. 19). It is "a particular, systematic arrangement of teaching/learning events designed to put our knowledge of learning into practice in a predictable, effective manner to attain specific learning objectives" (Heinich, Molenda, and Russell 1982, p. 19). Some of the components of educational technology include instructional television, audiovisual kits such as filmstrips, videocassette technology, closed-circuit television, and computers.

One problem with educational technology is that it is associated too closely with mechanization, machinery, and gadgetry. For educational technology to be better understood and accepted, a more humanistic and aesthetic approach must be taken. The following would enhance this perception of educational technology:

- Educational technology should address broader goals than simply instruction and training.

- Educational technology must be more oriented to humanistic compassion than simply mechanical activities.

- Educational technology must attempt to solve educational problems using a holistic approach.

- Educational technology must use scientific inquiry as a guide, not as a dictum.

- Educational technology should address concerns such as school organization and community involvement in addition to immediate learning by students. (Chan 1984)

Educational technology, therefore, includes many components. While it is often equated with machinery, mechanical responses, and restricted creativity, it can and should go beyond these perceived parameters. The most obvious technologies are in the area of machines and equipment (Hatch 1984); however, many other forms of educational technology can be effective in public schools for instructional purposes.

HIGHLIGHT

CONSIDERATION OF AETN FOR SCHOOLS SUPPORTED
Committee Also Notes Satellite Programing

By Cary Bradburn
Gazette Staff

Eight of nine persons appointed by Governor Bill Clinton to study the feasibility of using television to help schools meet new education standards agreed at their first meeting Thursday that the Arkansas Educational Television Network, as well as satellite programing from other states, should be considered for the schools.

Diane Blair of Fayetteville, chairman of the state Educational Television Commission, said the mission of the Governor's Task Force on Satellite Television Instruction was to look at the "whole spectrum" of telecommunications technology and make recommendations that would be financially practical and offer quality instruction.

Robert Nelson of Batesville, a member of the group and superintendent of the Cushman School District, said school districts should have flexibility in choosing systems for television instruction programs. "We need a multimedia approach," he added later.

AETN has the capability and funds now to provide "soft feed" programing districts could tape during nonbroadcast hours, John Cheek, a representative of the station, said. To provide live programing, however, AETN would have to modify its schedule that provides six hours of preschool instruction on weekdays, and members of the group raised questions about the desirability of doing that. Cheek said AETN now could not provide live instruction broadcasts to school districts at the same time the scheduled shows are broadcast. That would require a change of licensing and additional transmitters, he said.

James Vaughn of Delaplaine (Greene County), a farmer and member of the Commission, said AETN transmitters offered an existing resource, but the lack of "live interaction" between students and the "master teacher" on an AETN program had been noted as a drawback.

One of the strengths of satellite programing is the live interaction it affords, Nelson said. The Cushman district subscribes to a satellite system, TI-IN Network of San Antonio. John Smith, superintendent of the Paron School District, said his district received a Spanish course by satellite from a network funded by the Utah Office of Education, IBM and Bonneville International, a communications company. Nelson and Smith made video presentations to the group.

The satellite systems broadcast on a live or delayed basis from a studio. A master teacher conducts the course and a "classroom manager," who does not have to be certified in the subject, monitors the class. Nelson said the TI-IN Network enables students to talk directly by telephone to the teacher and students from other areas who are enrolled in the course.

Nelson said the initial cost for installation of a "down link," receiving dish, classroom equipment, computer and four cordless phones was $8,000.

The basic TI-IN subscription fee is $4,450 a year and $240 per student for a course, or $290 per student for a foreign language course. Nelson said 18 students in grades 9 to 12 had enrolled in psychology, sociology, French 1, personal business management and art history courses next semester, all courses which would not have been offered otherwise.

Smith said the Paron District spent $2,025, with $20,000 from the state, to install its system, which includes three television screens, five microcomputers, two video cassette recorders, a receiving dish and printer. He said it costs about $1,600 a year per student enrolled in the Spanish course.

Arkansas Gazette. May 16, 1986. Reprinted by permission of the Arkansas Gazette.

INSTRUCTIONAL TELEVISION

Instructional television (ITV) began in the United States in the 1960s. It was presented as a way to solve many of the problems facing educators and the schools: providing high-quality teaching to students, increasing the productivity of students and teachers, and providing education in the home as well as the school. Because of the sudden adoption of ITV, the development of ITV materials grew dramatically. Schools of education bagan to include ITV as a part of the teacher training curriculum. Demonstration projects were funded, and some states initiated statewide distribution plans of ITV materials (Rockman 1985).

The ITV movement has now leveled off; some would even say that it was a failure. Still, recent data collected by the Corporation for Public Broadcasting, the National Center for Education Statistics, and Quality Education Data, Inc. indicate that many schools still use ITV. These findings included:

- 70 percent of the classrooms in the United States have televisions.

- 55 percent of the classrooms in the United States use televisions for instruction.

- 18.5 million students receive some of their instruction through television.

- 14.5 million students use televisions as a regular part of their instructional day. (Rockman 1985)

These figures indicate that ITV is still heavily used in public school programs for instructional purposes. Although not considered as glamorous as computers, ITV continues to be a form of educational technology that is often used in schools.

Some benefits demonstrated by ITV include (1) increased student motivation, (2) illustration of material that is difficult to teach, and (3) ability of teachers to use a common stimulus for teaching (Rockman 1985). Additional advantages include the facts that information is presented using color, moving pictures; programs can be transmitted over long distances; cost per student can be low; and learners can even be reached in their own homes (Heinich, Molenda, and Russell 1982).

Along with benefits and advantages of ITV come disadvantages, which include:

- The complexity of the technology creates opportunities for problems.
- Many programs are poorly developed and produced.
- Weather conditions may disrupt signals.
- Images received on TV monitors may be too small for large classes.
- ITV is a one-way mode of communication. (Heinich, Molenda, and Russell 1982)

CLOSED-CIRCUIT TELEVISION

Another use of televisions for instructional purposes is through closed-circuitry. In closed-circuit television the sender and receiver are physically linked with wires. The most simple arrangement is a single camera hooked to a single television; more elaborate systems would have several classrooms connected to a television studio (Heinich, Molenda, and Russell 1982). By using closed-circuit television (CCTV), many advantages can be gained in various teaching situations. Menis (1982) suggested the use of closed-circuit television as a substitute for the science laboratory. Instead of having all students do actual work in the lab, live demonstrations can be provided that can enable students to see directly what is taking place in the lab. In days of high costs for lab equipment and materials, this method of presentation could greatly reduce costs and still allow students to see actual experiments conducted.

Other advantages of closed-circuit televisions include:

1. CCTV enables teachers to focus the students' attention to a particular task while neutralizing the effects of the surrounding environment.
2. CCTV enables the enlargement or magnification of small items on the screen for easy viewing and detail recommendations.
3. CCTV introduces different effects by using different cameras with different lighting and angles.
4. CCTV inserts enriching sections during the lecture and/or explanation of activities.
5. CCTV provides students with the opportunity to see successful experiments. Unsuccessful experiments are discarded or taped over so students only see what should occur. (Menis 1982)

Still another advantage, primarily administrative, is that since the signals used in CCTV do not travel over the airways, they are not regulated by government agencies; therefore, anyone with the equipment can use CCTV without a great deal of bureaucratic red tape.

Closed-circuit television as an educational technology has not been utilized as often as possible. Video cameras can be purchased relatively inexpensively (approximately $1,000), and videocassette recorders and tapes are readily available to make the necessary equipment accessible to most schools. Teachers should explore ways to use closed-circuit television instruction in their classes.

AUDIOVISUAL KITS

Audiovisual kits, usually in the form of filmstrips, tapes, or other audiovisual items and printed information, have been used in schools for instructional purposes for several decades. These kits enable teachers to focus on a particular topic and provide individual learning experiences to students (Smith and Ingersoll 1984). Like ITV, audiovisual kits are not the glamorous component of educational technology today. While computers are in the limelight as the possible "salvation" for American education, audiovisual kits continue to be used a great deal by teachers. They are effective, cost efficient, and available. Other advantages are that filmstrips and filmstrip projectors are portable, easy to manipulate, present information in a sequential manner for learning purposes, enable the pace and level of instruction to be controlled by the teacher, and are especially useful in independent studies (Heinich, Molenda, and Russell 1982). Smith and Ingersoll (1984) conducted a study in 1982, with a follow-up study in 1983, to determine the use of audiovisual kits in public schools in the United States (see table 14–1). These studies showed that there is not a growth trend in the use of audiovisual kits, but the use of these materials is fairly steady. The vast majority of teachers felt that audiovisual kits were available for their use, and approximately one-third of the teachers used the kits at least weekly. The use of the kits was greater in elementary schools than high schools.

Even though audiovisual kits are not considered as important as some other forms of educational technology, future teachers should be aware of the availability of such materials and of their usefulness in the teaching process. These kinds of materials can still motivate students and enable teachers to focus on specific learning tasks.

TABLE 14–1   Use of Audiovisual Materials in Schools

	Elem. Schools	Middle Schools	High Schools	All
% Teachers Reporting Availability of Audiovisual Kits in 1982	81.8	74.0	77.9	80.2
% Teachers Reporting Availability of Audiovisual Kits in 1983	72.8	70.3	71.3	71.0
% Teachers Reporting Weekly Use of Audiovisual Kits in 1982	41.2	23.2	17.9	32.9
% Teachers Reporting Weekly Use of Audiovisual Kits in 1983	29.4	19.5	20.8	26.0
% Teachers Reporting No Use of Audiovisual Kits in 1982	4.5	10.6	20.4	7.8
% Teachers Reporting No Use of Audiovisual Kits in 1983	7.7	14.5	14.0	11.0

Source: Smith and Ingersoll, 1984.

Teachers use a variety of audiovisual kits to focus on particular topics.

VIDEOCASSETTE TECHNOLOGY

A relatively new entry in educational technology is videocassette recorders and recordings. The first videocassette recorders were marketed in the early 1970s. The growth of this industry has been phenomenal; sales of videocassette recorders in 1984 alone topped fifteen hundred thousand units, which represented a 100 percent increase over the 1983 sales figures (Reider 1984).

Although expensive in their early availability, videocassette recorders (VCRs) can currently be purchased for less than four hundred dollars and blank videocassette tapes can cost as little as five dollars. The mass production of these devices, as well as their limited cost, makes the acquisition of VCRs easy for many individuals and most school districts.

Professionals in education have begun to realize the value in VCR technology to instruction. Some of the advantages to using this technology in education include:

- VCR technology is a conventional type of media.

- VCR technology is very accessible (due to cost and production levels).

- VCRs can be used to tape all kinds of educationally relevant materials.

The use of videocassettes in teaching has increased dramatically during the past several years.

- VCR technology can easily be controlled by teachers.

- VCR technology has many of the advantages of film while not including many of the disadvantages.

- VCR technology has many advantages over filmstrips, primarily the utilization of a moving image. (Reider 1984)

VCR technology is available today, relatively inexpensive, can take advantage of materials presented on television at any time, and provides students with a highly motivating audiovisual mode of processing information. Again, even though this device is not the glamour item in educational technology today, teachers need to be aware of the potential for using VCR's.

COMPUTERS

The newest, most talked about, and most highly sought after technology for education today is the computer. Computers are here to stay. Somewhat of a computer revolution has taken place in the United States since the beginning of the 1980s. Whereas computers were once thought of as big, expensive, and difficult-to-operate machines, today's computers are portable, relatively inexpensive, and easily operated. A large number of people who are not in the least into computer vocations have computers in their homes. People who just a few years ago would have said that computers are for "intellectual" people now have their own computers at home for home management, instruction, games, and a host of other activities.

HIGHLIGHT

Computer Bug Bytes More Schools

By Andy Kanengiser
USA Today

There's no stopping the computer invasion in USA public schools, shows a new survey.

States requiring public schools to offer computer courses have increased from five to 25 in the past two years, says the new *Electronic Learning* magazine.

"It's a dramatic jump," says editor Robert Burroughs.

Students must pass a computer literacy course in nine states: Louisiana, New Hampshire, New York, Rhode Island, South Dakota, Tennessee, Texas, Utah and Wisconsin. Only South Dakota and Rhode Island had such requirements in 1982–83.

Requirements vary. In New Hampshire, students in grades nine-12 must pass a half-year course called Computer Education. In New York, by the eighth grade, students must take a one-year technology education course that runs three hours each week.

Schools are required to offer computer courses in:

Arkansas, Delaware, Florida, Hawaii, Indiana, Louisiana, Minnesota, Maine, Nebraska, Nevada, New Hampshire, New Mexico, New York, North Carolina, Oregon, Pennsylvania, Rhode Island, South Dakota, Tennessee, Texas, Utah, Wisconsin, Vermont, Virginia, Washington and the District of Columbia.

Burroughs predicts the number of states pushing computers in schools will continue to grow as computer costs drop and parents keep up the demand for high-tech equipment in their kids' districts.

The survey also shows:

- Computer certification requirements exist for teacher candidates in 11 states, up from four two years ago.

- A state computer coordinator works full time to promote computer education in 36 states.

- Forty-one states have software evaluation materials available to schools and districts.

USA Today. October 8, 1985. Copyright, 1985, USA Today. Reprinted with permission.

Computers in Education

Computers are the most active form of educational technology in the schools today. The growth of the number of computers and the use of computers in schools is difficult to imagine. The number of schools with microcomputers increased from 13,986 in 1982 to 30,493 in 1983, an increase of 118 percent (National Center for Education Statistics 1984). Although estimates vary, by April 1984 approximately 350,000 microcomputers were available for students in grades 1–12 (Bork 1984). Schools not only have computers available, but many are using computers in computer-assisted instruction (CAI). A survey of 202 schools indicated that the use of computers in CAI ranged from a low of 56.5 percent in kindergarten to a high of 81.5

percent in the third grade. At the secondary level, the greatest use of computers in CAI was in math (92.1 percent) and science (85.7 percent) (Nelson and Waack 1985) (see table 14–2). Another study of the use of microcomputers determined that the number of teachers who used computers in their classrooms increased from 29 percent in 1982 to 53 percent in 1983 (Grossnickle, Laird, Cutter, and Tefft 1983).

History of computer usage in education. In the 1960s and 1970s the idea of using computers for educational purposes received a great deal of attention. Proponents of using this technology in public schools viewed computers as an unprecedented aid to teaching and learning. Still there were skeptics. Computers of this era were large monsters. They were designed for carrying out complicated mathematical calculations, for which they were very effective if the user understood the highly sophisticated language required to operate the hardware (Heinich, Molenda, and Russell 1982).

Then, about 1975, microcomputers were developed. The development of microcomputers was made possible by the invention of the silicon chip, a tiny microprocessor that could perform functions previously possible only on large mainframe computers. By 1980 approximately one million microcomputers were already in use (Heinich, Molenda, and Russell 1982). The development of microcomputers renewed the enthusiasm of some concerning the future role of computers in education. Microcomputers, the "Model T of the computer industry," have made computer technology readily accessible to most school districts (Holmes 1982).

The number of microcomputers on the market and their relatively low cost has enabled public education to implement computer technology into daily instructional activities. The movement to incorporate computer technology into education has basically been a grassroots phenomenon, led by classroom teachers who were inter-

---

TABLE 14–2   Uses of CAI

Grade Level	% Using CAI
K	56.5
1	73.2
2	76.9
3	81.5
4	80.6
5	75.5
6	66.6
7	21.4
8	28.7
Secondary/Math	92.1
Secondary/Science	85.7
Secondary/Business Education	82.2
Secondary/English, Language Arts	75.1

Source: P. Nelson and W. Waack, 1985.

ested in adding a new dimension into their classrooms (Donhardt 1984). The use of microcomputers in education is growing at a tremendous rate and should continue to increase in the future.

Close investigation of the use of computers in classrooms, however, indicates that their use has not been as successful as the numbers might indicate. Problems that continue to block the widespread use of microcomputers in education include (1) availability of computers in schools; (2) lack of policy in schools related to computer usage; (3) inadequate software; and (4) teacher training (Bonner 1984).

The use of computers, which potentially could revolutionize education, could end up as a failure similar to other technologies in the past where the purchases have come before the adequate planning and preparation of practitioners. To avoid this, Boyer (1984) suggests three priorities. First, students need to learn about technology. This includes teaching students about the social impact of technology and computers, not hands-on instruction. The second priority is to teach students how to learn with computers. Learning with computers includes using computers to gather information. Finally, students should learn from computers. This requires interactive learning between students and computers, or "conversing" between students and computers to improve thinking skills.

While computers are capable of becoming a major force in education, some concerns need to be mentioned. Some professionals argue that the overuse of computers and other technologies can have a negative effect on education. For example, the technology in education can "isolate us from the very processes by which we define our humanity" (Hatch 1984, p. 243). These human processes, defined as those things that differentiate humans from other living organisms, such as loving, knowing, and making decisions, can become devalued as a result of overdependency on technology.

Uses of Computers in Education

Computers, primarily microcomputers because of their low cost, high availability, and easy operation, can be used in education in several different ways. The three primary uses include computer-assisted instruction (CAI), computer science, and administration.

Computer-assisted instruction. Computer-assisted instruction is a main use of computers in schools today. This use of the computer is individualized and ranges from remediation for students having problems to enrichment for gifted students. The goal of CAI, simply stated, "is to use computers as a tool to increase student learning" (Long 1985, p. 27).

Advantages and disadvantages. As with any instructional methodology, CAI has both advantages and disadvantages. Specific advantages include

- individual pacing;

- immediate feedback;

- opportunities for drill;

- overlearning. (Smith, Price, and Marsh 1986)

Still other advantages include generating a high level of interest in students, enabling some students to learn materials that they would not be capable of learning in a normal classroom situation (Long 1985), and relieving teachers of some responsibilities (Holmes 1982).

Although these advantages appear to support the implementation of CAI, certain disadvantages must be considered. First, CAI is directly related to the teacher's ability to structure the course and to impose order on the content. Because many teachers have not been trained in CAI, this may create significant problems. Second, CAI has traditionally been used as a supplement to traditional classroom instruction. Also, the content of CAI programs is usually single-concept material, human interactions are missing, and the CAI program may have little relationship to the curriculum (Smith, Price, and Marsh 1986). Long (1985) adds that only a limited amount of software is available for CAI, and there is a dearth of materials appropriate for lower elementary students.

Barriers to implementing CAI. Regardless of the advantages and disadvantages in CAI, schools that want to implement the use of such methodologies should be aware of some barriers that are likely to present problems. These include the costs of equipment and software, maintenance, the attitudes of personnel, attitudes of parents, and attitudes of students (Holmes 1982). Schools that want to implement CAI must consider these barriers, as well as the disadvantages of CAI before attempting to develop a CAI component.

Roles of personnel in CAI. Certain individuals both inside and outside the school play a vital role in the development of a CAI program. These include administrators, teachers, and students. Administrators have been characterized as key individuals in change and attitude development of school staff. They have been found to be vital in the success of almost every school activity. For example, Smith, Flexer, and Sigelman (1980) determined that the amount of support high-school principals showed for secondary special education programs was directly related to the effectiveness of those programs.

School administrators, basically because they control the budget, have to be positive about CAI before it can be successfully implemented. Individuals in these roles usually proceed with change cautiously, because change itself can be extremely disruptive to the school. If CAI can be shown to be beneficial to administrators, their support is more likely than if they cannot see any positive result from implementing some new program. In the area of CAI, two possible benefits that administrators might respond to include peer approval and the possibility of receiving outside funding for the program (Holmes 1982). Individuals interested in receiving administrative support for CAI programs must work to garner this support. Examples of ways to get this support include

- inviting principals and other school administrators to visit schools that have implemented effective CAI programs;

- seeking outside funding from government or private sources to support the implementation of CAI programs;

- inviting school administrators to participate in a CAI planning session;

- making administrators realize that a great deal of positive publicity could result for the school following the successful implementation of a CAI program.

While these actions may not win over administrators, they at least plant the idea that could result in administrative support over a period of time.

Teachers are also key individuals in the successful implementation of a CAI program. If teachers are supportive, CAI will more likely be successful than if teachers have negative attitudes about the program. After all, teachers are the ones who will have to implement the CAI program. Administrators can purchase computers and software and even mandate that CAI be used; however, without the willing cooperation of the teachers who are responsible for implementing CAI, the program will not likely be successful.

Often teachers are apprehensive about change because they do not understand their new role. As long as they are expected to teach five sections of history, or four sections of math, or all subjects to second graders, they understand where they fit in the system. CAI creates the possibility that their role in the educational process will be lessened. Although this is not the case, many teachers may fear that computers will replace them or undermine their status in the schools (Holmes 1982). To garner the support necessary from teachers for CAI, they must be made to understand their new role in a CAI program. Teachers must see the personal advantages inherent in CAI. Administrators could do this by encouraging teachers to attend workshops on computer usage in instruction, providing funds for in-service programs, providing funds

Computers are the most active form of educational technology in schools today.

for college-credit courses, and simply indicating that administrative support would be available when CAI is implemented.

The third group of individuals who are critical to the successful implementation of CAI are the students (Holmes 1982). Students must want to use computers and software before they will be successful in using them. Although computers have been shown to be a motivating factor for many students, all students may not be receptive to their use. Computer anxiety is a real issue that must be overcome if students are to feel comfortable enough to try CAI, which is a major change from the traditional student-teacher learning process. One way to change students' attitudes about computers is to orient them to the technology. Administrators and teachers could sponsor a computer day for students, where local industries and computer dealers bring displays to the school and students get the opportunity to take a computer for a "test drive." Once students have the opportunity to see, touch, and operate a computer, many anxieties will be alleviated.

Parents of students also play a role in the successful implementation of CAI. If the community has a group of parents who want CAI in the schools, and this group is vocal in its support, the local school board will probably attempt to implement the program. Likewise, a group of vocal parents who oppose the introduction of computers could have a negative impact on the school's attempting to implement a CAI program. Parents, like students, could be invited to the school for the computer day so that they can gain a better understanding of the role computers would play in instruction were a CAI program initiated. One definite component for parents in the computer day should be a session pointing out the many personal and educational advantages students would have if they were computer literate.

Other community members could also have an impact on CAI. For example, school districts in towns with certain industries are likely to get support, both political and financial, from private sources if students trained in CAI would be more likely candidates for jobs. The private sector is one group that public schools often overlook in their attempts to implement new programs. School administrators need to court this group when attempting to implement new programs, especially those that have a high start-up cost like CAI.

Components of CAI. One of the problems pointed out about CAI is the lack of materials and the sometimes unrelatedness of CAI to the curriculum. If CAI is to be successful, the computer-based curriculum must address the following: "first, it must have sound educational objectives; second, it must reflect an awareness of how students will learn from an interaction with the computer; and finally, its objectives and their tests must be measurable" (Donhardt 1984, p. 30) (see table 14–3).

Software. CAI depends on programs commonly called *software*. The *hardware* is the machine, the computer, and peripherals (input-output devices); the software is the material that makes up the computer program (the step-by-step instructions that tell the computer what to do and how to do it). A lack of available, good software has been one of the criticisms often voiced about CAI. The software available for educators has increased dramatically in the 1980s, along with the use of computers in classrooms. Although much software is available, educators must be cognizant of how to select software to get the best for the money. Just because numerous programs dealing with certain educational areas are available, they are not necessarily all good and worth the money.

TABLE 14-3 Components of CAI

Component	Description
Educational Objectives	Objectives must be well thought out, based on a philosophy of education, and describe what attitude/value or skill/knowledge a student will possess after a learning session.
An Awareness of How Students Learn	Curriculum must consider such concepts as timely reinforcement, closure, limitations of short-term memory, and the length of time to gain mastery of the subject matter.
Objectives and Tests That are Measurable	Objectives and tests must be measurable in order to determine the effectiveness of the learning process.

Source: Donhardt, 1984.

Software in CAI is similar to textbooks in traditional instruction. To avoid selecting textbooks of poor quality, explicit procedures are followed by state departments of education and local school districts in textbook adoption. Reviewers determine if the textbook

- fits into the curriculum;

- is at the correct reading level;

- is of good quality;

- is compatible with the teacher's style;

- reflects sound educational practice. (Wallace and Rose 1984, p. 35)

Unfortunately, similar procedures are not always followed in the selection of computer software. Too often teachers are asked to purchase materials without adequate information. They may be told one morning that they must spend five hundred dollars before the end of the day in order to keep from losing the money, and that they should buy computer programs. After looking at computer software catalogs, teachers might decide to purchase certain programs because of many variables unrelated to the quality of the program, such as format of the advertisement, testimonials presented in advertisements by other supposed teachers, and cost. The end results are often that schools purchase programs that are of little value to students.

Selecting good software for CAI presents many problems. First, many companies do not like to loan software to schools for review purposes for fear that the programs will be copied and returned without a sale. Also, most teachers are unaware of the different types of educational software and do not understand proper methods of reviewing computer programs (Wallace and Rose 1984).

Reviewing educational software should include a review of the content, the screen presentation, the interaction process, and the human values criteria. If this is done, then educators will more likely purchase software that (1) fits the curriculum, (2) is at the appropriate reading level for students, (3) reflects quality, (4) is compatible with the teacher's style, and (5) maintains sound educational practice (Wallace and Rose 1984). A systematic form could be used when reviewing educational software for CAI

Educational Software Review Form

PART I: SUMMARY

Identification

Program name: ....

.... Single program   .... Series

Program available for microcomputer brands: ....

Memory required: .... 4K .... 16K .... 32K .... 48K 64K
Format: .... Cassette Tape   .... 5'' Diskette
.... Cartridge   (Drives .... One   .... Two)

Peripherals required:

.... Printer
.... Paddles/joystick   .... Voice/sound
.... Color monitor   Other: ....

Description of Program: ....
....
....

Recommendation About Use:

Appropriate for intended group: .... Yes   .... No
Group: ....
Not appropriate
for: ....

	Excellent	Acceptable	Poor
Appropriateness for student users	....	....	....
Instructional Approach	....	....	....
Content	....	....	....
Presentation design of material	....	....	....
Interaction process	....	....	....
"Human values" criteria	....	....	....

Other Comments: ....
....
....

(Continued)

Figure 14–1 Educational Software Review Form

(see figure 14–1). Although this form can be modified to meet any school's particular needs, it does reflect the necessary components to ensure adequate software review.

Computer science. Some schools actually offer computer science courses to their students. This application of computers in education is more likely to occur at the middle- and high-school level rather than elementary schools. Computer science instruction is basically advanced computer literacy. Students learn about computing and some programming skills (Long 1985). The basic difference between computer science and CAI is that CAI is a means of instructing students in courses found in the

Use:

Single user ....   Small team/group ....   Class ....

.... Drill/practice   .... Simulation   .... Testing

.... Instructional game   .... Problem solving   .... Management

.... Tutorial   .... Data base

Other ....

Target Audience: ....

Average Run Time: .... minutes

Management System:

Yes	No	
....	....	Keeps track of individual student performance.
....	....	Allows teacher to determine individual student levels within the program.

Directions for student user:

Yes	No	
....	....	Appropriate reading level.
....	....	Clear and understandable.
....	....	All contained and presented in the program.
....	....	Can be easily reviewed during use of the program.

PART II: EDUCATIONAL VALUE

Content:

Yes	No	None or NA	
....	....	....	Instructional objectives clearly stated.
....	....	....	The program has instructional significance.
....	....	....	Is compatible with other instructional materials.
			Levels of difficulty available:
			Determined by: program pretest ....,
			user selection ...., teacher selection ....
....	....	....	Material is free of content errors.
			Language free of:
....	....	....	sex bias,
....	....	....	race bias,
....	....	....	cultural bias.
....	....	....	Women are proportionately represented in text.
....	....	....	Minority group members represented in text.
....	....	....	Contributions of all racial and ethnic groups and women and men presented in realistic and/or accurate ways.
....	....	....	A variety of ages are represented.
....	....	....	Disabled are represented in a variety of roles.

(Continued)

Figure 14–1 (Continued)

regular curriculum. Computer science is not a method, but rather a course in itself. CAI is a means, computer science is a product.

Computer science courses in schools have some advantages and disadvantages. The chief advantage is that computer science will help students understand about computers. Since computers are here to stay and our society and world will become more and more computerized, students would be at an advantage to learn about and understand computers. Some advocates of computer science courses also believe that learning how to program can actually lead to improved logical thinking skills in students. The major disadvantage of computer science courses is that too often

Instruction and Motivation:

...'s	No	None or NA	
....	....	....	User clearly knows when the computer is waiting for input.
....	....	....	User knows what kind of input the program expects.
....	....	....	The program runs without disruption.
....	....	....	The screen display is easy to read and understand.
....	....	....	The user can correct entries.
....	....	....	The software provides correct answer after the user responds incorrectly: Number of entries (errors/guesses) allowed ....
....	....	....	The input into the computer is appropriate for the objective of the program.
....	....	....	User can exit from the program without completion of the full program.
....	....	....	Motivators for the user are non-violent.
....	....	....	Motivational rewards are for correct rather than incorrect responses.
....	....	....	Motivators will be effective for racial and ethnic minority students.
....	....	....	Motivators will be effective for female students.
....	....	....	The program emphasizes cooperation.
....	....	....	The program emphasizes thinking and creativity.
....	....	....	Provides a summary of performance: .... during, ... at the end of program.

PART III: TECHNICAL VALUE

Check the appropriate boxes for use of different presentation styles.*

Presentation	ATTRACT ATTENTION	DIRECT INSTRUCTION	SUPPORT INSTRUCTION	MOTIVATION FOR USER
Highlighted Text	....	....	....	....
Color	....	....	....	....
Sound	....	....	....	....
Still Graphics	....	....	....	....
Animation	....	....	....	....

*If different segments of the program use different presentation styles, code the segments.

ADDITIONAL COMMENTS:

Note to Readers: This evaluation form may be reproduced for education and training activities, provided that credit is given to *Educational Technology* Magazine and stating that it is used with permission.

Source: *EDUCATIONAL TECHNOLOGY*, October 1984

Figure 14–1 (Continued)

schools do not have faculty with the expertise necessary to teach such courses (Long 1985). Schools that implement computer science courses simply because of popularity may end up with poor programs. Administrators would better serve students if the development of computer science courses resulted from long-range planning and the capabilities of teachers were taken into consideration. If a school wanted to develop such a program, but no qualified teachers were in the school to serve as the instructor, the school might want to send an interested teacher to school to become prepared to teach such a course and to share learning received with colleagues.

Administration. The third use of computers in schools is in the area of administration or management. Frequently schools do not restrict the use of available computers to students. Two primary areas where computers are used in management activities are in the school office by school administrative staff and by teachers (Long 1985). In the school office, computers are often used for attendance records, student records, enrollment projections, or bus routing. Teachers most often use computers for management purposes, for word processing, grade keeping, scoring tests, and calculating grades.

Teacher Training in Computers

Computer usage in education is here to stay; the applications have been tested too often with favorable results. CAI, computer science, and management are three important uses of computers in the educational setting. Unfortunately, too few teachers take advantage of this technological revolution. Granted, many teachers have made a prompt and positive response to the use of computers in education (Sandoval 1984). Many have purchased their own computers, designed and/or purchased their own programs, and implemented the use of computers in their classrooms. This still is a minority of teachers. The majority do not have the skills or knowledge necessary to take advantage of the computer technology available.

The majority of teachers still do not use computers in their classrooms for several reasons, including:

1. Training and experience requirements for certification for teaching computer-related courses are generally lacking.
2. Many educators know very little about the potential for computer applications in the classroom.
3. Teacher training programs and courses are few and far between.
4. Computers seem to have a low priority in relation to other areas. (Milner 1980, p. 544)

That teachers need training in computer applications in education is understandable. The question is what kind of training and how much. Traditional teacher training programs focus on training in the teaching content area(s) and training in how to teach (Sandoval 1984). Although changing, training in how to use computers in the classroom has not been included in either of these two areas.

For teachers to understand how to use computers in the classroom, they need to have "(1) knowledge about the computer, its development, uses, and potential; (2) knowledge about how to design and/or operate programs for computers; and (3) knowledge of the computer as a teaching device" (Sandoval 1984, p. 31). For example, computer users need to have an understanding of some basic terms frequently used related to computers (see table 14–4). To prepare teachers with this knowledge, teacher training programs need to be redesigned to include the development of skills in using computers in the learning process, selection of appropriate software, and development and evaluation of programs (Sandoval 1984).

Milner (1980) suggests that teacher training programs incorporate six preservice courses that focus on the acquisition of the necessary skills to enable teachers to

---

TABLE 14–4   A Brief Glossary of Computer Terminology

BASIC—(Beginner's All-purpose Symbolic instruction Code) a simple programming language based on the English language.

Bit—smallest unit of information (from BInary digiT).

Byte—generally, a single, alphanumeric character (e.g., one letter of the alphabet).

CRT—(Cathode Ray Tube) a computer display screen, same as television set.

Hardware—physical components of computer system.

Mainframe—a large, high speed business/scientific computer; often entails time sharing.

Microprocessor—a tiny chip incorporating an integrated circuit that is able to execute complex instructions electronically.

MODEM—(MOdulator/DEModulator) device that translates computer signals for transmission over telephone lines.

Peripherals—auxiliary devices that can be attached to a basic computer (e.g., a voice synthesizer, hard-copy printer, MODEM).

PLAN—(Program for Learning in Accordance with Needs) a computer-based instructional management system for diagnosis and record-keeping developed in 1967 by Westinghouse with American Institutes for Research and 13 school districts.

Plato—a powerful computer system designed especially for instructional use; begun in 1960 at University of Illinois, now marketed by Control Data Corp.

RAM—(Random Access Memory) the major memory mechanism of a computer; a "blank slate" to hold the program currently being used and then to be erased.

ROM—(Read Only Memory) contains program(s) permanently wired into the circuitry of the computer (e.g., the BASIC language).

Software—the programs that control the computer operation.

TICCIT—(Time-shared Interactive Computer-Controlled Information Television) like Plato, a computer system custom designed for instructional purposes; it was developed by Mitre Corp. and Victor Bunderson of Brigham Young University, and is now marketed by Hazeltine Corp.

Reprinted with permission. Heinich, Molenda, and Russell, 1982, 323.

In order to implement the use of computers in schools, teachers must receive inservice training.

better utilize computers in the classroom. These include instructional design, designing computer-based learning materials, programming, hardware and software organization, computer uses in education, and computers and society (see table 14–5).

OTHER EDUCATIONAL TECHNOLOGIES

In addition to ITV, CCTV, audiovisual kits, and computers, there are many other components of educational technology. These include (1) programmed instruction, (2) programmed tutoring, (3) personalized system of instruction, (4) audio-tutorial systems, and (5) simulations and gaming. Although not often thought of as educational technology, these components are definitely a part of the overall area (see table 14–6).

EDUCATIONAL TECHNOLOGY: NEEDED DIRECTIONS

The computer revolution in the world affects everybody's daily lives. Bank machines, soft-drink machines with audio components, cash registers that talk are all possible

TABLE 14–5   Description of Computer Courses for Teachers

Course	Description
Instructional Design	• Overview of instructional technology • Aspects of instructional planning • Ways to individualize instruction
Designing Computer-Based Learning Materials	• Computer programming for instruction • Review of computer-based materials • Development of instructional modules • Implementing and evaluating modules
Programming Course One	• Development of algorithms • Design, coding, debugging, and documentation of programs
Programming Course Two	• Structured programming techniques • String processing and searching and sorting • Data structures
Hardware and Software Organization	• Assembly language programming • File processing • Computer organization • Operating systems • Programming language
Computer Uses in Education	• Computer systems fundamentals • Instructional usage modes • Developing and evaluating computer-based instruction
Computers and Society	• Systems fundamentals • Programming • Applications

Source: Milner, 1980.

TABLE 14-6 Characteristics of Technologies of Instruction

	Programmed Instruction	Programmed Tutoring	Personalized System of Instruction	Audio-Tutorial Systems	Simulation and Gaming	Computer-Assisted Instruction
A teaching/learning *pattern*	Small units of information requiring practice, followed by feedback	Small units of information requiring practice, followed by feedback	Large units of information in sequential order; passing a test is required before proceeding (mastery)	Core of instruction is on audio tape, used in lab setting independently; small group and large group sessions are added	Small group activity, may entail representation of reality and/or competition	Small units of information presented on display screen frequent practice required, followed by immediate feedback
Designed to provide *reliable*,	Program recorded in printed form	Tutor follows directions; learner uses structured workbook	Course organization is clearly spelled out; based on print materials and standardized tests	Core material recorded on audio tape and other audiovisual materials	Procedures are enforced by means of game directions and play materials	Instructions are coded into a computer program and displayed on a screen
Effective instruction	Programs must be learner tested and revised during development process	Programs are learner tested and revised during development process	Materials themselves are not validated, but mastery is assured by testing/correction cycle	Materials themselves are not validated, but mastery is encouraged by small group test/review sessions	May be learner tested for effectiveness	Programs must be learner tested and revised during development process: computer capability facilitates data gathering
To *each* learner	Allows individual pacing	Allows individual pacing plus highly flexible, responsive branching via human tutor	Allows individual pacing plus one-to-one discussion of test errors and questions	Allows individual pacing in independent study portion of course	Usually group paced, with individuals assigned to compatible groups	Allows individual pacing and some branching
Through application of *scientific* principles of human learning	Reinforcement theory: verbal response followed by knowledge of results	Reinforcement theory: verbal or other overt response followed by knowledge of results plus social reinforcers Constant personalized human contact Variety	Rather frequent response to tests over content followed by immediate correction Occasional personalized human contact Mastery requirement ensures that learner is working at his level of comprehension	Conversational relationship with instructor via tape High use of audiovisual and other concrete media Occasional personalized human contact Active involvement in challenging tasks	Meaningful organization of content (in simulation) Frequent practice with immediate feedback Social interaction with small group Emotional involvement Repetition of drill-and-practice without tedium High motivation	Reinforcement theory: verbal response followed by knowledge of results plus branching May involve audiovisual display Appearance of personalized human contact May apply mastery concept Highly motivational for at least some learners

Reprinted with permission. Heinich, Molenda, and Russell, 1982, 284.

because of computer technology. Without question, computers and other electronic technologies will have a major impact on education. If educators are to meet the challenges of these electronic technologies, several actions must be taken.

1. As the electronic technologies become the defining technologies, educators must gain an understanding of the history of technology, the role of technology in change, the social and psychological impacts of technology, and the implications of current changes for education.
2. Education must take a hard look at its traditional goals, particularly in the area of literacy.
3. Educators must devise new definitions of classroom learning consistent with the revolution in the cognitive sciences.
4. Educators must find a new metaphor for the learning environment. The school as factory is anathema.
5. Educators must abandon the lockstep, competency-based curriculum and devise new instructional strategies.
6. Educators must not only know about the electronic technologies, they must learn how to develop software for use with the visual media and the computer that facilitate learning.
7. Educators need to devise a curriculum whose content prepares students for thinking "by" computers, thinking "about" computers, and thinking "with" computers.
8. Education must emerge from its disciplinary narrowness. (Norton 1985, p. 18–20)

SUMMARY

This chapter focused on educational technology. The first section dealt with the perceptions about educational technology. Too often educational technology is associated only with machinery and gadgetry, not learning. If educational technology is to be better understood, efforts must be made to "humanize" the ways educational technology is used in public schools.

The next section presented the major educational technologies found in schools today. Included were instructional television, closed-circuit television, audiovisual kits such as filmstrips, videocassette technology, and finally computers. Each of these technologies was presented with information related to its use in schools, as well as its advantages and disadvantages in the learning process.

The final section of the chapter focused on computers in education. Computers are currently the major area of interest in educational technology. The three methods of using computers in schools were presented, including computer-assisted instruction, computer science, and management. Methods of application for each of these were presented, along with barriers to their use in the schools.

Finally, programs to better train teachers in the area of computer-assisted instruction were discussed. Too few teachers are capable of using computers in instruction adequately. Suggestions to alleviate this situation were presented. The major suggestion discussed, related to increased teachers' skills, was preservice training. Colleges and universities that train teachers must do a better job of preparing teachers to work with computers and CAI.

IN THE FIELD

1. Does the school use instructional television? If so, how?

2. Does the school use closed-circuit television? If so, how?

3. Does the school use audiovisual kits? If so, how?

4. Does the school use videocassette machines? If so, how?

5. Are computers used in the school? If so, how?

6. How many microcomputers are available for instruction?

7. Has the number of microcomputers available for instruction increased during the past three years?

8. Does the administration use computers?

9. Does the school have a review process before purchasing computer software?

10. Have teachers in the district received any in-service training regarding computers in education? If so, what has been the nature of the training?

REFERENCES

Bonner, P. 1984. Computers in education: Promise and reality. *Personal Computing 8*(9), 64–77.

Bork, A. 1984. Computers in education today—And some possible futures. *Phi Delta Kappan 66*(4), 239–43.

Boyer, E. L. 1984. Education's new challenge. *Personal Computing 8*(9), 81–85.

Chan, T. V. 1984. In search of the artistry in educational technology. *Educational Technology 24*(4), 7–12.

Donhardt, G. L. 1984. Microcomputers in education: Elements of a computer-based curriculum. *Educational Technology 24*(4), 30–32.

Grossnickle, D. R., B. A. Laird, T. W. Cutter, and J. A. Tefft. 1983. Profile of change in education: Microcomputer adoption status report. *Educational Technology 23*(9), 17–20.

Hatch, J. A. 1984. Technology & devaluation of human processes. *Educational Forum 48*(2), 243–51.

Heinich, R., M. Molenda, and J. D. Russell. 1982. *Educational media and the new technologies of instruction.* New York: John Wiley and Sons.

Holmes, G. 1982. Computer-assisted instruction: A discussion of some of the issues for would-be implementors. *Educational Technology 22*(9), 7–13.

Long, C. 1985. How are today's elementary schools using computers? *Educational Technology 25*(5), 27–29.

Menis, Y. 1982. Educational technology research: Substituting closed-circuit television for the science laboratory. *Educational Technology 22*(4), 24–27.

Milner, S. D. 1980. Teaching teachers about computers: A necessity for education. *Phi Delta Kappan 61*(8), 544–46.

National Center for Education Statistics. 1984. *The condition of education 1984 edition.* Washington, DC: Department of Education.

Nelson, P., and W. Waack. 1985. The status of computer literacy/computer-assisted instruction awareness as a factor in classroom instruction and teacher selection. *Educational Technology 25*(2), 23–26.

Norton, P. 1985. An agenda for technology and education: Eight imperatives. *Educational Technology 25*(1), 15–20.

Reider, W. L. 1984. Videocassette technology in education: A quiet revolution in progress. *Educational Technology* 24(10), 12–15.

Rockman, S. 1985. Success or failure for computers in schools? Some lessons from instructional television. *Educational Technology* 25(1), 48–50.

Sandoval, H. R. 1984. Teacher training in computer skills: A call for a redefinition. *Educational Technology* 24(10), 29–31.

Smith, C. B., and G. M. Ingersoll. 1984. Audiovisual materials in U.S. schools: A national survey on availability and use. *Educational Technology* 24(9), 36–38.

Smith, T. E. C., R. W. Flexer, and C. K. Sigelman. 1980. Attitudes of secondary principals toward the learning disabled, the mentally retarded, and work-study programs. *Journal of Learning Disabilities* 13(2), 11–13.

Smith, T. E. C., B. J. Price, and G. M. Marsh. 1986. *Mildly handicapped children and adults*. St. Paul: West Publishing Company.

Wallace, J., and R. M. Rose. 1984. A hard look at software: What to examine and evaluate (with an evaluation form). *Educational Technology* 24(10), 35–39.

Chapter 15
THE FUTURE

OBJECTIVES

After reading this chapter, you will be able to

- define futurism;
- describe the purposes of futurism;
- discuss the difficulties in predicting the future;
- describe worldwide population trends;
- discuss the impact of declining natural resources;
- list reasons for studying the future of education;
- describe population trends in the United States and their impact on public education;
- discuss the likelihood that school reform will continue;
- describe forces that will impact the curriculum in the future;
- discuss the future role of technology in education;
- list predictions made in 1974 concerning education.

OUTLINE

ADVANCE ORGANIZERS
INTRODUCTION
FUTURISM
GLOBAL CONCERNS AND THE FUTURE
    Population Trends
    Natural Resources
    Food
    Geopolitics
THE FUTURE OF PUBLIC EDUCATION
      IN THE UNITED STATES
    Population Trends in the United States
    Maintaining the School Reforms

Curriculum for the Future
Technology in the Future
PAST PREDICTIONS OF THE FUTURE OF
    EDUCATION
    Predictions by Theodore Hipple (1974)
    Predictions by Max Rafferty (1974)
    Conclusions on Predictions of 1974
AUTHOR'S PREDICTIONS
SUMMARY
IN THE FIELD
REFERENCES

ADVANCE ORGANIZERS

1. What is futurism?
2. Why should futurism be studied?
3. What is the global population trend?
4. What are the projected dates for the depletion of some natural resources?
5. What role does geopolitics play in the future?
6. How can the educational system change to meet the needs of the future?
7. What is the population trend in the United States?
8. How does the U.S. population trend affect planning for public education?
9. How can educational reforms be evaluated?
10. What will the curriculum in the future include?
11. What role will technology play in the future?
12. What is the status of predictions made in 1974 concerning education?

INTRODUCTION

Predicting the future is difficult, if not impossible. However, the challenges that face the educational system in the United States today will basically be the same in the next century (Anthony 1984). The future of public education is a big question mark. Interest in public education in the United States has been back and forth, on a pendulum. At various periods of history, the public has been heavily involved and interested in public education. At other times, unfortunately, other issues have usurped education in the public focus. Beginning with the critical reports issued concerning public education in the late 1970s and early 1980s, the public interest has skyrocketed. Politicians, parents, professionals, business leaders, and people from other sectors have all been clamoring for better educational programs and more influence in the public education provided for students. Whether this interest and involvement will continue remains to be seen. What can be stated is that the future of education, and the future of humanity, are very complex issues. Studying the future and applying predictions to specific issues like education is no easy task. Predicting the future of education is definitely linked, however, to the future of our society.

FUTURISM

The future is tomorrow and the day after. It is the entire period ahead of us. It "holds great promise for each of us if we think rather than daydream about it, if we plan rather than wait, if we accept rather than reject the inevitability of change" (Day and Speicher 1985, p. 7). The study of the future has been called futurism. "Futurism is concerned with forecasts, trends, and ideas, and the purpose of its study is to assist policymakers in choosing wisely among alternative courses of action available to them as they look to the future" (Johnson, Collins, Dupuis, and Johansen 1982, p. 417–18). Several different topics of study interest futurists, including world geopolitics, population, human resources, and natural resources. Education, also, is a topic studied by futurists.

Studying and forecasting the future is important for several reasons. First, people cannot continue to let history repeat itself. The world has experienced many failures; if people can learn from these failures and prevent their recurring, then humanity will be better off. While people are capable of destroying the planet, they are also able to save it (Schreyer 1980).

The future, from the 1980s on, will change rapidly and dramatically. The year 2000 will undoubtedly be significantly more different from 1980 than 1800 was from 1780 (Platt 1980). Toffler (1980) stated that "we are the final generation of an old civilization and the first generation of a new one . . ." (p. 11). During the past two decades major changes have occurred. For example, we now live in the shadow of nuclear holocaust; television may be changing the family, school, commerce, politics, and our thinking; electronics has changed science, government, and will affect every future society (Platt 1980). For the first time in history, we are able to

- manipulate, control, and change our own biological genetic substance;
- carry out collective self-destruction by interacting with the elementary building blocks of our world;
- create a worldwide communications and information network of an extent and effectiveness never dreamed before;
- throw off the shackles of our planet in the course of spreading out in the universe. (Puttkamer 1983, p. 4)

With changes occurring so rapidly, trying to study and predict the future becomes extremely difficult. However, without these efforts, humanity may be faced with problems too overwhelming to conquer.

GLOBAL CONCERNS AND THE FUTURE

Several concerns of the future are not unique to any one community, discipline, or country. These global concerns include changes in the population, geopolitics, and human and natural resources. Changes that occur in these areas and others across the planet can affect each of our lives in our local communities (Amara 1980). Without knowing what to expect in these global areas, predicting public education is perfunctory. Unfortunately, forecasting the future often has proved to lead to inaccurate predictions (Pulliam and Bowman 1975). Efforts in the area of futurism, however, are necessary to prepare for occurrences, that, unanticipated, could lead to global catastrophies.

Population Trends

The world population is increasing extremely rapidly. In 1975 the world population was estimated to be 4,090,000,000. This number is expected to increase to 6,350,000,000 by the year 2000, representing a 55 percent increase in only twenty-five years (Almanac and yearbook 1986). The rate of population increase has climbed steadily through history.

Efforts to curb the spiraling increase in the population have met with religious, economic, and even governmental barriers. The Roman Catholic church, for example,

Overpopulation threatens the availability of natural resources.

while supporting population control, is officially opposed to birth control methods. That the largest increases in the population are occurring in third world countries where poverty is frequently rampant, and where the education level of individuals is low, only hampers efforts at world population control. The largest projected population increases from 1975 to 2000 are in Africa (104 percent) and Latin America (96 percent) (Almanac and Yearbook 1986).

Natural Resources

The worldwide population explosion has had a severe effect on natural resources. Petroleum, once considered in sufficient supplies to be used uncontrollably by the large industrial countries, is now realized to be in dwindling quantities. Current rates of consumption would deplete petroleum reserves by the year 2021 (Almanac and Yearbook 1986). Although the oil shortage of the 1970s, which was primarily caused by world political forces, was reversed in the mid-1980s by an oil surplus, projections still indicate a real shortage of oil after thirty-five more years.

A world without oil could spell disaster for industrialized nations and have a devasting effect on developing countries Researchers, therefore, are trying to develop alternative energy sources, such as nuclear power, solar power, and wind power, to take the place of much of the oil-dependent activities of the world. The efforts of this research will undoubtedly determine, to a great extent, many aspects of the future.

Many other natural resources are also being depleted rapidly. These include water, natural ores, and forests. For example, the U.S. Energy Department forecasts that natural gas reserves could be used up by the year 2047 and uranium reserves could be depleted by the year 2017 (Almanac and Yearbook 1986). Scientists are working diligently to guard against exploitation of these and other natural resources. Developing substitutes and determining ways to replenish natural supplies are among the many alternatives being investigated.

━ HIGHLIGHT ━

6 African Nations Noted for Famine Threat

A United Nations report at Nairobi said Tuesday urgent action is needed to provide emergency food relief this year to six African nations faced with a famine that has already claimed more than 1 million lives.

The report, published in Nairobi by the UN Food and Agriculture Organization, named Angola, Su-

dan, Ethiopia, Cape Verde, Botswana and Mozambique as areas where acute food shortages and the threat of famine exist. Mozambique was said to have the worst problem. (UPI)

Arkansas Gazette. April 23, 1986. Reprinted by permission United Press International.

Food

The overpopulation of the world not only affects natural resources, but also the ability of the world to feed itself. Third world, developing countries are often not able to produce enough food to feed their people. In the early 1980s droughts and natural disasters, political struggles, and poor planning resulted in hundreds of thousands of people starving to death. The mass starvation in the Sudan and Ethiopia in the early 1980s brought the plight of millions of individuals to the television screens of the United States and other countries. The world responded with aid; even rock singers banded together in an effort to provide relief to the hundreds of thousands of individuals starving to death. While the efforts were somewhat successful, the future will see many other crises related to a lack of food and the resultant starving masses.

Geopolitics

The world of the 1980s is not at peace and will probably never be. Although global conflicts have not occurred since the 1940s with World War II, hundreds of localized military conflicts have continued to plague many parts of the world. Civil wars in many African and South American countries, the Arab-Israeli conflict, and other smaller wars have continued unabated. Add to this the continuing political differences among the superpowers and the result is constant world tension.

Whether humanity survives these conflicts and possible future conflicts will depend on the common sense of the world's leaders. Living under the constant threat of nuclear holocaust will definitely affect the lives of all individuals living on earth. That many countries hold different political ideologies that create tension will only make it more difficult to solve the problems that will face earth for the remainder of the twentieth century and into the twenty-first century.

━━━━━━━━━━━ HIGHLIGHT ━━━━━━━━━━━

'Customized' Education is Predicted for 1990s

NEW YORK (UPI)—Education will become more specialized in the 1990s as schools develop customized education plans for all students and stay open 24 hours a day to train adults for new jobs, a study released Friday said.

Cable television and computers also will play a key role in future education, says the report. It was prepared by the American Association of School Administrators.

"As standards rise, schools will be expected to develop individual education plans for all students," the report predicts.

"We expect that the findings of this study will be controversial," said William B. Royster, the association's president. "However, we believe a discussion of these predictions will be healthy for educators and other citizens and will ultimately lead to better education."

Research for "Schools of the Future" was conducted by Marvin Cetron, president of Forecasting International Inc. of Arlington, Va.

The 24-hour schools, the report says, may be necessary as schools and industry work together.

Among the other predictions in the report:

—Students will learn at home or in their communities one or two days a week, thanks to cable television and computer communication.

—Teachers will get greater status as education becomes recognized as basic to a strong economy, a sound defense and a competitive position among nations.

St. Louis Post-Dispatch. March 9, 1985. Reprinted by permission United Press International.

THE FUTURE OF PUBLIC EDUCATION IN THE UNITED STATES

Like predicting the future of global issues, predicting the future of education is complex and difficult. Making predictions is easy; making accurate predictions, on the other hand, is extremely difficult (Broudy 1974). Even with these realities, forecasting educational trends is necessary to best prepare for the future. "The educational arena is filled with numerous examples of once-proud and effective school districts that failed to anticipate or accept purposeful change to enhance educational programs for students" (Day and Speicher 1985, p. 7).

Many different elements in education will change throughout the twentieth century. These include population trends, the fate of reforms that began during the early 1980s; curriculum; emerging technologies; and the support of citizens for public education. Specific developments that will impact education in the future include computers, materials, fiber optics, and science (Day and Speicher 1985).

Many individuals have tied the future of the world to the future of education. While the future cannot be forecasted totally accurately, the nature of changes that will occur can be determined (Lewis 1983). The many problems that citizens of earth will face during the next twenty to thirty years may be insurmountable unless educational systems adapt to better prepare the children of today for the world of to-

The general public agrees that the role of education to the future of the United States is critical.

morrow. To meet the challenges of the future, Allen (1974) believes that the educational system must make the following changes:

1. Education should move to the center of societal interaction by implementing cross-generational, nonformal, location-free social service programs.
2. Education should reorient itself to a new conception of information based on interdependence and cooperation, and on a new psychology of man based on Maslovian principles and diversity.
3. Our present values about educational change—sameness and objectivity—must be radically altered.
4. In the schools that remain after we have transposed to education for social service, flexible scheduling and differentiated staffing should be implemented. (Allen 1974, p. 18)

By the year 2000 the population will need education to a greater extent than today (Broudy 1974). "More and more careers will require backgrounds in science, mathematics, and computer science. Fewer careers will be open to the undereducated" (Lewis 1983, p. 10). Schools will have to adjust to meet the needs of the future population. The changes required of the public education system in the United States are significant. The question is whether the system can be altered to meet the challenges of the future.

The general public agrees that the role of education to the future of the United States is critical. In the 1984 Gallup Poll of the Public's Attitudes Toward the Public Schools, 95 percent of the respondents indicated that developing the best educational system in the world was very important or fairly important in determining America's strength over the next twenty-five years (Gallup 1984). In contrast, only 81 percent felt that building the strongest military force in the world was very important or fairly important. With the acknowledgment from the public that the role of education is critical to the future of the United States, implementing reforms that improve American public education should be easier.

Population Trends in the United States

Just as the population of the world affects the future, the population of the United States has a major impact on the future of public education. Unlike world population, which will have a significant impact due to massive expansion, the population trends in the United States have resulted in fewer schoolchildren. While this trend may have recently been reversed at the lower elementary level, a decreasing school population will continue for several more years to impact the educational system.

Since the middle 1960s, the population growth in the United States has slowed markedly. Between 1955 and 1965 the average increase in the U.S. population was 2.8 million. Since 1965 the average has decreased to less than 1.9 million. During the 1980s the growth is estimated to be approximately 2.2 million per year, with only 1.5 to 2.0 million projected for the 1990s (Morrison 1979).

What this population trend means to schools is fewer students. With lower school enrollments, schools must contend with excess staff and buildings. Also, as the population increases in average age, persons in the work force will decline further eroding tax bases and possibly creating a situation where older Americans, without children in schools, will be less likely to pass tax increases for public school support. "Seven million fewer young people will reach working age in the 1990s than in the 1970s" (Lewis 1983, p. 10). By the year 2000 approximately 30 percent of the U.S. population will be over fifty years of age (Cage 1984).

School administrators at the local and state levels must plan for decreasing enrollments. How to reallocate staff and resources and provide increasing services and better educational programs on fewer tax dollars will create difficulties. Without some creative uses of public funds, school administrators may find themselves having to do more with less, and for fewer children.

Another problem created by declining enrollments is staffing. Administrators may find themselves faced with a situation of too many teachers and difficulties in decreasing their numbers. Teachers' unions, for example, will lobby hard for protection from layoffs that result from declining enrollments. While an oversupply of teachers could result from lower enrollments, the projections are for a teacher shortage. Many prospective teachers are opting not to enter teacher education programs due to some of the shortcomings of the teaching profession, which have included (1) an oversupply of teachers, (2) poor salaries and benefits, (3) negative public image of teaching, and (4) increased opportunities in fields other than education.

Maintaining the School Reforms

Many extensive educational reforms were initiated in the early 1980s as a result of the critical reports published concerning public education. The content of these reports and the resulting reforms have been substantially documented in previous chapters. The question now is whether the reform movement can be maintained. Will the general public continue to support educational changes, at a financial cost, or will the public interest in improving education wane and be replaced by other issues, such as the economy or geopolitics?

Kirst (1986) predicted that the pace of educational reforms will slow significantly during the latter 1980s. This will result from states passing fewer and fewer major reform acts and local districts implementing fewer and fewer sweeping changes at the district level. What could result is the same thing that has happened to other major reform movements in this country, such as cleaning up the environment and revitalizing inner cities. In each of these cases, the reform movements started out strong but fizzled after the initial discovery and crisis phases to mere policy phases.

To prevent the same negative results from happening to the educational reform movement, policymakers and the public must be kept apprised of the results of the reforms and the need for additional changes. This leads to the need for comprehensive evaluation of the reforms that have been implemented. Several different kinds and levels of evaluation should occur, including

1. performance indicators;
2. overall studies of the financial impact of reforms;
3. analysis of cost-effectiveness of various state interventions with the same specific objectives;
4. program evaluation;
5. impact of evaluation of several state interventions with the same general goal;
6. studies of the cumulative effects of all state reforms in omnibus bills;
7. research that isolates cause-and-effect relationships. (Kirst 1986, p. 343–45)

The South Carolina Education Improvement Act of 1984 mandates that community members be involved in the implementation of educational improvements. It is anticipated that interaction and collaboration among community business and industry leaders with local and state educational professionals will ensure the continued implementation and evaluation of educational reforms (Riley 1986). This sort of planning for ongoing reform activities should help maintain the reform momentum begun in the early 1980s and ensure that the public educational system in this country will continue to improve.

Curriculum for the Future

Predicting the curriculum of future public schools is difficult. Various factions will contend for control of the curriculum in the future, reflecting the "splintering of common interests and the polarization of the larger society" (Apple 1983, p. 321).

Two of the political issues that will affect the curriculum will be (1) determining the "basics" and (2) determining the relationship among schools, business, and labor. The movement to return schools to teaching basic subjects has been present for several years. The issue is who will determine what should be included in the basic curriculum. Conservative groups have begun to exert influence on the curriculum and seem to focus on basic academic subjects at the exclusion of other topics. Other groups, however, want to include courses beyond the basic academic subjects. For example, what role should be reserved for bilingual education? Should creation-science be taught along with or to the exclusion of evolution? These types of conflicts will continue in determining what exactly should be included in the basic curriculum (Apple 1983).

Along with the controversy over what should be included in the basic curriculum will come increased pressures from business and labor to influence the curriculum content of the schools. In times of declining tax bases, and therefore limited school budgets, schools have to rely on a closer relationship with the private sector for support. Too often coupled with this support comes efforts to control (Apple 1983).

Regardless of the difficulties associated with predicting the curriculum for the future, certain trends have been identified. The Virginia Beach, Virginia School District established a task force to predict future trends in curriculum planning. The fifteen implications that were selected included

- basic academic skills;
- computers and other information technologies;
- curriculum flexibility;
- curriculum revision;
- democratic ideals;
- early childhood programs;
- futures perspective;
- global interrelationships;
- lifelong learning;
- mass media;
- personal fulfillment;
- process approach;
- staff development;
- use of community;
- vocational and career education. (Troutman and Palombo 1983, p. 49)

These implications for curriculum planning were developed to help the local school district adequately plan for the future.

Some conclusions concerning the future curriculum for schools can be drawn from the literature. First, the basic academic curriculum will continue to be stressed. The nature of this "basic curriculum" will be determined at state and local levels. There will, however, be an increased emphasis on math and science (Apple 1983), along with technology. Certain professional groups, such as the Conference Board of Mathematical Sciences, are certain to influence the teaching of various subjects in the schools (Willoughby 1983/1984). Professional groups should have a major influence in the development of curricular content in their areas. Topics such as ecology and peace are also likely to receive a new emphasis in the school curriculum (Apple 1983).

A general conclusion concerning the curriculum of the future is that many groups previously not involved in curricular planning will want to participate. These groups include conservatives, liberals, business, labor, professional groups, and even state legislatures. While the outcome of such heterogeneous input is difficult to predict, it at least should lead to a curriculum well planned and debated, which has not always been the case in the history of American education.

Technology in the Future

The role of technology in education has been increasing dramatically. With the advent of the microcomputer age, schools have literally joined the technological revolution. The question is not whether technology, particularly computers, will be a major part of education in the future, but exactly what role it will play.

Just within the current decade, advances made in technology will have the potential to

1. improve instruction in conventional subjects;
2. allow the efficient teaching of types of knowledge and skills previously too expensive to include in the curriculum (such as sophisticated laboratory procedures and advanced music);
3. improve research into the teaching/learning process;
4. expand the number of students per teacher without increasing costs or decreasing quality. (Dede 1983, p. 22)

Certain obvious facts are predictable regarding technology and computers in the future of education, including:

- the number of computers in schools will increase;

- commercial companies will increase efforts to sell computers to schools and develop more educational software;

- computers will continue to become more sophisticated at even lower prices. (Bork 1984)

What is yet to be determined is the exact role computers and other technology will play in instruction. On the one hand, schools and teachers could continue to operate as today, using computers and technology as mere supplements to teacher-oriented instruction. On the other hand, schools and teachers could revolutionize education with the use of technology. Computers could become the impetus for new curricula, new instructional techniques, and a different organization of the school and the role of the teacher (Bork 1984). Only time will tell which direction the role of computers and technology take. Many other educational innovations, such as educational television, never lived up to their expectations. Although computers should, the verdict is still out.

PAST PREDICTIONS OF THE FUTURE OF EDUCATION

The preceding pages have outlined some predictions about the future of public education in the United States. Whether these predictions will be proved accurate remains to be seen. Throughout history, professionals have attempted to predict the future of education, noting that such predictions are difficult. In a 1974 publication, *The Future of Education: 1975–2000*, several authors made predictions about the future of education. The predictions of two of the authors are listed below to be evaluated by today's realities. While reading these predictions, determine which ones have proved accurate to this point, which ones are still under consideration, and which ones are obviously going to be proved wrong.

Predictions by Theodore Hipple (1974)

1. Financing of public education will be enlarged and its base broadened.
2. A concomitant of increased funding for education will be an increase in teacher's salaries.
3. Alternative forms of education will continue to flourish, especially beyond elementary school.
4. The school will be a community center as well as a user of community facilities to enhance its educational program.
5. To permit students to use the community facilities constructed near the schools, it seems probable that the time students spend in actual classrooms will be shortened.
6. Some of the "teachers" at the nearby playgrounds and youth centers will be high school youth who are using their free time to work, on a paid basis, at the centers.
7. The curricula of the schools—that which is taught in them and which students are presumed to learn—will change in the last quarter of the twentieth century, but perhaps not as radically as some educational seers have suggested.
8. Curricula that focus on problem solving and on values clarification activities will call for new instructional strategies.
9. Education for young children will expand; colleges and universities will become more specialized; private colleges will continue to have a difficult time; and junior and community colleges will expand.
10. Many problems will continue to plague education.
11. Educators should make schooling enjoyable.

Predictions by Max Rafferty (1974)

1. The oversupply of teachers will get worse and will have perfectly splendid spin-offs.
2. There will be better education in the big cities without forced busing.
3. The frequency of teacher strikes will decline to zero.
4. Mandated statewide use of standardized tests will be universal.
5. More and better vocational education is in the cards, and for a lot more children than are getting it now.

6. Ethnic studies will be as important in the curriculum as Etruscan tomb-carving, and no more so.
7. Merit pay for teachers and modifications of tenure laws are coming up around the bend of the time stream.
8. Better textbooks are already on the way.
9. Both a longer school year and school day seem in the cards.
10. More student participation in school administration will be occurring.
11. More part-time students and off-campus courses.
12. School and teacher accountability will be demanded.
13. There will be a change in the selection and training of school administrators.

Conclusions on Predictions of 1974

Obviously some of these predictions made more than a decade ago are on their way to coming to fruition; others will obviously never occur. Still others, while not achieved at this point, still have a chance to occur. Predicting the future of education is difficult; however, without futurists attempting to predict what will occur in the schools of tomorrow, there would be no time to prepare for needed changes. Futurism in schools is vital; without it the educational system would attempt and accept changes much less easily than is necessary. Everything needed to solve the problems of the future cannot be taught to children. However, two things must be done. These include helping students develop basic academic skills and encouraging students to become responsible for their own learning (Lewis 1983).

AUTHOR'S PREDICTIONS

With knowledge of past predictions made concerning the future of education, and with more insight into the future than was available in 1974, the author makes the following predictions.

1. Education will continue to become lifelong education. The education of young children, birth through age six, will expand. With more and more mothers joining the work force, the need for day care will continue to escalate. Traditional day-care centers will become more formalized educational centers. Likewise, education for older Americans will expand. With the American population becoming older, the need for formalized, publicly supported educational programs for adults will increase.
2. Financing of public education will broaden to include a major involvement with the private sector. Business and industries will expand their role of financial support to education. Along with this support will come an increased demand for influence in the curriculum.
3. Teachers will be better trained. The reform movement of the 1980s related to teacher education will continue. More emphasis will be placed on field experiences and psychology, with less emphasis on traditional methods courses. Along with better training for teachers will come better salaries and merit-pay plans.
4. Accountability will increase both for teachers and students. Standardized testing will unfortunately be the primary method of ensuring accountability, although alternative quality-assurance methods will be developed.

Although much is at stake, no one can predict exactly what course education will take in the future.

5. Schools will become year-round centers for learning. This will include longer school years for all students, but also flexible scheduling so that school plants are open and activities occur all year.
6. Opportunities for minorities will continue to be a priority. This includes improved educational opportunities for students with disabilities as well as minority racial and cultural groups.
7. School curricula will expand to include required subjects such as peace education, ecology, and geopolitics. Increased emphases on math, science, and computer technology will continue.
8. Computers will become a major part of each school. The role of the teacher, while changing, will remain the primary instructional leader in each classroom.
9. The role of the federal government will continue strong in public education. Federal funding, as well as federal regulation, will increase to ensure equality of educational opportunity for all segments of the society. The federal government will realize that a sound educational system is the best guarantee of a strong country.
10. The influence of various public groups, such as conservatives and liberals, will become less noticeable due to the increased involvement of more citizens, the private sector, and government.

SUMMARY

This chapter focused on the future of education in the United States. The beginning section dealt with futurism and the broader implications of the future of the world. Several variables will have a significant impact on the world and consequently the United States. These include the population explosion, depletion of natural resources, food shortages, and geopolitics. All of these variables are interrelated. For example, the population explosion directly affects the depletion of natural resources and the world hunger situation. World geopolitics can create an environment that is conducive for solving these problems or one that presents a barrier for common actions that could reduce the impact of these negative forces.

The focus of the chapter then moved to the future of education. Although predicting the future of education in the United States is a difficult process, a lack of predictions could lead to an inadequate educational system, one not capable of dealing with the problems of the next generation. Several different aspects of the future of education were discussed, including population trends in the United States, the future of school reforms, curriculum of the schools, and technology. Each of these factors was discussed, with implications presented for future planning.

The final section presented predictions of education provided by two authors in 1974 and the predictions of the author. Some of the earlier predictions were viewed as having been accomplished, while others were still considered in progress or were determined to be unattainable. The future of education in the United States definitely is tied to the future of the world. While predicting the future is extremely difficult, it is an exercise that must be constantly undertaken and updated. The problems faced by humanity in the twenty-first century will be substantial; without adequate predicting and planning, these problems could be overwhelming. Planning for the future increases the likelihood that humanity will endure.

IN THE FIELD

1. Does the school have a long-term plan (five years or more)?

2. What enrollment changes are predicted for the district?

3. Are educational reforms that have been implemented being evaluated? If so, how?

4. Does the district have a plan to deal with teacher shortages or too many teachers? If so, what is it?

5. How are computers currently being used and how will they be used in the future?

6. What are some predictions concerning education in your district made by teachers and administrators? Is there consistency in these predictions?

REFERENCES

Allen, D. 1974. What the future of education might be. In T. W. Hipple, Ed. *The future of education: 1975–2000*. Pacific Palisades, CA: Goodyear Publishing Company.

Almanac and yearbook. 1986. Pleasantville, NY: Reader's Digest.

Amara, R. 1980. Thinking globally, acting locally. In F. Feather, Ed. *Through the 80s: Thinking globally, acting locally*. Washington, DC: World Future Society.

Anthony, R. B. 1984. Education in the year 2000. *The Clearing House 58*(3), 104.

Apple, M. W. 1983. Curriculum in the year 2000: Tensions and possibilities. *Phi Delta Kappan 64*(5), 321–26.

Bork, A. 1984. Computers in education today—And some possible futures. *Phi Delta Kappan 66*(4), 239–43.

Broudy, H. S. 1974. Education: 1975–2000. In T. W. Hipple, Ed. *The future of education: 1975–2000*. Pacific Palisades, CA: Goodyear Publishing Company.

Cage, B. N. 1984. Educational changes for the 1990s. *Record 20*(4), 121–23.

Day, C. W., and A. D. Speicher. 1985. Planning for the 21st century. *American School & University 58*(3), 7–8.

Dede, C. 1983. The likely evolution of computer use in schools. *Educational Leadership 41*(1), 22–24.

Gallup, G. H. 1984. The 16th annual Gallup poll of the public's attitudes toward the public schools. *Phi Delta Kappan 66*(1), 23–36.

Hipple, T. W. 1974. Some (specific and not-so-specific) notions about the (distant and not-so-distant) future of education. In T. W. Hipple, Ed. *The future of education: 1975–2000*. Pacific Palisades, CA: Goodyear Publishing Company.

Johnson, J. A., H. W. Collins, V. L. Dupuis, and J. H. Johansen. 1982. *Introduction to the foundations of American education*. Boston: Allyn and Bacon.

Kirst, M. W. 1986. Sustaining the momentum of state education reform: The link between assessment and financial support. *Phi Delta Kappan 67*(5), 341–45.

Lewis, A. J. 1983. Education in the 21st century. *Educational Leadership 41*(1), 9–10.

Morrison, P. 1979. Beyond the baby boom: The depopulation of America. *The Futurist 13*(2), 131–38.

Platt, J. 1980. The greatest evolutionary jump in history. In F. Feather, Ed. *Through the 80s*. Washington, DC: World Future Society.

Pulliam, J. D., and J. R. Bowman. 1975. *Educational futurism: In pursuance of survival*. Norman, OK: University of Oklahoma Press.

Puttkamer, J. V. 1983. The future: Do we have a choice? *Educational Leadership 41*(1), 4–8.

Rafferty, M. 1974. American education: 1975–2000. In T. W. Hipple, Ed. *The future of education: 1975–2000*. Pacific Palisades, CA: Goodyear Publishing Company.

Riley, R. W. 1986. Can the school reform effort be sustained? *Educational Leadership 43*(5), 40–41.

Schreyer, E. R. 1980. The mystery of the future. In F. Feather, Ed. *Through the 80s: Thinking globally, acting locally*. Washington, DC: World Future Society.

Toffler, A. 1980. The third wave. In F. Feather, Ed. *Through the 80s: Thinking globally, acting locally*. Washington, DC: World Future Society.

Troutman, B. I., and R. D. Palombo. 1983. Identifying futures trends in curriculum planning. *Educational Leadership 41*(1), 49.

Willoughby, S. S. 1983/1984. Mathematics for 21st century citizens. *Educational Leadership 41*(4), 45–50.

EPILOGUE

Education in the United States is indeed at a crossroads. Never before in the history of public education in this country has so much attention been focused on public schools, teachers, administrators, students, and teacher education institutions. The reform movements that began with critical reports of education issued in the late 1970s and early 1980s are having an impact on education. The end result, however, the actual state of public education in the future after the current hoopla, remains cloudy. Certainly there have been other periods in the history of education in this country when the public clamored for reforms and more of a commitment to the public schools. Reforms definitely resulted from these periods. Whether the current activities in education have long-term effects remains to be seen. To summarize the text, the following few pages will present some of the major themes previously discussed and possible future directions of these areas.

CONTROL OF AMERICAN EDUCATION

The control of American education is a complex issue. Long thought of as being controlled by local boards of education, public schools are actually controlled by a complex group of forces. These include local, state, and federal governments; teacher unions; parent groups; textbook publishers; accreditation agencies; and administrators. All these groups have some influence over public education.

No one group has more control than the others. While local boards of education establish policies, these policies must conform to certain state standards. Federal legislation and litigation must also be considered when developing policies for the public schools. Although boards may develop policies, the actual implementation of those policies rests with teachers and administrators, two groups that have a great deal of freedom within individual schools and classrooms.

Still other groups that exert influence are textbook publishers, who control the curricula used in schools to a great extent, and accreditation agencies, private groups that decide that schools must offer certain courses and or experiences to students and that teachers and administrators must meet certain standards if schools receive accreditation.

In the future, state governments and the federal government are likely to continue to have a great impact on schools, especially in this era of reform when legislation and court decisions are mandating certain educational practices. Even in the current era of reform, other forces exert great influence over education. Publishing companies and authors will continue to have a great impact on the curriculum; accreditation agencies will continue to set standards; teacher unions will continue to have an impact on what occurs in classrooms; administrators will still implement policies in their schools; and parents will have some control through direct contact and school board elections. Control will continue to be determined by a complex, interrelated set of variables.

REFORM MOVEMENTS OF THE 1980s

Educational reform reached a fever pitch in the United States in the early 1980s. Resulting from several stinging critical reports on the status of American public education, the reform movements included

- improved teacher education;
- increased standards for teachers, including teacher testing;
- longer school days and more days in the school year;
- more emphasis on basic academic subjects, including math and science;
- more required courses for graduation;
- less emphasis on athletics and other extracurricular activities;
- better pay for teachers;
- merit pay for teachers;
- requirements for students to do homework;
- more funding for educational programs;
- applied research to investigate learning and teacher training.

While some of these changes will undoubtedly have positive effects on the quality of education offered in American public schools, others are questionable. For example, more of the same, if the same is inferior, is not necessarily a solution to quality educational programs. Therefore, simply extending the school day and the school year will not automatically lead to better educational programs. Still, the reform movements of the 1980s have had a positive effect by focusing the nation's attention on education. A subject not particularly popular, education has become publicized in newspapers, magazines, television, and even election campaigns.

The increased awareness of the need to improve the educational system in the United States can only benefit the public school system and American schoolchildren. The key is not to let the attention focused on education in the early 1980s disintegrate when other issues become more popular. Education needs to stay in the limelight.

ELEMENTARY AND SECONDARY EDUCATION

The basic elements of the American public educational system are the elementary and secondary schools. Elementary schools were the beginning level of public education in the United States. They developed out of private schools and the common school movement of the mid-1800s. Secondary schools, on the other hand, were not established on a large scale in the United States until the twentieth century. Still, they were the model for secondary education for the world. Few countries had publicly supported educational programs for adolescents until well into the twentieth century.

The future of elementary and secondary public schools rests with many issues. The organizational structure of the elementary school will undergo few changes. At the secondary level, however, changes are possible. Some critics believe that the comprehensive high school, the one that tries to be all things to all different types of children, is obsolete. These critics would argue for differentiated education at the secondary level, where brighter students are afforded opportunities in academic areas and other students have options that would focus more on vocational areas. The comprehensive high school, however, has been the basic element of public education at the secondary level for many years and will probably not change dramatically in the near future.

SPECIAL EDUCATION

A subject not requiring much attention ten years ago, special education today is a relevant issue for all educators. As a result of federal and state legislation, and a multitude of litigation, providing appropriate educational programs for handicapped children is now a shared responsibility among all educators, both regular teachers and special education teachers. Administrators, who previously had little to do with special education programs, were also affected by the changing service model.

The major legislation mandating services for handicapped children was Public Law 94–142. Passed in 1975, and effective in 1978, this legislation mandated that every handicapped school-age child be afforded a free, appropriate education, regardless of the severity of the handicapping condition. A major requirement of the legislation was that the education provided had to be in the least-restrictive environment; that is, these children have to be educated in regular classrooms with nonhandicapped children, by regular classroom teachers, as much as is feasible. This requirement has had a tremendous impact on regular classroom teachers. Before the legislation went into effect, regular teachers rarely saw handicapped children; after the requirement was passed, handicapped children were mainstreamed into regular classes a large portion of each school day.

Even though some attempts have been made to alter the requirements of P.L. 94–142, especially by the Reagan administration in the early 1980s, the requirements have not been changed. The lobby for the handicapped population is so strong that a major retrenchment from the requirements of P.L. 94–142 is highly unlikely. This means that all educators must continue to share in the responsibility of educating this group of children. Closer collaboration as well as better training will greatly facilitate this shared responsibility and enable handicapped children and nonhandicapped children to receive a better, higher quality education.

VOCATIONAL AND CAREER EDUCATION

Another major component found in many American schools is vocational and career education. Career education is a concept that was developed in the 1970s. The basic purpose of career education was to prepare students for the world of work. Career education, when implemented properly, begins in elementary school with career awareness activities. Teachers are encouraged to infuse ideas about possible careers into their daily instructional activities. Career education is not a separate course and does not require elaborate equipment or materials. Creative teachers find ways to implement career awareness activities into their daily routines.

Other components of career education are installed at the junior-high and senior-high levels. These components focus more on finding out about specific jobs and even training for these jobs. The actual job training is vocational education, which is one component of a comprehensive career educational program.

Vocational education programs are most normally found in secondary schools. Students are able to select a particular job skill area and receive training in that particular area. Part of the vocational training program may actually take place on site, at the regular job location. Vocational education programs include many different options, some of the more common being power mechanics, drafting, building trades, cosmetology, and woodworking. Comprehensive high schools offer a wide variety of vocational training options to their secondary students. Unfortunately, smaller, rural schools often are limited in the vocational training options available.

Vocational and career education programs will continue in the future. Career education, unfortunately, never caught on as its proponents had hoped. Schools that tried the idea often lost interest after a few years. Although career education programs are still found in some classrooms, the adoption of career education programs at the district level is limited.

Vocational education, on the other hand, is strong in American public schools and will likely continue to grow. Although the reform movements of the 1980s caused some concern among vocational educators, this concern is probably not necessary. While there is a movement to require more academic courses for all students, there is not a systematic drive to reduce the availability of vocational education opportunities for students who wish to complete high school with a salable, marketable skill. Vocational education programs will continue to grow in number and sophistication.

EDUCATION AS A PROFESSION

While many would agree that there can be no more noble a profession than teaching, many negative aspects are associated with teaching as a career. These include low pay, low status, high stress, burnout, and being a scapegoat for education ills. However, teaching does have its rewards, many of which cannot be related to material benefits. Some have said that teachers are the ones who help shape the future more than any other group, including parents. Often teachers spend more time, especially one-to-one, with children than the children's parents. As role models and imparters of knowledge, teachers play a critical role in the lives of children.

Teachers provide knowledge and information to students; facilitate students' learning; act as a role model for social skills, values, and attitudes; and act as a friend and stand-in parent. Teachers are definitely involved in more than instruction. If the only activities teachers did were lecture and make assignments from textbooks, computers could more easily and efficiently do the job. Teachers do a tremendous job in American schools. Even though they are frequently accused of being uncaring members of labor unions, most teachers are dedicated to the job of educating children and youth. The future should continue to find excellent individuals serving as teachers in public schools.

Teachers, thus, are key individuals in the instructional process. How they become teachers has been an issue during the early 1980s. Along with criticisms of the educational programs offered in public schools have been criticisms of teacher education programs. Some of the common criticisms have included (1) low quality of students, (2) too much emphasis on how to teach, rather than child growth and development and educational psychology, (3) easy curriculum, (4) easy entrance and exit requirements for teacher education majors, and (5) poor quality of instruction from professors in teacher education.

While not all of these issues are valid, some of the criticisms have resulted in needed reforms. For the most part, these reforms have been initiated by colleges of education. While some of the criticisms have been considered valid and have been addressed, others have been determined to be an attempt to make teacher education the scapegoat for the current perceived crisis in American public education. Many quality teacher education institutions are doing an excellent job training teachers. Although all colleges of education could improve in some areas, most are already doing an excellent job of preparing teachers.

Some of the reforms initiated by colleges of education in response to critics have included

- increased admission standards to teacher education;

- modified curriculum that focuses less on an abundance of methods courses;

- increased emphasis on applied research by faculty in college of education;

- higher exit standards for teacher education graduates.

These are but a few of the reforms initiated by many teacher education institutions. The future should reveal that more colleges of education have taken a hard look at their programs and instituted many valuable reforms. The end result will definitely be better-trained teachers for American schools.

TECHNOLOGY IN THE SCHOOLS

The uses of technology in education include videotape, filmstrips, films, educational television, and microcomputers. Since the late 1970s, microcomputer technology has exploded. Millions of machines are currently on the market, and the area of educational software has become a major business.

As more schools purchase, or are given, computers for their students, the selection and use of software becomes more important. Schools should use precise, careful methods in selecting software, similar to the selection of textbooks. Once purchased, school officials must ensure that teachers know how to use both the machinery and software for maximum educational purposes. Computer technology is too valuable in education to wind up on a shelf collecting dust.

During the past decade, great strides have been made in the uses of computers in education. Initially they were primarily machines for drill. However, recent uses have included activities that actually facilitate learning in ways other than rote memory or drill. The appropriate uses of computers in instruction can greatly enhance the educational program of any school. In addition to being used in instruction, computers can also be useful in administration. School personnel are just beginning to learn how to best utilize computer technology in areas other than instruction. The future should see increased uses of computers in schools, both in instructional and administrative areas.

ORGANIZATION AND FUNDING OF SCHOOLS

Schools are similar to businesses in that they have to have leaders. In schools these individuals are called administrators. School administrators serve many varied functions, depending to a large degree on their actual administrative role. For example, superintendents are the chief school officers of the district. They are employed by a lay board of directors, usually elected by the community. In turn superintendents recommend that the school board employ principals to act as the chief administrative officer of a particular school. Administrators have roles that range from communicating with the school board to establishing and implementing a discipline policy for a particular school.

Administrators must be managers, disciplinarians, evaluators, facilitators, communicators, change agents, and fiscal managers. School administration is no longer a job that should go to retired athletic coaches simply because they contributed to the district. The roles of school administrators are so complex that the job requires a highly skilled, highly trained individual to be successful. In the future more school administrators will be career administrators, individuals who move up to administration through the teaching ranks. These individuals will have an inside view of the classroom and other aspects of public education and should lead the way to more effective administration in public schools.

A major requirement of schools is to educate students. To do this, they must have money. Public schools are supported by taxes at all levels of government: local, state, and federal. Types of taxes generally used to support schools include income taxes, primarily at the federal level, sales taxes at the state level, and property taxes at the local level.

One problem that has plagued educational finance since public support was first started has been the issue of equitable educational programs. Some schools, because of their local tax base, are able to offer higher cost, probably more effective programs than other districts that have limited funds. States have made serious efforts to equalize the finances available to local districts. Unfortunately, most of these efforts have not been totally successful. Still, efforts must be made to develop methods of equity in school finance. Children in all districts should have access to equal educational opportunities. The future should see improved efforts in equitable school financing, as well as increased efforts at all levels of government in financing quality public education programs.

CONCLUSIONS

Public education in the United States is big business. The public schools employ more people and serve more individuals than any other industry or agency in the country. While many problems do exist in American public schools, for the most part the educational system is sound. Compared with other educational systems in the world, the American system is excellent. The reform movements of the 1970s and 1980s have resulted in public attention being focused on quality education. The outcomes from this refocusing of attention will be more quality educational programs.

Public schools are sound. The ideas on which public education is based are sound. Teacher training is sound. Governmental and public support for public education are sound. Although there are problems, the most critical of these are being addressed, and the results will be a major improvement in an already excellent national program. Individuals wanting to become teachers will have an exciting career in public education. The future is ours; if mediocrity is our goal, it can be easily achieved. If excellence is our goal, it can also be achieved through extraordinary investment and effort. The final determination rests with the attitudes and willingness of the American public to fund, support, and rally for quality educational programs for children.

APPENDIX 1

AGENCIES AND PROFESSIONAL ASSOCIATIONS

American Association of Colleges for Teacher Education
One Dupont Circle
Washington, D.C. 20036

American Association for Counseling and Development
5999 Stevenson Avenue
Alexandria, Virginia 22304

American Society of Educators
1511 Walnut Street
Philadelphia, Pennsylvania 19102

American Vocational Association
1410 King Street
Alexandria, Virginia 22314

American Federation of Teachers
555 New Jersey Avenue, N.W.
Washington, D.C. 20001

Association for Childhood Education International
11141 Georgia Avenue, Suite 200
Wheaton, Maryland 20902

Association for Supervision and Curriculum Development
125 North West Street
Alexandria, Virginia 22314

Association of Teacher Educators
1900 Association Drive
Reston, Virginia 22091

Council for Exceptional Children
1920 Association Drive
Reston, Virginia 22090

Home Economics Education Association
1201 Sixteenth Street, N.W.
Washington, D.C. 20036

International Reading Association
800 Barksdale Road
P.O. Box 8139
Newark, Delaware 19714–8139

Kappa Delta Pi
P.O. Box A
West Lafayette, Indiana 47906

National Association of Biology Teachers
11250 Roger Beacon Drive, #19
Reston, Virginia 22090

National Association of Elementary School Principals
1801 North Moore Street
Arlington, Virginia 22209

National Association of Secondary School Principals
1904 Association Drive
Reston, Virginia 22091

National Council for the Social Studies
3501 Neward Street, N.W.
Washington, D.C. 20016

National Council of Teachers of English
1111 Kenyon Road
Urbana, Illinois 61801

National Council of Teachers of Mathematics
1906 Association Drive
Reston, Virginia 22901

National Education Association
1201 16th Street, N.W.
Washington, D.C. 20016

National School Boards Association
1680 Duke Street
Alexandria, Virginia 22314

Parent Teachers Association
700 North Rush
Chicago, Illinois 60611–2571

Phi Delta Kappa
Eighth and Union
P.O. Box 789
Bloomington, Indiana 47402

Society for Research in Child Development
5801 Ellis Avenue
Chicago, Illinois 60637

United States Department of Education
Washington, D.C. 20202

APPENDIX 2

IN–THE–FIELD ACTIVITIES REPORT FORM

NAME: _____ Date: _____

CHAPTER NUMBER AND TOPIC: _____

CLASSROOM SETTING WHERE OBSERVATIONS TOOK PLACE: _____

_____

QUESTION/ACTIVITY: _____

FINDINGS: _____

_____

QUESTION/ACTIVITY: _____

FINDINGS: _____

_____

QUESTION/ACTIVITY: _____

FINDINGS: _____

_____

QUESTION/ACTIVITY: _____

FINDINGS: _____

_____

QUESTION/ACTIVITY: _____

FINDINGS: _____

_____

GENERAL COMMENTS:

FEDERAL LEGISLATION AFFECTING EDUCATION

LAND ORDINANCE OF 1785
- First legislation passed at the national level that had an impact on education.
- Required one section of each township established in the Northwest Territory be reserved for the establishment of public schools.

NORTHWEST ORDINANCE OF 1787
- Expressed general commitment for education by the federal government.
- Stated that "Religion, morality, and knowledge being necessary to good government and the happiness of mankind, schools and the means of education shall forever be encouraged."
- Considered by many as the foundation for public education.

MORRILL LAND GRANT ACT OF 1862
- Gave thirty thousand acres of federal land to each state for each elected representative to Congress.
- Purpose of the land was to establish a college for agriculture and mechanical arts.
- Eventual donation of seventeen million acres of land.

THE SMITH–HUGHES ACT OF 1917
- Provided funds to states to train teachers in the area of vocational education.
- Primarily assisted high schools, however, some funds used in junior colleges.
- Helped establish an extensive network of vocational education in the country.

NATIONAL DEFENSE EDUCATION ACT OF 1958
- Passed after the launching of Sputnik.
- Primarily enacted as a defense action.
- Provided unprecedented amounts of federal money for public education.
- Emphasized educational improvement in the areas of science and foreign languages.

VOCATIONAL EDUCATION ACT OF 1963
- Expanded federal support for vocational education.
- Main purpose was to assist states in maintaining, extending, and improving existing vocational education programs and provide part-time employment for youths.
- Provided for $60 million during fiscal year 1964 and $225 million per year thereafter.

BILINGUAL EDUCATION ACT OF 1964
- Provided funds for school districts to develop and operate special programs for students with limited-English-speaking skills.
- 1974 amendment removed requirements that students in the program be from low income homes.

ELEMENTARY AND SECONDARY EDUCATION ACT OF 1965
- Most extensive federal legislation passed dealing with public education.
- Focused public education efforts on children from poverty homes.
- Provided funds for library support.

- Established services for academic support and remedial instruction.
- Provided funding for research activities by universities.
- Funded programs at state education agencies to support personnel training and planning.

ECONOMIC OPPORTUNITY ACT OF 1965

- Continued efforts at providing services to poor children.
- Funded Head Start programs.

REHABILITATION ACT OF 1973

- Basically civil rights legislation for the handicapped.
- Prevented discrimination against children and adults due to disabilities.
- Applied safeguards for school-age disabled children.

EDUCATION FOR ALL HANDICAPPED CHILDREN ACT OF 1975

- Required the provision of a free, appropriate public education for all handicapped children.
- Mandated that all handicapped children have an Individualized Educational Program (IEP).
- Required that handicapped children be educated with nonhandicapped children as much as possible.
- Provided parents, students, and schools with due process safeguards.
- Required that parents be involved in the education of their handicapped children.
- Mandated that nondiscriminatory assessment practices be used with children.

IMPORTANT COURT CASES AFFECTING EDUCATION

COMMONWEALTH v. HARTMAN (1851)
  The Pennsylvania Supreme Court ruled that the state constitution and school laws only establish minimum requirements and that schools could establish more stringent requirements, in this case, mandatory education.

SPRINGFIELD v. QUICK (1859)
  The United States Supreme Court ruled that states could collect taxes and tax funds for public educational programs.

KALAMAZOO CASE (1874)
  The Michigan Supreme Court ruled that the Kalamazoo school district could levy taxes to support high schools.

PLESSY v. FERGUSON (1896)
  The United States Supreme Court upheld a Louisiana law that required railways to provide separate-but-equal facilities for white and black individuals.

ATTORNEY GENERAL OF MICHIGAN v. LOWREY (1905)
  The United States Supreme Court upheld the right of state legislatures to make and change boundaries of school districts.

PIERCE v. SOCIETY OF SISTERS (1925)
  The United States Supreme Court ruled that state laws may require the attendance of children in school, but could not regulate whether the school is private or public.

COCHRAN v. LOUISIANA STATE BOARD OF EDUCATION (1930)
  The United States Supreme Court ruled that state funds could be used to purchase textbooks for all school-age children, including those attending private, sectarian schools.

ILLINOIS ex rel. v. BOARD OF EDUCATION (1948)
  The United States Supreme Court ruled as unconstitutional a school program that permitted students to attend religious instruction in school during school hours.

ILLINOIS ex rel. McCOLLUM v. BOARD OF EDUCATION (1948)
  The United States Supreme Court ruled that school programs permitting religious instruction during school hours, and allowing students to leave their regular classes for the religious classes, was unconstitutional.

SWEATT v. PAINTER (1950)
  The United States Supreme Court ruled that a black student could not be denied admission to the University of Texas Law School for the sole reason of race.

BROWN v. BOARD OF EDUCATION, TOPEKA KANSAS (1954)
  The United States Supreme Court ruled that children could not be denied admission to public schools on the basis of race; ruling declared segregated public schools to be unconstitutional

based on the Fourteenth Amendment to the Constitution.

ENGEL v. VITALE (1962)

The United States Supreme Court ruled that a New York State law that required the reading of a twenty-two-word, nondenominational prayer unconstitutional.

ABINGTON SCHOOL DISTRICT v. SCHEMPP, MURRAY v. CURLETT (1963)

The United States Supreme Court ruled as unconstitutional a law that required the reading of ten Bible verses and recitation of the Lord's Prayer during school hours, on school grounds, conducted by school personnel.

EPPERSON v. ARKANSAS (1968)

A law forbidding the teaching of evolution was ruled unconstitutional by the United States Supreme Court.

GREEN v. COUNTY SCHOOL BOARD (1968)

The United States Supreme Court declared that a "freedom of choice" plan in a previously segregated school district offers little likelihood for desegregation. The ruling required that an effective plan for desegregation be implemented.

TINKER v. DES MOINES INDEPENDENT COMMUNITY SCHOOL DISTRICT (1969)

The United States Supreme Court ruled as unconstitutional the suspension of students wearing armbands or other symbolic expressions unless the wearing of such interferes with school.

SWANN v. CHARLOTTE–MECKLENBURG BOARD OF EDUCATION (1971)

Federal court ruling upheld busing as a legitimate means for desegregating schools. It gave district courts wide discretion in remedying longstanding segregated school systems.

PENNSYLVANIA ASSOCIATION FOR RETARDED CITIZENS (PARC) v. PENNSYLVANIA (1971)

Federal court required local schools to provide a free, appropriate public education for all school-aged mentally retarded children.

SAN ANTONIO INDEPENDENT SCHOOL DISTRICT v. RODRIQUEZ (1973)

Federal court upheld a state funding model where local property taxes are used to provide a minimum educational program for all students.

SLOAN v. LEMON (1973)

The United States Supreme Court ruled as unconstitutional a law allowing for partial reimbursement by the state for tuition paid by parents sending their children to private schools.

MILLIKEN v. BRADLEY (1974)

The United States Supreme Court, in a five to four decision, overturned lower court rulings that required the busing of children between Detroit and suburban school districts to desegregate the Detroit system.

BAKER v. OWEN (1975)

The United States Supreme Court ruled that a statute allowing for reasonable corporal punishment was constitutional as long as certain procedural rights were afforded.

WOLMAN v. WALTER (1977)

The United States Supreme Court ruled that states may supply secular texts, standardized tests, diagnostic speech, hearing, and psychological services, and guidance and remedial services provided on religiously neutral territory to religious, private schools.

BATTLE v. COMMONWEALTH (1980)

Third Circuit Court of Appeals ruled that some handicapped children should be afforded extended school year services in cases where significant regression would occur during the summer.

BOARD OF EDUCATION v. ROWLEY (1982)

The United States Supreme Court ruled that Public Law 94–142 guaranteed the right of disabled children to a minimally appropriate educational program, not a program designed to maximize the educational performance of students.

IMPORTANT DATES IN AMERICAN EDUCATION

1636	Harvard University chartered.
1642	Law of 1642 enacted in Massachusetts.
1647	Old Deluder Satan Act passed in Massachusetts.
1690	First appearance of the *New England Primer*.
1693	William and Mary College chartered.
1701	Yale University chartered.
1746	Princeton University chartered.
1749	Benjamin Franklin introduced his Proposal Relating to the Education of Youth in Pennsylvania.
1751	First academy established in United States.
1754	Columbia University chartered.
1785	Land Ordinance of 1785 passed by national government.
1787	Northwest Ordinance of 1787 enacted by national government.
1788	United States Constitution ratified.
1802	Pauper School Act in Pennsylvania.
1806	First Lancastrian School established in New York.
1812	New York State has first state school officer.
1818	First Infant school begun in Boston.
1821	English Classical School of Boston established, first American high school.
1825	University of Virginia opens.
1827	Massachusetts law compelling high schools passed.
1837	Massachusetts first state school board established. Horace Mann becomes first secretary.
1839	First public normal school established.

1840   Rhode Island compulsory education law becomes effective.

1849–50 General tax support for education supported in New York.

1852   Massachusetts compulsory education law.

1855   First American kindergarten established.

1857   National Education Association (NEA) established.

1859   Darwin's *On the Origin of Species* published.

1861   Massachusetts Institute of Technology founded; first engineering school.

1862   Morrill Act passed.

1866   Federal Department of Education established; became the Office of Education after one year.

1872   Kalamazoo law case establishes legal right of city to establish high school.

1881   Tuskegee Institute, first black normal school, founded.

1890   Second Morrill Act passed.

1892   Committee of Ten established by NEA to standardize high schools.

1896   *Plessy v. Ferguson* law case.

1899   Dewey's *The School and Society* published.

1909   First junior high school established at Berkeley, California.

1910   First junior college established at Fresno, California.

1916   American Federation of Teachers (AFT) established.

1917   Smith-Hughes Act passed.

1918   NEA establishes Commission on the Reorganization of Secondary Education.

1919   Progressive Education Association organized.

1924   Scopes "monkey" trial.

1926   Establishment of the Commission on the Social Studies in the Schools.

1944   First G. I. Bill passed.

1950   Establishment of the National Science Foundation.

1950   National Commission on Accrediting established.

1954   *Brown v. Board of Education* law case.

1957   Soviet Union launches Sputnik.

1957   Federal troops ordered to Little Rock to ensure school desegregation.

1958   National Defense Education Act passed.

1964   Civil Rights Act passed.

1965   Elementary and Secondary Education Act passed.

1968   Bilingual Education Act passed.

1971   *Swann v. Charlotte-Mecklenburg* court case.

1975   Education for All Handicapped Children Act (P.L. 94–142) passed.

1979   Department of Education created.

1983   *Nation at Risk Report* issued.

GLOSSARY

Academy: American secondary school during co-lonial times; stressed practical subjects.

Accountability: Responsibility related to quality of educational programs.

Accreditation: Acknowledgment by an outside group that an educational institution or program meets certain standards.

Administrative Hierarchy: Administrative organi-zation of a local school district.

Aesthetics: Philosophy related to beauty.

Alternative Certification: Teacher licensure ob-tained through other than traditional course-work in education courses.

American College Testing Program (ACT): Col-lege entrance exam used by many universities.

American Federation of Teachers (AFT): A na-tional teachers' organization second only to the National Education Association in membership.

Assistant Principal: Administrative position in an individual school that primarily assists the princi-pal in administrative duties.

Assistant Superintendent: Administrative position in a school district that primarily assists the su-perintendent in administrative duties.

Attitude: Preconceived notions or ideas that affect behavior toward certain groups of people or programs.

Audiovisual Kit: Instructional materials, usually in the form of filmstrips, tapes, and other audiovi-sual items and printed information.

Axiology: Area of philosophy that focuses on val-ues.

Back-to-the-basics: Movement to return schools to emphasizing basic academic subjects in the curriculum.

Behaviorism: Educational philosophy and prac-tice that emphasizes reinforcing appropriate be-havior or learning. Includes the concepts of stim-ulus and response.

Bilingual Education: Educational programs aimed at providing equal opportunities to limit-ed-English-speaking students.

Bill for the More General Diffusion of Knowl-edge: Bill presented by Thomas Jefferson in Virginia that would have made three years of elementary education available for all children. Although defeated, this bill laid the foundation for public education.

Board of Education: A group of citizens at the local and state levels, usually elected but occa-sionally appointed, that set policies for schools.

Building Level Administration: Administration of individual schools.

Burnout: The process of losing interest and moti-vation in teaching or other fields.

Cardinal Principles: Seven goals for secondary education developed by the NEA in the early twentieth century.

Career Education: A concept that aims at prepar-ing students for adulthood, with emphasis on careers and vocations; can be infused into ex-isting curricula K–12.

Categorical Aid: Financial assistance provided to local schools for specific programs or purposes.

Censorship: The act of censuring materials such as library books and textbooks.

Central Office: Refers to the district administration level of local school districts.

Certification: Teacher licensure.

Change Agent: A role of school administrators re-lated to making and influencing innovations in schools.

Classical Conditioning: A theory of learning based on stimulus response.

Closed-Circuit Television: A form of educational technology using a television and video camera.

Cognition: Process of thinking.

Colonial Period: Period in American education from 1607 to 1788.

Committee of Fifteen: A committee appointed in 1895 by the National Education Association that reversed the findings of the Committee of Ten.

Committee of Ten: NEA committee established in 1893 to standardize high schools.

Common School: Free, publicly supported schools for all children; movement began in the mid-1800s.

Competency: Ability to perform certain skills at appropriate levels.

Comprehensive High School: Secondary schools that provide a variety of curricular options for students.

Compulsory Education: Legal mandated education for all students within certain age groups.

Computer-Assisted Instruction (CAI): Programmed instruction using a computer.

Computer Science: The study of computers and computer programming.

Concrete Operational State: Stage of Piagetian development for children ages seven to eleven in which logical thinking begins.

Conservative Movement: Movement to influence educational programs by conservative groups.

Consolidation: Combining smaller school districts into larger districts.

Core Curriculum: Required curriculum for all students.

Creation-Science: The study of the development of humanity based on the Bible.

Criterion-Referenced Tests: Tests that are designed to assess a student's progress or ability in a particular area.

Cultural Pluralism: A society composed of many varied cultures forming a unified cultural group.

Curriculum: All experiences provided students in schools.

Curriculum Reform: Movements to change basic curricular options for students.

Declining Enrollments: Trend in schools during the past decade.

Department of Education: Cabinet-level office within the federal government responsible for education.

Discipline: Actions in response to inappropriate behavior or actions that prevent inappropriate behaviors.

Discretionary Funds: Federal funding for specific programs granted after specific needs are identified and documented.

Due Process: Procedural safeguards afforded students, parents, and teachers that protects individual rights.

Eclectic Learning Theory: Learning theory that includes a combination of the major learning theories.

Educational Psychology: Applications of psychological principles to education.

Educational Technology: Technology applied to educational practices, primarily instruction.

Educational Television: Educational programs broadcast by either commercial stations or specialized educational networks that emphasize educational subjects.

Education Trends: Forecasted patterns in education.

Elementary Schools: Grades 1–6 or K–6.

Enactive Representation: Earliest form of symbolization in which infants represent their worlds in terms of interaction with the environment.

English Grammar School: Model of elementary education in colonial America.

Enlightenment Period: Period in Europe during eighteenth century.

Epistemology: Branch of philosophy that focuses on the nature of knowledge.

Essentialism: Area of philosophy that believes a common core of knowledge and ideals should be the focus of the curriculum.

Ethics: Philosophy that studies values.

Evaluation: Assessing the quality and effectiveness of programs for individuals and groups.

Evolution: The study of the development of humanity based on scientific data that proposes human beings developed from lower life forms.

Exceptional Children: Students with disabilities or talents that require specialized programs.

Existentialism: Philosophy that emphasizes individuals and individual decision making.

Federal Government: Governmental actions that occur within the national government of the United States.

Federal Role: Role of the federal government in education.

Formula Grants: Educational funding based on the number of children eligible for various programs.

Fringe Benefits: Any number of benefits provided employees in addition to salary. Examples include insurance programs, retirement programs, and liability insurance.

Full-Time Equivalency (FTE): Funding model used at many universities where programs are funded based on the number of full-time students enrolled.

Futurism: The study of the future, including global concerns and more regional or local matters.

General Curriculum: Basic curriculum required of all students.

Geopolitics: Political status of all countries in the world.

Gifted and Talented: A group of students whose abilities are above those of most students; these students require specialized programs.

Global Trends: Forecasted developments that have an impact on the entire world, such as geopolitics, hunger, population.

Graded Schools: Schools organized using a step system whereby students are usually grouped related to chronological age rather than abilities.

Graduation Requirements: Courses required of all students for graduation.

Handicapped Children: Students who deviate from the norm due to physical, emotional, or mental disabilities.

History of Education: Historical study of education.

Hornbook: A single page, usually attached to a wooden paddle, containing the alphabet, syllables, a prayer, and other simple words; this "book" was used extensively in colonial schools.

Human Development: Study of the development of humans from infancy through adulthood.

Iconic Representation: Representation of the world through mental imagery.

Idealism: A philosophy that emphasizes global ideas related to moral teachings.

Individualized Educational Program (IEP): Individual program of study mandated by federal and state laws for all handicapped students in special education programs.

Individualized Instruction: Instruction designed to meet the needs of an individual student. Every student's individualized program is different.

Instructional Television: Televised lessons broadcast for schools usually on educational television.

Intermediate Unit: A level of educational organization between local school districts and the state department of education.

Kindergarten: School programs for preschool age children; term coined by Froebel.

Latin Grammar School: Secondary school whose curriculum emphasized Latin and Greek and focused on preparing students for college.

Learning Disability: A handicapping condition where students of average or above-average intelligence have difficulty with academic subjects.

Least-Restrictive Environment: Educational setting that is closest to a normal classroom for handicapped learners.

Legislation: Acts passed by state legislatures and Congress that become laws.

Litigation: Court actions, suits.

Local Education Agency (LEA): Local school districts. This is the basic educational unit in all states.

Mainstreaming: The practice of integrating handicapped students into regular classrooms and programs as much as possible; implementation of the least-restrictive environment.

Measurement: Another term used interchangeably with evaluation.

Medieval Period: Period in Europe from 476 to 1300.

Melting Pot Theory: Theory that people from all cultures form a common culture.

Mental Retardation: A handicapping condition related to intellectual deficits; usually defined in terms of limited IQ scores and adaptive behavior.

Merit Pay: Salary paid to an employee based on the employee's abilities or competencies, irregardless of number of years of service.

Metaphysics: Philosophy that studies the nature of reality.

Microcomputer: Personalized computer the approximate size of a television set or smaller.

Middle School: An organized educational unit between elementary school and high school; usually includes grades 5–8.

Mill: A tenth of a cent or a thousandth of a dollar. Used to assess the rate of property taxes.

Minimum Competency Testing: Evaluations to determine if students have minimum skills necessary for progressing to the next grade or graduation.

Minimum Foundation Program: Funding model found in most states that attempts to guarantee a basic educational program for children funded at an average minimal level.

Monitorial Schools: School model where brightest students were instructed and in turn they taught other students.

Motivation: Willingness or drive to accomplish something.

Nation at Risk Report: National report developed by the National Commission that indicated public education in the United States has serious problems.

National Commission on Education: A study group formed in the early 1980s to investigate the status of public education in the United States.

National Council for the Accreditation of Teacher Education (NCATE): Accreditation agency that certifies the quality of teacher education programs nationwide.

National Education Association (NEA): Largest teachers' organization in the United States.

National Period: Period in American education from 1788 to the present.

Negative Reinforcement: Removal of an adversive stimulus when appropriate behavior is exhibited.

New England Primer: Early textbook used in colonial schools.

New Right: Term used to refer to extremely conservative groups that attempt to influence educational programs.

Nongraded School: An organizational pattern for schools that use students' abilities for grouping rather than assigning students to certain grades based on chronological age.

Normal School: First college training programs that trained teachers.

Norm-Referenced Tests: Tests that enable the comparison of students' scores to a "norm" group.

Northwest Ordinance: Early legislation passed by the national government prior to the ratification of the United States Constitution.

Open Classroom: Physical organization of schools where rooms are deleted; students are educated in groups in large, open areas.

Operant Conditioning: Learning theory based on positive reinforcement.

Overpopulation: A condition when there are more people than a particular landmass can accommodate.

Paraprofessional: Teachers' aides and others who assist teachers in educational programs.

Parent Teachers Association (PTA): National organization composed of parents and teachers that advocates for public education.

Pedagogy: Science and art of teaching.

Perennialism: Educational philosophy that believes in the existence of unchanging universal truths.

Personnel Evaluation: Evaluation of individual teachers and administrators.

Philosophy of Education: Application of philosophy to educational programs and practices.

Piagetian Theory: Theory of child development based on the writing of Jean Piaget.

Population Trends: Forecasted patterns of population growth and decline.

Positive Reinforcement: Application of something positive to someone following appropriate behavior.

Pragmatism: Philosophy that focuses on practical application of knowledge; John Dewey was a leading proponent.

Preoperational Stage: A stage in development, according to Piaget, for children ages two through seven in which the ability to symbolize is developed.

Primary Reinforcer: The positive reinforcement that the child receives following appropriate behavior.

Principal: Administrator in charge of individual schools.

Program Evaluation: Evaluation of specific programs regarding their effectiveness.

Progressive Tax: A tax where individuals with higher incomes pay more taxes than individuals with lower incomes.

Progressivism: Educational philosophy emphasizing experiences.

Property Assessment: Determination of property values to assign taxes to individuals.

Property Tax: Taxes assessed on local properties to use to finance public education.

Proportional Tax: Taxes that require individuals to pay the same percentage of their incomes regardless of income level.

Public Law 94-142: Education for All Handicapped Children Act. Passed in 1975, this act mandates a free, appropriate public education for all handicapped children.

Punishment: Application of something unpleasant to a child following inappropriate behavior.

Puritan Influence: Influence over education by Puritans in the New England colonies during colonial America.

Realism: Philosophy that emphasizes natural sciences and gaining knowledge through experiences.

Reform Movements of the 1980s: Educational reforms initiated in the early 1980s in response to several national reports concerning the quality of public education.

Reinforcement: Stimulus provided following a behavior; may be positive or negative.

Reinforcement Schedule: Schedule used to determine when reinforcers are given to a person.

Regressive Tax: Taxes where persons with lower incomes pay proportionally more taxes than individuals with higher incomes.

Reliability: The technical aspect of a test that indicates that students' scores will be stable over time.

Renaissance and Reformation: Period in Europe between 1300 and 1700.

School Counselor: Professionals in schools who provide counseling for students who need affective intervention.

School Social Worker: Social worker who works in schools to provide social work services to students and their families.

School Superintendent: Chief school administrator at the local district level; usually appointed by the local board of education.

Secondary Reinforcer: A reinforcer paired with a primary reinforcer designed to influence behavior after the primary reinforcer is no longer provided.

Secondary Schools: Schools that provide educational programs for older students; usually includes grades 9–12 or 10–12.

Secretary of Education: Cabinet-level official in charge of the United States Department of Education.

Self-Contained Classroom: Classroom organization where students remain in the same room with the same teacher all day.

Sensorimotor Stage: A stage in Piagetian theory from birth to approximately two years where the development of the senses is paramount.

Sexism: Practice of discrimination based on gender.

Shaping: The process of providing reinforcers to alter a child's behavior into appropriate forms.

Software: Computer programs.

Special Education: Specialized programs developed for the education of children with disabilities.

Standardized Test: A test that is norm-referenced and has specific administration standards so scores can be compared.

State Department of Education: State unit responsible for public and private educational programs in states.

Symbolic Representation: Most abstract of representation commonly referred to as verbal learning or problem solving.

Superintendent: Chief school administrative officer in local school districts.

Supervisor: Administrator responsible for specific programs in public schools, e.g., supervisor of special education, vocational education supervisor, supervisor of elementary education.

Supply and Demand: Comparison between the number of teachers trained and the number needed for open positions.

Taxes: Payments to a government to pay for various services.

Tax Revolt: Movement to decrease taxes during the 1970s.

Tax Shifting: The process of having someone else or some other group pay taxes for you.

Tax Sources: Sources of tax revenue.

Teacher Education: Programs designed to train prospective teachers in pedagogy.

Teacher Testing: A movement begun in Arkansas in the early 1980s to test teachers in basic skills.

Teacher Unions: Teachers' organizations that lobby for educational programs and teachers' rights and benefits. The NEA and AFT are the two largest national teacher unions in the United States.

Teacher Unit: A method of funding public education programs based on the number of teachers needed for a particular district or program.

Technology: Use of technical materials and equipment in schools.

Tenth Amendment United States Constitution: Amendment that reserves to states areas not specifically mentioned in the Constitution.

Tenure: An employee benefit that makes it difficult to terminate someone; usually provided to teachers after several years of successful teaching experience.

Textbook Censorship: The process of groups determining which textbooks meet their standards.

Tracking: Practice of channeling students into certain courses based on ability levels.

Ungraded Schools: School organization where students progress based on their ability level rather than chronological age.

Validity: Technical aspect of tests indicating that they measure what they purport to measure.

Values Clarification: A teaching program that focuses on students understanding and expressing their own values.

Videocassette Technology: Equipment consisting of a television and videocassette camera for use in educational settings.

Vocational Education: Educational programs that emphasize career preparation. Training of students for particular jobs or skills.

Weighted Pupil Method: A method of state funding for public education based on the needs of types of students.

INDEX

A

Abington School District v. *Schempp,
Murray* v. *Curlett* (1963), 77, 388
Academic performance, problem of declining, 151–152
Academic Preparation for College, 6
Academy movement
in middle colonies, 37
origin of, 38–39
Accommodation, 263–264
Accreditation agencies, 83–84
Action for Excellence, 7
Activity mode of teaching methodology,
116
Administration
careers in, 235, 307
benefits, 235–237
process of achieving, 235
in the elementary school, 102–104
future trends in, 380
hierarchy, 217
local board of education, 217–218
powers and responsibilities of, 218–
220
professional staff, 220
building-level, 223–235
districtwide, 220–223
superintendents, 220–221, 222
roles of, 94
uses of computers in, 351
Agencies, listing of educational, 382–383
Alcohol abuse, problem of, in schools,
152
Amaral, Ed, 305
American Association for Counseling
and Development, 382
American Association of Colleges for
Teacher Education, 382
American Association of Mental Deficiency (AAMD), 199
American College Testing (ACT) Program, 82, 83
test scores on 5, 152

American Federation of Teachers (AFT),
14, 80, 382
as labor union, 290–291
formation of, 82
impact of, on education, 82
influence of, 26
on competency testing of teachers,
324
state chapters of, 90
American Historical Association, 86
American Industry, 176
American Normal School Association,
82
American Society of Educators, 382
American Vocational Association, 382
Analytic philosophy, 66
Appalachian Regional Development,
171
Appearance codes, problem of, in
schools, 147
Aquinas, St. Thomas, 61, 63
Aristotle, 35, 59, 270, 287
Armstrong v. *Kline* (1979), 196
Articulation problems, 202
Assimilation, 263
Assistant principals, 234–235
salaries earned by, 236, 237
Association for Childhood Education In-
ternational, 382
Association for Children with Learning
Disabilities (ACLD), role of, in passage
of P.L. 94–142, p. 190
Association for Supervision and Curricu-
lum Development, 382
Association of Teacher Educators, 382
Athletics, 139–141
"no pass/no play" rule, 139–141
Attorney General of Michigan v. *Lowrey*
(1905), 77, 387
Audio-tutorial systems, 353, 354
Audiovisual kits, 338–339
Austin, Joe, 227–228
Avoidance, 274
Axiology, 58

B

Back-to-the-basics movement, 10, 64,
133, 287, 367–369
Baker v. *Owen* (1975), 388
Bandura, Albert, 278
Basic Educational Opportunity Grants,
171
Battle v. *Commonwealth* (1980), 388
Bedame, Ish, 250
Behavioral chaining, 274, 278
Behavioral engineering, 64
Behavioral theory, 271–274
classroom applications, 274–275
Behavior disorders, 201
Behaviorism, 62–63
impact of, on education, 62–63
Behavior modification, 64
Bell, Clarence, 251
Bell, Terrell, 4, 25
Bennett, William J., 187, 194, 319
Bibb, David, 173
Bilingual education, 12–13
Bilingual Education Act of 1968, p. 72,
73, 385
Bill for the More General Diffusion of
Education, 38
Binet, Alfred, 186–187
Blair, Diane, 335
Block grants, for education, 256
Board of education, 217–218
composition of, 219–220
discretionary powers of, 218
duties of, 218
influence of, on education, 91–92
responsibilities of, 219
*Board of Education of the Hendrick
Hudson Central School District Board
of Education* v. *Rowley* (1982), 196,
388
Boyer, Ernest, 319
Brainstorming, 143–144
Braun, Werner von, 130
Brown v. *Board of Education, Topeka,
Kansas* (1954), 50, 73, 76, 77, 189,
195, 287, 387–388

Bruner, Jerome, 276
Burnout, 303
Burroughs, Robert, 341
Business, role of, in vocational education, 171–172

C

Cable television, 364
Calvin, John, 36, 185
Calvinism, influence of, on education, 36
Camayd-Freixas, Yohel, 151
Career education, 174–175. *See also* Vocational education
  components of programs in, 175–177
  future of, 377–378
  in elementary schools, 177–178
  in secondary schools, 178
  objectives of, 175
  relationship between vocational education and, 179
Careers, 287–289. *See also under specific career.*
  as professional support personnel, 308
  in administration, 307
  in school counseling, 307–308
  in school health, 308
  in social work, 308
  in teaching, 287–306
Carnegie report, 319
Carter, Jimmy, support of, for Department of Education, 79
Cascade of Services Model, and special education, 207, 210
ment of Education, 79
Cascade of Services Model, and special education, 207, 210
Case study, 144
Catterall, James S., 150
Central office staff, 221, 223
Cetron, Marvin, 364
Charlemagne, 34–35
Cheek, John, 335
Chomsky, Noam, 267
Citizenship education, as goal of elementary education, 101
Civilian Conservation Corps. (CCC), 254
Civil Rights Act of 1964, p. 73
Civil rights legislation, and education, 73
Classical conditioning, 271
Classification, 266
Classroom discussion, 141–143
Classroom materials, use of, in elementary education, 114
Classroom milieu, in elementary education, 117–118
Clements, Bill, 141
Clinton, Bill, 288, 335
Closed-circuit television, 337–338

Cochran v. *Louisiana State Board of Education* (1930), 387
Cognitive structuralism, 276
Cognitive theory, 275–277
  classroom applications, 277
Collective bargaining, teachers' rights in, 93
College Entrance Examination Board, 83
Colonial America, education during, 35–37
Commission for Reorganization of Secondary Education, issuance of Cardinal Principles of Secondary Education by, 129
Committee of Ten (NEA), 42–43
Common school movement, 3, 39–41, 99
  state legislation supporting, 41
Commonwealth v. *Hartman* (1851), 387
Competency testing, for teachers, 14, 306, 319, 322–324
Computer(s), 364
  brief glossary of terminology, 352
  potential of, in education, 20–21
  teacher training in, 351, 353
  uses of, in education, 343–351
Computer-assisted instruction (CAI), 341–342, 354
  advantages and disadvantages of, 343–344
  barriers to implementing, 344
  components of, 346, 347
  hardware for, 346

  components of, 346, 347
  hardware for, 346
  roles of personnel in, 344–346
  software in, 346–348
  uses of, 342
Conant, James, 4, 46
Concept learning, 278
Conduct disorders, 201
Conference Board of Mathematical Sciences, 368
Conference of Executives of American Schools for the Deaf, 201
Connecticut Laws of 1650, p. 218
Conservation, 265–266
Conservative movement, and public education, 17
Context, Input, Process, Product Model (CIPP), 229
Continuum of services model, and special education, 206–207
Council for Exceptional Children, 91, 382
  role of, in passage of P.L. 94–142, p. 190
Counseling services, 120

Creation science, in the secondary school, 136–137
Criterion-referenced test, 281
Cultural pluralism, 11
Curriculum
  in elementary schools, 107–110
    variations in, 112–118
  for the future, 367–369
  reforms in
    back-to-the-basics as, 10, 64, 133, 287, 367–369
    state initiatives in, 11
  in secondary schools, 132
    common, 132–134
    creation science, 136–137
    death education, 135–136
    math, 133–134
    multicultural education, 137
    nuclear threat, 136
    science, 132–133
    sex education, 135
    social studies, 134
    specialized areas, 135–138
    steps of development, 138

D

Darwin, Charles, 58–59, 61
Deaf, schools for the, 186
Death education, in the secondary school, 135–136
Debating, 144
Deductive logic, 59
Deinstitutionalization, 205
Demonstration mode implementing, 344
Deductive logic, 59
Deinstitutionalization, 205
Demonstration mode of teaching methodology, 116
Departmentalized elementary schools, 106–107
Descartes, René, 270
Desegregation, 50
  effects of, 48–49
  in Ohio, 78–79
  judicial decisions on, 50, 73, 76, 77, 189, 196, 287, 387–388
Dewey, John, 4, 33, 43, 61
Diana v. *State Board of Education* (1970) and (1973), 196
Discipline, problem of, in schools, 145–147
Discrepancy evaluation model (DEM), 228, 229
Discretionary funding, for education, 255–256
Discriminative stimulus, 273
Dix, Dorothea, 186
Dressing codes, problem of, in schools, 147

Dropouts, problem of, in schools, 149–151

Drug abuse, problem of, in schools, 152

Due process hearings
  and the handicapped child, 192–193
  and multicultural special education, 197
  in expulsion and suspension cases, 147–148
  under P.L. 94–142, p. 193

Dysfluency, 202

E

Eclectic theory, 277–278

Economic Opportunity Act of 1965, p. 72, 386

Educating Americans for the 21st Century, 7

Education
  control of American, 375–376
  future outlook of, 26–27
  important dates in American, 389–391

Education, Federal Department of, 79

Education, U.S. Department of, 383
  establishment of, as cabinet level department, 79–80
  organizational structure of, 81

Educational Consolidation and Improvement Act (1981), 255

Educational philosophies, 55–56
  and educational practice, 64–67
  and school policies, 107
  axiology, 58
  behavioral engineering, 64
  behaviorism, 62–63
  definition of, 56
  epistemology, 57–58
  essentialism, 64
  existentialism, 61–62
  idealism, 58–59
  metaphysics, 57
  perennialism, 63
  pragmatism, 61
  purposes of, 56–57
  realism, 59–61
  reconstructionism, 64

Educational practices, impact of philosophy on, 64–67

Educational psychology, 261
  human development
    development of language, 266–267
    development of morality, 268–270
    development of thinking, 262–266
  learning principles, 270–271
    behavioral theorists, 271–275
    cognitive theorists, 275–277

eclectic theorists, 277–278
measurement and evaluation, 281–282
motivation, 279–281

Educational reforms. *See* Reform movements.

Educational Research Analysts, 89

Educational Services Incorporated (ESI), 85

Educational technology, 334–335
  audio-tutorial systems, 353, 354
  audiovisual kits, 338–339
  closed-circuit television, 337–338
  computer(s), 340–353
  computer-assisted instruction (CAI), 353, 354
  future of, 369, 379–380
  instructional television, 336–337
  needed directions for, 353, 355
  personalized instruction system, 353, 354
  programmed instruction, 353, 354
  programmed tutoring, 353, 354
  simulation and gaming, 353, 354
  videocassette technology, 339–340

Educational Testing Service (ETS), 82–83

Educational trends
  changing federal role, 25–26
  conservative movement, 17
  curricular reform, 10–11
  declining enrollments, 24–25
  fiscal problems, 22–24
  home schooling, 18–19
  improved teachers, 15–16
  melting pot theory, 11
  multicultural education, 11–14
  new right, 17–18
  teacher unions, 26
  technology, 20–21

Education Amendments of 1976, p. 164

Education Commission of the States, 5, 11

Education for All Handicapped Children Act of 1975. *See* P.L. 94–142.

Education history
  European foundations, 33–35
    Enlightenment, 35
    Greek period, 34
    Medieval period, 34–35
    Reformation, 35
    Renaissance, 35
    Roman period, 34
  in the United States
    colonial period, 35–37
    in the nineteenth century, 39–43
    in the twentieth century, 43–51

national period, 37–39

Educators for Social Responsibility (ESR), 136

Efficacy studies, and special education, 205–206

Egocentricism, 265

Eisenhower, Dwight, and federal funding for education, 256

Elementary and Secondary Education Act (ESEA) of 1965, pp. 72–73, 255, 287, 385–386

Elementary school(s), 99
  administration of, 102–104
  career education in, 177–178
  classroom materials, 114
  classroom milieu, 117–118
  curricular variations within classrooms in, 112–118
  curriculum in, 107–110
  future of, 376–377
  instructional grouping in, 116–117
  measuring student achievement levels in, 100–101
  methods of instruction, 115–116
  organizational arrangements of, 104–107
    horizontal organization, 106–107
    vertical organization, 104–106
  philosophy in, 107, 108
  purpose of, 99–100, 101–102
  space utilization, 114–115
  teachers in, 110–112
  testing to measure student achievement levels, 100–101
  textbooks in, 113–114

Emotional disturbance/behavior disorders, 200–201

Enactive representation, 276

Engel v. *Vitale* (1962), 388

English Classical School (Boston), 42

Enlightenment, education during, 35

Enrollments, problem of declining, 24–25, 366

Epistemology, 57–58

Epperson v. *Arkansas* (1968), 77, 388

Essentialism, 64

Existentialism, 61–62
  impact of, on education, 62–63

Experimental extinction, 272

Experimental Program for Orientation (EXPO), 149

Expository mode of teaching methodology, 116

Expulsion, problem of, in schools, 147–148

Extinction, 273

Extracurricular activities
  athletics, 139–141
  in the secondary school, 138–140

F

Federal government
  role of, in education, 25–26, 71–80, 375, 385–386
  role of, in special education, 184
  role of, in vocational education, 163–164, 171
  support of education, 254–255
    discretionary funds, 255–256
    formula grants, 255
    future of, 256
Field-based learning, 172
Finance. *See* School finance.
Formative and Summative Evaluation, 228, 229
Formula grants, to education, 255
Franklin, Benjamin, 36, 38, 247
Freud, Sigmund, 262
Froebel, Friedrich, 118
Full time equivalent (FTE) model, for funding college programs, 324–325
Futrell, Mary Hartwood, 14, 319
Futurism, 360–361

G

Gabler, Donna, 89
Gabler, Mel, 89
Gagné, Robert, 277–278
Gallaudet, Thomas Hopkins, 186
Geiger, Keith, 243
George-Barden Act of 1946, p. 164
George-Dean Act of 1936, p. 164
George-Elizey Act of 1934, p. 164
George-Reed Act of 1917, p. 164
Gifted education services, 119–120
Global concerns, 361
  food, 363
  geopolitics, 363
  natural resources, 362–363
  population trends, 361–362
Goal setting, 281
Goodlad, J.I., 4
Graded elementary schools, 104–105
Graded secondary schools, 131
"Great Books" of history, curriculum based on, 63, 64
Greece
  education in, 34
  treatment of handicapped in, 185
Green v. County School Board (1968), 77, 388
Guaranteed Student Loan program, 171

H

Hahn, George, 136
Handicapped children. *See also* Special education.
  history of treatment of, 185–188
  judicial decisions involving, 50, 76
Hatch, Orrin G., 194
Hearing impairment, 201
Heterogeneous grouping
  advantages of, 116
  disadvantages of, 117
Higher Educational Act of 1965, p. 72
High schools, 128–129. *See also* Secondary schools.
Hipple, Theodore, 370
Holmes, Ruth D., 14
Home Economics Education Association, 382
Home schooling movement, 18–20
Hornbook, 36
Howe, Samuel, 186
Hume, David, 271

I

Iconic representation, 276–277
Idealism, 58–59
  influence of, on education, 58–59
Illinois ex rel. v. *Board of Education* (1948), 77, 387
Illinois ex rel. McCollum v. *Board of Education* (1948), 387
Impact Aid to education, 256
Individual educational program (IEP)
  and multicultural special education, 197
  right of handicapped child to, 191–192
Individual instruction, 143, 144
Inquiry mode of teaching methodology, 116
Instructional groupings, in elementary education, 116–117
Instructional methods, in elementary education, 115–116
Instructional objectives, 281
Instructional television, 336–337
Instruction methods, 141
  brainstorming, 143–144
  case study, 144
  classroom discussion, 141–143
  debating, 144
  individual instruction, 143, 144
  lectures, 141
  project approach, 144
  role playing, 144
  simulation, 144
  teacher demonstration, 145

  team learning, 145
  telelecture, 145
Intermediate schools, 127–128
International Reading Association, 382
Intuition, 265
Iowa Test of Basic Skills, test scores on, 5
Itard, Jean, 185–186

J

Jefferson, Thomas, 38, 247
Jobs for Delaware Graduates (JDG), 172
Judicial decisions, 73–79, 387–388
  on desegregation, 50, 73, 76, 77, 189, 196, 287, 387–388
  on handicapped children, 50, 76
  on school finance, 251
  on special education, 195–196
Junior high schools, 127–128

K

Kalamazoo case (1874), 387
Kant, Immanuel, 270
Kappa Delta Pi, 382
Kean, Thomas, 288
Kindergarten education, 118
Kirby, Bill, 140
Kohlberg, Lawrence, 268

L

Labor movement, teaching and, 290–291
Lancaster, Joseph, 39
Lancasterian schools, 39
Land Ordinance Act of 1785, pp. 72, 247, 254, 385
Landures, Diane, 305
Language development, 266–267
Lanham Act of 1941, pp. 72, 256
Latin Grammar School, 34, 36
Lazenby, Larry, 227–228
Learning centers, 115
Learning disabilities, 199
  characteristics associated with, 200
  definition of, 200
Learning theory, 270–271
  behavioral theory
    classroom applications, 274–275
    Pavlov, 271–272
    Skinner, 273–274
    Watson, 272–273
  cognitive theory
    Bruner, 276–277
    classroom applications, 277
    Piaget, 275–276
  eclectic theory, 277
    Bandura, 278
    Gagné, 277–278

Lectures, 141
Legislation, 385–386. *See also specific acts.*
  and civil rights, 73
  and the common school movement, 41
  and special education, 189–195
  and vocational education, 164
Literacy, public schools' responsibility for, 99–100
Litigation, *See* Judicial decisions.
Local advisory groups, influence of, on education, 92–93
Local education agencies (LEAs), 88
Local government, influence of, on education, 92–94
Locke, John, 185, 271
Luther, Martin, 35, 185

M

Mainstreaming, 112, 191, 204, 206, 209
Making the Grade, 6
Mann, Horace, 4, 39, 40, 41, 99
Manpower Development Training Act of 1962, p. 72
Marland, Sidney, 174, 175
Maslow, Abraham, 280
Massachusetts School Ordinance of 1642, pp. 36, 217
Massachusetts School Ordinance of 1647, p. 218
Massey, Harold, 141
Math education
  in the secondary school, 133–134
  supply and demand for teachers in, 297
Mattheis, Duane, 175
Measurement and evaluation, 281–282
Melting pot theory, 11
Mental retardation
  characteristics of categories of, 199
  definition of, 199
Merit pay program, for teachers, 15–16, 306
Metaphysics, 57
Middle Ages, treatment of handicapped in, 185
Middle schools, 128
Mildly handicapped, 203–204
Mill, John Stuart, 271
Miller, John E., 250–251
Milliken v. Bradley (1974), 388
Mill v. Board of Education of the District of Columbia (1972), 196
Minimum Foundation Program, concept of, as solution to equalize school finance, 252–254

Modern Language Association, 86
Monitorial schools, 39
Moore, Charles R., 250, 251
Moral development, 268
  stages of, 268–270
Morrill Act of 1890, pp. 72, 164, 254
Morrill Land Grant Act of 1862, pp. 72, 164, 254, 385
Motivation, 279–281
Multicultural education, 11, 196
  and vocational education, 163
  as goal of elementary education, 102
  components of, 12–13
  concerns in, 197
  future of, 13–14
  in the secondary school, 137
  melting pot theory, 11
  purposes of, 11
  responding to the problem, 197
Multiple discrimination learning, 278

N

National Association of Biology Teachers, 382
National Association of Retarded Citizens (NARC),
  role of, in passage of P.L. 94–142, p. 190
National Association of School Superintendents, 82
National Association of Secondary School Principals, 382
National Commission on Excellence in Education, 4, 5, 6, 151
National Commission on Secondary Vocational Education, 173
National Council for Accreditation of Teacher Education (NCATE), 84
National Council for the Social Studies, 382
National Council of Teachers of English, 86, 383
National Council of Teachers of Mathematics, 383
National Defense Education Act (NDEA) (1958), 385
  passage of, as response to Sputnik, 46, 47, 60, 72, 132, 255
National Education Association (NEA), 80, 383
  as labor union, 290–291
  Commission on the Reorganization of Secondary Education, 44–45
  establishment of Committee of Ten, 42–43
  formation of, 82
  growth of membership, 82

influence of, 26
  on competency testing of teachers, 14, 324
  on education-spending rate, 21–22
  on nuclear threat education, 136
  on teacher characteristics, 292
  on teachers' salaries, 300
  state chapters of, 90
National School Boards Association, 383
National Science Foundation (NSF), 255
National Teachers Association, 82
National Teachers Examination (NTE), 323–324
National Youth Administration (NYA), 254
Nation at Risk, 4, 6, 7
Natural resources, 362–363
Needs theory, 280
Negative reinforcement, 62
Nelson, Robert, 335–336
New England Association of Secondary Schools, 83
New England Primer, 36–37
New Right, and public education, 17–18
Newton, Sir Isaac, 61
Nondiscriminatory assessment procedures, and the handicapped child, 192
Nongraded elementary school, 105–106
Nonverbal children, 202
"No pass/no play" rule, 139–141
Normalization, 204, 206
Normative philosophy, 66
Norm-referenced testing, 281
  as discriminatory, 197
Northwest Ordinance of 1787, pp. 38, 72, 247, 254, 385
Nuclear threat, education about in the secondary school, 136

O

Object permanence, 264
"Olde deluder Satan" law of 1647, pp. 36, 246
Operant conditioning, 62, 64, 273, 275
Orthopedic impairment, 202

P

P.L. 19–8 (1823), 189
P.L. 45–186 (1879), 189
P.L. 66–236 (1920), 189
P.L. 80–617 (1948), 189
P.L. 83–531, p. 189
P.L. 85–926, p. 190
P.L. 88–164, p. 190
P.L. 89–10, p. 190
P.L. 89–36, p. 190
P.L. 89–750, p. 190

P.L. 91–205, p. 190
P.L. 91–61, p. 190
P.L. 93–112, p. 190
P.L. 93–380, p. 190
P.L. 94–142, pp. 50, 72, 73, 119, 189, 377, 386
  and multicultural special education, 197
  effect of, on amount of time a principal devotes to special education, 223
  effect of, on role of teachers, 288
  effect of, on teacher training, 112
  expansion of, 194–195
  forces leading to passage of, 189–190
  key components of, 191–194
  purposes of, 190–191
P.L. 815, p. 256
P.L. 874, p. 256
Parent advocacy groups, role of, in passage of P.L. 94–142, p. 190
Parent involvement, in education, 231, 232–233
Parent Teachers Association (PTA), 383
  influence of, on education, 93
Pavlov, Ivan, 62, 271–272, 278
Pennsylvania Association for Retarded Citizens (PARC) v. *Pennsylvania* (1971), 50, 76, 77, 195, 388
Perennialism, 63, 64
Perry, Sue, 228
Personal development, as goal of elementary education, 101–102
Personalized instruction system, 353
PERT (program evaluation review technique), 228
Phi Delta Kappa, 383
Philadelphia Academy, 36
Physically handicapped, 202. *See also* Handicapped children; Special education.
Physical Science Study Committee (PSSC), 85
Piaget, Jean, 262–263, 268
  and cognitive developmental theory, 275–276
  stages of cognitive development, 264
    concrete operational stage, 265–266
    formal operational stage, 266
    preoperational stage, 265
    sensorimotor stage, 264–265
Piagetian theory, 263
  adaptation, 263
  equilibration, 263
  schema, 263
Pierce v. *Society of Sisters* (1925), 387
Plato, 58, 270, 287

Plessy v. *Ferguson* (1896), 50, 387
Population trends, 361–362
  in the United States, 366
Positive reinforcement, 62
Pragmatism, 61
  impact of, on education, 61
Principals, 223
  assistant, 234–235
  as change agent or innovator, 230–231
  as conflict mediator, 230
  as instructional leaders, 103
  and personnel evaluation, 227–228, 229–230
  and program evaluation, 228–229
  benefits available to, 238
  effectiveness of, 234
  expectations of, 231–233
  roles of, 223–231
    in elementary schools, 102–103
  salaries earned by, 235, 236, 237
  typical day of, 233
Private education, 8–9
Problem solving, 278
Professional associations, listing of educational, 382–383
Program evaluation
  context, input, process, product model (DIPP), 228, 229
  discrepancy evaluation model (DEM), 228, 229
  Formative and Summative Evaluation, 228, 229
  program evaluation review technique (PERT), 228, 229
Program Evaluation Review Technique (PERT), 228, 229
Programmed instruction, 353
Programmed tutoring, 354
Progressive Education Association (PEA), 86
Progressivism, 64
Project approach, 144
Project Feast, 176
Property taxes, 248–252
Proposition 2 1/2 (Massachusetts), 23–24, 248
Proposition 13 (California), 23, 248
PROTEACH, 324
Public education
  development of customized programs in, 364
  future of, 364–369, 371–372
  magnitude of, 8–9
  number of students in, 8
  origin of, 38
  past predictions on the future of, 370

  by Max Rafferty, 370–371
  by Theodore Hipple, 370
  purposes of, 9
  spending rate for, 21–22
Public Works and Economic Development Acts of 1965, p. 171
Punishment, 274
Puritanism, impact of, on education, 36–37

R
Rafferty, Max, 370–371
Reagan, Ronald
  on Department of Education, 80
  on federal funding for education, 256
Realism, influence of, on education, 59–62
Reconstructionism, 64
Reformation
  education in, 35
  treatment of handicapped in, 185
Reform movements
  and competency testing for teachers, 14, 306, 319, 322–324
  and merit pay for teachers, 15–16, 306
  and vocational education, 173
  back-to-the-basics, 10, 64, 133, 287, 367–369
  in the 1980s, pp. 367, 376
  in teacher education, 320–325
  state initiatives, 11
Rehabilitation Act of 1973, p. 386
Reinforcement, 272, 274
Religious realism, 61
Renaissance
  education in, 35
  treatment of handicapped in, 185
Resource room model, for special education, 203, 205, 208–209
Reversibility, 265
Ricketts, Ann, 153, 154
Rickover, Hyman G., 130
Riegel, Julie, 305
Robb, Charles, 288
Robinson v. *Cahill,* 251
Role playing, 144
Roman Catholic church, influence of, on education, 34–35, 61
Rome, education in, 34
Royster, William B., 364
Rule learning, 278
Rural Development Act, 171
Russell, Marvin, 250

S
San Antonio Independent School District v. *Rodriquez* (1973), 77, 251, 388

Scholastic Achievement Test (SAT), 82, 83
    test scores on, 5, 151, 152
Scholasticism, 61
School administration. *See* Administration.
School boards. *See* Board of education.
School counseling, careers in, 307–308
School districts, 8
School finance, 22–24, 243
    development of, 246
    federal support of education, 254–255
        discretionary funds, 255–256
        formula grants, 255
        future of, 256
    future of, 380
    local support, 248
        property tax, 248–250, 251–252
    momentum for change in, 250–251
    state spending for education, 243–244, 252
        growth in, 243–244
        minimum foundation programs, 252–254
    taxes, 244
        classification of, 244–245
        shifting of, 245
        sources of, 246
School health, careers in, 308
School library censorship, New Right support for, 18
Schwartz, Robert B., 150
Science education
    in the secondary school, 132–133
    supply and demand for teachers in, 297
Search and seizure, problem of, in schools, 148
Secondary school(s)
    curriculum of, 132
        career education in, 178
        common curriculum, 132–134
        creation science, 136–137
        death education, 135–136
        development and revision, 138
        math, 133–134
        multicultural education, 137
        nuclear threat, 136
        science, 132–133
        sex education, 135
        social studies, 134
        specialized areas, 135–138
    development of, 41–43
    extracurricular activities in, 138–140
    future of, 376–377
    growth of, 126
    instructional methods, 141

brainstorming, 143–144
case study, 144
classroom discussion, 141–143
debate, 144
independent study, 143
individual instruction, 143, 144
lectures, 141
project approach, 144
role playing, 144
simulation, 144
teacher demonstration, 145
team learning, 145
teleclecture, 145
objectives of, 129–131
organization of, 131–132
origin of, 126
philosophy and policies, 145
    appearance codes, 147
    discipline, 145–147
    expulsion and suspension, 147–148
    search and seizure, 148
problems facing, 148–155
    alcohol and drug abuse, 152
    declining academic performance, 151–152
    school dropouts, 149–151
    suicide, 154–155
    teenage pregnancy, 153–154
structure of, 126–129
    high schools, 128–129
    intermediate schools, 127–128
Second Mile Plan, 16
Self-contained classrooms, 106, 205, 206, 210
Sequin, 186
Seriation, 266
Seriously emotionally disturbed (SED), 200–201
Serrano v. *Priest,* 251
Sex education
    in the secondary school, 135
    and teenage pregnancy, 153–154
Shanker, Albert, 14, 324
Shaping, 273
Signal learning, 278
Simulation, 144
Simulation and gaming, 353, 354
Skinner, B.F., 62, 64, 273–274
Sloan v. *Lemon* (1973), 77, 388
Smith, John, 336
Smith-Hughes Act of 1917, pp. 72, 164, 247, 254, 385
Social studies curriculum, in the secondary school, 134
Social work, careers in, 308
Society for Research in Child Development, 383

Society of Associated Teachers of New York City, 81–82
Socrates, 270
South Carolina Education Improvement Act of 1984, p. 367
Space, use of, in elementary education, 114–115
Special education, 119, 184
    current service delivery model, 205
        continuum of services model, 206–210
        efficacy studies, 205–206
    future of, 377
    handicapped children, 198
        generic/noncategorical model, 203–204
        traditional classification system, 198–202
    history of treatment of the handicapped, 185–186
    legislation on, 189–195
    litigation in, 195–196
    mainstreaming, 112, 191, 204, 206, 209
    multicultural programs, 196–197
    normalization, 204
    students served by, 188–189
    supply and demand for teachers in, 297
    traditional service delivery model, 205
        categorical grouping, 205
        institutional settings, 205
        self-contained classes, 205
        special schools, 205
Speech and language disorders, 202
Springfield v. *Quick* (1859), 387
Sputnick, passage of National Defense Education Act as response to, 46, 47, 60, 72, 132, 255, 385
State education agencies (SEAs), 88–89
State government
    influence of, on education, 86–91
    responsibility of, for education
        beginnings of, 38
    role of, in education, 375
Stimulus discrimination, 272
Stimulus generalization, 272
Stimulus response learning, 278
Stitham, Susan A., 14
Strayer-Haig formula for state aid for education, 252
Suicide, problem of, in schools, 154–155
Summerhill school, 62
Superintendents, 220–221, 222
Supreme Court, U.S. *See* Judicial decisions.

Suspension, problem of, in schools, 147–148

Sutherland, David, 305

Swann v. *Charlotte-Mecklenburg Board of Education* (1971), 77, 388

Sweatt v. *Painter* (1950), 77, 387

Symbolic representation, 277

Synoptic philosophy, 66

Systematic desensitization, 274

T

Taxes, 244
  classification of, 244–245
  property, 248–252
  shifting of, 245
  sources of, 246

Taylor, Jim, 172–173

Teacher(s)
  benefits of, 301, 302
  burnout, 303
  characteristics of, 291–295
  collective bargaining rights of, 93
  competency testing of, 14, 306, 319, 322–324
  elementary
    characteristics of good, 111–112
    roles of, 110–111
  future of profession, 378–379
  influence of, on local educational practices, 93
  and the labor movement, 80–82, 290–291
  low job status, 303–305
  merit pay program for, 15–16, 306
  need for dedication of, 308–309
  professional status of, 289–291
  role of principal in evaluation of, 227–228
  salary level, 300–301, 302, 306
  supply and demand, 295–300

Teacher certification, 325
  alternative programs, 327, 329
  recertification requirements, 326, 328
  secondary standards, 327
  traditional programs for, 325–326

Teacher demonstration, 145

Teacher education, 112, 314
  criticisms of, 316–318, 329–330
  in computers, 351
  reforms in, 320–325
  status of, 314–316
  student teaching programs, 321–322

Teacher unions, 80–82, 290–291
  growth of, in membership and influence, 26
  and protection from declining enrollment, 366

Teaching methods
  activity mode, 116
  demonstration mode, 116
  expository mode, 116
  inquiry mode, 116

Team learning, 145

Teenage pregnancy, problem of, in schools, 153–154

Telelecture, 145

Testing agencies, 82–83

Testing movement, and special education, 186–187

Textbooks
  impact of, on education, 85–86, 375
  state influence over content of, 89–90
  use of, in elementary education, 113–114

Time for Reform, 6

Tinker v. *Des Moines Independent Community School District* (1969), 77, 388

U

Unfinished Agenda, The, 173

United States Office of Education (USOE), 79

V

Validity, 282

Vaughn, James, 335

Verbal association, 278

Videocassette technology, 339–340

Visual impairment, 201–202

Vocational education, 161–162. *See also* Career education.
  current status of, 164–166
  definition of, 162–163
  effectiveness of, 166–170
  future of, 173–174, 378
  history of, 163–164
  institutions offering, 168, 172–173
  legislation affecting, 164
  purposes of, 163
  reform movements and, 173
  relationship between career education and, 179
  role of business in, 171–172
  role of federal government in, 163–164, 171
  student enrollment in, 165, 169
    earnings of, and hours worked by, 170
  variables of, 166

Vocational Education Act of 1963, pp. 72, 164, 171, 385

Vocational Education Amendments of 1968, p. 164

W

Wasson, William J., 20

Watson, John, 62, 272–273

Weicker, Lowell P., Jr., 187, 194

Wilkening, Leonard, 154

Will, Madeleine, 184

Williams, Betty, 305

Wilson, Laval S., 150

Witcher, Murry, 228

Wolman v. *Walter* (1977), 388

World of Manufacturing, 176